FILM/GENRE

FILM/GENRE

Rick Altman

 Publishing

First published in 1999 by the
British Film Institute
21 Stephen St, London W1P 2LN

Reprinted 2000, 2002, 2003

The British Film Institute is the UK national agency with responsibility for encouraging
the arts of film and television and conserving them in the national interest.

Cover design: Ketchup
Cover images: Dorothy Malone in *Tarnished Angels* (1958) and Peter Fonda in *Easy
Rider* (1969)

Picture research: Sarah Prosser

Set in 10/12pt Minion by Fakenham Photosetting Limited, Fakenham, Norfolk
Printed in Great Britain by St Edmundsbury Press Limited, Bury St Edmunds, Suffolk

British Library Cataloguing-in-Publication Data
A catalogue record for this book is available from the British Library
ISBN 0–85170–718–1 hbk
ISBN 0–85170–717–3 pbk

Contents

Preface   vii
1 What's at stake in the history of literary genre theory?   1
   Classical genre theory   1
   Neoclassical genre theory   4
   Nineteenth-century genre theory   · 5
   Twentieth-century genre theory   7
   Ten tendencies of literary genre theory   11

2 What is generally understood by the notion of film genre?   13
   Genre is a useful category, because it bridges multiple concerns   14
   Genres are defined by the film industry and recognized by the
      mass audience   15
   Genres have clear, stable identities and borders   16
   Individual films belong wholly and permanently to a single genre   18
   Genres are transhistorical   19
   Genres undergo predictable development   21
   Genres are located in a particular topic, structure and corpus   22
   Genre films share certain fundamental characteristics   24
   Genres have either a ritual or an ideological function   26
   Genre critics are distanced from the practice of genre   28

3 Where do genres come from?   30
   The musical   31
   The Western   34
   The biopic   38
   Producers as critics   44
   Joel Silver, the 'Selznick of schlock'   46

4 Are genres stable?   49
   Adjectives and nouns   50
   Genre as process   54
   Noir as adjective and noun   60
   Genrification as process   62

5 Are genres subject to redefinition?   69
   Post-mortem for a phantom genre   70
   Rebirth of a phantom genre   72
   Critics as producers   77
   Selling The Creature from the Black Lagoon   78

6 Where are genres located?   83
    A multiplicity of locations   84
    Genre and nation   86
    Genre as textual structure: Semantics and syntax   87
    Genre as institution, institution as genre   90
    More than just a game?   96

7 How are genres used?   100
    A day at Walt Disney World   101
    Majors and independents   102
    Hollywood and Washington   107
    Genres as good and bad objects   110
    Ratings as genre   110
    Name-brand marketing strategies   113
    Brand-name movies   115
    Generic discursivity   121

8 Why are genres sometimes mixed?   123
    Critical investments   123
    Studio strategies   128
    The genre-mixing game   130
    Hollywood cocktail   132
    Classical versus postmodern   139
    Mixing instructions   142

9 What role do genres play in the viewing process?   144
    The generic crossroads   145
    Genre films on television   150
    Generic economy   152
    The generic community   156
    How spectators use genres   164

10 What communication model is appropriate for genres?   166
    The four-hoot call of the barred owl   166
    Modelling generic communication   169
    Saussure revisited   173
    How it works in practice   175
    A new communication model   178

11 Have genres and genre functions changed over time?   179
    The neoclassical nature of standard genre theory   180
    Audience or 'audience'?   182
    Genre in the age of remote consumption   184
    Pseudo-memorials   188
    The passed-along song   190
    Sports, stars and advertising   192
    Genre in the new millennium   193

12 What can genres teach us about nations?   195
    Hegel's newspaper   196
    Regenrifying the national anthem   199
    The name of the father   202
    Hyphenating the margins   203
    Genre/nation   205

Conclusion: A semantic/syntactic/pragmatic approach to genre   207
    A semantic/syntactic/pragmatic approach   208
    Reception, opposition, poaching   211
    Planning and using cities and texts   213

Appendix: 'A semantic/syntactic approach to film genre'   216

Bibliography   227

Index   237

This book is dedicated
to the memory
of
Michael Erec Altman
1976–1995

Preface

This book began over two decades ago. When I first came to the University of Iowa in the mid-70s, I found a group of students that included future genre theorists and historians Jim Collins, Jane Feuer and Thomas Schatz. Together we spent many happy hours critiquing popular American films, discussing how they work as aesthetic systems, and debating the roles they play in American life. Our lively exchanges led to several books and articles on genre, written by Collins, Feuer and Schatz, and by others who taught or studied American film genres at Iowa in the late 70s and early 80s: Ed Buscombe, Mary Ann Doane, Thomas Elsaesser, Wes Gehring, Paul Hernadi, Henry Jenkins, Barb Klinger, Phil Rosen and Alan Williams. Daily interaction with this talented group of genre theorists also induced me to begin my own writing about genre.

My work on genre was slow to mature, however, and not just because most of my time in those days was spent on French film and medieval narrative. Before I could feel comfortable writing about specific American film genres, I felt a need to think broadly about the theoretical underpinnings of genre. This concern eventually led to a *Cinema Journal* article titled 'A Semantic/Syntactic Approach to Genre' (1984), which tried to bring clarity and structure to generic textual analysis and history (and which is reproduced as an appendix to the present book). This line of reasoning was followed up in the theoretical chapters (1, 5 and 9) of *The American Film Musical* (1987); in one sense that entire book was a demonstration of the methods and theory outlined in the 1984 article. Since that time I have had the satisfaction of seeing the 'semantic/syntactic approach' adopted by colleagues and students working on a wide range of problems.

Nevertheless, the present book grows directly out of misgivings regarding the theoretical foundations of my earlier work. We are often our own best critics, but only rarely do we let our hesitations surface and do the critical work of which they are capable. For years I fought off my own doubts, but eventually started taking them seriously. The result is the semantic/syntactic/pragmatic theory presented in this book, which began to take shape in 1994. Not until the drafting of the later chapters, however, did I begin to realize that my relatively focused reflections on American film genre had turned into a broader theory of communication in the modern world.

I have worked hard to make this a readable book that will concentrate attention on important, enduring problems. Where possible I have endeavoured to lighten the theoretical burden; some readers may find that I have oversimplified complex problems, but I remain committed to the notion that an accessible style empowers readers and encourages them to do their own theorizing. I have also laboured to lighten the scholarly apparatus. Parenthetical citations replace traditional notes; where the reference is obvious, I have even dispensed with a separate citation. While this approach encourages neither direct dialogue with other scholars nor full documentation of competing points of view, it has the virtue of concentrating attention on the argument at hand. As a further device to pinpoint problems and positions, I have provided regular summaries of hypotheses and conclusions.

The theses presented in *Film/Genre* were worked out in a number of places and with the help of many people. I owe a debt of gratitude to those who invited me to present parts of this material at the University of California at Irvine Center for Advanced Studies, the annual meeting of the Association Québécoise des Etudes Cinématographiques in Montreal, the University of California at Los Angeles, the Chicago Film Seminar, and the Universities of Copenhagen, Bergen, and Trondheim, as well as those who encouraged me to publish earlier versions and related texts in *Cinema Journal, IRIS, The Oxford History of World Cinema, Refiguring American Film Genres: History and Theory*, and *Storia del cinema*. For their support I want especially to thank Nick Browne, Gian-Piero Brunetta, Alain Lacasse, Andrew Lockett, Geoffrey Nowell-Smith, Lauren Rabinovitz, and my students at the University of Iowa. Thanks are also due to my father, Frederick J. Altman, for taking time out from his patent applications to help me prune gallicisms and trim solecisms. Special thanks to my wife, Janet Gurkin Altman, for her continued support.

1
What's at stake in the history of literary genre theory?

> We discover that the critical theory of genres is stuck precisely where Aristotle left it. The very word 'genre' sticks out in an English sentence as the unpronounceable and alien thing it is. Most critical efforts to handle such generic terms as 'epic' and 'novel' are chiefly interesting as examples of the psychology of rumor.
>
> Northrop Frye, *Anatomy of Criticism* (1957, p. 13)

Of all the concepts fundamental to literary theory, none has a longer and more distinguished lineage than the question of literary types, or genres. From Aristotle to Todorov and from Horace to Wellek and Warren, the topic of genre has remained one of the staples of theoretical discourse. As much as has been written on genre, however, the historical study of genre theory can hardly be characterized as a satisfying enterprise. The debate over genre has consistently taken place in slow motion. The decades – or even centuries – that have separated major genre theory statements have all too often led the debaters alternately to take disputed propositions for granted or to forget the very topic of the debate.

The history of genre theory thus traces a particularly zigzag trajectory. Sharing major claims with their predecessors, theoreticians on the straight stretches evince no need to justify their positions, while genre theorists in the turns rarely explain why a change of direction is necessary. Yet, quietly, the genre theories of the past have nevertheless set certain standards that continue tacitly to underlie recent attempts to theorize genre. If this chapter contains many of the familiar names of generic thinking, it is not, however, simply to rehearse what these thinkers have said about genre. In other words, what follows is in no sense a history of literary genre theory. Rather, in the hope of discovering the origins of our own blindness, the purpose here is to highlight the very claims that genre theorists have failed to recognize they were making, the constitutive assumptions that theoreticians have neglected to acknowledge in their own work, the habits and positions that have been silently passed on, often at cross-purposes with official positions and conscious claims.

Classical genre theory

'I propose to treat of poetry in itself and of its various kinds, noting the essential quality of each', says Aristotle at the outset of *Poetics*.

> Epic poetry and tragedy, comedy also and dithyrambic poetry, and the music of the flute and of the lyre in most of their forms, are all in their general conception modes of imitation. They differ, however, from one another in three respects – the medium, the objects, the manner or mode of imitation, being in each case distinct.

1

Certainly, one of the most attractive features of Aristotle's famous treatise – and one of the sources of its continued influence – is the clarity, indeed the apparently incontrovertible simplicity, with which every claim is made. Everything is straightforward. Or rather, as with all great rhetoricians, every claim is made to seem straightforward. In fact, every one of Aristotle's apparently transparent expressions conceals a set of assumptions tacitly adopted by virtually every subsequent genre theorist. An expanded version of the first sentence of the *Poetics* should help to underscore the assumptions that Aristotle asks us to make with him:

> I propose to treat of *the form of activity that our society has labeled* poetry *which I claim can best be considered as an isolated phenomenon* in itself and of *what I will treat as* its various kinds, noting *or rather claiming that there is such a thing as* the essential quality of each.

In order to begin his work, Aristotle must define an object of study. By borrowing an already defined object rather than defining his own, however, Aristotle provides a model for centuries of genre thinkers. Surprisingly, this most careful of thinkers thus opens his thought to whatever Greeks the Trojan horse of 'poetry' might carry. Who defined poetry? To what end? On the basis of what assumptions? With what ramifications for the proposed generic breakdown? Aristotle's spare, declarative style makes it unlikely that these questions will be asked, and very likely that subsequent theoreticians will remain oblivious to the slippery slope of the underlying terrain on which their theories are built.

The very notions that poetry exists 'in itself' and that a kind can have an 'essential quality' involve unsubstantiated claims with far-reaching effects. These unopposed assumptions justify Aristotle's famous claim that the types of poetry differ in medium, object and manner of imitation, along with the implication that no other differences are involved. Note that the author of the *Nicomachean Ethics* does not suggest that the types of poetry differ in the uses to which they are put, the places in which they are used, or the groups that use them. He does not propose distinctions based on the actions that differing types of poetry inspire, but instead assumes that poems with similar 'essential' qualities will produce similar effects on their audiences. Thus all poems that arouse pity and fear are not necessarily tragedies, but all tragedies may be expected to arouse pity and fear.

My purpose here is not to show that Aristotle is in any way wrong, but rather to show that (a) the *Poetics* is based on unspoken and apparently incontrovertible assumptions, (b) these assumptions sanction certain types of conclusion, while precluding others, and (c) alternatives do exist to the positions taken by Aristotle. For example, given the origin of Greek poetic forms in diverse rituals, a categorization of poems based on their differing ritual uses would have produced a fascinating and fully defensible generic breakdown. From within the *Poetics*, however, such an approach remains invisible, unthinkable – not only to today's readers, but more importantly to readers across the ages who have taken their generic cues from Aristotle. As influential as it may have been, Aristotle's categorization of the kinds of poetry has had the effect of narrowing genre theory ever since. By accentuating poetry's internal characteristics rather than the kinds of experience fostered by poetry, Aristotle set genre theory on to a virtually unbroken course of textual analysis. Not that textual concerns and experiential concerns are entirely unrelated, but their relationship requires theorization – and that is precisely what Aristotle's spare style and unanswerable rhetoric preclude.

By the time Horace drafted his *Ars Poetica*, three centuries after Aristotle's death, the Greek philosopher's arguments about poetic types had achieved the status of received truth. Whereas Aristotle opens his *Poetics* with the stealth of a rhetorician schooled in the delicate art of Platonic debate, Horace begins his epistle on the art of poetry with all the bravado of an author sanctioned by the ancients.

> Suppose a painter meant to attach a horse's neck to the head of a man, and to put fancy-work of many colored feathers on limbs of creatures picked at random; the kind of thing where the torso of a shapely maiden merges into the dark rear half of a fish; would you smother your amusement, my friends, if you were let in to see the result?
> Believe me, Pisones, a book will be very much like that painting if the meaningless images are put together like the dreams of a man in a fever, to the end that the head and the foot do not match the one body.

Wrapped in the authority of (his culture's notion of) nature, Horace need not argue for the existence of genres. The only natural and healthy thing to do, Horace implies, is to recognize the differences among genres. If nature and health exist, then so do genres. Confident as if backed up by the combined Roman legions, Horace leaves the recipient of his epistle little room to manoeuvre. Each genre must be understood as a separate entity, with its own literary rules and prescribed procedures. Tragic verse forms, Horace affirms, must not be used for comic situations. 'Let each form of poetry occupy the proper place allotted to it.' Inaugurating a long tradition whereby genre and decorum are allied in critical discourse, with proper behaviour expected of literature and citizens alike, Horace also initiates the equally tenacious tradition according to which the authority behind the 'proper' and the method of allotting a separate place to each form of poetry remain outside the genre theorist's range of analysis.

Quoted continually from the late Renaissance to the eighteenth century in support of neoclassical poetic and theatrical practices, Horace's *Ars Poetica* contains more than detailed prescriptions regarding specific genres. More important are two changes in emphasis with relation to the Aristotelian model. For Aristotle, imitation means *mimesis*, sketching from nature; for Horace, the same term implies imitation of a literary model and adherence to the standards represented by that model, as described by distinguished critics (such as Horace himself). In other words, the notion of genre is now fully conscripted into the legion of techniques whereby writers are trained to respect current standards of cultural acceptability.

With this redefinition of generic imitation as a major form of cultural indoctrination, a fundamental bifurcation occurs in generic thinking. Whereas Aristotle aims primarily at description of existing works of art, sometimes speaking solely as critic, sometimes addressing the problems of poets and their audiences, Horace is mainly concerned to prescribe appropriate modes of writing poetry. Having devoted the first half of the *Poetics* to a historical and theoretical analysis of poetic genres, only in the latter half of the treatise does Aristotle begin to sketch out appropriate writing practices. To the Greek master's historical preterites and descriptive present tenses correspond Horace's incessant imperatives:

– Let the work of art be whatever you want, as long as it is simple and has unity. (96)
– Adopt material to match your talents ... (96)
– Let each form of poetry occupy the proper place allotted to it. (97)
– Do not bring out on stage actions that should properly take place inside, and remove from view the many events which the descriptive powers of an actor present on the stage will soon relate. Do not have Medea butcher her sons before the audience ... (100)
– Do not let a play consist of less than five acts. ... Do not have a god intervene. ... Have the chorus carry the part of an actor ... and do not let them sing anything between the acts which does not contribute to the plot and fit properly into it. (100)
– Whatever you have in the way of a lesson, make it short ... (103)

At every turn, Horace is concerned to provide clear rules for generically faithful literary composition. To Aristotle's concern for the structure of generic texts is now added a durable interest in the production of generic texts.

Curiously, for all his emphasis on the production of poetry, Horace radically dissociates the processes of creation and criticism. The critic does the reading of previous poetry and criticism, while the writer carries out the critic's prescriptions. As we will see in later chapters, this split has a significant effect on the future of genre theory. Whereas Aristotle saw history and theory, criticism and practice, audience and poets, as somehow all intertwined, Horace sets up a simple generic model for the ages: poets produce by imitating a predefined original sanctioned by the literary-critical oligarchy.

Neoclassical genre theory

As filtered through Horace and the power of Roman literary institutions, Aristotelian notions of genre provided the very foundation of the neoclassical critical system. Rediscovered by Italian Renaissance authors, Aristotle inspired virtually non-stop publication of poetic treatises throughout the sixteenth century, in three volumes (Marco Girolamo Vida, 1527), in six (Ugento Antonio Minturno, 1559), in seven (Julius Caesar Scaliger, 1561), or in a single-volume summary (Lodovico Castelvetro, 1570). For nearly two centuries, the adaptation of neo-Aristotelian principles would be chronicled and justified in the writings of such important writer-critics as Torquato Tasso, Pierre Corneille, Nicolas Boileau, John Dryden and Alexander Pope.

Perhaps the most celebrated cause of this period is the battle over the ultimate generic crossbreed: tragicomedy. Ever the incontrovertible naturalist, Horace had set limits on the poet's right to mix genres: 'it does not go to the extent that savage should mate with tame, that serpents should couple with birds, or lambs with tigers'. Reacting strongly against the medieval grotesque tendency to mix the sublime and the ridiculous, the sacred and the secular, the tragic and the comic, seventeenth-century French neoclassical critics at first found it quite impossible to accept the new composite. Yet little by little the production of new plays by Pierre Corneille and Jean Mairet in the second quarter of the seventeenth century, along with the apparent Roman precedent of Plautus' *Amphitryon*, broke down critical resistance and led to acceptance of the hybrid genre.

4

For our purposes, one particular lesson stands out from this unexpected development. That a new genre should be born in an expanding culture hardly provides cause for surprise. More important is the way in which this genre develops out of the coupling of two genres previously thought diametrically opposed. In spite of the Horatian commitment to keep genres separate and the neo-Aristotelian refusal to recognize genres not mentioned by Aristotle, the rise of tragicomedy demonstrates the possibility of generating new genres through the monstrous mating of already existing genres. For the first time, genre theory must accommodate itself to genre history, rather than vice versa.

During the latter half of the eighteenth century, a new genre began to edge its way between tragedy and comedy. At first called simply the 'serious genre', as opposed to the classical genres, deemed incapable of dealing with contemporary reality, the new genre was denigrated as the 'weepie genre' (*genre larmoyant*) by its conservative opponents. Eventually baptized simply 'drama' (*drame*) by its radical supporters (Denis Diderot, Pierre de Beaumarchais, Louis-Sébastien Mercier), this is the theatrical form that would eventually give rise to melodrama – the most popular theatrical mode of the nineteenth century and cinema's most important parent genre. The details surrounding the new genre's rise to popularity and its post-revolutionary transformation into popular melodrama are less important here than genre's new role as the object of critical and political strife.

If Aristotle has remained a favourite with twentieth-century genre theoreticians, it is in part because his primary purpose was to describe and codify existing practice rather than to exercise any direct influence over that practice. While most recent genre critics and theorists continue to accept genres – including melodrama – as classically attested pre-existent forms, the history of (melo)drama reveals that critics once understood their role as far more active and interventionist. The example of melodrama stresses the critic's potential role in making genre a living, changing, active part of cultural development and self-expression. From this point on in the history of genre theory, classically motivated genre separation will never again hold sway, yet, as we shall see, many of the hidden institutional commitments underlying the classical system will never fully die.

Nineteenth-century genre theory

As with the classics, so with the romantics, but in reverse. Whereas the neoclassical approach to all composition began with identification and separation of genres, romantic inspiration was based on the breaking down of all generic differences. German theoretician Friedrich Schlegel provided the philosophical underpinnings, recommending abolition of all generic classifications in his *Dialogue on Poetry* (1800), while two French renegades led the assault. Stendhal spearheaded the first attacks in his tract, *Racine et Shakespeare* (1823 and 1825), with Victor Hugo's theatrical works and their prefaces soon providing able reinforcement (*Cromwell* in 1827, *Hernani* in 1830). In support of its genre-mixing aesthetic, the romantic movement rapidly established a new canon, including such unlikely bedfellows as Isaiah, Aeschylus, Rabelais and Shakespeare, all masters of the mixed genre.

Here again we encounter an unexpected contribution to the broader realm of genre theory. The neoclassical canon was fully furnished by centuries of tradition; the only remaining questions were of the order of whether Homer or Virgil was the greater epic poet. The romantics quickly discovered that new genre theories can be skillfully buttressed by adducing a carefully concocted new canon. Choosing works from different countries and even different periods (Hugo throws in Homer, Saint Paul, Tacitus, Dante and Cervantes for good measure), the romantics fully revealed for the first time just how effectively genre theory (and even the production of generically marked literary works) can be pressed into the service of broader institutional goals. Often forgotten, this lesson will be recalled in later sections of this book.

The final decades of the nineteenth century witnessed a development of particular importance for the future of genre theory. While the binomial nomenclature system of Carolus Linnaeus had provided a new basis for the classification systems used in the world's increasingly numerous natural history museums, it took the evolutionary schemes of Charles Darwin and Herbert Spencer to attract the literary community to a scientific model. Especially in the work of French literary historian Ferdinand Brunetière, the evolutionary model was directly applied to the problem of genres (particularly in the multivolume *L'Evolution des genres*, 1890–94). Believing in the reality of genres as if they were biological species, Brunetière was of course only providing scientific underpinnings for the already familiar Horatian model. The strength of this added argument, however, can scarcely be overestimated. Reinvented by virtually every student of genre since Brunetière, scientific justification of genre study serves to convince theorists that genres actually exist, that they have distinct borders, that they can be firmly identified, that they operate systematically, that their internal functioning can be observed and scientifically described, and that they evolve according to a fixed and identifiable trajectory.

It is indeed surprising just how far the influence of this attitude extends. Within a page of the beginning of *The Fantastic* (1970), for example, as careful a scholar as Tzvetan Todorov quotes Karl Popper's claim that 'no matter how many instances of white swans we have observed, this does not justify the conclusion that all swans are white' (p. 4). Anxious to establish the validity of a deductive, scientific method, Todorov retorts:

> On the other hand, a hypothesis which is based on the observation of a limited number of swans but which also informs us that their whiteness is the consequence of an organic characteristic would be perfectly legitimate. To return from swans to novels, this general scientific truth applies not only to the study of genres, but also to that of a writer's entire *oeuvre*, or to that of a specific period, etc.
>
> (1970, p. 4)

Given the well-known genre of swans, claims Todorov, I can take a small number of specific swans at random, study their organic make-up, and come to legitimate conclusions regarding the entire genre. But who will define the genre of swans, we might well object, when 'swan' stands for 'fantastic novel'? And how will we know how to recognize a 'swan' when we see one? And just what are the organic characteristics of 'swans'? And so on. The scientific model offers an extraordinarily powerful rhetorical ploy, yet, begging basic questions, it often leads unsuspecting readers astray. Perhaps more important still, by obscuring very real theoretical problems the scientific model all too often keeps serious genre theorists from coming to terms with all aspects of their own object of study.

Twentieth-century genre theory

Not surprisingly, twentieth-century genre theory begins with a resounding 'No!' to the scientific schemes of Brunetière and his many imitators. From his very first important publication in 1902 (*Aesthetic as Science of Expression and General Linguistic*), Italian theorist and critic Benedetto Croce launched a frontal attack on the very concept of genre. Indeed, by his own admission, the critique of genres provided the impetus for Croce's entire philosophy. Noting that attempts to prescribe the code of a genre are consistently defeated by poets' efforts to exceed or subvert that code, Croce sought to sweep away virtually all generalizing critical discourse. Ironically, where he might have become the father of postmodernism, with its distaste for totalizing discourse, Croce instead sired an unexpected combination of nihilism and aestheticism, along with a fundamental shift in the definition of genre problematics.

For over a century before Croce, virtually all genre theory involved some version of the classic versus romantic genre dialectic, opposing the so-called pure genres handed down by tradition to modern mixed genres more attentive to human multiplicity and complex reality. Croce's strong critique of genres had the effect of shifting genre theory towards a new dialectic opposing generic categories and individual texts. Whereas all literary composition, as well as all interpretive acts, had for centuries been seen as occurring within generic boundaries, the new model figured genre as one pole of an opposition featuring modernist innovators at the other pole. Eventually played out by Anglo-American New Criticism, this new dialectic also had an important influence on post-war film theory, which neatly opposed bedrock genres to the creative efforts of auteurs capable of subverting and personalizing them.

One of the most influential and level-headed attempts to renew genre theory in the post-Croce era came from René Wellek and Austin Warren, in their *Theory of Literature* (1956), written during the 1940s while both were faculty members at the University of Iowa. Distinguishing between what they call 'inner' and 'outer' form, Wellek and Warren propose a bifurcated approach:

> Genre should be conceived, we think, as a grouping of literary works based, theoretically, upon both outer form (specific metre or structure) and also upon inner form (attitude, tone, purpose – more crudely subject and audience). The ostensible basis may be one or the other (e.g., 'pastoral' and 'satire' for the inner form; dipodic verse and Pindaric ode for outer); but the critical problem will then be to find the *other* dimension, to complete the diagram.
>
> (Wellek and Warren, 1956, p. 231)

Encouraging critics to investigate the relationship between structure and technique, Wellek and Warren clearly provide both a conscious model for analysis,

7

and criteria according to which the existence and extent of a genre may be conveniently judged.

In providing such a reasonable model, however, they reveal a strange blindness. On the one hand, they recognize that genres are more than just convenient classification aids: 'The literary kind is an "institution" – as Church, University, or State is an institution. It exists, not as an animal exists or even as a building, chapel, library, or capitol, but as an institution exists' (*ibid.*, p. 226). Thus distancing themselves from Brunetière and the biological model, Wellek and Warren open up a potentially new domain for genre theory. Providing critics with the wherewithal not just to recognize genres, but to redraw the generic map, based on concordances of inner and outer form, Wellek and Warren nevertheless fail to recognize the role of the theorist or critic in founding generic institutions, thus missing the opportunity to bring radical change to genre theory.

The possibility of redrawing generic charts, only vaguely evoked by Wellek and Warren, was rapidly realized in the work of Canadian scholar Northrop Frye, whose *Anatomy of Criticism* (1957) remained at the centre of international genre theory debate for two decades. Taking his cue from Jung, Frye links literary forms with broader archetypal categories. Especially in his 'Theory of Mythos', Frye singlemindedly follows up his intuitions and observations regarding inner and outer literary form to the point of redescribing and thus ultimately redefining such familiar generic categories as comedy, romance and tragedy. No longer would the establishment of a corpus of texts depend on tradition alone. Adducing a wide spectrum of sometimes unexpected texts in support of his revised definitions, Frye treats literary criticism and its categories not as institutions but as the object of a new scientific endeavour, based on a broad inductive approach and the positing of coherence. How ironic that Frye, as the first theorist perhaps of all time singlehandedly to succeed in imposing a new generic classification, should fail to recognize the institutional nature and ramifications of his own activities, which he instead defines as transparently and selflessly scientific.

While Brunetière borrowed the evolutionary content of Darwin's *Origin of Species* (1859), Frye adopts its revolutionary method and its idealistic vision of apolitical scientific endeavour. With the Scopes trial, Darwinians learnt once and for all that new scientific paradigms, however rational, would always be seen by certain sectors of society as unacceptable competition. If literary questions could cause the 'battles' associated with Corneille's *Le Cid* in 1636–7 and Hugo's *Hernani* in 1830, it hardly seems surprising that a problem of 'pure' literary theory should lead to academic strife in the 1960s. Appearing in French in 1970, the first chapter of Tzvetan Todorov's *The Fantastic* was in a sense Frye's Scopes trial. He doesn't lose the trial, in spite of strong criticism levelled at him by Todorov, but at a time when North American and European literary theories were clearly locked in battle over the terrain of young academic minds (including my own at the time), Frye's trial-by-critique certainly sent out a clear signal to all would-be followers of Frye: 'In spite of what you may have heard [e.g., from Geoffrey Hartman's article in the 1966 *Yale French Studies* issue on Structuralism], *Anatomy of Criticism* is not consonant with French structuralism'. Todorov begins by expressing six articles of faith that he shares with Frye, and that have been adopted by most subsequent genre theorists:

1. Literary studies must be conducted in a scientific manner.
2. Value judgments have no place in literary studies.
3. Literature is systematic; chance has no part in it.
4. Literary analysis should be synchronic, as if all texts existed simultaneously.
5. Literary discourse is not referential.
6. Literature is created from literature, not from reality.   (1970, pp. 9–10)

Such a set of assumptions might well have led Todorov to welcome Frye into the structuralist camp.

Instead, Todorov castigates Frye for a series of failings, including the inability to recognize the difference between 'theoretical' genres, which are deduced from a theory of literature, and 'historical' genres, which are the result of an observation of literary phenomena. Seeking to dissociate himself from previous unsystematic genre study, and to stake out a firm ground on which a durable analysis might be built, Todorov distinguishes between the types traditionally recognized by our culture (epic, short story, lyric poetry, and so forth) and the new types suggested by the modern systematic critic. Types accepted by the culture are thus labelled 'historical', while 'theoretical' types are defined by the critic. But this opposition begs the question of the critic's position within the culture. All historical genres or types were once theoretical genres, defined by the critics of a former culture (who may have been known by other names – essayists, journalists, or simply men or women of taste and influence – but who played the role of critic none the less) according to a theory then current (not a self-consciously elaborated theory like that championed by Todorov, but a theory none the less).

In spite of the repeated pronouncements of Todorov and others, there is no place outside of history from which purely 'theoretical' definitions of genre might be made. In substituting his so-called 'theoretical' definition of the fantastic for a series of historical categories (fairy tale, ghost story, gothic novel, etc.), Todorov is only substituting a *current historical* understanding of literature (heavily dependent on contemporary fashions of psychoanalysis and formal analysis) for a *former historical* definition of literature (referring instead to literature's mimetic function and thus dependent on content paradigms). Reading *The Fantastic* a generation after its publication, we already recognize its vocabulary, its methodological tools, and its classification of literature as marked by a particular period which only recently was the present, which may once have appeared not-yet-historical, but which we now identify with the historical phenomenon of French structuralism. The 'fantastic' as defined by Todorov is already (*was always already*) a historical genre. 'Theoretical', when it is opposed to 'historical', defines a utopian space, a 'no place' from which critics may seemingly justify blindness to their own historicity. Just as the critic is always part of a culture, thus undermining any attempt to oppose the critical to the cultural, so the theoretician always stands on the historically marked ground of a particular era.

Whether or not Todorov's justification of theoretical genres makes historical sense, *The Fantastic* certainly furthers the tendency – already posited by Wellek and Warren, and developed by Frye – towards critic-defined genres. Indeed, Todorov goes so far as to place the primary determinant of the fantastic genre within the reader. Does the reader hesitate between two explanations – one uncanny, the other marvellous – of the phenomena encountered in the text? Then the text must be considered part of the fantastic genre. While this approach perhaps raises more problems than it solves (can the same text be fantastic for one reader, but not fantastic for another? can the same text be fantastic on first reading but not on subsequent readings? does the genre exist among the impressionable and on dark nights, but not among scientists or in the daytime?), it paradoxically throws Todorov's readers, trained to respect self-conscious theory over all else, back on the mercy of untutored readers, capable of making decisions of generic magnitude simply by deferring reading past nightfall.

This dependence on readers' attitudes exactly reverses the order of priorities that we noted earlier in Aristotle's logic. For the Greek philosopher, tragedies are defined by their essential properties, and because they share essential properties they can be expected to have similar effects on viewers (i.e., arousing pity and fear). How different the history of genre theory might have been had Aristotle taken the opposite position, identifying all texts that arouse pity and fear as tragedies (rather than vice versa). Indeed, this is precisely what Todorov does. Rather than claim that all fantastic texts cause readers to hesitate between two readings, he suggests that all texts producing hesitation between uncanny and marvellous readings are part of the fantastic genre. *The Fantastic* thus stands as a potentially important turning point in literary genre theory, not because it out-structures and out-theorizes Frye's *Anatomy of Criticism* in the front room, but because it opens the back door to ordinary historical readers and their reading habits.

In many ways, Todorov's project thus parallels that of E.D. Hirsch, Jr., whose *Validity in Interpretation* (1967) reintroduced the notion of genre into the reading process – not only for generic readings or interpretation of specific literary genres, but for every act of reading, literary or not. Hirsch's project develops the simple and apparently unexceptionable insight that 'the details of meaning that an interpreter understands are powerfully determined and constituted by his meaning expectations. And these expectations arise from the interpreter's conception of the type of meaning that is being expressed' (1967, p. 72). This basic tenet of schema theory is proved every day when we manage to understand dialogue that we can hardly hear, simply because we have a clear idea of the general type of meaning involved. From time to time, of course, we confirm Hirsch's hypothesis more negatively, by misconstruing a message that we heard perfectly well, simply because we had wrongly identified the type of meaning involved.

From this broad assumption, Hirsch moves directly to the claim that 'an interpreter's preliminary generic conception of a text is constitutive of everything that he subsequently understands, and that this remains the case unless and until that generic conception is altered' (p. 74). Sliding all too easily from 'type of meaning' to 'genre', Hirsch is able to affirm that 'every disagreement about an interpretation is usually a disagreement about genre' (p. 98). By equating 'genre' with 'type of meaning', however, Hirsch has broadened the notion of genre to the point where it no longer coincides with the meaning usually ascribed to the term in literary theory. Certainly, Hirsch is right to claim that a husband's comment on returning home late, 'I'm very tired tonight', may carry a variety of meanings, depending on the conventions that have been established between husband and wife (p. 53). Yet the word genre will have changed meanings too much to be of any use to us if it must refer to general types of meaning like 'expression of physical state', 'admission regarding previous whereabouts', or 'refusal to participate in love-making activities'. While Hirsch offers eloquent evidence for the role of genres in the meaning-making process, he unintentionally spotlights the extent to which literary and filmic genres are more than just general classes of texts expressing determinable types of meaning.

More than previous genre theorists, Todorov and Hirsch tie questions of textual structure to reader expectations regarding textual structure. Within their methodology, this strategy serves as yet one more way to focus attention on a text's formal properties. If it were released for general usage, however, this emphasis on reading patterns would risk provoking what we might call a 'sorcerer's apprentice' effect: once the magic word 'reader' is pronounced, there might be no controlling the ultimate effect. Once labelled by writers and critics, genres might well fall into the hands of untutored readers or out-of-control audiences.

Thus far, this threat has not materialized. On the contrary, the most important English-language genre theory of the last two decades, Alastair Fowler's *Kinds of Literature: An Introduction to the Theory of Genres and Modes* (1982), resolutely returns to classical emphasis on textual structure within traditional genres and canons of texts, instead of releasing responsibility for genres to readers and audiences. 'The kinds, however, elusive, objectively exist', says Fowler (p. 73), permanently closing off debate.

Ten tendencies of literary genre theory

At the conclusion of even as cursory an overview as that presented here, it should be possible to outline the major principles of genre theory established by two millennia of genre theorists. Yet this is precisely what we cannot do. Even so simple a question as the meaning and extent of the term *genre* remains confusing, for the term inconsistently refers to distinctions derived from a wide variety of differences among texts: type of presentation (epic/lyric/dramatic), relation to reality (fiction versus non-fiction), historical kind (comedy/tragedy/tragicomedy), level of style (novel versus romance), or content paradigm (sentimental novel/historical novel/adventure novel).

While this overview of literary genre theory has been far too limited to provide anything like a history of the topic, it has served to bring to the surface a number of important tendencies, questions and contradictions that deserve to be recalled as we move to the area of film genre. The following list thus attends to unexpressed assumptions shared by genre theorists, along with some of the theoretical problems that remain unaddressed over the long history of genre-oriented literary speculation.

1. It is generally taken for granted that genres actually exist, that they have distinct borders, and that they can be firmly identified. Indeed, these facts have seemed so obvious to theoreticians that they have rarely seemed worthy of discussion, let alone of questioning.
2. Because genres are taken to be 'out there', existing independently of observers, genre theorists have generally sought to describe and define what they believe to be already existing genres rather than create their own interpretive categories, however applicable or useful.

3. Most genre theory has attended either to the process of creating generic texts in imitation of a sanctioned predefined original, or to internal structures attributed to those texts, in part because the internal functioning of genre texts is considered entirely observable and objectively describable.
4. Genre theorists have typically assumed that texts with similar characteristics systematically generate similar readings, similar meanings, and similar uses.
5. In the language of theoreticians, proper genre production is regularly allied with decorum, nature, science and other standards produced and defended by the sponsoring society. Few genre theorists have shown interest in analysing this relationship.
6. It is regularly assumed that producers, readers and critics all share the same interests in genre, and that genres serve those interests equally.
7. Reader expectation and audience reaction have thus received little independent attention. The uses of generic texts have also largely been neglected.
8. Genre history holds a shifting and uncertain place in relation to genre theory. Most often simply disregarded by its synchronically oriented partner, genre history nevertheless cries out for increased attention by virtue of its ability to scramble generic codes, to blur established generic tableaux and to muddy accepted generic ideas. At times, genre history has been used creatively in support of specific institutional goals, for example by creating a new canon of works supportive of a revised genre theory.
9. Most genre theorists prefer to style themselves as somehow radically separate from the objects of their study, thus justifying their use of meliorative terms like 'objective', 'scientific', or 'theoretical', to describe their activity, yet the application of scientific assumptions to generic questions usually obscures as many problems as it solves.
10. Genre theoreticians and other practitioners are generally loath to recognize (and build into their theories) the institutional character of their own generic practice. Though regularly touting 'proper' approaches to genre, theorists rarely analyse the cultural stakes involved in identifying certain approaches as 'improper'. Yet genres are never entirely neutral categories. They – and their critics and theorists – always participate in and further the work of various institutions.

Regarding a number of important interrelated questions, literary genre theory has come to no firm conclusion. For some, the important dialectic constitutive of genre theory and practice involves the opposition of pure genres to mixed genres, while others stress the antithesis between genres and individual texts. Some theorists pay attention to the contrast between rule-driven production and spontaneous creation, while other theoreticians are more interested in the difference between inner and outer form. Does genre reside in a pre-existing pattern, in texts, in criticism, or somewhere else? Are genres classificatory conveniences or are they representations of reality? What difference do genres make? How and to whom do they make that difference? Even the term 'genre' is itself extremely volatile, in extent as well as in object and content.

But it cannot be taken for granted that film genre is the same thing as literary genre. Nor should we assume that film genre theory is coterminous with literary genre theory, even if it does largely derive from the work of literary theorists. In the next chapter we will discover whether any of these questions receives more satisfactory treatment in the work of film genre theorists.

2

What is generally understood by the notion of film genre?

> Genre isn't a word that pops up in every conversation about films – or every review – but the idea is second nature to the movies and our awareness of them. Movies belong to genres much the way people belong to families or ethnic groups. Name one of the classic, bedrock genres – Western, comedy, musical, war film, gangster picture, science fiction, horror – and even the most casual moviegoer will come up with a mental image of it, partly visual, partly conceptual.
>
> Richard T. Jameson, *They Went Thataway* (1994, p. ix)

In many ways, the study of film genre is no more than an extension of literary genre study. While film genre critics rarely quote Horace or Hugo, they do regularly cite Aristotle and a litany of more recent literary theorists. Leo Braudy invokes Samuel Johnson; Frank McConnell harks back to John Dryden; Ed Buscombe looks to Wellek and Warren; Stuart Kaminsky, John Cawelti and Dudley Andrew cite Northrop Frye; Will Wright leans on Vladimir Propp; Stephen Neale quotes Roland Barthes and Tzvetan Todorov. Clearly, much that is said about film genre is simply borrowed from a long tradition of literary genre criticism.

Nevertheless, there are significant differences between film genre criticism and its literary predecessors. Starting in the late 60s, publication on film genre mushroomed, eventually producing an intellectual space in which film scholars and critics now respond primarily to each other rather than to the literary critics who provided the backdrop for previous generic speculation. Whereas the bibliography of Will Wright's *Sixguns and Society* (1975), for example, still depended heavily on assorted literary theoreticians, linguists and anthropologists, almost every film genre study of the last decade repeats the same litany of film genre theorists, all published in the last quarter-century: Altman, Buscombe, Cawelti, Doane, Elsaesser, Neale, Schatz, Williams, and the very same Will Wright. In short, film genre study has over the last two decades established itself as a field separate from literary genre study. As such, it has developed its own assumptions, its own *modus operandi*, and its own objects of study.

This chapter will be devoted to a sketch of recent approaches to film genre. This overview is based primarily on book-length studies of major genres, along with particularly influential articles. The positions described are not necessarily the ones touted on book jackets or in theoretical introductions, however, but derive from the actual praxis of current genre study, i.e., the theory that emerges from the practice of genre criticism and history. I do not agree with all the methods or conclusions presented in this chapter. Indeed, the rest of this book will offer alternatives to many of the positions presented. Nevertheless, it is important for readers to understand the classical tradition of film genre studies as a basic context for the proposals that will be made in subsequent chapters. For this reason, the following ten claims have been presented in as straightforward a manner as possible, with little attempt to present variant positions or to criticize potentially problematic stands and strategies.

Genre is a useful category, because it bridges multiple concerns

Comic books are full of contraptions capable of performing multiple tasks. Genre is usually seen as just such a device. Only slightly short of magical in its versatility, genre endures within film theory because of its ability to perform multiple operations simultaneously. According to most critics, genres provide the formulas that drive production; genres constitute the structures that define individual texts; programming decisions are based primarily on generic criteria; the interpretation of generic films depends directly on the audience's generic expectations. All of these aspects are covered by the single term of genre.

As Dudley Andrew puts it in *Concepts in Film Theory* (1984), genres serve a precise function in the overall economy of cinema, an economy involving an industry, a social need for production of messages, a vast number of human subjects, a technology, and a set of signifying practices. Genre is a rare category in that it overtly involves every aspect of this economy; these aspects are always at play whenever the cinema is concerned but their interrelation is generally very difficult to perceive (1984. p. 110). Genre, it would appear, is not your average descriptive term, but a complex concept with multiple meanings, which we might identify as follows:

- genre as *blueprint*, as a formula that precedes, programmes and patterns industry production;
- genre as *structure*, as the formal framework on which individual films are founded;
- genre as *label*, as the name of a category central to the decisions and communications of distributors and exhibitors;
- genre as *contract*, as the viewing position required by each genre film of its audience.

While not every genre theorist attends to each of these four meanings and areas of generic operation, genre theorists typically justify their activity by the concept's polyvalence. Stephen Neale's *Genre* (1980), for example, begins by quoting Tom Ryall's claim that 'The master image for genre criticism is the triangle composed of artist/film/audience. Genres may be defined as patterns/forms/styles/structures which transcend individual films, and which supervise both their construction by the filmmaker, and their reading by an audience' (p. 7). From the film-maker through the individual film to the eventual audience, the same term suffices.

It is of course this ability to serve multiple functions that gives genre the power to secure privileged relations among cinema's various components. Film genre's special power is nearly always expressed in terms of stylistic devices or metaphors that figure a special ability to establish connections. According to Thomas Schatz (1981), film genres 'express the social and aesthetic sensibilities not only of Hollywood filmmakers but of the mass audience as well' (p. 14). In preference to this simple 'not only ... but ... as well' construction, Dudley Andrew offers an active balancing metaphor, asserting that 'genres equilibrate spectators and that vast technical, signifying, and ideological machine of the cinema' (1984, p. 111). It is Jim Kitses (1969), however, who achieves the most dynamic expression of film genre's communicative powers. 'Genre,' affirms Kitses in *Horizons West*, 'is a vital structure through which flow a myriad of themes and concepts' (p. 8). At one and the same time, genre is a structure and the conduit through which material flows from producers to directors and from the industry to distributors, exhibitors, audiences and their friends. While it is easy to understand how genre's multiple definitions and associations might lead to some confusion, it is even easier to appreciate how a concept of such versatility should capture the imagination of film critics (leading some to mistake the concept of genre for a critical panacea).

In passing, it is perhaps worth noting that film genre's consistent connections to the entire production-distribution-consumption process make it a broader concept than literary genre has typically been. Where the Horatian system emphasizes appropriate models for textual production and the Aristotelian tradition stresses textual structure and its effects on reception, film genre theorists have systematically assumed that the main virtue of generic criticism lies in its ability to bind and explain *all* aspects of the process, from production to reception. In fact, by regularly choosing examples from genres where all definitions (production, text, exhibition, consumption) neatly line up, critics have managed to avoid difficult questions regarding possible conflicts among those definitions.

Genres are defined by the film industry and recognized by the mass audience

Universally assuming that genres are broadly recognized public categories, film critics regularly find themselves faced with a tricky problem: if the existence of a genre depends on general public recognition rather than on individual spectator perception, then how does that public recognition come about? While this problem might have been resolved by reference to general cultural circumstances (following Siegfried Kracauer's argument in *From Caligari to Hitler* [1947]) or to the institutions of film reception (following Tony Bennett's [1983] 'reading formation' model), film genre theorists have preferred to trace a direct path from industrial origins to generalized audience acceptance of generic existence, description and terminology. While this conclusion depends on the somewhat doubtful assumption that genres shaped by the film industry are communicated completely and uniformly to audiences widely dispersed in terms of time, space and experience, it serves to close off further debate about the constitution and naming of genres.

When Frye and Todorov call for a 'scientific' approach to genre study, they mean that critics must be free to discover new connections, to form new textual groupings, and to offer new labels. Only in this way can Frye offer his theory of *mythoi* or Todorov describe the genre that he calls the *fantastic*. Film genre criticism has not followed this lead, particularly in constituting its objects of study. Instead of the romantic model of privileging individual critical analysis, film genre theory has followed the classical line, stressing the primacy of industry discourse, along with its broad effect on the mass audience.

Refusing to locate genre in textual properties alone, film genre theorists have systematically assumed a quasi-magical correspondence between industry purposes and audience responses – quasi-magical because the mechanics of the relationship between industry and audience have been described in only the most primitive manner. Leo Braudy's version of the relationship, for example, goes as follows: 'Genre films essentially ask the audience, "Do you still want to believe this?" Popularity is the audience answering, "Yes" ' (1977, p. 179). As Schatz says, after quoting Braudy's formula approvingly, 'The genre film reaffirms what the audience believes both on individual and on communal levels' (1981, p. 38). Paradoxically, then, the standard view of film genre sets up industry and audience each as an agent of the other. While in one sense 'genres are "made" by the collective response of the mass audience' (Schatz, 1981, p. 264), in a more fundamental way they are originally established and named by the film-producing industry. In an apparently continuous loop, like two serpents biting each other's tails, industry and audience are seen as locked in a symbiotic relationship leaving no room for a third party.

Explaining that genres are 'the product of audience and studio interaction', Schatz stresses that genres are 'not the result of some arbitrary critical or historical organization'. Neither organized nor discovered by analysts, film genres are instead 'the result of the material conditions of commercial filmmaking itself' (*ibid.*, p. 16). This point is echoed throughout the film genre tradition in the methods used by critics to constitute their generic canon. Whether the topic is the musical (Feuer), the Western (Cawelti), the biopic (Custen), the historical adventure film (Taves), the war film (Basinger), or even British genre films (Landy), the generic corpus is assumed to be a given, pre-defined by industrial fiat. As we will see in Chapter 5, by constructing their own versions of industry genre definition and corpus constitution, most genre studies actually do not fully respect the industrial activity to which they systematically pay lip service. Nevertheless, the theory behind current genre study clearly turns on the importance of industrial action to define what Neale calls 'institutionalized classes of texts' (1990, p. 52). If it is not defined by the industry and recognized by the mass audience, then it cannot be a genre, because film genres are by definition not just scientifically derived or theoretically constructed categories, but are always industrially certified and publicly shared.

Genres have clear, stable identities and borders

The theoretical clarity of film genre criticism is quite obviously challenged at every turn by the historical dimensions of film production and reception. Where film genre theory assumes coincidence between industrial and audience perceptions, history furnishes example after example of disparity. Where the theory of generic reception requires texts whose genres are immediately and transparently recognizable, the most interesting texts supplied by film history are complex, mobile and mysterious. Where Linnaeus' scientific binomial nomenclature model assumes pure specimens, genre history offers crossbreeds and mutants.

Yet film genre studies have too great a stake in generic purity to pay overmuch attention to history. Though the history of cinema might well have turned the study of film genre towards romantic notions of generic mixing, the theoretical programmes adopted by genre critics depend instead on careful adherence to

16

classical standards, not only in terms of genre separation, but also in terms of rule-based creation. The reasons for this are quite clear. Because genre is conceived as a conduit down which are poured textual structures linking production, exhibition and reception, genre study produces satisfactory results only when it has the right type of material to work with, i.e., texts that clearly and simultaneously support all aspects of the standard generic trajectory: blueprint, structure, label and contract. Only when the label and the structure provide a clear blueprint for production and a demonstrable basis for reception can this particular approach to genre operate properly.

In order to furnish appropriate material for this type of genre study, critics have regularly performed two complementary operations. First, they have systematically disregarded films that fail to exhibit clear generic qualifications. Second, each major genre has been defined in terms of a nucleus of films obviously satisfying the theory's fourfold assumptions:

(a) Each film was produced according to a recognizably generic blueprint.
(b) Each film displays the basic structures commonly identified with the genre.
(c) During its exhibition each film is regularly identified by a generic label.
(d) Audiences systematically recognize each film as belonging to the genre in question and interpret it accordingly.

However the privileged corpus of an individual genre is defined, one characteristic stands out: most genre critics prefer to deal with films that are clearly and ineluctably tied to the genre in question. No romantic mixed genres, no crossbreeds, no anomalies.

In fact, one of the common first moves made by genre theorists and historians is to justify reduction of the enormous corpus implied by the book's main title to the narrow corpus expressed in the title's colonated small print. Robert Lang, for example, begins a book titled *American Film Melodrama* (1989) by explaining that he is really dealing with 'family' melodrama as it appears in three films each by Griffith, Vidor and Minnelli. Will Wright (1975) reduces multiple thousands of Westerns to fifty films grossing more than four million dollars. Many more books conceal a *de facto* selection process beneath broad titles and claims. For Jane Feuer (1982) the musicals that really count are those produced by MGM's Freed unit. Thomas Schatz (1981) expresses his conclusions about the history of the Western in terms of selected films directed by John Ford. There is no sense in doing genre criticism, it would seem, without first constituting a corpus that is incontrovertibly generic.

A second method of assuring genres that are neat, manageable and stable is simply to subdivide broad genres into smaller units. Rather than take on the whole comic genre or even all of romantic comedy, Stanley Cavell (1981) trims down Hollywood comedy in *Pursuits of Happiness* to six comedies of remarriage. Brian Taves in *The Romance of Adventure* (1993) provides a remarkably clear example of this process in the opening words of the first chapter:

Ask six different individuals – lay person, scholar, critic, or filmmaker – to name the first adventure film that comes to mind, and there will probably be a half-dozen widely divergent answers. One person mentions *Raiders of the Lost Ark*, the second champions *Star Wars*, another replies *The Guns of Navarone*, a fourth cites *Quo Vadis*, a fifth champions the James Bond movies, and the sixth suggests *Robin Hood*. I believe that of these examples only *Robin Hood* is truly an adventure film. The others represent genres that are distinct in their own right. *Raiders of the Lost Ark* is a fantasy ... *Star Wars* is science fiction ... *The Guns of Navarone* is a war movie ... *Quo Vadis* is a biblical epic ... James Bond is a spy ... in a world of espionage and secret agents. *Robin Hood*, by contrast, deals with the valiant fight for freedom and a just form of government, set in exotic locales and the historical past. This is the central theme of adventure, a motif that is unique to the genre.

It is essential to determine what comprises an adventure film, to analyze the genre's central tenets, and to distinguish its borders from other forms with similar elements.

(pp. 3–4)

Concerned to remain faithful to the true nature of the genre, Taves demonstrates the importance currently attributed to aligning a genre's 'central tenets' and a narrow generic corpus with clear 'borders'. The nationalistic overtones of this dedication will receive further commentary in Chapter 12.

Individual films belong wholly and permanently to a single genre

Just as genres must have clear borders in order to facilitate the kind of genre criticism described here, so the individual films of any particular generic canon must clearly serve as examples of that genre. While a film may be seen as combining several lighting or camera styles, as juxtaposing radically different sound models, or as mixing location, studio and process images, it is usually treated as *either* a Western or a film noir, *either* a musical or a melodrama, *either* a historical adventure film or a biblical epic. When Hollywood converted to sound, films were designated by percentages, as 20 per cent talkie, or 50 per cent talkie, or even all-talkie. With genres, no such gradations are commonly deemed possible. Because of the uses to which the notion of genre is put, only an all-or-nothing approach to corpus building has appeared acceptable.

If spectators are to experience films in terms of their genre, films must leave no doubt as to their generic identity; instant recognizability must be assumed. Statements about generic spectatorship typically take this for granted. For example, Stephen Neale says that 'The existence of genres means that the spectator, precisely, will always know that everything will be "made right in the end", that everything will cohere, that any threat or any danger in the narrative process itself will always be contained' (1980, p. 28). It is of course not 'the existence of genres' alone that guarantees spectator comfort. A text conflating two genres, say romantic comedy and documentary reporting or exploitation violence, might well put spectators in a potentially uncontainable quandary. Where one genre seems to assure the young lovers' safety, the other offers only an atrocious death. This too is a type of reading that could be made possible by 'the existence of genres', but it is emphatically not the one regularly chosen by recent critics.

For this reason, terms used to describe relationships between individual films and genre typically follow the type/token model. That is, each film is imaged as an example of the overall genre, replicating the generic prototype in all basic characteristics. Thus films are often said to 'belong to' or to be 'members of' a genre. While the inclusive lists provided at the end of many genre studies show great concern to divide the genre into its constitutive subgenres, they almost never reveal any doubt about whether each and every film deserves to be considered as a token of the genre in question. Termed simply 'Major and representative westerns' (Cawelti, 1975), 'Musicals by subgenre' (Altman, 1987), 'Biopics by studio' (Custen, 1992), or 'Adventure films by type' (Taves, 1993), these listings provide eloquent testimony to the doctrine of generic exclusivity practised by recent critics, theorists and historians. If genres are regularly treated like nation-states, then dual citizenship has clearly been proscribed by current genre studies.

Rare is the city that has forever flown the same flag. Just as it might seem logical to think that some films simultaneously exhibit the characteristics of more than a single genre, it would appear reasonable to believe that some films might have changed colours over the years. In the 20s, virtually every film was identified as either a melodrama or a comedy; in the 40s films were regularly identified by multiple designators (such as comedy melodrama, juvenile comedy, or comedy-fantasy); by the 70s an entirely new set of generic types was available (road film, big caper film, disaster film, and the like). Instead of considering that changes in terminology modify the generic identity of previous films, however, critics have always assumed that new terms should have no effect on already existing films and that generic identification is a once-and-for-all affair. When Stuart Kaminsky introduces the big caper genre, he suggests that, 'as a formula, big caper movies are as old as Westerns' (1974, p. 75). Yet he mentions only three pre-1950 films and reaches the conclusion that 'The big caper film did not emerge as an identifiable genre, however, until the 1950s' (*ibid.*, p. 76). The next twenty-three pages and the entire film list are thus given over to the genre since 1950.

Stephen Neale (1990; 1993) has pointed out that many films have undergone a change in genre designation over the course of their lives. Far from concluding that films may indeed under some circumstances change genre, however, Neale simply castigates recent critics for misapprehending the genre of the films in question. The basic, broadly accepted assumption thus stands: once generically identified by the industry, films are typed for life.

Genres are transhistorical

In current practice, the very act of identifying a genre requires that generic texts be lifted out of time and placed in a timeless holding area as if they were all contemporaries. Responding to a classical sense of tradition popularized by Matthew Arnold, T.S. Eliot and Northrop Frye, this synchronic approach strips away historical differences, thus offering a stage where similarities among texts may readily be recognized. Also operative here is the influence of Lévi-Strauss and of anthropology in general. Commonly dealing with texts that are undatable or virtually unchanging over time, structural anthropologists offer the perfect model for genre critics who would see genre as somehow beyond history.

Even more than Jungian psychology, Lévi-Straussian influence on literary structuralism heavily contributed to a persistent tendency either to compare genre to myth or to treat genres as current embodiments of myth. For Bazin, 'The western was born of an encounter between a mythology and a means of expression' (1971, p. 142). Altman claims that 'the musical fashions a myth out of the American courtship ritual' (1987, p. 27). Schatz confesses that 'in the final analysis, the relationship of genre filmmaking to cultural myth-making seems to me to be significant and direct' (p. 263). Will Wright dots the 'i's': 'the Western, though located in a modern industrial society, is as much a myth as the tribal myths of the anthropologists' (1975, p. 187).

Likening genre to myth provides clear gains for genre theorists. This strategy provides an organizing principle for genre study, transmuting what might have been a hollow commercial formula into a culturally functional category, and thus lending the prestigious support of cultural anthropology to the heretofore lowly study of popular genres. In return for these benefits, however, genre critics have been forced to forego serious historical considerations in favour of the transhistorical model offered by myth. Says John Cawelti: 'Genre is universal, basic to human perceptions of life' (1975, p. 30). Following Peter Brooks, Robert Lang speaks of the 'melodramatic imagination' (1989, pp. 17–18), while Gerald Mast (1973) speaks of the 'comic mind'. Each film genre is thus figured as a representational form deriving directly from a basic human capacity.

The need to treat genre as a transhistorical category has an interesting effect on recent accounts of genre beginnings. Whereas genres might have been seen as developing within the film industry, according to a historically specific logic, they tend instead to be seen either as continuations of genres pre-existing in literature (the Western), theatre (melodrama) and non-fiction writing (the biopic), or as volcanic eruptions of mythic magma, brought to the surface by the vagaries of technology (the musical), censorship (screwball comedy), or modern life (sci-fi). Whatever role current circumstances may play in formulating the surface structure of genre films, much recent genre theory has assumed that the deep structures come directly from the archetypal depths of myth, whether already apparent in other domains or newly brought to the surface by cinema itself.

The transhistorical nature of current generic speculation often leads to treatment of a single film or group of films as having a special role in defining a genre or expressing its 'essence'. Stanley Cavell claims that 'a genre emerges full-blown ... and then works out its internal consequences ... it has no history, only a birth and a logic' (1981, p. 27). Like many others, Thomas Schatz refers to a 'generic prototype' (1981, p. 264), as if genres were typically set in place on an industrial model: create a prototype, put it into production, continue to produce the new product as long as it sells. Jerome Delamater slightly varies this metaphor by treating a particular type of musical (the 'integrated' musical) as the genre's Platonic ideal (1974, p. 130), i.e., as the mythically pure form to which this earthly genre aspires. The musical was born by mistake in the wrong form, as Delamater tells the story, but the genre's 'natural' tendency towards replicating the myth's pure form assured the musical's eventual adherence to the integrated model.

If all philosophy is a footnote to Plato, then all genre theory is little more than a footnote to Aristotle. The current tendency to figure genres transhistorically simply extends Aristotle's intention to note the *essential* quality of each poetic kind. It is precisely the notion that genres have essential qualities that makes it possible to align them with archetypes and myths and to treat them as expressive of broad and perdurable human concerns.

Genres undergo predictable development

By defining genres in a transhistorical fashion, recent critics facilitate the identification and description of genres, while stressing the extent to which genres regularly repeat similar strategies. Yet genres do exist in history. Unlike the exact replicas produced by other consumer industries (clothing, appliances, cars), genre films must not only be similar in order to succeed, they must also be different. As Robert Warshow has pointed out, 'variation is absolutely necessary to keep the type from becoming sterile; we do not want to see the same movie over and over again, only the same form' (1974, p. 147). Genre critics have long deemed it necessary to construct a model that would properly describe and account for this tendency towards variation.

Two closely related paradigms, both dependent on organic metaphors, have been developed to configure and explain the restricted variations of genre film. The first treats the genre as a living being, with individual films reflecting specific age brackets. As Jane Feuer points out, 'film genres, especially long-lived ones such as the Western and the musical, follow a predictable life cycle' (1993, p. 88). John Cawelti details the stages of this development: 'One can almost make out a life cycle characteristic of genres as they move from an initial period of articulation and discovery, through a phase of conscious self-awareness on the part of both creators and audiences, to a time when the generic patterns have become so well-known that people become tired of their predictability' (1986, p. 200). The metaphor is pervasive. Brian Taves (1993) notes the development of the adventure genre from 'a time of comparative innocence' (p. 73) to a period of 'experience .. . and disillusionment' (p. 74). Schatz (1981) returns repeatedly to life-cycle terminology, outlining 'a newborn genre's status as social ritual' (p. 41), evoking a genre's habits 'at the earliest stages of its life span' (p. 38), and concluding with evocations of maturity and death. Two different section headings in Schatz's book *Hollywood Genres* employ the expression 'comes of age' to describe generic development (with reference to the musical, p. 189, and melodrama, p. 223), while the Western's growth is traced from youth through self-confident maturity to neurotic professionalism.

The notion that a genre grows according to a human developmental scheme accompanies a more general anthropomorphism whereby genres are regularly said to develop, to react, to become self-conscious, and to self-destruct. Whether the parallel is simply suggested metaphorically or programmatically developed, generic anthropomorphism always provides a rhetorically effective model of variation within a context of fundamental fixity. Convinced of the sacrosanct nature of personal identity, our society easily accepts the human life metaphor as guarantor of continuity.

Critics who stress change over continuity typically also turn to a second model, that of biological evolution. Brian Taves traces the 'evolution' of the adventure genre through four cycles (1993, 56ff). Thomas Schatz (1981) shuttles between Christian Metz's classic-parody-contestation-critique model and Henri Focillon's quadripartite version of the life of forms: the experimental age, the classic age, the age of refinement, the baroque age. Designed to account for variety within a genre's overall homogeneity, these evolutionary schemes paradoxically stress generic predictability more than variation. Whereas biological evolution depends heavily on unexpected mutations, the evolutionary model used to describe generic evolution always dwells on entirely predictable patterns. Jane Feuer's treatment of the backstage musical clearly exemplifies this tendency:

> The backstage musical provides a textbook illustration of a genre's development from a period of experimentation in which the conventions are established (1929–33) to a classical period during which a balance reigns (1933–53) to a period of reflexivity dominated by parody, contestation and even deconstruction of a genre's native tongue. Indeed, the neat unfolding I have just been enumerating has about it an almost mathematical precision, as if one could out of a table of permutations have predicted the emergence of certain new combinations at certain periods in the genre's history.
>
> (1993, p. 90)

Feuer's unfolding metaphor identifies her evolutionary stance as pre-Darwinian. Genres are like genetically programmed seeds, she seems to say, bound for a particular destiny and no other.

Both of the models typically evoked to explain generic development – the well-known stages of a human life and the prescribed pattern of an unfolding evolution – thus offer precious little elbowroom. Like a train, genre is free to move, but only along already laid tracks. This tendency to subordinate history to continuity by restricting change to prescribed limits helps us to understand the sleight of hand whereby genre history can regularly be written without contradicting genre's transhistorical nature. Like railroad tracks, teleological history assures that genres will be free only to shuttle back and forth between experimentation and reflexivity. Always contained, generic types are forever separated by the isolating action of a historical logic according to which genres can only unfold, but never mate or select. Genre history so eschews change that it resembles no other modern form of history. Yet genre history's organic model serves a particular type of genre theory especially well, effectively containing the significant challenge that serious historical consideration would pose to genre, thereby preserving recent genre theory's overall commitment to a transhistorical definition of clearly separate genres.

Genres are located in a particular topic, structure and corpus

Films might reasonably be categorized – indeed have been categorized – according to a wide spectrum of variables. Films are produced by major, minor, or independent studios, in live-action or animation form, on a big budget or a shoestring, as personal projects or programmers. Short or long, widescreen or academy ratio, in black and white or colour, films are distributed as 'A' or 'B' pictures, initial- or re-release, with an age rating of, for example, 'PG' or 'X'. Exhibited in first-run or local theatres, in standalones or multiplexes, with mono sound, Dolby stereo, or THX, films inspire audiences to giggles and laughter or pity and fear, to silence or whistling, to buy popcorn or not. Any one of these differences, and many more, might have been deemed pertinent to generic classification. Yet genres are typically defined according to a far more limited range of characteristics.

Consider the famous *Variety* headline: 'STIX NIX HICK PIX'. Are 'hick pix' a genre, including rural melodramas, regional musicals, small-town crime movies, and any other film dealing with rural America? Generations of American genre critics have answered this question in the negative. We understand what 'hick pix' are, but we don't treat this category as a genre. Instead, genres are thought to reside in a particular topic and structure or in a corpus of films that share a specific topic and structure. That is, in order to be recognized as a genre, films must have both a common topic (and here rural America might well do) and a common structure, a common way of configuring that topic. Even when films share a common topic, they will not be perceived as members of a genre unless that topic systematically receives treatment of the same type (which is where 'hick pix' falls short, for it is a

Shots like this one of gunfighter Harrison Ford led many critics to assimilate Star Wars *(1977) to the Western.*

category based solely on a broad topic). The inverse of this proposition has also remained true in recent criticism. When *Star Wars* took American theatres by storm, many viewers recognized in its structure the familiar epic configuration of the Western. In fact, some critics described *Star Wars* as a Western. Their desire to integrate this film into the corpus of the Western did not hold sway, however, for the general tendency of genre theorists and the popular audience alike is to recognize genre only when both subject and structure coincide.

If genre-ness is thought to reside in a particular complex of topic and structure (or 'semantics' and 'syntax', the terms used in my 1984 article printed as an appendix to this volume), the genre itself is typically thought of as a corpus of films. When we hear the expression 'the Hollywood musical' we understand that someone is referring not to production, exhibition, or reception concerns, but to an existing, largely agreed on corpus of films. It is not by chance that most genre studies close with a list of films, for it is that very corpus that constitutes the author's object of study. This attitude has become so familiar as to seem natural. The entire history of genre theory has trained us to expect critics to start with a predefined genre and corpus.

In passing, it is worth noting that the corpus typically identified with a specific genre is not single, but double. Nearly every genre critic offers a long list of films, but only treats a few of them. Sometimes this restriction is done consciously and openly (Thomas Elsaesser [1973] reducing melodrama to family melodrama), but more often, in imitation of Northrop Frye's slippage from comedy in general to the more restrictive domain of New Comedy, the narrowing of a standard corpus fails to be acknowledged (as in the common auteurist tendency to equate the suspense film with Hitchcock, the melodrama with Sirk, the Western with Ford, and the musical with films produced by MGM's Freed unit). Because of this tendency towards generic gerrymandering, it is important to recognize the effective difference between the full list of films identified as the critic's object of study and the far more limited list of films that represent the critic's version of the genre's putative Platonic ideal.

Genre films share certain fundamental characteristics

Given the critical tendency to locate genre in a shared topic and structure, films within the same genre must obviously share certain basic attributes. Curiously, though, the resemblance does not stop there: critics have noted that all Hollywood genre films share certain essential properties.

Constantly opposing cultural values to counter-cultural values, genre films regularly depend on dual protagonists and *dualistic* structures (producing what I have called dual-focus texts). In the archetypal Western scene, the sheriff confronts an outlaw in a shoot-out; the gangster is doubled by a rival gang leader or FBI agent; the US Army commander is matched by a German or Japanese counterpart; the human hero is pitted against a monster from prehistory or outer space; even Fred Astaire must share the billing with Ginger Rogers. When a single individual manages to hold the spotlight throughout, it is often because he is himself schizophrenic, divided like Dr Jekyll and Mr Hyde into separate and opposed beings.

24

Both intratextually and intertextually, the genre film uses the same material over and over again. A common complaint levelled against genre films, 'If you've seen one you've seen 'em all', correctly describes their *repetitive* nature. The same fundamental conflicts are resolved over and over again in similar fashion – the same shoot-out, the same sneak attack, the same love scene culminating in the same duet. Each film varies the details but leaves the basic pattern undisturbed, to the point where shots used in one film are often recycled in another (for example, battle action from the 1929 *Divine Lady* is pressed into service in the 1935 *Captain Blood* and yet again in the 1940 *Sea Hawk* – see Behlmer, 1985, p. 109). The extras of adventure and war movies truly die a thousand deaths – once shot they must change costume or location in order to repeat the exercise. The genre film seems to represent nothing more than the endless repetition of the same confrontation, the same two-shot, the same love scene.

The repetitive nature of genre films tends to diminish the importance of each film's ending, along with the cause-and-effect sequence that leads to that conclusion. Instead, genre films depend on the *cumulative* effect of the film's often repeated situations, themes and icons. Early critics of the gangster film were already well aware of this fact; the deaths of Cagney, Robinson and Muni at the end of *Public Enemy, Little Caesar* and *Scarface* are insufficient to reverse the impression left by the rest of the film. In its totality, the gangster film glorifies the gangster by accumulating scenes of bravado, wit, good sense, fidelity and just plain guts. Who can follow or remember the cause-and-effect sequence presented in *The Big Sleep*? Yet no one forgets the interaction between Bogie and Bacall. Far more important than the ending of a road movie are the repeated and similar encounters that make up the middle of the film. From *Bonnie and Clyde* to *Thelma and Louise* it is the cumulative effect of the couple's interactions that stays with the viewer, rather than any particular decision or result.

The repetitive and cumulative nature of genre films makes them also quite *predictable*. Not only can the substance and the ending of most genre films be predicted by the end of the first reel, but the repeated formulaic use of familiar stars usually makes them predictable on the basis of the title and credits alone. Such names as Boris Karloff, Errol Flynn, Jeanette MacDonald, John Wayne, Gene Kelly, Sylvester Stallone, Goldie Hawn and Arnold Schwarzenegger designate more than just actors and actresses – they guarantee a certain style, a particular atmosphere and a well-known set of attitudes. The pleasure of genre film spectatorship thus derives more from reaffirmation than from novelty. People go to genre films to participate in events that somehow seem familiar. They may be looking for strong emotions, exciting scenes, novel situations and fresh dialogue, but like those who go to the amusement park in search of adventure, they would rather enjoy their excitement in a controlled environment that they recognize. Genre film suspense is thus almost always false suspense: in order to participate in the film's strong emotions we must provisionally pretend we don't know that the heroine will be rescued, the hero freed, and the couple reunited.

Films with weak generic ties usually depend heavily on their own internal logic, whereas genre films make heavy use of *intertextual* references. The Western respects and recalls the history of the Western more than it does the history of the West. Musicals constantly refer back to earlier musicals. As if each genre were itself a complete and closed universe, discussions among film genre fans regularly evoke other genre films rather than the real world. Implicitly, each new genre film ingests every previous film, a process often literalized by the recycling of popular titles. In order to understand the later films we must also know the earlier films that they contain.

In spite of a strong tendency to close in on themselves, genre films nevertheless maintain a strong connection to the culture that produced them. Whereas other films depend heavily on their referential qualities to establish ties to the real world, genre films typically depend on *symbolic* usage of key images, sounds and situations. Actual location matters less for the Western's incessant long shots of the landscape than the way the landscape is used to figure the simultaneous danger and potential that the West represents. Similarly, a train crossing the prairie (*The Man Who Shot Liberty Valance*), a contested gun (*Winchester '73*), and the building of a church (*My Darling Clementine*) or a schoolhouse (*Oklahoma!*) all carry a symbolic weight that outstrips the historical referent. More than just part of history, these symbols evoke the taming of nature's dangers and the resultant civilization of the West. Often castigated for oversimplification of history and human relations, genre films also gain from their simplicity, for it is the very concentration derived from simplification that allows cowboys, gangsters, dancers, detectives and monsters to take on symbolic value so easily and systematically.

As Malinowski and Radcliffe-Browne discovered with ritual, as Langer and Cassirer claimed of myth, as Freud suggested for dreams and Huizinga for play, film genres are *functional* for their society. Whereas producers and exhibitors see genre films as 'product', critics increasingly recognize their role in a complex cultural system permitting viewers to consider and resolve (albeit fictively) contradictions that are not fully mastered by the society in which they live. Seen as referential documents, musicals are a lie; they offer a view of male–female relationships that simply does not square with real life. Musicals make much more sense when they are seen as working out the sexes' different expectations within American culture, thus justifying cultural practices that might otherwise be judged unacceptable. Musicals – and other genres – thus function to satisfy a society that its practices, almost always problematic from some point of view, are fully defensible and deserving of public support.

Genres have either a ritual or an ideological function

During the 60s and 70s, renewed interest in popular culture and its genres was spurred on by two critical currents. On the one hand, literary structuralism followed the lead of Vladimir Propp and Claude Lévi-Strauss in concentrating on folk narratives without any apparent source other than the very audience of those narratives. From Lévi-Strauss and other structural anthropologists, genre critics learnt that narrative can serve as a form of societal self-expression, directly addressing the society's constitutive contradictions. During the same period, a growing number of Marxist critics followed the example of Louis Althusser, who demonstrated the ideological investment that governments and industries place in the symbolic and representational systems that they produce.

During the 70s and 80s, these two basic tendencies were transformed into exemplary theories regarding the function of genre in popular texts. Had genre theorists turned instead to other available models, for example quantitative uses and gratifications research, Freudian psychoanalysis, or the New History of the Annales School, they would certainly have reached different conclusions about the function of genre. With Lévi-Strauss and Althusser serving as primary models, however, it is hardly surprising that they split into two counterposed groups – what might be called the ritual and ideological camps.

Following the example of primitive or folk narrative, the ritual approach considers that audiences are the ultimate creators of genres, which function to justify and organize a virtually timeless society. According to this approach, the narrative patterns of generic texts grow out of existing societal practices, imaginatively overcoming contradictions within those very practices. From this point of view, audiences have a very special investment in genres, because genres constitute the audience's own method of assuring its unity and envisioning its future. Particularly welcome to champions of popular culture because of its ability to lend meaning to a previously neglected or condemned domain, the ritual approach has been applied to cinema by a wide range of critics, including Altman, Braudy, Cawelti, McConnell, Schatz, Wood and Wright.

Based on an entirely different narrative model, the ideological approach reaches radically divergent conclusions. Imaging narrative texts as the vehicle for a government's address to its citizens/subjects or an industry's appeal to its clients, Althusser's system attributes greater importance to discursive concerns than the ritual approach, more sensitive instead to questions of narrative structure. Whereas ritual critics interpret narrative situations and structural relations as offering *imaginative* solutions to a society's real problems, ideological critics see the same situations and structures as luring audiences into accepting *deceptive* non-solutions, while all the time serving governmental or industry purposes. Here too, genres have a particular role and importance, for it is through generic conventions that audiences are lured into false assumptions of societal unity and future happiness.

Taking their cues from demonstrations by Roland Barthes and Theodor Adorno that popular texts lull audiences to sleep by apparently doing the reading for them, ideologically oriented theorists treat genres as particularly soporific tunes in the overall ideological lullaby programme. Originally propounded by Jean-Louis Comolli and other writers for the Parisian journal *Cahiers du cinéma*, along with Jean-Louis Baudry and his colleagues at *Cinéthique*, the film-oriented version of ideological criticism was initially popularized in the English-speaking world by the British journal *Screen*; in the United States it was first championed by the Marxist-inspired *Jump Cut*, but moved rapidly to *Camera Obscura* and other feminist venues before suffusing virtually the entire field during the 80s.

One might expect the proponents of each of these approaches to champion a separate corpus of films, like conservative and liberal Christians quoting complementary passages from the Bible in support of their irreconcilable positions. Curiously, the debate has never turned on the kind of complex textual gerrymandering characteristic of religious conflict. On the contrary, both sides regularly cite films by the same beloved directors (Ford, Hitchcock, Minnelli, Sirk) and with the sole exception of the film noir, which ritual critics have still not managed to crack, both sides regularly evoke all major genres and a wide variety of minor ones. One reasonable conclusion – that Hollywood genres owe their very existence to their ability to serve both functions at once – has been advanced (Altman, 1987, pp. 98–9), but not generally adopted.

Genre critics are distanced from the practice of genre

The role of film criticism and the status of speculation about genre occupy an unexpected place in recent genre theory. The genre critic might well have been accorded a special function in our overall understanding of genre. As a *primus inter pares* within the genre audience, the genre critic might have been seen as an especially important player in the game of determining generic existence, boundaries and meaning. This position follows quite reasonably from the ritual approach, whereby audiences are said to mould genres to their own needs. The critic would thus play the role of shaman, interceding between the audience and the text, the society and the industry.

Instead, the stance typically assumed by genre critics follows a different model, where texts are seen as handed down by a distant, powerful government or industry. Here, the role of the critic is to stand aside and watch the effect of institutionally produced texts on unsuspecting subjects. Following a time-honoured humanist tradition, further developed by Cartesianism, Enlightenment science and nineteenth-century positivism, critics are assumed to have the power to rise above the very audiences with whom they viewed the films they write about. The kindest words that genre theorists of the last half-century can apply to themselves – such terms as scientific, objective, or theoretical – are all words that implicitly separate them from the masses of viewers who are unable to see with the specially trained eyes of the critic. While this configuration was not surprising in post-war high culture attacks on popular culture, it is to say the least unexpected in the entertainment-oriented domain of genre film.

The ramifications of this position are many. Though originally developed in order to empower critics, who were thus all the better able to look down from their cultured heights on the masses, the distancing of critics from the genre audience has had the effect of excluding them, at least in theory, from the active constitution of genres. The 'industry' is regularly treated by Stephen Neale and other writers as the only effective creator and sustainer of genres. While this position no doubt overlooks the extent to which genre criticism has itself become a substantial industry, it does have the virtue of maintaining the purity of the critic's role as observer, rather than as player, in the genre game. All the more curious in a post-structuralist context, where every reader is expected to be a rewriter of texts, the objective and distanced genre theorist has chosen the strange position of a high culture commentator in order to comment on a popular culture form.

The extent to which current genre theory places the genre critic 'out of the loop' is all too consistent with the way in which genre critics actually view films, for it must be admitted that critics are the only viewers of genre films who so regularly do their viewing alone, whether in screening rooms, on a Moviola, or a VCR. However consistent this position may be with other aspects of traditional journalism and academic endeavour, it is important to recognize that it does not constitute the only possible solution. Chapter 5 will evoke examples of the generic changes that might be made by critics and audiences who would see their appropriate role as active and engaged rather than as theoretical and objective.

The overall account that emerges from these ten partial views is surprisingly coherent – far more so than literary genre study has ever been. According to this account, the film industry, responding to audience desires, initiates clear-cut genres that endure because of their ability to satisfy basic human needs. While they do change in predictable ways over the course of their life, genres nevertheless maintain a fundamental sameness both from decade to decade and from production through exhibition to audience consumption. Guaranteeing the broad applicability of generic concepts is the broad range of meanings attributed to the term genre, along with the conduit-like nature of textual structure. Seen from the vantage point of the distanced critic, genres at times appear to function ritually, and at other moments to operate ideologically.

This traditional view of genres thus presents a neat and welcome package. Still, the very coherence of this approach remains somewhat disconcerting. Several times during this chapter, the question of genre history has been raised as a potential threat to traditional views of genre. The time has now come to take that problem seriously. Can the current understanding of genre be squared with genre history? Or might careful consideration of historical questions shake the very ground on which traditional genre theory is built?

3
Where do genres come from?

> The more promising possibility, for the moment at least, is to return to film history and try to produce individual genre studies with real historical integrity. This would mean (1) starting with a genre's 'pre-history', its roots in other media; (2) studying all films, regardless of perceived quality; and (3) going beyond film content to study advertising, the star system, studio policy, and so on in relation to the production of films.
>
> Alan Williams, 'Is a Radical Genre Criticism Possible?' (1984, p. 124)

Much of what passes for genre history is actually no more than description of a genre's putative life cycle. Once identified, the genre's first appearance on film is treated as a generic prototype, born of the marriage between a pre-existing form and a new technology. The new genre then develops, matures and enjoys a stable career before eventually succumbing to reflective old age. Critics regularly assume that film genres are simply borrowed from already existing genres in another medium. Both industrial decision-making and critical evaluation of each new film genre are taken to be simplified by the prior existence of the same genre in other media.

This is the logic that has given such films as *The Broadway Melody* (1929), *The Great Train Robbery* (1903) and *Disraeli* (1929) such a prototypical place of honour in the history of, respectively, the musical, the Western and the biopic. The notion that these films and others like them serve as generic models would of course be problematic without the bolstering effect of non-filmic generic precedents. Stephen Neale expresses the commonly held opinion when he says that 'each new genre film constitutes an addition to an existing generic corpus and involves a selection from the repertoire of generic elements available at any one point in time' (1990, p. 56). While these claims appear logical enough, they make sense only as long as nobody asks, 'But where did the genre come from?' In recent theory, myths of origin have rightly been criticized for their tendency to dissimulate problems rather than to solve them. Film criticism's recourse to generic prototypes anchored in previously existing, non-filmic genres solves this problem all too cleverly: by locating the generic origin in some other medium, this approach indefinitely defers explanation of that origin.

This chapter will offer an entirely different method of understanding generic beginnings. Instead of describing generic origins with terminology developed *post facto* and retroactively applied to early films, I will look closely at the terms actually used by contemporaries to describe the films that today are widely recognized as a genre's early masterpieces. Instead of taking for granted the existence of generic links postulated by recent critics, I examine production decisions in order to determine the types of connection foregrounded and furthered at the time. Instead of assuming that yesterday's film industry and today's critics know what constitutes 'the repertoire of generic elements available at any one point in time',

I propose to show that the film production industry plays a far more creative and yet tentative role than has been concluded in the past. Contributing to the elaboration of a new theory of generic origins will be three case studies, covering the early years of three major genres: the musical, the Western and the biopic.

The musical

It is commonly alleged that the musical burst on to the Hollywood scene with the coming of sound. Virtually every history of the genre lists *The Jazz Singer* as the first musical and the years 1929 and 1930 as the genre's heyday. In 1931 and 1932, these same histories all agree (I ought to know, I wrote one of them), the production of musicals fell off precipitously, because the public tired of the genre. Commentators on the early history of the musical have generally assumed that the genre is a direct import from Broadway, predetermined by new sound film technology. The circumstantial evidence certainly points in that direction: not only are Broadway songs and plots reused, but even when Hollywood produces its own original musicals it simply borrows Broadway personnel to get them off the ground. This debt is clearly reflected in the Broadway orientation of early musical titles (*The Broadway Melody, Broadway, Broadway Babies, Broadway Scandals, Gold Diggers of Broadway, Broadway Bad, Broadway Thru a Keyhole, Broadway to Hollywood*).

Yet the first sound films built around entertainers and their music were not actually identified at the time as 'musicals'. Instead, the presence of music was at

The Broadway Melody *(1929) is now regularly treated as the granddaddy of all musicals, but it was originally described by MGM as an 'all talking, all singing, all dancing dramatic sensation'.*

31

first treated simply as a manner of presenting narrative material that already had its own generic affinities. During the early years of sound in Hollywood, we thus find the term 'musical' always used as an adjective, modifying such diverse nouns as comedy, romance, melodrama, entertainment, attraction, dialogue and revue. Even films currently considered classics of the early musical were not labelled as musicals when they first appeared. *The Broadway Melody* was described in MGM publicity as an 'all talking, all singing, all dancing *dramatic* sensation' (my emphasis), while Warner Bros. characterized *The Desert Song* as an 'all talking, all singing *operetta*' (my emphasis).

The variety of generic terms used to categorize films now regularly described as musicals is remarkable. Here, for example, is a selection of the terms used by *Photoplay* to describe films that appeared between early 1929 and mid-1930:

Weary River: epic
My Man: drama
Hearts in Dixie: singing, dancing comedy with music
The Time, the Place and the Girl: all-talking comedy drama
Broadway: underworld drama
Street Girl: musical drama
The Vagabond Lover: romantic musical comedy
College Love: 100% talking, singing college picture
Rio Rita: musical comedy
The Love Parade: light opera
Sally: musical romance
Devil May Care: romance punctured with subtle comedy
Roadhouse Nights: melodrama and button-busting comedy
The Rogue's Song: operetta
Broadway Hoofer: backstage comedy
The Big Pond: straight romantic comedy
Top Speed: musical comedy, with emphasis on the comedy
Let's Go Native: musical farce

Ironically, use of the term 'musical' as a freestanding label designating a specific genre was not broadly accepted until the 1930–31 season, when the public's taste for musical films took a nosedive. From 55 musical films in 1929 and 77 in 1930 (figures equalled only during the war years), production fell to 11 musical films in 1931 and 10 in 1932 – the industry low point until the 60s. Only after this demise was the term 'musical' regularly used as a standalone substantive, usually to denigrate earlier films, which in retrospect appeared standardized and limited. Here are some samples of *Photoplay*'s 1930–31 terminology (my emphasis):

Whoopee: Don't say you're fed up on musical comedies. Go to see 'Whoopee' instead. ... This is the new type of screen *musical*. There is no attempt at realism.
Half Shot at Sunrise: Incidentally, while it's not a *musical*, there are a few good song numbers.
Follow the Leader: Why must *musicals* be going out, when some are like this?
Sunny: Who said *singies* were through? A gem of a picture like this makes us wonder.
Children of Dreams: Another reason why the box-office turned thumbs down on *musicals*.

Palmy Days: Ten-to-one, this will bring back film *musicals* in a veritable inundation. It's *that* good! ... If they can make *musicals* like this, then there's no reason at all why they shouldn't come back.

Prior to late 1930, the standalone term 'musical' was almost never used. Surprisingly, current terminology post-dates the production of scores of films regularly identified today as musicals. Only retrospectively could films of such differing natures appear to constitute a coherent grouping. Not yet musicals when they were *in*, certain films became musicals retroactively precisely because they constituted a general style that had gone *out*. Paradoxically, it was their late 1930 fall from grace that helped to unify a theretofore heterogeneous collection of films with music. Thus, in June of 1931, *Photoplay* could offer a short article about the strange career of John Boles:

> No matter what way you may look at it, it's still a funny business – this movie-making.
> For instance, John Boles was originally put on contract by Universal because of not so much his good looks as his good voice. So they had him sing and sing.
> Then musicals 'went out,' as Hollywood believes, and they put John Boles, the singer, into the leading rôle in 'Seed,' wherein he doesn't sing a note.
> And now they're talking about 'bringing musicals back!'
> Is there NO reason?
>
> (Quoted in Kreuger, 1975, p. 276)

What is it that films must have in common in order to be perceived as a separate genre? Ironically, an initial hypothesis would seem to be in order:

1. Films often gain generic identity from similar defects and failures rather than from shared qualities and triumphs.

From the time of the public premiere of Vitaphone in 1926, featuring opera singers, classical musicians, a banjo picker and a troupe of Spanish dancers, sound technology had been mated with every type of programme, from feature films and cartoons to documentaries, travelogues and news. Fiction films alone had been based on legitimate drama, nightclub acts, vaudeville turns, minstrel shows, burlesque routines, circus numbers, show boats, ventriloquists, radio programmes and Hollywood films. Music had been added to melodramas, Westerns, romances, college comedies, biographies and even science fiction films. Every style of singer had been pressed into service: crooners, grand opera stars, light operetta favourites, Irish tenors, cabaret singers, and even zany comics. It is hardly surprising, then, that early films with music were not identified by either their makers or their viewers as part of a single well-delineated genre.

The early history of the musical reveals that film genres are not always borrowed intact from non-film sources. The musical has far too many sources for all of them to be unproblematically extended in a single filmic form. Furthermore, the standalone term 'musical' was not invented until the consolidation of the film musical. Not until 1933, with the merger of music-making and romantic comedy, would the term 'musical' definitively abandon its adjectival, descriptive function and assume its identity as a generic noun – as when Warner Bros. *42nd Street* is referred to in *Photoplay* as an 'out-and-out musical'.

The musical also suggests a second hypothesis:

2. The early history of film genres is characterized, it would seem, not by purposeful borrowing from a single pre-existing non-film parent genre, but by apparently incidental borrowing from several unrelated genres.

As counterintuitive as it may seem, as unthinkable as it may be, there was no musical genre as such in 1929. The 1929 films that we now identify with the musical already had clear generic identities, which had to be dissolved, or at least significantly attenuated, before the musical could become an established independent genre.

The Western

Of all received notions about cinema, few are so widely shared as the sure knowledge that Edwin S. Porter's 1903 film *The Great Train Robbery*, based on Scott Marble's recently revived play, was the cinema's first Western. Filed by histories of the West and the Western (Fenin & Everson, 1962, p. 49; *The Wild West*, 1993, p. 348) as well as general cinema surveys (Cook, 1990, p. 25; MacGowan, 1965, p. 114), *The Great Train Robbery's* claim to priority is also forwarded by genre theorists (Cawelti, 1975, p. 110; Schatz, 1981, p. 45). Until recently, the few scholars who contested the claim of Porter's film did so on the ground that some other film with Western trappings had been exhibited earlier, such as *Poker at Dawson City*, *Cripple-Creek Bar-room*, or *Kit Carson* (for example, Buscombe, 1990, pp. 22–3). Underlying these claims is the unspoken assumption that the film genre known as the Western is a straightforward extension of the nineteenth-century treatment of the 'American West as Symbol and Myth', as the subtitle to Henry Nash Smith's (1950) influential *Virgin Land* puts it. What makes a Western a Western, this implicit theory holds, has nothing to do with cinema. The Western is not, as it were, cinema's biological offspring, but its adopted child.

A 1984 article by Charles Musser, extensively quoted in 1990 by Stephen Neale, offers an entirely new perspective. Against all expectation, Musser represents the first half of *The Great Train Robbery* as an example of the railway subgenre of the currently popular travel genre, and the second half of the film as 'part of the violent crime genre which had been imported from England a few months earlier' (1984, p. 130). According to Musser, *The Great Train Robbery* was not primarily perceived in the context of the Western. Its success did not encourage other Westerns but other films of crime – Lubin's *The Bold Bank Robbery*, Paley and Steiner's *Burned at the Stake*, and Porter's own *Capture of the Yegg Bank Burglars* (*ibid.*, p. 131).

Musser's claims are interestingly supported by the evidence of casting and directorial precedents. The most versatile member of *The Great Train Robbery's* cast was surely a young man named Max Aronson, also known as G.M. Anderson, who played the parts of the passenger shot trying to escape, the tenderfoot who dances to the rhythm of pistol fire, and one of the outlaws (Musser, 1990, p. 352). Considered retrospectively, this young actor is neither Max Aronson nor G.M. Anderson but 'Broncho Billy' Anderson, after the character he played in a highly successful series of later films. If he were to be recognized at all in 1903, however, it would have to be as the daring but unfortunate young man in *What Happened in the Tunnel* (Edison, 1903). At the beginning of this one-minute film that takes place on a train, Anderson attempts to kiss a young woman as he returns her handkerchief. Just then, the train enters a tunnel and the screen goes dark. When the image finally returns, the ardent young man is caught in the act of kissing not the girl but her black maid. In 1903, Anderson was not a Western star, but a railway vedette.

Similarly, in historical treatments of the Western, Edwin S. Porter is usually identified as the director not only of *The Great Train Robbery*, but also of the 1906 *Life of a Cowboy* (the film that Porter considered his first Western). To later viewers, these two films may seem to exist as part of a timeless generic corpus, each reinforcing the structures of the other. Yet in November 1903, *The Great Train Robbery* would more likely have reinforced the structures of Porter's most recent film, *Romance of the Rail*, the tongue-in-cheek story of young Phoebe Snow – clothed in white – who meets her true love – also in white – on the coal-carrying Lackawanna Railroad. Their resplendent white clothing never becoming the least bit dirty, the young lovers are finally married from the train's observation platform by a minister – clothed, of course, in white.

In the years following its release, the identification of *The Great Train Robbery* with the travel genre's railway subgenre was strongly reinforced by the development of a hyperrealistic railroad-based exhibition practice. Started by George C. Hale in Kansas City in 1905 (or perhaps at the 1904 St. Louis World's Fair), Hale's Tours rapidly grew into a national chain of railroad-car-shaped theatres in which the audience was offered moving images identified with train travel. Not surprisingly, such films as *What Happened in the Tunnel* and *The Great Train Robbery* were staples of the Hale's Tours circuit, along with later films like Biograph's *Interior N.Y. Subway* and *Hold-up of the Rocky Mountain Express* and Selig's *Trip Through the Black Hills*. The production of these and many other films – some of them stressing crime or danger – for a railway-oriented exhibition context had the effect of perpetuating *The Great Train Robbery*'s identity as a combination of travel and crime genres.

It wasn't until much later in the decade (and probably not by the 1906 date of *Life of a Cowboy*) that the Western took on the self-conscious trappings of an accepted genre. In some ways, this is an entirely strange notion. Scholars assure us that the Western existed in late nineteenth-century fiction. We know that it existed as a major film production category throughout the teens. Yet at the beginning of the century the Western was not yet a film genre. Whether scholars have actually located a Western genre in the last century, or just projected contemporary terminology on to similar material from an earlier period, must remain for the time being an open question. But we can confirm a third hypothesis:

3. Even when a genre already exists in other media, the film genre of the same name cannot simply be borrowed from non-film sources, it must be recreated.

Not surprisingly, this recreation process may very well produce a genre that is decidedly *not*, in spite of the shared name, identical to the non-film genre.

We easily recognize that much of what has been written about the early Western derives from a tacit assumption that any visual or plot element associated with the post-teens Western is always a sign of the presence of the Western, even prior to 1910. For example, Indians are a staple of the Western as it is described in dozens of manuals. 'Next to the cowboy, the American Indian is the most prominent figure in the Western,' affirms Ed Buscombe in the *BFI Companion to the Western* (1990, p. 155). This fact has regularly led hasty scholars to conclude that the common use of Indians in pre-1910 plots is a marker of the presence of the Western genre. Yet during the first decade of this century, Indian films clearly constituted a separate genre, featuring noble 'red men' mistreated by dissolute 'whites'. When 'Broncho Billy' Anderson's Essanay company chose its Indian-with-headdress trademark in 1907, it could thus not have been referring to the Western genre, whatever meanings the trademark may have taken on since.

In fact, it might reasonably be claimed that many of the pre-1910 films produced in the West by Essanay, Kalem and Selig were actually not Westerns. That is, they may have imitated the outward trappings of the currently popular Wild West shows, and offered identifiably Western scenery, but always in association with a dominant already existing genre, and without the civilization versus savagery plot motifs that later come to characterize the genre. In other words, such films fail to constitute a Western genre, because they are still primarily associated with other genres. We thus find confirmation for a fourth hypothesis:

4. Before they are fully constituted through the junction of persistent material and consistent use of that material, nascent genres traverse a period when their only unity derives from shared surface characteristics deployed within other generic contexts perceived as dominant.

While the presence of similar material may lead later critics to identify these early texts with a later genre, such a claim is clearly retrospective and historically unjustified.

To describe the exact process whereby the Western developed as an independent genre would require a full-length study based on major research into the generic spawning ground constituted by the nickelodeon period. Such a study would show how a growing production of 'Wild West films', 'Western chase films', 'Western comedies', 'Western melodramas', 'Western romances' and 'Western epics', solidified into a genre called simply the 'Western'. In its early manifestations, as the many possible associations of the adjective clearly suggest, the Western could take on any of a multitude of different plots, characters or tones. By 1910, however, the possibilities implied by a simple geographical designator (along with diverse influences from a growing Western iconography and literature) were being explored, sifted, and codified. Once only a geographical adjective, designating a favoured location for films of various types (just as 'musical' had once been only a technological designator), 'Western' quickly became the name for a loosely defined film genre capitalizing on public interest in the American West. Within a very few years, a strengthened and conventionalized generic concept would inspire the repeated production of genre films systematically interpreted by spectators according to standards particular to the 'Western'.

A careful study of the Western's early development would certainly point to a

Before the Western was fully constituted as a genre, there were 'cowboy pictures', as evidenced by this Moving Picture News *ad, 29 April 1911.*

combination of the travel genre's exotic locations (and the industry's timely move to southern California) with the crime genre's suspenseful situations (and their melodramatic trappings). It would also demonstrate the impact of redefining Indian roles according to melodramatic models, as well as the localizing effect of casting Indians as villains. From an economic standpoint, it would be important to note the product differentiation value of films that are both popular with Europeans and difficult to produce in Europe (due to different scenery, lack of authentic props, absence of trained cowboys, and so forth). From a cultural point of view, it would be essential to highlight the Western's value as a clearly American genre, a prime melting-pot recipe, in a period of growing unrest regarding virtually unlimited immigration.

Like the musical, the Western consolidated its identity through criticism. 'The vast amount of letters sent to us regarding the Western film stories if published in our columns would about fill three issues,' noted *The Moving Picture News* in 1911, 'and out of this batch there is not one single letter in favour of the production of this class of films. . . . In fact, they are so farfetched that we might describe them as an abomination or tissue of false impressions' (p. 6). Castigating Westerns as artificial, unrealistic and violent, attractive only to young boys and Europeans lacking in knowledge of the real West, reformers helped to solidify the new genre. A study of Western origins would even cite the limited available demographic evidence demonstrating the youth of the Western audience, such as the 1916 University of Iowa thesis revealing the steady decline in preference for the Western starting as early as the sixth grade (Short, 1916, p. 43). But this is not the place for such a study.

The biopic

If genre theory as currently practised were conceived as a game, then a list of the rules according to which that game is played might begin as follows:

1. From industry or critical sources, glean the existence of a genre.
2. Analysing the characteristics of the films most often identified with the genre, establish a description of the genre.
3. Scouring filmographies, compile a full listing of films that share enough generic traits to be identified as belonging to the genre.
4. On this basis, begin analysis of the genre.

This game might well be called the 'Critic's Game', to stress its retrospective nature. Fundamentally synchronic in nature, the Critic's Game is diametrically opposed to the entirely prospective 'Producer's Game', which has quite different rules:

1. From box-office information, identify a successful film.
2. Analyse the film in order to discover what made it successful.
3. Make another film stressing the assumed formula for success.
4. Check box-office information on the new film and reassess the success formula accordingly.
5. Use the revised formula as a basis for another film.
6. Continue the process indefinitely.

Critics never tire of explaining how Hollywood used generic formulas in order to assure production simplicity, standardization and economy. Yet, curiously, they always seem to prefer the Critic's Game to an approach that would deal directly with production decisions. In this section I propose to play a version of the Producer's Game. Instead of looking backward to constitute the corpus of a genre that

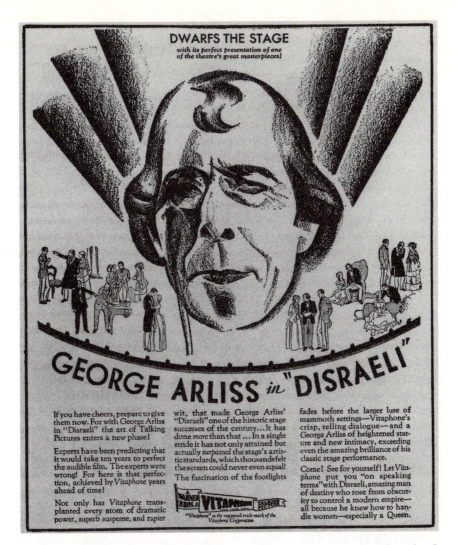

DWARFS THE STAGE
*with its perfect presentation of one
of the theatre's great masterpieces!*

GEORGE ARLISS *in* **"DISRAELI"**

If you have cheers, prepare to give them now. For with George Arliss in "Disraeli" the art of Talking Pictures enters a new phase!

Experts have been predicting that it would take ten years to perfect the audible film. The experts were wrong! For here is that perfection, achieved by *Vitaphone* years ahead of time!

Not only has *Vitaphone* transplanted every atom of dramatic power, superb suspense, and rapier

wit, that made George Arliss' "Disraeli" one of the historic stage successes of the century...It has done *more* than that ... In a single stride it has not only attained but actually *surpassed* the stage's artistic standards, which thousands felt the screen could never even equal! The fascination of the footlights

WARNER BROS. & VITAPHONE TALKING PICTURES

"Vitaphone" is the registered trade mark of the Vitaphone Corporation

fades before the larger lure of mammoth settings—Vitaphone's crisp, telling dialogue—and a George Arliss of heightened stature and new intimacy, exceeding even the amazing brilliance of his classic stage performance.

Come! See for yourself! Let *Vitaphone* put you "on speaking terms" with Disraeli, amazing man of destiny who rose from obscurity to control a modern empire—all because he knew how to handle women—especially a Queen.

Not yet a biopic, Disraeli (1929) *was initially advertised as a stage success brought to the silver screen through the magic of the new Vitaphone process.*

didn't establish itself firmly until the late 30s, I propose to start with a successful 1929 film and from there to trace producer decisions until the genre is fully recognized.

When Warner Bros. produced *Disraeli* as their prestige production for 1929, they were simply choosing a pre-sold script (from the still popular 1911 Louis Napoleon Parker play) and a ready-made leading man (George Arliss, who had played the lead on the stage and in a silent film version), at a time when every studio was scrambling to locate suitable properties for sound films. Expected to succeed primarily with the carriage trade, *Disraeli* enjoyed a popular triumph exceeding all expectations: a six months' stay in New York, a consecutive worldwide run of 1,697 days in over 29,000 separate theatres, and a total audience of over 170 million spectators speaking twenty-four different languages. The film also won an Academy Award for Best Actor for George Arliss.

Even though it was clearly recognized as a star vehicle for the man now called *Mr.* George Arliss, *Disraeli* was too great a moneymaker not to invite imitation. In short, this is clearly a film that launches a Producer's Game. But how can we know just how *Disraeli* was viewed and what films were made in imitation of this film? In the past, in the Critic's Game, the answer would be simple: *Disraeli* is a biopic, just look and see what other biopics were made. It is this type of logic that leads the few critics who deal with early Warner Bros. biopics to jump from the 1929 *Disraeli* to Arliss' subsequent success in the 1931 *Alexander Hamilton* and the 1933 *Voltaire*, his last film for Warner Bros., or even to the actor's later triumphs for 20th Century Pictures (before the studio's merger with Fox): *The House of Rothschild* in 1934 and *Cardinal Richelieu* in 1935 (Sennett, 1971, pp. 270–1; Roddick, 1983, p. 182; Custen, 1992, p. 61). In the Producer's Game, however, we may not take for granted the existence of a genre that producers did not evoke at the time. Instead, we must look carefully at subsequent films to discover the extent to which they appear to be imitations of, or at least derived from, the blockbuster success.

In Warners' view, what might have caused *Disraeli*'s success? What does the film have that might be worth imitating? In 1929, Warner Bros. saw *Disraeli* not as a biopic – a non-existent category at the time – but as a film whose success was due to its primary emphasis on British history, political intrigue and international strife, with secondary attention to financial concerns, Jewishness and expansive speech-making, plus perhaps a nod to director Alfred E. Green and the film's stage-play source. It is thus not surprising that the studio immediately assigned their two current British stars to complementary 'very British' films. Opening in February 1930 was *The Green Goddess*, the previously staged and silently filmed story (with Arliss both times) of an Indian potentate who holds a group of Britishers prisoner; once again the British empire and international strife are in play, but this time Arliss is the Rajah rather than the British Lord. The following month, John Barrymore opened as a Scottish peer, playing British situations for comedy instead of adventure in a film version of the stage play, *The Man from Blankley's*. While both films played well in initial New York and Los Angeles runs, a third 1930 Alfred E. Green British-oriented film, *Sweet Kitty Bellairs*, based on the eighteenth-century musical heroine, did not fare so well.

Warner Bros. thus dropped the music and the lady in order to seek out other appropriate vehicles with a British political or financial flavour. By August 1930, Green had directed Arliss for the last time, with Arliss playing the head of a bankrupt shipping firm in a John Galsworthy play, *Old English*; here all trace of *Disraeli*'s political intrigue is gone, but the Victorian English interest is heightened, as are the financial dealings of the earlier film. So successful was *Old English*, with the best initial run of any 1930 Warner Bros. film, that the financial thread was followed up in Arliss' next film, *The Millionaire*, his first of many directed by John Adolfi. As the eponymous millionaire, Arliss fills the boredom of retirement with the purchase of a gas station, a clever disguise, shady financial dealings, and revenge on his family.

Hot on the heels of *The Millionaire*, in 1931 Arliss starred in the film version of his own play, *Alexander Hamilton*. In the Critic's Game, this film of course appears as a direct biopic successor to *Disraeli*. While the British interest is absent from the 1931 film, both offer biographical treatment of a well-known statesman involved in political intrigue. In order to connect the two films, Warners would only have had to play down the American context of the later film and play up the speech-making and political jockeying common to both films. Yet this is precisely what they did not do. In their publicity for the film, the studio stressed the American side of *Alexander Hamilton* so strongly as virtually to obliterate all connections with *Disraeli*. Furthermore, Hamilton's scandalous affair with a married woman was emphasized in such a way as to place the film into a category with Paramount's 1927 *Madame Pompadour*, Warners' *Glorious Betsy* (the 1928 account of a romance between a Baltimore socialite and Napoleon's younger brother Jerome) and *The Divine Lady* (the 1929 story of the liaison between Lord Nelson and Emma Hamilton) and United Artists' 1930 *Dubarry, Woman of Passion*. Indeed, scandalous affairs involving statesmen or royalty would be a topic of choice in the years following *Alexander Hamilton*. In making *Alexander Hamilton* the studio was decidedly not self-consciously producing a biopic.

Seeking to duplicate the success of *Old English* and *The Millionaire*, Arliss and Adolfi would soon abandon statesmen and the Old World altogether. Their new method: replicate the earlier films' central character (an older madcap rich businessman), his supporting cast (a combination of sympathetic and cantankerous family members), major themes (honesty in financial dealings) and major plot devices (based principally on the main character's fondness for disguises). This technique was put into play in *A Successful Calamity* (1932), described in studio publicity as 'the story of a Millionaire who went on strike', and *The Working Man* (1933), as well as in the *The Last Gentleman* (1934) after Arliss had moved to 20th Century Pictures. In the meantime, Barrymore had triumphed as *Svengali* (1931), like Disraeli a mesmerizing British speech-maker, and in its lookalike *The Mad Genius* (Barrymore's last Warners film in 1931), to the point where Arliss was cast in a similar plot featuring a handicapped artist, *The Man Who Played God*, which claimed the longest initial run of all Warners' 1932 films.

Parenthetically, it is important to note that overall financial figures are not as useful to the Producer's Game as initial box-office strength. Producers cannot react rapidly to current trends if they must wait a year for complete domestic figures or even longer for foreign returns. Information on initial east and west coast runs thus looms much larger in production logic.

What lessons can be learnt from this turn with the Producer's Game? As a critic, it must be admitted that there is something disconcerting about playing the Producer's Game. Not even the simplest description of a film holds up throughout the game, because each new film undermines our previous understanding. At first, *Disraeli* seemed decidedly British and political, as reinforced by *The Green Goddess*. Little by little, however, Warners' successive attempts to capitalize on the film's prestige led different aspects to be accentuated. In *Svengali*, *The Mad Genius* and *The Man Who Played God*, Arliss and Barrymore together bring out the bizarre qualities of Disraeli, the very attributes that gave him the nickname of 'Dizzy'. In *Old English* it is the financial intrigue, along with Disraeli's clever repartee and speech-making ability, that come to the fore. The farther we go, the more frustrating the process becomes, for these very attributions are in turn under-

Though Voltaire *(1933) now seems to be a biographical film about a famous European thinker and statesman, Warners sought to attach it instead to a currently modish cycle of films recounting the affairs of famous men.*

mined by still later films. When *The Millionaire*, *A Successful Calamity* and *The Working Man* take Arliss away from England and give him a multi-generational family, a large personal fortune and a penchant for disguise, we find not only that the financial aspects of *Disraeli* become more salient, but we discover that previously invisible aspects of *Old English* begin to materialize. And so on down the line. Since producers don't stop evaluating successful films in order to produce further hits, no film can ever achieve a stable definition in the Producer's Game.

When Arliss appears in *Voltaire* in 1933, therefore, yet another new set of configurations appears in *Disraeli*. As configured by Warner Bros., *Voltaire* – publicised as 'The Affairs of *Voltaire*' – is an attempt to capitalize on the political romance strain recently exploited in *Alexander Hamilton*. In spite of the studio's initial posturing, however, *Voltaire* includes more than a famous philosopher with Madame Pompadour in his boudoir while he decides the fate of a nation. Several other aspects of *Voltaire* reverberate with *Disraeli* and thus succeed in redefining the earlier film. Previously, Disraeli had always been British; now his association with Voltaire dissolves specific national identity and makes them both simply foreign. In developing the Suez Canal project, Disraeli had been identified with banking and financial interests; seen in the context of *Alexander Hamilton* and *Voltaire*, he becomes an independent thinker with no debts to anyone. Before, Disraeli had seemed to be pleading for a coherent British empire; now, associated with Alexander Hamilton and Voltaire, he appears to be fighting for human rights. In the light of his later comedies, Arliss as Disraeli is just a kooky older man; with distinguished statesmen for companions his strangeness becomes a mark of genius and commitment rather than simply a stylistic leftover from silent film. Defined and redefined by subsequent films (especially, but not solely, those starring George Arliss), Disraeli now takes on, along with Voltaire, a set of characteristics that will sound familiar to biopic buffs: he is a foreigner, an independent thinker, a human rights fighter, an eccentric genius – as in Louis Pasteur, Emile Zola, Benito Juarez, Paul Ehrlich and Paul Reuter, the subjects of the more famous Paul Muni/Edward G. Robinson Warner Bros. biopics directed by William Dieterle during the latter half of the 1930s.

Retrospectively it is easy to see *Disraeli* as a distinguished predecessor of the Dieterle biopics and as the first important token in the biopic type. But that is Critic's Game logic and we are playing the Producer's Game. Here an entirely different line of reasoning reigns, suggesting this chapter's fifth hypothesis:

5. Films are always available for redefinition – and thus genres for realignment – because the very process of staying in the black involves reconfiguring films.

Hardly restricted to Warner Bros., this trait is one of the defining characteristics of studio production. As seasoned RKO and MGM director George Stevens explained in 1947,

> Producers, writers and directors have got into the habit of screening over and over again the pictures that have been proved in the past to possess something that made them box office successes. I don't mean that they simply make them over. They break them down into their component elements, study these carefully, and then use them again in different arrangement, as parts of a new story, depending on them to assert the same appeal they did the first time.
>
> (Quoted in Bordwell *et al.*, 1985, p. 111)

Practically speaking, this approach regularly puts studio personnel in the place of the critic.

It is not by chance that one of Hollywood's most clichéd scenes takes place in the screening room, for it is there that the recipes of past triumphs are discovered. When producer George Jessel was labouring to develop a concept for the life story of composer Joe Howard, 20th Century-Fox studio chief Darryl Zanuck simply instructed Jessel to 'scientifically analyze and study the fundamentals' of previous Fox successes (which in Critic's Game logic would certainly all appear to deserve the label of 'musical biopics', but which Zanuck systematically referred to by title, in accordance with the rules of the Producer's Game). 'If you study the previous pictures I am certain you will find the necessary elements', insisted Zanuck in his memo (Custen, 1992, p. 144). Comments like this led Todd Gitlin to quip that 'the logic of maximizing the quick payoff has produced that very Hollywood hybrid, the recombinant form, which assumes that selected features of recent hits can be spliced together to make a eugenic success' (*ibid.*, p. 64).

In the art of assaying former triumphs to locate their most valuable elements, for two decades nobody in Hollywood could match Darryl Zanuck. Indeed, when the thirty-one-year-old Zanuck left Warners in 1933 to establish 20th Century Pictures, he immediately grabbed George Arliss to star in a series of films depicting the lives of famous foreigners. Anxious to launch his new company with a series of prestige productions, in 1934 Zanuck cast Arliss as the head of *The House of Rothschild*, while other actors were depicting *The Affairs of Cellini* and *The Mighty Barnum*. The following year, Arliss played *Cardinal Richelieu* while Ronald Coleman appeared as *Clive of India*. Hollywood's ultimate assayer, Zanuck continued throughout this period to point back to the successful formulas of the films he knew at Warners. Is Richelieu not sympathetic enough? Is he too old for romantic treatment? Zanuck's response in a 7 January 1935 story conference: just use the device from *Disraeli*, where a single mission is used to outsmart the French and to demonstrate the elder statesman's support for young love (Custen, 1992, p. 61).

However tempting it may be to identify *Disraeli* and other early sound films as biopics, the record suggests instead that the genre was not created until multiple studios, playing the Producer's Game, repeatedly replicated specific biographical elements of the earlier films. The direction taken by Zanuck and 20th Century

Pictures constantly spotlights older foreign figures. Under the tutelage of Hal Wallis and Henry Blanke, the Warners assaying office regularly emphasizes young freedom fighters. Concurrently, the musical biopic remains faithful to the musical genre's systematic subordination of professional success to romantic coupling.

Producers as critics

In stressing the studios' power to redefine previous films, to build new cycles and genres out of elements gleaned from earlier successes, it might seem that I am simply agreeing with the critics (for example, Neale, 1990) who stress the power of the producing industry to define genres. On the contrary, my purpose here is to show that the process by which studios define genres is an *ex post facto* operation that is not conceptually different from the methods used by critics. Whence the sixth hypothesis:

> 6. Genres begin as reading positions established by studio personnel acting as critics, and expressed through film-making conceived as an act of applied criticism.

We tend to think of the producing industry as somehow not only chronologically but also logically prior to the critical industry, but as we have seen in this chapter, film production constantly involves a process of criticism that actually precedes the act of production. Almost every film is meant to serve the function of creating synergy by locating a successful device and carrying it to another film where, if it again succeeds, still further success is guaranteed. Yet these attempts are by definition multiple, inconsistent, contradictory, and thus in constant internal competition.

Our vision of the film industry as a self-confident machine producing clearly delimited generically defined products must be abandoned. Current understanding of genre depends on the assumption that generic terms and concepts are few, neat and clear. Dudley Andrew provides a telling example. Explaining the production-standardizing value of the notion of genre in *Concepts in Film Theory*, he suggests that in 1933 Warners' production chiefs probably said something like 'let's make nine gangster films this year' (1984, p. 110). In fact, good fortune provides us with Darryl Zanuck's December 1932 *Hollywood Reporter* article, outlining Warners' plans for 1933:

> It is my sincere belief that the moving picture public will continue to respond to the 'headline' type of screen story that it has been the policy of Warner Brothers-First National Pictures to produce during the past two years.
> A headline type of story must not be confused with the gangster or underworld cycle of productions that have flooded theatres in the past. Somewhere in its makeup it must have the punch and smash that would entitle it to be a headline on the front page of any successful metropolitan daily.
> Sometimes the story is a biography or an autobiography, like *I Am a Fugitive from a Chain Gang*. Sometimes the story is that of a fictitious character, based on headline incidents from the life of a real character, such as *The Match King*. ... Sometimes the story is of an exposé nature, like *Grand Slam*. ...
> The first of these productions was *Doorway to Hell*. Then came *Little Caesar*, *Public Enemy*, *Smart Money*, *Five Star Final*, etc. We have touched on a great variety of subjects; ... a maternity ward in *Life Begins*, labor problems of the new South in *Cabin in the Cotton*, etc., etc.

Of the productions we are handling at the present time, the most pretentious are *Silver Dollar* and Warden Lewis E. Lawes' *Twenty Thousand Years in Sing Sing*. ...

We have just completed a musical exposé, *Forty-second Street* ... *Frisco Jenny*, featuring Ruth Chatterton, is based on the life of a very notorious San Francisco Barbary Coast hostess. ...

It is my belief that the producer of pictures today, in searching for entertainment, finds himself in a position very similar to that of the editor of a metropolitan newspaper. By this I don't mean that romance and romantic stories are not 'headline material'. Love stories and sex stories make very good headlines, and sometimes very good pictures. *Baby Face* with Barbara Stanwyck, and *Ex-Lady*, with Bette Davis, are two of these particular types we are now producing. ...

You can't go on telling the same story forever. The triangle is rusty. That is why we originally adopted the headline type of story, and that is why we intend to continue with it.

(Quoted in Behlmer, 1985, pp. 9–10)

I have quoted this article at length, for it has clear ramifications for any genre theory that would take industry discourse as both the first and the last word regarding genre identification and definition.

As Warner Bros. entered 1933, the studio production head clearly planned to produce a large number of 'headliners' – a category that we do not recognize today as having any more than a distant descriptive value. Yet for Darryl Zanuck, this

Darryl Zanuck, seen here receiving an illuminated testimonial from Fox, was one of the best at assaying studio properties in order to take advantage of their qualities in subsequent films.

concept was far more important than the 'gangster', 'biography', or 'musical' types to which he refers (and to which he attaches the term 'headline' in exactly the same way that the terms 'musical' or 'Western' were attached as adjectives to recognized genres before they themselves came to be recognized as separate genres). Even a powerful studio production chief – a gifted critic and Hollywood's ultimate assayer – cannot impose generic conceptions on the public at large.

A seventh hypothesis regarding generic origins thus suggests itself:

7. If the first step in genre production is the creation of a reading position through critical dissection, and the second is reinforcement of that position through film production, the required third step is broad industry acceptance of the proposed reading position and genre.

According to this hypothesis, other studios would have had to rally behind Zanuck's headline-oriented position in order for the headline qualities of existing films to be perceived. Instead, these studios read existing films (and thus produced

Joel Silver, the 'Selznick of schlock'

What Darryl F. Zanuck and David O. Selznick were to Hollywood's Golden Era, Joel Silver is to the New Hollywood of the 80s and 90s: an extraordinarily successful assayer of film properties, and thus an active cycle-maker and genrifier. The hit that started him on his way was *48Hrs.* (1982), an action comedy pairing Nick Nolte's world-weary cop with escaped con Eddie Murphy in his film debut. Almost immediately, Silver set to work emulating the offbeat multiracial buddy team. In 1985, *Brewster's Millions* paired John Candy with Richard Pryor and *Commando* teamed Arnold Schwarzenegger with Rae Dawn Chong. In 1986, Silver tried to stretch the formula across gender lines by engaging Whoopi Goldberg in *Jumpin' Jack Flash*. Yet none of these films replicated the success of *48 Hours*, perhaps because Silver's repeated multiracial pairings had induced other studios to produce their own teams, thus leading to recognition of the buddy film as a genre, thereby destroying Silver's virtually proprietary hold on the multiracial buddy formula.

Undaunted, Silver – now head of Silver Pictures – simply assayed his competitors' mid-80s successes (*The Terminator*, *Rambo II*, *Crocodile Dundee*) and consequently increased the action quotient of his own films. Switching directors from Walter Hill to Richard Donner and John McTiernan, in 1987 Silver paired Mel Gibson and Danny Glover in *Lethal Weapon* and then Arnold Schwarzenegger and Carl Weathers in *Predator*. These massive successes were matched a year later by another hit, *Die Hard*, with action and comedy elements this time fused in the same actor, Bruce Willis. Whereas early 80s action films like *First Blood* and *Conan the Barbarian* stressed guns, hardware and male survival, and stretched over an indeterminate period of time, Silver and his alter ego scriptwriter Steve de Souza regularly combined tongue-in-cheek dialogue with thrills and action heightened by time pressure. Though recognizing the importance of 'edge-of-your-seat action, suspense, blood, sweat, [and] emotion' in *Die Hard*, critics noted the equal emphasis on 'wiseass cracks, new films) according to more specific semantic content. While during Prohibition it is hard to imagine a gangster film that would not in some way be a contemporary and thus headline-type film (whence the origin of both the gangster genre and the would-be headline genre in the same list of films: *Doorway to Hell, Little Caesar, Public Enemy, Smart Money*), the other films mentioned by Zanuck were eventually assimilated by Hollywood at large to the biopic, the musical and the social problem film. In fact, it is a mark of Zanuck's ability to roll with the punches that his biopics at 20th Century Pictures should be so markedly uncontemporary, and that most of his folksy musicals for Fox should take place so far from the headlines. It's not that other studios failed to imitate Warners' successes; other studios just read those successes differently from Zanuck and thus imitated other parts of them.

When we play the Critic's Game, it is reasonable to look back at film history and to concentrate on the moment when a studio has concretized its generic reading position in the development of a coherent and durable production unit (like the one constituted by Warner Bros. around the biopic in the late 30s: producer

Die Hard *(1988) was the high point of a long-running action film collaboration between producer Joel Silver and writer Steven E. de Souza.*

bad-guy body counts, funny limo driver sidekick, [and] funny fat cop sidekick' (Triplett, 1988).

According to Silver, this composite strategy purposefully targets the female audience. 'The action-genre audience roughly tops out at $60 million,' he claims. 'The shitty ones do 40, 45. But if women come, it'll go more than that. *Die Hard* did $82 million because it attracted women' (Richardson, 1991, p. 112). Perhaps this explains why *Die Hard* became an instant target of industrywide imitation. 'Since the movie came out in 1988,' quipped one writer, 'we've had *Die Harder, Die Hard With a Vengeance, 'Die Hard* on a bus' (*Speed*), '*Die Hard* on a boat' (*Under Siege*), '*Die Hard* on a plane' (*Passenger 57*), '*Die Hard* on *the president's* plane' (*Air Force One*) and '*Die Hard* at a Pittsburgh Penguins hockey game' (*Sudden Death*)' (Triplett, 1998).

Always attentive to the benefits of attracting crossover audiences, Silver started his career by using multiracial pairings to put the buddy film on Hollywood's financial and generic maps, he then combined action with comedy to expand audience appeal to women, in the process spawning a new genre. Like Zanuck and Selznick, Silver seems to have a gift for isolating the box-office appeal of successful films. And like the studio heads of old, his competitors have a knack for turning his ideas, through imitation, into the industry standards that we call genres.

Henry Blanke, director William Dieterle, cinematographer Tony Gaudio, actor Paul Muni). When we play the Producer's Game, on the contrary, the solidification of a reading position into an automatic, institutionalized mechanism signals the end of the game, or at least a reduction in its interest.

What does our turn at playing the Producer's Game with the biopic mean for *Disraeli* and for the many other retroactively designated 'generic prototypes'? Does it mean that we should avoid calling *Disraeli* a biopic, *The Great Train Robbery* a Western, or *The Broadway Melody* a musical, because they clearly were not so identified by their contemporary audiences? On the contrary, I would suggest that just as Zanuck assayed *Disraeli* and found in it what he needed, so each generation must use the films of the past to meet its own needs.

We cannot, however, justify calling *Disraeli* a biopic according to the needs of our generation and at the same time maintain the claim that we are only respecting the categories proposed by producers and guaranteed by the industry. If producers are able to make meaning by making films, it is only by virtue of those films' ability to serve as vehicle for the film-makers' analyses of previous films. We thus reach a final hypothesis:

> 8. The generic terminology we have inherited is primarily retrospective in nature; though it may provide tools corresponding to our needs, it fails to capture the variety of needs evinced by previous producers, exhibitors, spectators and other generic users.

In fact, we are never working with the original producers' vocabulary but with a motley assemblage of terms jury-rigged by decades of film user groups: producer critics, journalistic critics and academic critics, to name only the most visible. In other words, institution after institution has used whatever product it produces as an act of criticism designed to reconfigure previous films and thus to define genres in a manner that suits its own institutional needs.

For the time being it is enough to have defined the initial process whereby producers forge critical readings of successful films in order eventually to confect successful 'imitations' of those films, in the process producing the shared structures that will eventually precipitate into genres (thus convincing latter-day viewers that those 'imitations' are really full-blown, authentic copies of the generic prototype). Eventually, however, we shall have to face the fact that this process is a never-ending one, and thus requires a theory stretching well beyond the first moment when genres become sufficiently substantial to be recognized by producers and audiences alike. In Chapter 5 we will consider what it might mean to see ourselves – today's critics – not only as the objective external describers of a past genre formulation process, but as the current actors in an ongoing genrification process.

4
Are genres stable?

Genre can be defined as a structural pattern which embodies a universal life pattern or myth in the materials of language. ... Genre is universal, basic to human perceptions of life.

John Cawelti, *The Six-gun Mystique* (1975, p. 30)

Prior to the mid-twentieth century, discussions of genre almost always invoked historical precedents. The late Renaissance rise of generic consciousness was specifically predicated on a revival of the genres of classical Greece and Rome: comedy, tragedy, satire, ode and epic. Even the anti-genre romantics could not escape the tyranny of genre history as they sought to destroy generic specificity and with it the weight of the past. When science provided a model of apparently stable biological species permanently separated by reproductive incompatibility, the concept of biological evolution – immediately adapted to social and literary categories – quickly re-established the traditional link between generic thinking and historical observation. In a turn-of-the-century world dominated by Ferdinand Brunetière's *Evolution of Genres*, there could be no question of genres existing outside of history.

Half a century later, however, under the influence of Jungian psychology and structural anthropology, genres found themselves in new company. Instead of being read in the context of Horace and Boileau, they found themselves surrounded by pagan rituals, native ceremonies, undated traditional texts and descriptions of human nature. No longer was attention concentrated on the appearance, transformation, combination and disappearance of genres, and thus on new, modified, or vanishing genres, but on generic continuity and in particular on genres that might justify claims of generic permanence. With Northrop Frye identifying genres as embodiments of myth and Sheldon Sachs connecting genres to stable characteristics of the human mind, it is hardly surprising that a generation of film critics should have considered film genres as nothing more than the latest incarnation of broader, older, more permanent generic structures. Although, following John Cawelti and his culture-specific notion of formula fiction, critics have seen Hollywood genres as specifically American, they nevertheless happily attribute to film genres a distinguished ancestry including Greek comedies, Western novels, stage melodramas and Viennese operettas.

Not surprisingly, the myth-oriented rediscovery of genre criticism during the third quarter of this century seriously jeopardized our ability to think of genres as anything other than the stable manifestations of more or less fundamental and permanent human concerns. In one sense, this is only reasonable, because the prestige associated with the term *genre* over the past few decades derives from a belief that the notion of genre, like Alice's rabbit hole, provides a magic connection between this fallen world and the more satisfying, more permanent realm of archetype and myth. Once filled by prayer, the role of mediating between man and the eternal has now fallen to genre. In short, we must see genres as stable if they are to do the work we require of them.

In placing so much emphasis on generic fixity – necessary for access to the benefits of archetypal criticism – two generations of genre critics have done violence to the historical dimensions of genre. Stressing the apparently representative straight stretches of the mighty genre river rather than its tortuous tributaries, its riverbed-defying floods, or its tidewater-dominated estuary, recent genre theory has devoted too little attention to the logic and mechanisms whereby genres become recognizable as such. This chapter offers a corrective to that tendency.

In the recent past, all genre study has begun with questions of permanence and coherence: What do these texts have in common? What shared structures permit them to make more meaning as a genre than the sum of their meanings as individual texts? What forces explain, and what patterns reveal, generic longevity? Here, however, I look instead at problems of transience and dissemination. How is it that some structures fail to achieve generic recognition? What changes are required for others to be constituted as genres? If genres are the temporal reflection of transhistorical values, what explains the regular conflicts regarding their definition, extent and function? Traditionally, by stressing coincident structures and concerns, genre criticism has laboured mightily to conceal or conquer difference and disagreement; the principle observed in this chapter instead underscores discrepancies in order to explain what makes difference possible. Only when we know how difference is spawned in the apparently universal generic context will we be in a position to arbitrate the many border disputes growing out of genre's role as a representative of permanence in a world of change.

Adjectives and nouns

Stressing discrepancy rather than coincidence, we cannot help but notice that generic terminology sometimes involves nouns, sometimes adjectives, a distinction also noted by Leutrat and Liandrat-Guigues (1990, pp. 95, 105–7). Indeed, the very same word sometimes appears as both parts of speech: *musical comedies* or just plain *musicals*, *Western romances* or simply *Westerns*, *documentary films* or film *documentaries*. Interestingly, there would seem to be some kind of historical consistency in these generic doublets. Earlier uses of the term are invariably adjectival in nature, describing and delimiting a broader established category. Not just *poetry*, but *lyric poetry* or *epic poetry*. Later uses involve stand-alone substantival treatment, with a corresponding change in the status of the new category. Lyric poetry is a type of poetry; the more types of poetry we name, the more we reinforce the existence of poetry as an independent category, with each type corresponding to a different potential aspect of poetry. When we drop the noun and promote the adjective to substantival status – *a lyric* – we have done quite a bit more than simply pass from a general type – *poetry* – to a specific case – *a lyric poem*. By giving the adjective the status of a noun we imply that *lyric* exists as a category independent of *poetry*, the noun that it originally modified.

When a descriptive adjective becomes a categorical noun, it is thus loosened from the tyranny of that noun. *Epic poetry* calls to mind Homer, Virgil or Milton, poets all. But what mental images does the stand-alone substantive *an epic* call forth? *The Song of Roland? War and Peace? Alexander Nevsky? Lonesome Dove?* No longer is our imagination bound to poetic form; instead it seeks out similar texts across media. Before, epic was one of the possible qualities of the primary category *poetry*; now film is one of the possible manifestations of the primary category *epic.*

The number of generic terms that have gone through this substantifying process is surprising. *Narrative poetry*: the nature of *narrative. Scenic photography*: a *scenic* (one of the staples of silent film exhibition). *Serial publication*: a *serial. Commercial message*: a *commercial. Roman noir, film noir*: just plain *noir.* In some cases a neologism is required in order to incorporate the adjective into a noun. A *biographical picture* becomes a *biopic. Musical drama* turns into *melodrama.* On the same model, *documentary drama* can be termed *docudrama. Science fiction* stories are *sci-fi.* Often, the exigencies of journalism even generate clones of these substantified terms: musicals are *singies*, Westerns are *oaters*, melodramas are *mellers, tearjerkers* or *weepies.*

In each case the development of the stand-alone noun signals the liberation of the former adjective from its noun and the formation of a new category with its own independent status. Consider the history of comedy. Over the centuries comedy has been characterized in a variety of ways, according to its source, tone, costuming, exhibition, and the like. Now we have a series of categories that have become more or less loosened from the parent genre: burlesque, farce, masque, screwball, slapstick, and so on. In fact, this progression recalls the fact that *comedy* itself did not start as a noun, but as one of a set of adjectives designating the possible types of theatre or song: the word *comedy* comes from the kind of singing associated with revelling (Greek *komoidos* < *komos* = revel + *aiodos* = song), whereas *tragedy* comes from the type associated with goats, i.e., satyrs (Greek *tragoidia* < *tragos* = goat + *oide* = song).

In other words, even such apparently basic terms as *comedy* and *tragedy*, like *epic* and *lyric*, had to earn substantival status. What initially were simply descriptive adjectives had to commandeer entire texts and demonstrate a clear ability to pilot them independently. Alistair Fowler is right to recognize that types expressed in noun form (which he calls kinds or genres) can eventually give rise to types expressed as adjectives (which he calls modes), but since he takes for granted both the existence of genres and the 'structurally dependent status of mode vis-à-vis kind' (1982, p. 108) he fails to note the importance of adjective-to-noun progression in the creation of genres.

Burlesque comedy was once simply a form of the comedy genre belonging to the mode of burlesque, characterized by travesty, caricature, and nonsense jokes (the original meaning of the adjective 'burlesque'). But history doesn't stop there. What initially appeared as *(burlesque) comedy*, a known genre dressed in modal garb, with the noun outweighing the adjective, took on a new identity when accompanied by burlesques of other genres, thus becoming *burlesque (comedy)*, with the adjective now outweighing the noun. Soon the single substantive 'burlesque' was introduced, with the slight discomfort accompanying neologisms. Eventually, the only thing left was just plain *burlesque*, standing alone on the generic stage, stripped of any necessary connection with comedy.

51

Typical of early studio discourse about the Western, Moving Picture World *ads for Kalem's* The Tenderfoot *(27 July 1907) and* The Lost Mine *(16 November 1907) attach the adjective 'western' to already existing generic nouns: 'comedy' and 'romance'.*

The constant sliding of generic terms from adjective to noun offers important insight into film genres and their development. Before the Western became a separate genre and a household word, there were such things as Western chase films, Western scenics, Western melodramas, Western romances, Western adventure films, and even Western comedies, Western dramas and Western epics. That is, each of these already existing genres could be and was produced with settings, plots, characters and props corresponding to current notions of the West. In 1907 the West was a drawing card, so even familiar melodramas could be given new life if they could be staged with Western trappings (just as the popularity of high-tech sports shoes has given rise to such unexpected phenomena as commercials employing sports shoes to advertise everything from batteries to rental cars). In a similar manner, the musical was preceded by musical comedy, musical drama, musical romance, musical farce, and even the doubly redundant *all-talking, all-singing, all-dancing musical melodrama*. Just as turn-of-the-century America was fascinated by anything Western, the sliced bread of the late 20s was sound film; in 1929, a film seemed incomplete unless music was added to its existing generic framework.

As long as Western trappings, music, or a dark style were just add-ons, neither the Western, the musical, nor film noir could exist as a genre. Three changes had to occur before full genrification could take place:

a) Abandoning the add-on approach ('Let's just add music to this comedy'), studios had to shift attention away from pre-existing substantive genres toward transgeneric adjectival material. Musical *melodrama* and musical *comedy* have little in common, but *musical* melodrama and *musical* comedy reveal proto-generic relationships. The primary vehicle of this change is standardization and automatization of the reading formation through which previous successes are evaluated and imitated.

b) Films had to display shared attributes stretching beyond the genre's eponymous material (music, the Wild West, dark atmosphere), but nevertheless sufficiently connected to that material to justify using the name for that material as a generic label. In the Western, this began when Western material was combined with melodramatic plots and characters (villain, endangered woman, law-abiding young man). In the musical, it had to await the use of music as both catalyst and expression of heterosexual romance.

c) The public, whether self-consciously or not, had to become so aware of the structures binding disparate films into a single generic category that the process of viewing would always be filtered through the type concept. That is, the expectations that come with generic identification (character types and relations, plot outcome, production style, and the like) must become part and parcel of the process whereby meaning is attributed to films.

Conceptually aiding these three parallel processes, and like them taking place not all at once but over a period of time, the substantification of the generic label signals the beginning of a privileged period for film genre that we appropriately celebrate by use of the expression *genre film*. All too often in the past, *genre film* has been used interchangeably with the more general designator *film genre* or simply to designate a film with obvious connections to a widely recognized genre. A more precise use is in order:

1. Genre films are films produced after general identification and consecration of a genre through substantification, during the limited period when shared textual material and structures lead audiences to interpret films not as separate entities but according to generic expectations and against generic norms.

If one of the attractions of the very notion of genre is its ability to celebrate connections among the various players in the film game, then any short span of genre film production and reception is the ideal object of genre theory, because it is there that the various forces are most clearly aligned, and the overall power of generic terms apparently at its height. Indeed, so seductive is this alignment that many genre studies never stray outside its bounds.

Genre as process

Attention to coincidence having been banned from this chapter, another discrepancy now offers itself for analysis. Too often, attempts to understand origins have led to careful description of situations favouring change, evaluation of factors motivating change, and enumeration of devices revealing change, only to limit deployment of the resultant model to a single moment, that of origin. But what if the model thus constructed were applicable to other moments as well? What if genre were not the permanent *product* of a singular origin, but the temporary *by-product* of an ongoing *process*?

We begin with two discrepancies. The first we have already noted. The genres formed when adjectives become nouns in the process of genrification (for example, comedy, melodrama and epic) are themselves subject to replacement when they are in turn modified by other terms that then may graduate from adjective to substantive (for example, burlesque, musical and Western). Yet even the latter terms never achieve security, because they too can be displaced according to the same process that brought them to the fore. Thus at any given time we find an unselfconscious mixture of terminology. With no way to distinguish among the terms, we regularly intermingle current and former genres, either in an adjectival or a substantival state. Lumped in the same sentence are films made under a genre-film regime and films subsequently assimilated to that genre; genres that once existed, that now exist, and that have not yet fully begun to exist; genres recently substantified and others still adjectival in nature; genres currently boasting genre-film audiences and others that long ago lost those audiences. The usual response to such a dilemma is to walk quietly away.

A second discrepancy is more surprising in nature, because it contradicts virtually everything that has ever been said about the value of genre terms to the production process. Received wisdom suggests that genres provide models for development of studio projects, simplify communication among studio personnel and ensure long-term economic benefits. So far, so good. All of these functions are surely fulfilled by genres. The role played by generic concepts in production, it is claimed, is then reflected in studio film publicity, where generic concepts are prominently displayed. With few exceptions (for example, see Barrios, 1995, p. 66 on *The Broadway Melody*; Buscombe, 1992, p. 76 on *Stagecoach*; Jenkins, 1992, p. 125 on the television series *Beauty and the Beast*), this is the generally shared critical attitude towards the role of genre in Hollywood publicity. Never having looked closely at film publicity campaigns with this problem in mind, I too for a long time believed that Hollywood regularly overtly exploited the generic identities of its genre films. Surprisingly, when I took a genre-sensitive look at advertisements and press books, I found something quite different.

Whereas film reviews almost always include generic vocabulary as a convenient and widely understood shorthand, film publicity seldom employs generic terms as such. Indirect references to genre are of course regularly used, but they almost always evoke multiple genres. A widely distributed poster for *Only Angels Have Wings* (1939) is typical in this regard. The topmost prose promises 'Everything the Screen can give you . . . all in one MAGNIFICENT picture . . .!' A box on the lower left adds specificity to this general statement:

Like most Hollywood publicity, this poster for the 1939 Columbia picture Only Angels Have Wings *downplays direct generic references in favour of coded appeals to multiple categories of viewers.*

EACH DAY
a Rendezvous
with Peril!
EACH NIGHT
a Meeting
with Romance!
Set against the
mighty tapestry
of the
FOG-SHROUDED
ANDES!

The design of the poster reinforces this tripartite guarantee, with photographic close-ups of three different couples separated by sketches of a crashing plane and of a tropical port dominated by an enormous peak. The only specifically generic

This poster for the 20th Century-Fox musical version of The Three Musketeers *(1939) clearly works hard to complement the Dumas' novel's well-known adventure orientation with implications of additional genres: comedy, romance and the musical.*

vocabulary is located front and centre, but in small type overwhelmed by the names of the stars, Cary Grant and Jean Arthur, 'TOGETHER FOR THE FIRST TIME ... IN AN EXCITING ROMANTIC ADVENTURE!'

Hollywood has no interest, as this poster clearly suggests, in explicitly identifying a film with a single genre. On the contrary, the industry's publicity purposes are much better served by implying that a film offers 'Everything the Screen can give you'. During Hollywood's golden years, this usually meant offering something for the men ('EACH DAY a Rendezvous with Peril!'), something for the women ('EACH NIGHT a Meeting with Romance!'), and an added something for that *tertium quid* audience that prefers travel to adventure or romance ('the mighty tapestry of the FOG-SHROUDED ANDES').

Again and again in Hollywood publicity materials we find the same combination. DeMille's *Northwest Mounted Police* (1940) is 'the Mightiest Adventure Romance of All Time!!! ... two surging love stories woven into an unforgettable drama of human emotions ... told against the blazing beauty of the northern forests'. Starring Gable and Harlow, *Saratoga* (1937) is 'as exciting as the Sport of Kings it dramatizes ... and is the romance of a daring gambler and a girl who thought she wanted to ruin him'. *A Damsel in Distress* (1937) has Fred Astaire and 'Mad adventure! Daring deeds! White hot love with music!' Pub-

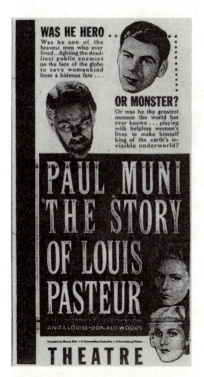

The Jekyll and Hyde characterization of Paul Muni in this poster for Warners' The Story of Louis Pasteur (1936) seeks to double the film's interest and its generic affinities.

licity for Warners' *The Singing Marine* (1937) reduces the formula to just a few words, promising 'the crowning martial musical'. At every turn, we find that Hollywood labours to identify its pictures with multiple genres, in order to benefit from the increased interest that this strategy inspires in diverse demographic groups.

When specific genre terms are used, they are invariably offered in adjective/noun pairs, thus guaranteeing an appeal to both sexes: Western romance, romantic adventure, epic drama, and so on. Whenever possible, still other generic affiliations are implied, especially when comedy is part of the mix. The key words in ads for the Ritz Brothers' version of *The Three Musketeers* (1939), for example, are 'CLASHING BLADES AND LOVABLE MAIDS! RINGING TUNES AND BALMY BUFFOONS!' Thus guaranteed adventure, romance, music and comedy, how can we possibly resist?

We now regularly identify *The Story of Louis Pasteur* (1936) and *The Story of Dr. Ehrlich's Magic Bullet* (1940) as biopics. Although Warners almost certainly did not think of the former as a continuation of the politically oriented tradition initiated by

As touted by this 1940 Warners poster, Hollywood films constitute a magic bullet for children, women and men alike.

Disraeli, they just as clearly considered the latter film as furthering the sequence begun by films depicting the life stories of Pasteur and Zola. Whereas Pasteur's story comes at the beginning of a cycle, Ehrlich's comes near the end. Nevertheless, certain aspects of the publicity for the two films are handled in similar fashion. *Pasteur's* posters feature two radically different vignettes of Paul Muni; seen from eye level, he is a good-looking, well-shaven ladies' man, but in high angle he is a bearded, backlit, heavily shaded, horror-film star. The caption reads: 'WAS HE HERO ... OR MONSTER?' Posters for *Dr. Ehrlich's Magic Bullet* of course never revealed what the magic bullet really was (a cure for syphilis). Instead, they reinforce the title's composite offer (a doctor for the ladies, a bullet for the men, magic for the *tertium quid*) with three scenes illustrating 'A CHILD'S LAUGHTER ... A WOMAN'S LOVE ... 1000 MEN'S HOPE'. Rarely has there been a better example of Hollywood's strategy: tell them *nothing* about the film, but make sure that everyone can imagine something that will bring them to the theatre.

Whether through sparsely used specific generic terms or the more common strategy of broad generic implication, Hollywood's stock-in-trade is the romantic combination of genres, not the classical practice of generic purity. In one sense, this is hardly surprising; by definition, genres are broad *public* categories shared across the entire industry, and Hollywood studios have little interest in anything that must be shared with their competitors. On the contrary, they are primarily concerned to create cycles of films that will be identified with only a single studio. After his 1929 success in *Disraeli*, for example, Warners moved George Arliss through a series of films, each time retaining one or more apparent money-

Secure in its own biopic success, Warners downplayed other studios' biographical films, whereas 20th Century-Fox here seeks to attach its star to Warners' success by associating The Story of Alexander Graham Bell *(1939) with its competitors' best-known biopics.*

making features from a previous success, but never falling into a fully imitatable pattern. Searching for something only Warners could sell, the studio stressed a Warners contract actor, Warners' hard-hitting style and Warners' recognizable cycles. When the time came to advertise *Dr. Ehrlich's Magic Bullet*, therefore, reference was made to Pasteur and Zola not because all three are biopics, but in order to tie *Ehrlich* to an ongoing cycle of Warners hits.

Once the biopic bandwagon got moving, of course, any studio could hop on and take advantage of its momentum. Having no cycle of its own to sell, 20th Century-Fox thus advertised *The Story of Alexander Graham Bell* (1939) in the context of the larger biographical genre, a strategy typically employed only after a genre has been recognized by industry-wide adherence.

Once fully formed, as these examples suggest, genres may continue to play an exhibition or reception role as convenient labels or reading formations, but they actually work *against* the economic interests of the studio that spawned the genre. This unexpected observation helps us to bring together the two discrepancies mentioned earlier. Both adjectives and nouns, we first noted, can be used to designate genres. Although heavily used by critics, such terminology is generally avoided by studio publicity, which prefers to imply generic affiliation indirectly, with at least two generic connections invariably implied. Putting these two observations together with the recognition that studios prefer to establish cycles (which are proprietary) rather than genres (which are sharable), we may make a number of unexpected hypotheses that can serve as a preliminary foundation for a new model of generic process.

2. By assaying and imitating the money-making qualities of their most lucrative films, studios seek to initiate film cycles that will provide successful, easily exploitable models associated with a single studio.

Stressing studio-specific resources (contract actors, proprietary characters, recognizable styles), these cycles always also include common features that can be imitated by other studios (subject matter, character types, plot patterns).

3. New cycles are usually produced by associating a new type of material or approach with already existing genres.

Noir as adjective and noun

Thanks to the research of Charles O'Brien (1996) and Jim Naremore (1996; 1998), we now realize that film noir also began as a loose, adjectival, add-on mode that took decades to mature into the substantival genre that we know today. Following Raymond Borde's and Eugène Chaumeton's 1955 *Panorama du film noir américain*, critics have long assumed that the articles written in 1946 by Nino Frank and Jean-Pierre Chartier offered the initial formulations of the new genre. As Charles O'Brien shows, however, these articles simply extend to American films a pre-war

Before it became one of film noir's founding films, Double Indemnity *(1944) was regularly called a 'murder melodrama'.*

The Great Train Robbery (1903) and its immediate successors associated crime films, railway films and scenics with the Wild West. *The Singing Fool* (1928) and its imitators were musical melodramas, musical comedies or musical romances. Early biopics applied the biographical model to historical romances, adventure films and melodramas.

4. When conditions are favourable, single-studio cycles can be built into industry-wide genres.

Conditions are more likely to be favourable for genrification when the cycle is defined by elements easily shared by other studios (common plots and settings rather than proprietary characters or contract players) and easily perceived by audiences.

5. When cycles become genres, adjectival genre labels are substantified.

tradition identifying certain French films with the narratives of Gallimard's proprietary 'Série noire', a cycle of particularly bleak tales in the popular French *roman policier* (detective novel) genre. At first, the term 'noir' is directly borrowed from the French expression *roman noir* and used simply as a descriptive adjective defining films with a gloomy atmosphere. In January 1939, Ernest Vuillermoz says that the subject of Jean Renoir's film *La Bête humaine* is noir, adding that black seems to be the 'in' colour in French studios these days. By July of the same year, sensing that the descriptive adjective was beginning to take on a classificatory meaning, critics and editorialists for *L'Intransigeant*, *Le Petit-journal* and *Pour vous*, describing such films as *Quai des brumes*, *Hôtel du Nord*, *Le dernier tournant* and *Le Jour se lève*, begin to confine the word noir or even the full expression film noir in quotation marks (O'Brien, 1996, p. 10), as do Frank and Chartier in the post-war era.

As with the Western and the musical, the first American films regularly described as noir already had their own generic identity. Frank and Chartier concur in identifying most of the films they discuss with the *policier* or detective genre; *Double Indemnity* is regularly called a murder melodrama; *Murder, My Sweet* is dubbed a thriller on both sides of the Atlantic; *Woman in the Window* is labelled a bourgeois tragedy by the French (Naremore, 1996, pp. 15–17). First used only as an adjective to describe a particular style of treatment adapted to several different types of film, noir settled into the noun phrase film noir only well after the war, achieving full substantival status only when, after crossing the Atlantic during the 50s, it was adopted by an American culture adept at making dark films but entirely unaware that noir had ever been an adjective.

I recall in the 70s constantly correcting the term 'noir', used as a noun, in the drafts of Thomas Schatz's dissertation. Oblivious to the winds of change, I wanted him to use the full noun-plus-adjective expression. By 1981, the Random House copy editors for *Hollywood Genres* were already willing to indulge the neologistic use of 'noir' as a stand-alone term. History has proved Schatz right, as noir has over the last twenty years become as much a part of film journalism as biopic, sci-fi and docudrama, thus completing the full adjective-to-noun trajectory.

Just as Kleenex tissues were soon referred to simply as *Kleenex*, and eventually reduced to the 'generic' term *kleenex*, so *musical comedy* became *the musical*. The difference lies in the fact that product names may be registered and protected, whereas genre terminology is shared by all. Knowing that their competitors may not use them, manufacturers strive for generalized application of their trademarks (Kleenex, Linoleum, Kodak, Hoover, and so on), whereas a film studio has little to gain from genrification.

> 6. Once a genre is recognized and practised throughout the industry, individual studios have no further economic interest in practising it as such (especially in their prestige productions); instead, they seek to create new cycles by associating a new type of material or approach with an existing genre, thus initiating a new round of genrification.

Without the ability to ensure a significant measure of product differentiation, studios cannot expect a substantial economic return on their investment. When a genre reaches the saturation point, studios must either abandon it, restrict it to 'B' productions, or handle it in a new way. Though this does not necessarily guarantee the creation of a new genre, it always recreates the circumstances out of which new genres are generated. At this point, then, the entire process has the potential to begin again.

The progression described here is by no means specific to *film* genre. As compared to literature and its approach to genre, however, cinema accentuates and accelerates the product differentiation aspects of the process.

Genrification as process

Over the past few millennia, every extant general term has been subjected to a version of the process described above. Discourse as a whole has been divided into poetry, painting and history. Poetry, in turn, has been characterized as epic, lyric or dramatic. Moving down yet another step, dramatic poetry – or theatre, as it came to be called – was considered as comic or tragic (and eventually even tragicomic). Note that the category-producing substantification process in these classic cases looks extremely measured and sensible. New types appear to be produced not one by one, but by an apparently scientific subdivision process. In other words, the terminology involved seems to represent the permanent and stable result of synchronic categorization. We commonly image such relationships through a branching diagram such as those that are used to locate a given species in a Linnaean configuration. Thus tigers are configured (in simplified form) as shown in figure 4.1. In order to establish such a chart, the charted animals must be imagined as existing in a timeless, unchanging museum (like the natural history museums erected around the world during the nineteenth century). In addition, we must imagine ourselves, as authors or users of the chart, as objective observers, radically separated from the animals that the chart classifies.

Generic terminology is commonly based on a classificatory model of this type – the classical origins, extended life and seeming permanence of the terms and the overall structure that contains them apparently justifying neglect of history and of

Through phrases like 'mirthful martial musical' and 'riotous regiment of singing', this 1936 Warners poster does it best to identify Sons O' Guns *with three separate genres.*

our own place within it. Consider the not-so-famous case of *mirthful martial musical romantic comic dramatic poetic discourse*. When we try to make sense of Warners' mid-30s series of annual musicals built around the service academies and related military motifs – including *Flirtation Walk* (1934), *Shipmates Forever* (1935), *Sons O' Guns* (1936) and *The Singing Marine* (1937) – we understand the contemporary label *martial musical* as part of the overall classification simplified

Figure 4.1

kingdom		animals		
phylum	protozoa	vertebrates	molluscs	arthropods
class	amphibians	mammals	reptiles	birds
order	primates	carnivores	rodents	insectivores
family	weasels	cats	dogs	bears
genus	lynx	panthers	wildcats	
species	leopards	tigers	lions	

in figure 4.2. The more recent categories are treated with the classificatory neatness of their classical predecessors, even when their status, title, characteristics and durability remain uncertain. Yet the accelerated genrification process characteristic of this century's fully commodified genres follows not a librarian's deliberate

Figure 4.2

kingdom		discourse	
phylum	painting	poetry	history
class	epic	dramatic	lyric
order	tragic	comic	tragicomic
family	slapstick	romantic	burlesque
genus	screwball	musical	remarriage
species	backstage	martial	college

Dewey-decimal desires, but the entrepreneurial spirit and its heightened adrenaline levels.

This is not the place to decide whether or not genrification was ever a fully scientific categorizing process, free from commercial or political interests. What we can affirm at this point, however, is that the constitution of *film* cycles and genres is a never-ceasing process, closely tied to the capitalist need for product differentiation. The 'martial' musical is at first neither a genre nor a species in the permanent sense that we borrow from Linnaeus. Instead, it is a Warners cycle, a well-differentiated product sure to return a good profit to the studio's backers. As such, it has the wherewithal to become (depending on the actual level of studio investment and audience reaction) what I have termed an 'adjectival' genre. But as an adjecti-

Figure 4.3

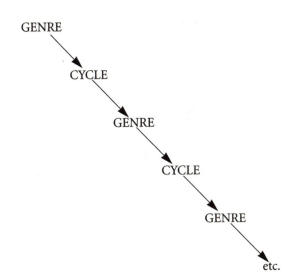

val genre, the martial musical gains the opportunity eventually to become a broadly practised substantival genre. Just as musical comedy spawned the musical, so martial musicals might (but will not necessarily) give rise to the 'martial' genre.

But why stop there? Posters for *Sons O' Guns* identified it as a '*mirthful* martial musical' (my emphasis). If romantic comedy can become the spawning ground for a new genre, eventually losing territory through squatters' rights to music and the values, situations and relations it vehicles, then why can't the process continue from the musical to the *martial or even eventually the *mirthful? (Used here according to the conventions of linguistics, the asterisk designates hypothetical categories never actually observed in the field.) Through this process-oriented logic we discover to our surprise that the number of levels is in no way fixed. Just as geology places us only on the latest level, not on the fundamental or final level, so a process-oriented understanding of genrification keeps us from thinking of the kingdom-phylum-order-class-family-genus-species sequence as complete or closed.

Genres are not just *post facto* categories, then, but part of the constant category-splitting/category-creating dialectic that constitutes the history of types and terminology. Instead of imaging this process in terms of static classification, we might want to see it, in terms of a regular alternation between an expansive principle – the creation of a new cycle – and a principle of contraction – the consolidation of a genre (see figure 4.3).

But this formulation fails to take account of the special relationship studied in the preceding section, namely the connection between adjective and noun genres. The proposed model must therefore be revised as suggested in figure 4.4 (overleaf). That is, a fresh cycle may be initiated by attaching a new adjective to an existing noun genre, with the adjective standing for some recognizable location, plot type, or other differentiation factor.

Under certain conditions, so much attention may be attracted to the tacked-on adjective that it changes parts of speech and inaugurates its own noun genre, only

Figure 4.4

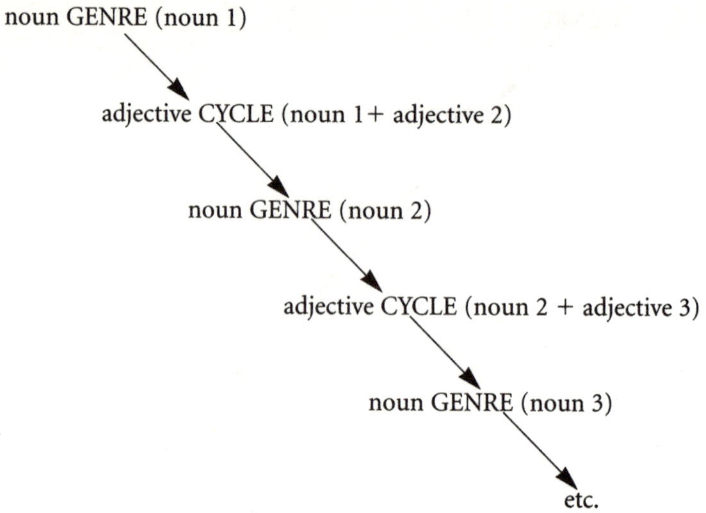

noun GENRE (noun 1)

adjective CYCLE (noun 1+ adjective 2)

noun GENRE (noun 2)

adjective CYCLE (noun 2 + adjective 3)

noun GENRE (noun 3)

etc.

to remain constantly subject to eventual regenrification through the constitution of yet another adjectival cycle. And so forth.

A process-oriented representation of our not-so-famous *mirthful martial musical romantic comic dramatic poetic discourse* would thus look something like figure 4.5. Yet even this model is too rigid, too linear, in its attempt to avoid stability at all costs.

The musical, for example, achieves cycle status not just by modifying the silent romance genre with the new musical technology; on the contrary, early musical forays involve modification of every genre in sight, drawn from every level of the historical genrification process. Indeed, promotion from adjective to noun genre is strongly favoured by the ability of adjectival material to be applied to multiple noun genres. Thus the ability of music to be attached to drama and comedy as well as to romance enhances the likelihood that a noun genre will be created out of a number of musical adjective genres.

As the asterisks in figure 4.5 suggest, not every cycle spawns a genre. In the 1929–30 period, for example, adjectival 'backstage' and 'musical' genres competed for promotion to noun genre status. According to *Photoplay, Close Harmony* (1929) is a 'vaudeville backstage hit', *Broadway Hoofer* (1930) is a 'backstage comedy' and *Puttin' on the Ritz* (1930) is a 'backstage story', while *Variety* styles *Glorifying the American Girl* (1929) as a 'backstage formula', *Behind the Make-Up* (1929) as a 'backstage picture', and *It's a Great Life* (1930) as a 'backstage yarn'. In 1930, the time was certainly right for someone to coin the term *backstager, on the model of 'soaper' and 'meller', yet no such term was forthcoming. Just as the *martial never gets beyond the adjectival level, so the backstage cycle never graduates to noun genre status. This is not, as might be assumed, because the backstage cycle is simply a subgenre of the musical. *Behind the Make-Up* and many other backstage formula films are either devoid of music or shunt the music to a single location and a few short passages, as film noir does with its sultry night-

66

Figure 4.5

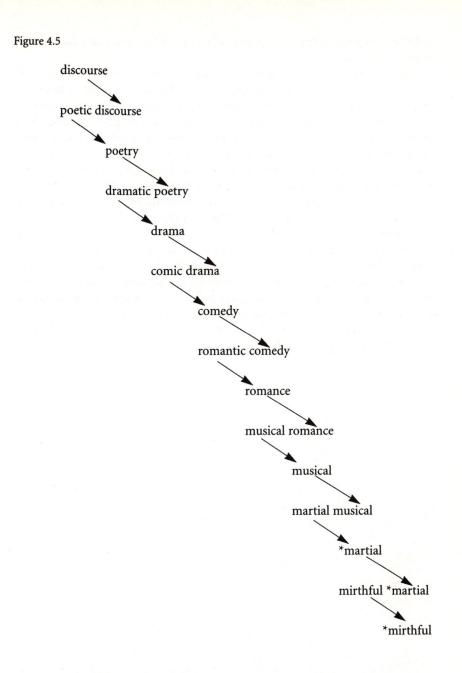

discourse

poetic discourse

poetry

dramatic poetry

drama

comic drama

comedy

romantic comedy

romance

musical romance

musical

martial musical

*martial

mirthful *martial

*mirthful

club singers; other backstage films offer scenes from legitimate rather than musical theatre. If some adjectival cycles are promoted to generic status while others are not, it is because some are more easily applicable in theory to a broad spectrum of film types, and actually adopted in practice by the industry as a whole. Ironically, it was the general demise of musical films that caused them, rather than backstage films, to be perceived and named as an independent genre. As the *martial and *backstager cases demonstrate, there is nothing automatic about the genrification process. For every dozen cycles, only a few genres ever emerge, and even fewer endure.

The cycle-creation process may at any point in time be initiated at any level of the generic past. Like the earth around us, genre history is marked by folds that bring previous generic levels to the surface, where they can once again serve as the basis for regenrification. Think of how many times the epic has been thrust back to the surface by the energy of enterprising producers. Western epics, historical epics, biblical epics, wartime epics, science fiction epics, and many others testify to the epic's permanent youth. Certainly, the ability of classical nouns to serve as host for modern adjectives lies at the heart of genre theory's many difficulties. The geological metaphor helps to explain the simultaneous presence of phenomena formed in radically different periods. The term *epic* dates from the first ice age, and *romance* from the second, whereas *Western* and *musical* are creations of the current era, yet all are simultaneously visible on the surface of the current generic lexicon. That the nonlinearity of this situation should create confusion is hardly surprising, especially since producers have tended to stress adjectives and cycle creation, whereas critics have paid attention instead to nouns and genre formation. When we understand the process whereby cycles and genres are created, we at least understand the source of our confusion and thus take the all-important first step towards dissipating it.

5
Are genres subject to redefinition?

> One question insists: why does the women's picture exist? There is no such thing as 'the men's picture', specifically addressed to men; there is only 'cinema', and 'the women's picture', a sub-group or category specially for women, excluding men; a separate, private space designed for more than half the population, relegating them to the margins of cinema proper. The existence of the women's picture both recognises the importance of women, and marginalises them.
>
> Pam Cook, 'Melodrama and the Women's Picture' (1983, p. 17)

Unlike new worlds discovered by early modern explorers, which were drawn on the other side of the globe, newly created genres must be drawn on the same mental sketch pad that holds the previous map. Instead of conveniently locating Florida or the West Indies somewhere across the western sea, we usually represent slapstick, romantic and burlesque comedy on the same map, within the very same space, that holds, say, epic, lyric and dramatic poetry or tragic, tragicomic and comic theatre. Even though the musical was not recognized as a separate genre until late 1930, and was not defined consistently with current usage until 1933, in today's criticism the term 'musical' nevertheless shares space with such generic terms as *backstage, Western, romantic, tragicomic,* and *slapstick* – none of which is in Aristotle, but all of which have specific historical origins that set them on a different hierarchical level from the musical. With genres, it is as if terms designating phylum, class, order, family, genus and species were all folded together willy-nilly, providing little clarity to would-be generic spectators.

Just as our knowledge of the changing borders of France underlies any current use of the term 'France', so categories like *poetry, drama* and *comedy* coexist with *the musical.* Consider the many events in French history that have had a direct impact on the national map. 'All Gaul is divided into three parts', Caesar had said, but the 843 Treaty of Verdun split the Carolingian Empire and granted west Francia to Charles the Bald. Then came the Norman Conquest, Henry the Fifth's victory at Agincourt, and the successful resistance of the French led by Joan of Arc. Eventually Alsace was annexed by the treaty of Westphalia under Louis XIV while Savoy and Nice became part of France by plebiscite in 1860. Lost again with the treaty of Frankfurt in 1871, Alsace-Lorraine was not returned to France until the 1919 Treaty of Versailles. While today's maps show no evidence of the shifting borders that these events have produced, the very name of the country continues to carry all of these events and the differing concepts of 'France' that they have occasioned.

Imagine the chaos that would result if we were regularly to alternate among the various maps to which the term *France* has been attached at differing points in time. It would be nearly impossible to communicate effectively without first specifying which map serves as a point of reference. Yet this is precisely what we do when we use generic terminology. The word *drama* no longer means the same thing as it meant before *musical drama* was drained away from the definition of just-plain-*drama* by creation of the term *melodrama*. The map looked one way when musical comedy, musical drama and the musical Western were cycles within the genres of comedy, drama and the Western, and quite another way when the musical was established as a stand-alone genre. We would surely benefit from careful description of successive generic maps, yet most critics remain unaware that generic cartography involves multiple superimposed maps of differing ages and extents – even though they use many of the same place names. The familiar questions of generic terminology (should the term genre be reserved for comedy and tragedy or may it be applied as well to epic, lyric and drama? Or are the latter modes rather than genres? Is film noir a genre or a style?) reveal the extent to which critics are convinced that their vocabulary is stable, fixed once, and forever after inert.

Working simultaneously with overlapping generic maps is the price we must pay for recognizing the continuous, process-based nature of generic creation. Zoologists working in the Linnaean tradition may succeed in convincing themselves that they are dealing with a fixed grid, but we have seen the process of genrification at work too clearly to return to a rigid, immutable model. According to the Darwinian approach to evolution, the specificity of a new genus is guaranteed by its inviolability. That is, no genus is interfertile with another genus. Besides the lack of fertility between genera, the purity and thus the identity of the species is also guaranteed by the fact that previous life forms, once extinct, disappear from the world forever. Only in the multi-era imaginary world of a 'Jurassic Park' do the categories of a previous evolutionary state continue to exist.

In the genre world, however, every day is Jurassic Park day. Not only are all genres interfertile, they may at any time be crossed with any genre that ever existed. The 'evolution' of genres is thus far broader in scope than the evolution of species. Unencumbered by the limitations of the flesh, the process of genre creation offers us not a single synchronic chart, but an always incomplete series of superimposed generic maps. Every time our eyes concentrate on the map we find that a new map, currently in the process of being drafted, is just coming into view within the same space. The map can never be completed, because it is a record not of the past, but of a living geography, of an ongoing process.

Post-mortem for a phantom genre

Recent writing about melodrama offers an interesting test case for this process-oriented approach to genre. The term melodrama has had a surprisingly lively existence since Rousseau borrowed it in 1770 from an Italian synonym for opera to describe his play *Pygmalion*. The longevity of the term derives at least in part from critics' willingness to imagine genres as similar to human bodies. Not a single molecule of my body today was present in my body even ten years ago, yet current notions of personhood make it easy for me to image myself as a continuous being, regardless of changes in my physical make-up. There have of course been societies where such individualism was unknown, where continuity was located in the universe as a whole rather than in any individual body seen as the temple of a specific personality. In the post-romantic world, however, continuity is mapped through bodies and the names attached to them. In this century, personal continuity is thus available to serve as a model for generic continuity. To be sure, melodrama changes, but so does each of us; like individual humans, it is claimed, melodrama maintains a core of continuity in spite of its evolving corpus.

One of the main strategies devised to ensure generic continuity involves treatment of a genre not as an evolving category or even as a corpus of films, but as a transhistorical tendency. Thus Lucien Goldmann speaks of a 'tragic vision', Gerald Mast imagines a 'comic mind' and Peter Brooks assumes a 'melodramatic imagination'. The titles of books and articles on literary and film genre regularly include terms that style the genre as the expression of a broadly shared human propensity: 'attitude', 'experience', 'imagination', 'inspiration', 'mystique', 'situation', 'spirit', 'vision'. The reason for holding on to generic terms so tightly, we must conclude, is that they enjoy a level of prestige that cannot easily be matched by other concepts or terms. Note that this statement applies less to film producers, who find too little product differentiation in unmodified genre terms, than to critics. We critics are the ones who have a vested interest in reusing generic terminology, which serves to anchor our analyses in universal or culturally sanctioned contexts, thus justifying our all too subjective, tendentious and self-serving positions. We are the ones who see to it that generic vocabulary remains available for use. While producers are actively destroying genres by creating new cycles, some of which will eventually be genrified, critics are regularly trying to fold the cyclical differences into the genre, thus authorizing continued use of a familiar, broad-based, sanctioned and therefore powerful term.

Several critics have drawn attention to the inconsistent way in which the term 'melodrama' has been used over the years. Starting with Russell Merritt in 1983, there has been persistent questioning of the critical tendency to define and understand melodrama through the 'feminine' excesses of 40s 'weepies' and 50s films directed by Douglas Sirk. Seen from a distance, this questioning fits into a broader current in film studies. As film history has progressed from poor cousin of the Parisian semiotic patriarch to fully-fledged New World head of family, a number of earlier generic analyses have been criticized for their tendency to reduce a broad and durable genre to a particularly successful cycle of films or to a limited period. Thus Tag Gallagher has castigated Thomas Schatz for limiting the Western to the films of John Ford and the post-1939 period. In the same manner, I myself have pointed out the tendency of Delamater, Schatz and Feuer to overemphasize MGM's Freed unit in their construction and analysis of the musical. A similar case might be made regarding Thomas Elsaesser's treatment of William Dieterle's Warner Bros. films as representative of the biopic. Others overemphasize the role of early Universal films in the history of the horror film.

But does the problem involve nothing more than stressing one group of films at the expense of others? Russell Merritt suggests that something else is at stake. Under the intriguing title 'Melodrama: Postmortem for a Phantom Genre', he points out that film critics have regularly written about melodrama as if the term were 'self-evidently clear and coherent' (1983, p. 26). For Merritt, however, melodrama is a slippery and evolving category. Citing examples from the first two decades of this century, Ben Singer provides still greater historical specificity in support of a similar argument. Although most recent critics have treated melodrama as an introspective, psychological, women's genre, Singer points out that in the early years of cinema melodrama was specifically associated with action, adventure and working-class men. Carefully attending to the critical practice of the silent period, Merritt and Singer successfully question current usage of the term *melodrama*. Indeed, a rapid glance at any standard treatment of silent film genres reveals the extent to which current definitions of melodrama fail to reflect earlier understanding of the term. In his treatment of the Western, family, society, rural, crime and military subgenres of silent-feature melodrama, Richard Koszarski emphasizes the villain-hero-heroine triangle, true-to-type characters and visually powerful dramatic confrontations rather than the self-sacrificing psychology of downtrodden women usually stressed in recent definitions of the genre (1990, pp. 181–6).

The first scholar to directly tackle the disparity between recent and traditional definitions of film melodrama is Steve Neale, who has exhaustively studied the use of melodrama and related terms (meller, melodramatic) in the trade journal *Variety* from 1938 to 1959, with extension for selected films to the 1925–1938 period. What Neale discovers is that, during this key period, the term melodrama 'continued precisely to mean what it did in the teens and twenties'. He finds that 'the mark of these films is not pathos, romance, and domesticity, but action, adventure, and thrills; not "feminine" genres and the woman's films but war films, adventure films, horror films, and thrillers, genres traditionally thought of as, if anything, "male" ' (1993, p. 69).

In other words, Neale claims that critics have been mistaken in their use of the term. Employing trade press usage of the term melodrama to exemplify his earlier claim that genres are established once and for all by the industry at the time of production (1990, pp. 48–52), Neale points out that films featuring women or clearly aimed at female audiences are rarely designated as melodrama, meller or melodramatic, 'because these films usually lack the elements that conventionally define these terms from the trade's point of view' (1993, p. 74). It is worth noting that Neale regularly conflates the trades of film criticism and film production as parts of the same industry. Yet we have seen how the interests and practices of these two activities may diverge.

For the time being, Neale's methods are less important than his purpose and his results. Though he never states specific conclusions, it seems clear that a major goal of the 1993 article is to demonstrate that scholars have misused the term melodrama and its derivatives in describing what are now often called 'women's films'. As Neale shows, in the 40s and 50s melodrama meant something else; recent critics thus make improper use of the term when they apply it to 'the weepies'. Yet a generation of feminist critics has systematically used the term melodrama in reference to the female-oriented films of the 40s and 50s. Their analyses have taken for granted – and thus reinforced – the existence and nature of this genre and its corpus. How are we to understand this discrepancy? Are current definitions of melodrama wrong, as Merritt, Singer and Neale imply? Or is another principle at work here? In order to come to terms with this problem, it is necessary to trace the history of the constitution of the woman's film as a genre, along with its connections to melodrama.

Rebirth of a phantom genre

For Molly Haskell, in 1974 the first of the recent critics to draw attention to the genre, a *woman's film* is a film that has a woman at the centre of its story. Just as initial generic recognition of the Western and the musical was facilitated by negative – and thus category-strengthening – evaluations, so Haskell acknowledges from the start the deprecatory connotations of the term *woman's film* as it had been intermittently employed by two generations of critics:

> Among the Anglo-American critical brotherhood (and a few of their sisters as well), the term 'woman's film' is used disparagingly to conjure up the image of the pinched-virgin or little-old-lady writer, spilling out her secret longings in wish fulfillment or glorious martyrdom, and transmitting these fantasies to the frustrated housewife. . . . As a term of critical opprobrium, 'woman's film' carries the implication that women, and therefore women's emotional problems, are of minor significance. . . . At the lowest level, as soap opera, the 'woman's film' fills a masturbatory need, it is soft-core emotional porn for the frustrated housewife. The weepies are founded on a mock-Aristotelian and politically conservative aesthetic whereby women spectators are moved, not by pity and fear but by self-pity and tears, to accept, rather than reject, their lot. That there should be a need and an audience for such an opiate suggests an unholy amount of real misery. And that a term like 'woman's film' can be summarily used to dismiss certain films, with no further need on the part of the critic to make distinctions and explore the genre, suggests some of the reasons for this misery.
>
> (1974, pp. 154–5)

Strong terms these, and extraordinarily revelatory of the purpose of feminist investment in the revitalization of *woman's film* as a term and a genre. Citing such well-known literary tragic heroines as Anna Karenina and Emma Bovary as generic models, along with examples drawn from films previously thought of as dramas, melodramas, films noirs or screwball comedies, Haskell delineates four subgenres of what she calls the 'woman's film', identifiable according to the type of activity engaged in by the heroine: sacrifice, affliction, choice or competition.

We recognize in Haskell's analysis a familiar technique of cycle and genre formation, though this time the critic rather than the producer appears to be the initiator of the process. By attaching the term *woman's* to a succession of already existing genres, Haskell succeeds in building an adjectival genre that was not fully constituted during the period of the films' production. We have already noted the extent to which the building of genres is often a critical, rather than a production-based, concern, so the only thing surprising about Haskell's attempt to rehabilitate the woman's film by broadening and strengthening its definition is the delay between the production of the films in question and the moment of critical intervention.

Indeed, Haskell's purpose is furthered by the many critics who have taken up her call. For Mary Ann Doane,

> the 'woman's film' is not a 'pure' genre – a fact which may partially determine the male critic's derogatory dismissal of such films. It is crossed and informed by a number of other genres or types – melodrama, film noir, the gothic or horror film – and finds its point of unification ultimately in the fact of its address.
>
> (1984, p. 68)

This is precisely the type of statement that might have been made in 1910 regarding the Western, in 1930 describing the musical, or in 1946 with relation to film noir. When they are still styled as cycles associated with multiple traditional genres –

whether by producers or critics – nascent genres never appear to be pure. Because the new generic content is expressed as an adjective modifying several different nouns, its very existence seems dependent on and derivative of those nouns. Doane's definition clearly images *woman's film* as a convenient term to describe a number of separate subgenres of diverse pre-existing genres: woman's gothic, woman's horror, woman's film noir and woman's melodrama. The application of the term *woman's* to each of these genres brings the four subgenres together, but the adjectival nature of its use precludes the woman's film from being seen as a fully independent genre.

In order to understand the process by which the *woman's film* eventually evolved into a fully-fledged genre, it is necessary at this point to subject certain aspects of mid-80s feminist criticism to such microscopic methodological and orthographic scrutiny that the original purpose of the essays analysed will be lost to view. However, this close inspection will ultimately bring the essays' broader goals and functions into focus.

For Doane in 1984, as for Haskell in 1974, the term 'woman's film' still had to be set off by quotation marks. A decade ago, what we now call the woman's film had a kind of starred existence, like a suspected but never actually witnessed Indo-European root word. The quotation marks are there not only for Haskell in 1974 and Doane in 1984, but also for many other critics in the mid-80s, including influential articles written in 1984 by Judith Mayne and Linda Williams. In fact, when in 1984 Doane mentions her book in progress, she refers to the book as ' *The "Woman's Film": Possession and Address*' (1984, p. 81). 'The book focuses,' she says, 'on "women's films" of the 1940s' (*ibid.*). In 1984, the quotation marks still seemed required.

When the book was published in 1987, however, it was titled *The Desire to Desire: The Woman's Film of the 1940s*. Following a practice begun in the United Kingdom by Claire Johnston, Annette Kuhn and Pam Cook, already adopted in the States by Tania Modleski, and soon to be followed by virtually the entire critical community (with the exception of a few male critics such as Robert Lang and David Cook), Doane strips the term *woman's film* of its quotation marks, thereby abandoning any remnant of doubt regarding the category's right to independent existence. Hesitation remains, however, regarding the generic status of the newly enfranchised category. In explaining the topic of her book, Doane regularly refers to the woman's film as a genre. In the opening methodological chapter, she notes a basic difference between the woman's film and other films: 'The cinema in general, outside of the genre of the woman's picture, constructs its spectator as the generic "he" of language,' says Doane. 'The woman's film is therefore in many ways a privileged site for the analysis of the given terms of female spectatorship and the inscription of subjectivity precisely because its address to a female viewer is particularly strongly marked' (1987, p. 3). A few pages later, Doane further specifies her purpose: 'The aim of this study is to outline the terms in which a female spectator is conceptualized – that is, the terms in which she is simultaneously projected and assumed as an image ... by the genre of the woman's film' (*ibid.*, p. 9). Doane goes on to explain that 'the conditions of possibility of the woman's film as a genre are closely linked to the commodity form' (p. 27). This is why, she contends, 'the woman's film as a genre, together with the massive extracinematic discursive apparatus, insure that what the woman is sold is a certain image of femininity' (p. 30). Doane's removal of the quotation marks from the expression

Scenes like this one between Irene Dunne and June Clyde led Back Street *(1932) to be ident-ified with the woman's film.*

'woman's film' is apparently justified by her acceptance of the woman's film as a fully-fledged genre.

Yet in the final section of the first chapter we unexpectedly read the following:

> The woman's film undoubtedly does not constitute a genre in the technical sense of the term, insofar as the unity of a genre is generally attributed to consistent patterns in the-matic content, iconography, and narrative structure. The heterogeneity of the woman's film as a category is exemplified by the disparity between gothic films such as *Under-current* (1946) or *Dragonwyck* (1946), influenced by film noir and the conventions of the thriller, and a love story such as *Back Street* (1941) or a maternal melodrama such as *To Each His Own* (1946). But the group does have a coherence and that coherence is grounded in its address to a female spectator. The woman's film, quite simply, attempts to engage female subjectivity.
>
> (1987, p. 34)

Initially, it may seem that Doane contradicts herself by first stressing and then contesting the generic nature of the woman's film. In retrospect, however, an entirely different attitude seems justified: *Doane hesitates about the generic status of the woman's film precisely because she is in the process of changing that status.* I do not mean to claim that Doane was by herself capable of turning a motley assortment of old films into a widely recognized genre, but I would suggest that a major purpose of *The Desire to Desire* is to establish the woman's film as a genre. One of the founding arguments for genrifying the woman's film is plain to see in the preceding quote: according to Doane, the coherence, and thus the generic status, of the woman's film 'is grounded in its address to a female spectator'.

The other telling argument involves the assimilation of the woman's film to an already established genre, capable of lending to the woman's film some of its long-standing genericity. Sliding conveniently from one category to another, Doane points out that 'the melodramatic mode is often analyzed in terms which situate it as a "feminine" form, linking it intimately with the woman's film in its address to a female audience' (1987, pp. 72–3). And a paragraph later: 'Because it fore-grounds sacrifice and suffering, incarnating the "weepie" aspect of the genre, the maternal melodrama is usually seen as the paradigmatic type of the woman's film' (*ibid.*, 73). In arguing for a privileged connection between the woman's film and melodrama, Doane is following a line initiated by Laura Mulvey and Tania Mod-leski, and widely circulated at conferences and colloquia from the early 80s on.

Though both Mulvey and Modleski end up at the same place – establishing an identity between melodrama and the woman's film – their strategies are quite dif-ferent. Identifying realism with Hollywood's address to men, Mulvey claims that in contrast 'the woman's film was identified with melodrama' (1986, p. 21), and that 'there appears to be no absolute line of demarcation between melodrama and the woman's film' (*ibid.*, p. 36). Following Geoffrey Nowell-Smith's insights regarding the connection between melodrama and hysteria, Modleski takes a dif-ferent tack. Pointing out the origin of the term hysteria in female anatomy, Modleski finds in the hysterical nature of melodrama 'a clue as to why for a large period of film history melodrama and the "woman's film" have been virtually syn-onymous terms' (1984, pp. 20–1).

Promotion of the woman's film as a genre has at the same time been abetted by borrowings from Thomas Elsaesser's 1972 article titled 'Tales of Sound and Fury: Observations on the Family Melodrama'. Though Elsaesser's topic is ostensibly a particular kind of melodrama dealing with family matters, most of his conclusions are broadly stated and have regularly been taken to apply to melodrama as a whole, whence the tendency over the past decade to assume that family melodrama is syn-onymous with melodrama as such. Robert Lang summarizes the standard position by claiming that 'if the notion of family is conceived of flexibly, the family can be said to represent melodrama's true subject, making the family melodrama a genre, where all other films are only to a greater or lesser degree melodramatic, but do not belong to the genre we call the melodrama' (1989, p. 49). All of this apropos of a term (*family melodrama*) that Neale never found once in his exhaustive study of the terminology applied to Hollywood women's films and melodramas.

Despite the fact that the notion of the woman's film was originally assembled out of female-oriented cycles within a variety of genres, woman's melodrama was promoted by critics during the 80s to the role of synecdoche for all of the others. In the same manner, family melodrama, once a peripheral melodramatic sub-genre, was saddled with the responsibility of representing all other types of melodrama. All that remained, in order to guarantee the generic status of woman's film and a redefinition of melodrama as family melodrama, was to link the two through their common feature of being primarily addressed to a female audience. Only when this junction took place – in conferences on both sides of the Atlantic as well as in passages like those quoted above from Doane – would the woman's film abandon its quotation marks in favour of full generic status. Since the late 80s the generic status of the category has never been in doubt (see, for example, the work of Caryl Flinn, Jane Gaines and Maureen Turim). Indeed, a new generation of introductory texts has begun to treat the woman's film as fully the equal of established genres (Dick, 1990, pp. 104–7; Sklar, 1993, pp. 116–17, 210–11; Maltby, 1995, pp. 133–6).

Until the 70s the term family melodrama was rarely used, and the term woman's film was never associated with the genre of melodrama. Yet during the 80s, critics regularly conflated the two categories, eventually styling the woman's film and family melodrama as the very core of melodrama as a genre. Introducing the term woman's film into serious critical discourse, Molly Haskell evinces a desire to use a new level of respect for the term itself as a weapon in the ongoing struggle to empower women. If we want to understand some of the reasons for women's misery, Haskell insists, we have but to look at the fact 'that a term like "woman's film" can be summarily used to dismiss certain films, with no further need on the part of the critic to make distinctions and explore the genre' (1974, p. 155).

One of the major tasks of feminist film criticism over the past twenty years has been to rehabilitate the term woman's film and thereby restore value to women's activities. In fact, not only has woman's film been rehabilitated, but the entire genre of melodrama has now been redefined through the woman's film (to the point of raising the hackles of historical critics aware that neither category – woman's film or family melodrama – had the contemporary existence that is attributed to it today). Like the parallel move made by Western and musical from adjective to substantive, the slide from 'woman's film' to woman's film carries far more than simple grammatical ramifications. Once it could be divorced from specific films and pre-existing genres, the woman's film was free to take on a life of its own, drawing to its corpus virtually any film apparently addressed to women.

But not just films. Tania Modleski (1982) and Jane Feuer (1984) stress the importance of gothic romances and television soap operas for any study of woman's film. Starting with Annette Kuhn's *Women's Pictures: Feminism and Cinema* (1982) and E. Ann Kaplan's *Women and Film: Both Sides of the Camera* (1983), the corpus was expanded to include not only classic Hollywood films, popular novels and television programmes, but also recent films and videos produced by women. Increasingly, the term woman's film has been used as a multimedia banner.

Critics as producers

Where does this leave us in our attempt to understand the process of genre constitution and transformation? It permits us to formulate a number of new hypotheses regarding the genrification process, complementing those offered in the previous chapters.

> 1. The genre constitution process is not limited to a cycle's or genre's first appearance.

It would be convenient if all generic categories, once constituted, could be counted on to remain forever stationary. The benefits of such a stable system shine so brightly that a number of critics have declared undying allegiance to original industry-spawned definitions. Yet it must be manifest that producers' interests in novelty guarantee a constantly shifting generic map. Neither melodrama as a category nor melodramatic texts have remained stable since Pixérécourt, Belasco and Griffith any more than comedy has remained stable since the Greeks. It would indeed be convenient if genre stability were guaranteed, but it is decidedly not so, and our genre theories must be established accordingly.

2. Taking one version of the genre as representative of the genre as a whole is not only a common practice, it is a normal step in the regenrification process.

Selling *The Creature from the Black Lagoon*

Regenrification is one of Hollywood's most ingenious rhetorical resources. When Universal released *The Creature from the Black Lagoon* in 1954, 'creature features' had long since been relegated to 'B' production and the bottom half of twin bills. Science fiction films, on the other hand, were quite the rage. Not a problem, said Universal's publicity department; all we have to do is define *The Creature from the Black Lagoon* as a sci-fi film. Radio spots thus touted *Lagoon* as the 'strangest science-fiction thriller of them all!' Audiences were invited to 'thrill to science-fiction shock filmed FOR THE FIRST TIME in amazing UNDERWATER 3-D'. A major studio advertising a major film would have sought to develop the film's individuality rather than tie it to a specific genre, but as a chronically impoverished minor studio, Universal used every available avenue to promote *The Creature from the Black Lagoon* as a science fiction film.

But why stop there? If careful generic posturing can breathe life into today's newly hatched creature then shouldn't it also have the power to resuscitate Universal's substantial creature-feature backlist? The accompanying advertisement from the pressbook distributed by Universal to exhibitors of *The Creature from the Black Lagoon* eloquently testifies to the power of revisionist history. Throughout the 20s and 30s, Universal had been the uncontested king of the horror film genre. From *The Phantom of the Opera* and *The Hunchback of Notre Dame* to *Frankenstein, Dracula, The Mummy, The Wolf Man* and *The Invisible Man,* Carl Laemmle's studio had experimented with every possible combination of man and animal, man and corpse, man and the unknown. With horror films falling out of fashion in the 50s, however, the only solution was to rebaptize all these films according to the new science fiction fad. Of the twelve films pictured, all but three (the Paramount films *The Golem, Dr. Jekyll and Mr. Hyde* and *War of the Worlds*) were produced by Universal. Through the magic of regenrification, Universal not only associated their latest production with the hot genre, but they even managed to pave the way for re-releasing their entire horror stock in the guise of science fiction.

Opposite:
If your vaults are full of horror films, but sci-fi is the current craze, then something must be done: this publicity mat from the pressbook for Universal's 1954 science-fiction thriller offers an object lesson in creative regenrification.

Rhetorically, the most effective method of redefining a genre is not to do so overtly, but rather to promote a subset of the genre to a representative position. When Northrop Frye needed to define comedy in a particular manner, in order to fit conveniently into his overall pattern of mythoi, he appointed New Comedy as the only worthy bearer of comedy's flag. Recognizing the importance to the Greeks of both Aristophanes' Old Comedy tradition and of Menander's New Comedy strain, Frye nevertheless claims that 'today, when we speak of comedy, we

normally think of something that derives from the Menandrine tradition' (1949, p. 58). Stretching the notion of comedy beyond its original theatrical meaning to cover all media, Frye effectively redefined comedy for generations of critics. A similar logic governs the common attempt, initiated by Jerome Delamater, to build an 'integrated musical' genre around films produced by Arthur Freed for MGM during the 40s and 50s.

> 3. Rewriting film history is one of the fundamental rhetorical strategies accompanying regenrification.

Convinced that genres are always transhistorical phenomena, popular opinion typically treats the phrase 'new genre' as an oxymoron. Genre critics often escape this quandary by adducing a tradition of texts and tendencies bearing witness to the genre's longevity. For some genres, like the Western, this may involve citing nineteenth-century literary and artistic precedents. For others, like the woman's film, it requires reshuffling period definitions, reconstructing contemporary canons and rediscovering films made by and addressed to women. Just as a rewritten history of melodrama provided a new and proud history for current women's productions, studios can furnish a made-to-order backdrop for their current projects simply by rewriting the history of their own past productions, as demonstrated in the case of *The Creature from the Black Lagoon*.

> 4. Most generic labels carry sufficient prestige that they are retained for the designation of newly formed genres, even when they are only partially appropriate.

Frye could have chosen to label one of his mythoi simply as 'New Comedy', but such a designation sounds limited and neologistic as compared to the traditional and powerful simplicity of 'comedy'. Delamater might well have treated the integrated musical as one of many subgenres of the musical. Instead, the integrated approach to the musical is termed the genre's Platonic ideal and attention to the MGM musical is justified accordingly:

> Choosing to concentrate on the MGM musical is based on more than judgmental whim, however. The MGM musical seems to contain every element which characterizes the musical as a genre. The concepts of the star vehicle, studio style, the producer's touch, and the Platonic ideal of the integrated musical come together at MGM and become manifest in many of that studio's films from the late-1930s to the mid-1950s.
>
> (1974, p. 130)

Delamater uses the term MGM inaccurately, if purposefully. During the period in question, MGM musicals were concurrently produced by three different units, led by producers Jack Cummings, Arthur Freed and Joe Pasternak, but only Freed systematically turned out integrated musicals. When Delamater identifies the integrated musical with 'the MGM musical', he thereby raises the Freed unit to representative status for all of MGM's musical production. In the same way, the association of the woman's film with family melodrama retains the power of the more general term, while applying that term to a corpus of films many of which do not fit the original action-oriented meaning of the term *melodrama*.

Originally propelled by its airfield antics toward the flyboy adventure genre, Tarnished Angels *(1957) would later be assimilated to the woman's film to take account of Dorothy Malone and Robert Stack's love on the wing.*

5. Any group of films may at any time be generically redefined by contemporary critics.

One of the founding principles of genre study is the importance of reading texts in the context of other similar texts. We have seen how, through the assaying process, studios may provide those very texts. Immediately following the success of *Disraeli*, Warners failed to produce films that would ensure a biopic-oriented reading of *Disraeli*. After the unexpected success of *The Story of Louis Pasteur*, however, Warner Bros. produced a series of films ensuring that *Pasteur* would be understood through a particular generic tradition, that of the newly identified biopic. But producers are not the only ones who can establish a context of films within which a given film will be read. Just as Frye saw to it that Molière would be read within a New Comedy context, rather than against the Old Comedy-related slapstick tradition, the romance-oriented comedy-ballet mode, or the tragic dark comedy strain (all of which many of Molière's plays fit just as well as New Comedy), so Elsaesser and the rehabilitators of the woman's film have ensured that, for example, Sirk's *Tarnished Angels* (1957), originally promoted as a flyboy adventure film, would be read in the unexpected context of *Stella Dallas* (1937) and *Rebecca* (1940), films that another era would have placed in entirely different genres. Situating films that include a great deal of male action, like most of Sirk's later work, in the context of movies built around female performers and domestic plots, has the effect of concentrating critical attention on Sirk's women, thus transferring his films effectively from one genre to another.

6. In the regenrification process, critics regularly take on the cycle-formation function previously associated only with film production.

To some recent genre theorists, for whom traditional genre definitions remain sacrosanct, the process of generic redefinition may seem unauthorized, interventionist and thus undesirable. Yet as argued in this chapter, critics' desires to use regenrification as part of their critical arsenal appears entirely expected, reasonable, and in any case unpreventable. Feminist critics are thus not wrong to redefine the woman's film and family melodrama, they are simply going about their business. Though we like to think of ourselves as objective and distanced from our objects of study, we too have objectives and needs, we too must differentiate our products from those of rival critics. In other words, today's critics find themselves in the same position *vis-à-vis* yesterday's critics and films as yesterday's producers found themselves *vis-à-vis* the-day-before-yesterday's films. Just as producers would assay a successful film, replicating certain aspects in order to initiate a successful cycle, so critics in all periods assess recent criticism, replicating certain aspects of successful publications in order to initiate a successful critical cycle. Those same critics also assay groups of films, creating new cycles in support of their own interests. The redefinition and rehabilitation of the woman's film and family melodrama provide a particularly clear example of this process.

7. Like studio-initiated cycles, critically inspired cycles become genres only through industry-wide imitation and adoption of their basic characteristics.

Until a cycle is consecrated as a genre by industry-wide recognition, it remains a cycle. Thus family melodrama, first constituted as a cycle by Thomas Elsaesser, became a genre virtually replacing melodrama when first Thomas Schatz (1981), and then the feminist critics previously cited, reiterated in their analyses Elsaesser's implied corpus, context and reading formation. The woman's film in turn remained no more than a cycle, slightly redefined from contemporary critical usage, until the removal of its quotation marks and assertion of its affinities with the newly redefined family melodrama. Once it gained generic independence, the redefined and regenrified woman's film garnered the freedom to associate with an entirely new class of texts: popular novels, radio programmes, television shows and films made by women.

When Stephen Neale demonstrates that recent critics' genre terms are inconsistent with the generic terminology originally used to describe those films, he appears to be suggesting that recent critics are using the wrong generic terms. This chapter has offered another way of looking at the problem. Instead of simply seeing some critics as right and others as wrong, we must interpret both approaches as attempts to capture jurisdiction over the right to redefine the texts in question. Rather than assume that generic labels have – or should have – a stable existence, we must heed the examples of the woman's film and family melodrama, recognizing the permanent availability of all cultural products to serve as signifiers in the cultural bricolage that forms our lives.

6
Where are genres located?

> Consider for example the proceedings that we call 'games'. I mean board-games, card-games, ball-games, Olympic games, and so on. What is common to them all? – Don't say: 'There *must* be some thing common, or they would not be called "games" – but *look and see* whether there is anything common to all. – For if you look at them you will not see some thing that is common to *all*, but similarities, relationships, and a whole series of them at that. To repeat: don't think, but look! . . .
>
> And the result of this examination is: we see a complicated network of similarities overlapping and criss-crossing: sometimes overall similarities, sometimes similarities of detail.
>
> I can think of no better expression to characterize these similarities than 'family resemblances'. . . . – And I shall say: 'games' form a family.
>
> Ludwig Wittgenstein, *Philosophical Investigations* (1953, pp. 66–7)

Because the notion of genre has often been brought to bear on apparently simple popular texts, serially conceived and mass produced, the complexity of the concept has rarely been recognized. When critics in other fields sit down to work, they have firmly identified a stable object of study; they know what it is and where it is, and they can count on its staying there. In the case of genres, quite to the contrary, critics seek their object in every corner, finding it in none. Consider the art critic writing about Michelangelo's 'David'. No picture, no description, no evaluation, can possibly displace the famous statue from its location in Florence. Centuries of tourists and scholars have viewed Michelangelo's masterpiece without compromising its identity. Art critics need have no hesitation regarding their object of study.

Most literary critics enjoy a similar sense of security. While there may exist thousands of copies of a Henry James novel, their similarity justifies treatment of, say, *The Portrait of a Lady* as a single, stable object of study. Theatre critics, it must be admitted, do have a more difficult time of it, given the performed nature of their target. Still, as long as they are seen as performances of Shakespeare's text, even multiple versions of *Hamlet* lead back once again to a relatively stable object. A similar logic has even been applied to the cinema by critics who subordinate differences in exhibition situation, film programme and audience constitution to similarities in a given film's projected image from one showing to the next.

Students of genre forever forego such security. Genre offers neither a unique object of study nor the stability of an exactly duplicated text. There exists no generic original of which particular events might be represented as performances. Present in no specific place at any particular time, the notion of genre cannot be adequately grasped through the models offered by art, literature, theatre or film. The oldest cliché in genre studies holds that a single text cannot constitute a genre. Less obvious, but no less important, stands the fact that genres are never made up of texts alone, however numerous. Because the very notion of genre depends on

83

the existence of audience activity (prior knowledge of similar texts, intertextual comparisons, specific cognitive tendencies and predictable schema-processing practices), no genre critic can afford to treat so-called generic texts in a vacuum. Furthermore, like all critical constructs, genres are created and sustained by repeated use of generic terminology – not only as part of recognizable generic criticism, but also in ads, posters, labels, iconography, quotations and other inter-textual references. Whereas no critical discourse, however prestigious or oft repeated, can become part of *Hamlet*, even the lowliest of genre critics cannot help but contribute to the genre itself.

A fundamental problem of genre studies stems from the ever-present desire for a stable and easily identifiable object of analysis. Ever simplifying, genre critics have simply borrowed an ontology, a methodology and an epistemology developed by critics of art and literature for other objects and other purposes, thereby reducing the notion of genre to a *corpus* of texts or to textual *structure*. We do better, I suggest, to treat genre as a complex *situation*, a concatenated series of events regularly repeated according to a recognizable pattern. For a genre to exist, a large number of texts must be produced, broadly distributed, exhibited to an extensive audience and received in a rather homogeneous manner. Traditional genre criticism has tended to treat a single aspect of this process as representative of the whole situation. Yet no isolated part of this process actually *is* the genre; instead, the genre lies somewhere in the overall circulation of meaning constitutive of the process. As the by-product of an extended series of events, a genre must be defined in a manner consistent with the complexity of an overall situation made up of three-dimensional events spread out over space and time.

A multiplicity of locations

In his book *Beyond Genre*, Paul Hernadi suggests that approaches to genre may conveniently be broken down into four fundamental categories, according to whether the critic's primary concern is the author, the reader, the verbal medium or the evoked world, thus producing generic criticism that he qualifies, respectively, as expressive, pragmatic, structural or mimetic (1972, p. 7). Hernadi's quadripartite division offers an appropriate starting point for our inquiry into the location of genre.

Literary and film critics alike often locate genre in the mind or models of generic authors. Rosalie Colie states that her primary purpose is 'to try to define some of the ways in which the idea of genre governed (– a vile phrase) and contributed to (– an O.K. phrase) writers and writing in one of the great outbursts of literary growth and change' (1973, p. 8). Whether genre actually governed or simply contributed to Renaissance writers, Colie clearly sees genre's major role as taking place in the process of composition. In a similar manner, Schatz locates genre in the material conditions of commercial film-making, where plots are copied and formulas forever reiterated (1981, p. 16).

Far more common, however, is the assumption that genres are located in the texts that are produced through dependence on generic models. Most books on genre begin by specifying the corpus of films that they will treat. Archetypically, Bruce Babington and Peter William Evans begin their book on *Biblical Epics* by delineating their field of inquiry: 'the term "Hollywood Biblical Epic" is taken to cover three sub-types of film: the Old Testament Epic; the Christ Film; and the Roman/Christian Epic' (1993, p. 4). Virtually every genre study includes in its opening pages a sentence such as this one, since most genre critics assume that the genre is located neither in the authors nor in the audience, but in the texts themselves taken as a group.

Still other critics stress genre's effects on reader or viewer expectation. Insisting that 'Genres do not consist only of films,' Steve Neale suggests that 'they consist also, and equally, of specific systems of expectation and hypothesis which spectators bring with them to the cinema, and which interact with films themselves during the course of the viewing process' (1990, p. 46). Differences between genres are thus measurable by what viewers accept as true, reasonable or verisimilar. According to Jonathan Culler, 'each genre constitutes a special *vraisemblance* of its own' (1975, p. 147). Aumont *et al.* go so far as to claim that 'the plausible maintains the necessary cohesion of the genre' (1992, p. 118). In other words, differences in verisimilitude are not just generated by differences in genre; they are instead the very location of the genres in question. Though generic differences are surely reflected in individual texts, according to this point of view they are driven by audience expectation.

More recently, genre theorists have begun to posit a new function and location for genre. Adena Rosmarin, for example, argues that 'genre is most usefully defined as a tool of critical explanation, as our most powerful and reasoned way of justifying the value we place or would place on a literary text' (1985, p. 49). Where others associate genre primarily with the author, the text or the audience, Rosmarin sees genre as a critical construct. 'Genre is not, as is commonly thought, a class but, rather,' claims Rosmarin, 'a classifying statement' (*ibid.*, p. 46). In a broader sense, we may fruitfully recognize the extent to which genres appear to be initiated, stabilized and protected by a series of institutions essential to the very existence of genres.

When discussing the question of generic location, genre theoreticians invariably adopt an exclusionary discourse, championing *either* the author(s) *or* the text(s) *or* the audience *or* generic institutions as genre's primary location. Depending on their preferred medium, period and genre, critics advance differing hypotheses about generic location, but usually within a fundamentally monological framework. This is a surprising situation, given the range of variables used to define individual genres. Lyric poetry, for example, is typically distinguished from other forms of verse on the basis of the author's mood and intention, while the epic is usually delimited according to textual content and structure. When Todorov defines the fantastic genre, however, he does so according to the reader's attitude. 'The fantastic,' he asserts, 'is that hesitation experienced by a person who knows only the laws of nature, confronting an apparently supernatural event' (1970, p. 29). Yet when scholars of nineteenth-century popular literature refer to the dime novel or the serial novel, their distinctions are clearly based not on auctorial, textual or audience concerns, but on the institutions and technology of book publication.

The same variety of generic logics reigns as well in the film world. Thanks to video store classification systems, the category of foreign films has become increasingly recognized as a separate genre. As with the category women's films (when it refers to films made by women), genre is here located in the details of authorship. However, most film genre distinctions depend heavily on textual concerns. Whether the Western is defined iconographically or structurally, Western-ness is virtually always assumed to be located in key aspects of the films themselves. In contrast, definitions of the horror genre usually stress viewer experience. Yet when critics seek to define avant-garde film, art cinema and blaxploitation as genres they do so through recourse to institutional concerns. The only reasonable alternative is to conclude that genre is not permanently located in any single place, but may depend at different times on radically differing criteria.

Like the notion of nation, the very idea of genre exists in the singular only as a matter of convenience – or ideology. Yet virtually all approaches to genre have assumed that genre is a single thing. They take it for granted that every time we use a genre term we are referring to the same type of category. Typically fetishizing textual characteristics or institutional influences, the standard method of containing generic complexity is to reduce the full genre situation to a single factor. The following sections of this chapter will look at some long-standing assumptions about the location of genre, before offering a more general hypothesis regarding generic location.

Genre and nation

With regard to location, it is instructive to note just how closely the notion of genre parallels that of nation. Where is the American nation located, for example? Is it to be found in the Constitution? Or is it in the Bill of Rights? Is it by virtue of a shared history that the States are United? Or is it because of shared values? Are we one by opposition to an ever changing set of others? Or do we cohere through commitment to a set of unchanging principles? Is the nation located in its elected officials or in the people whom they represent? As with genre the nation question offers up no simple, single answer. For at different times in the country's history, differing logics apply. During the Revolution, and in every foreign war since, geographical coherence has served as a strong basis for political differentiation. Yet during successive waves of immigration, American-ness has been connected to broader notions of identity, international in nature and caught up in the idea that *all* people are created equal and thus deserve equal opportunity.

For some, the nation is located in its flag, an inviolable symbol of national identity; for others, the flag is but a convenient emblem of the broader values in which the nation resides. Defying received notions of language's straightforward referential nature, the term 'nation' proves to be anything but a single coherent concept referring to a single coherent referent. On the contrary, the very notion of nation appears to depend on constant (but not necessarily visible) conflict among multiple competing but related notions. Though at times of external

Genre as textual structure: Semantics and syntax

The twin requirements of representation and communication always involve a strong tension between two opposed ideals: the need for *accurate* designations and the need for *sharable* terms. A language made up entirely of proper nouns, like the one used in horse racing forms, offers significant representational benefits; every name clearly corresponds to and identifies a single horse. For those who wager on horse races and for those who pay off their bets, such a high level of accuracy is essential. But what happens when a potential bettor, unfamiliar with a particular horse, asks for information? Such a question leads away from the comfortable domain of guaranteed accuracy towards sharable terms whose applicability to individual horses proves increasingly questionable. Labelling Jupiter's Girl a filly achieves a certain balance between accuracy and sharability, but when a tout goes on to call her a smallish quarter horse, a fast starter, a fair sprinter, a good mudder and a poor finisher, we easily recognize the uncertain reality and applicability of each quality evoked.

Ideally, proper nouns depend on a culturally sanctioned once-and-for-all act of linguistic creation timed to match an act of natural creation; when a horse is born, its name is stillborn, we might say, forever fixed (by custom and law) in a particular representational relationship with a single horse. Adjectives and common nouns, on the other hand, continue to evolve; they remain at the mercy of the very society sanctioning their use. Whenever we gain the possibility of sharing lan-

threats to national sovereignty a nation-wide tendency towards epic homogeneity commonly conceals the nation's fundamentally heterogeneous nature, peace time quickly restores the constitutive debate regarding the very meaning of the notion of nation.

In one sense this is nothing more than a particular case of the general rule whereby language and other cultural structures depend on the evolving circumstances of the linguistic or interpretive community. Every word, every cultural artefact remains implicitly a permanent site of conflict among multiple possible meanings and locations. With most words, however, the level of conflict is low and its ramifications minor. Only with the major building blocks of a culture are conceptual conflicts regularly and meaningfully highlighted.

This production still from Warners' wartime Yankee Doodle Dandy *(1942) suggests an uncomplicated relationship between the nation, the flag, Uncle Sam, and America as last bastion of liberty.*

guage we simultaneously expose that language to the unpredictable influence of those who share it. All sharable language thus remains perpetually under the constant risk of change, of reduced accuracy, and thus, ironically, of diminished sharability.

In response to this general problem of language, human communities have adopted a series of strong, conservative measures designed to assure that most language will approximate the high level of accuracy and sharability achieved by a term like 'filly'. Not only do we all know what that word means (and if we don't, its meaning can easily be taught by reference to universally recognized biologically fixed phenomena), but its applicability to any particular case is easily tested, thus assuring a high level of accuracy. Created in order to maintain a language's accuracy and sharability, dictionaries have commonly constituted a major aspect of a broad nationalistic project. Similar nation-binding benefits accrue from canonizing key texts, codifying grammar and stamping out dialects in favour of a single sanctioned phonological system. While none of these attempts at standardization actually arrests the development of language, each contributes to the creation of a level playing field, a space and a time during which individual practitioners of the language can be relatively sure that (a) the language is stable, and (b) their interlocutors understand the language as they do. Together, these two effects play a major role in reinforcing national unity.

A nearly identical logic reigns over genre. In order successfully to play the horses (designated by proper nouns), racing enthusiasts must have at their disposal a vocabulary of common nouns and adjectives; in order to understand the role of individual films within the overall history of cinema, film fans must be able to describe those films in sharable, generalizable terms. Theoretically, there exists no necessary connection between the individual film and the general term used to describe it. Yet the creators and users of those general terms have laboured mightily to foster the perception of such a connection. The preferred strategy is to locate each genre in a property or properties of the text itself, thus creating the illusion that the genre arises directly out of the film, rather than out of texts produced in reaction to the film. All text-based genre claims and descriptions thus serve a silent stabilizing purpose, simultaneously reinforcing the twin goals of applicability and sharability. The more texts a particular generic notion matches, the more that generic notion seems worthy of generalization and sharing; the stronger the match, the greater the stability achieved by the generic notion.

This is decidedly not the major manner according to which generic claims have typically been made or understood. Those who have located genres in a configuration of specific textual features have usually done so as part of an overall truth claim regarding the history and functioning of literature or cinema. While appearing to expand horizons and serve truth, the careful structural analysis and reasoned historiography of genre study actually enforce a rather limited and tendentious view of generic activity. My own semantic/syntactic approach to genre provides an appropriate example. Because it uses familiar and thus eminently sharable terminology to achieve a satisfactory level of accuracy in describing generic phenomena, both textual and historical, the semantic/syntactic approach has been broadly adopted as an acceptable method of describing the history of genre texts and the work of genre theorists. From the more fully discursive standpoint adopted throughout the present book, however, something quite different appears. However accurate and serviceable the semantic/syntactic approach may be, more is at stake in this – and any other – textual approach than applicability alone.

As first presented in *Cinema Journal* (Altman, 1984), slightly expanded in *Film Genre Reader* (Altman, 1986, reproduced as an appendix in this book), and then extended to a large generic corpus in *The American Film Musical* (Altman, 1987), the semantic/syntactic approach to genre is based on the recognition that generic labels are commonly attached to categories deriving their existence from two quite different sources. At times we invoke generic terminology because multiple texts share the same building blocks (these *semantic* elements might be common topics, shared plots, key scenes, character types, familiar objects or recognizable shots and sounds). At other times we recognize generic affiliation because a group of texts organizes those building blocks in a similar manner (as seen through such shared *syntactic* aspects as plot structure, character relationships or image and sound montage).

Attention to textual semantics produces generic statements that have the benefit of broad applicability, easy recognition, and general consensus. Stressing common iconography (including six-guns, horses and Western landscapes), a semantic approach to the Western, for example, is readily applied to a large number of films, producing a corpus so inclusive that it may even incorporate some films not usually treated as Westerns. Sorting through a pile of stills from Hollywood films, we readily identify those that come from Westerns, because the defining semantic elements lie on the easily recognizable surface of the image. Treating the Western as a cluster of semantic elements makes it possible to achieve a high level of consensus regarding the Western-ness of any particular film. Semantic approaches to genre thus serve the important social function of providing easily sharable and consistently applicable vocabulary. In this sense, you don't have to see a whole film to know whether it is a Western, and you can be pretty sure that your neighbour (or even an Italian or Venezuelan film fan) will share your conclusions.

Proponents of syntactic analysis regularly point, however, to the relative shallowness of the semantic approach. Where attention to semantic concerns produces little more than a label, they suggest, syntactic analysis offers understanding of textual workings and thus of the deeper structures underlying generic affiliation. Stressing an exclusive corpus of texts that share multilayered patterns, the syntactic approach requires attention to much more than individual objects or images. If a Western is a film with a six-gun (a stripped-down version of the semantic approach), then a single glance suffices to identify the genre, but if a Western is a film contrasting wilderness and community (Jim Kitses' version of a syntactic approach), then in-depth analysis will be required to confirm any particular film's association with the Western genre. The process may be more complex, and thus both slower and less consensual, but it has the benefit of facilitating comparison to extratextual syntactic patterns (like history, myth or psychology) that might be seen to explain or at least appropriately contextualize the genre.

Though not always using the terms semantic and syntactic, critics have for decades practised some version of these approaches, usually adopting one of two familiar attitudes toward the implicit rivalry between them. Many critics simply elect to practise one kind of generic analysis in preference to the other, with the heyday of structuralism in the 70s producing a sea change from earlier semantic tactics to more recent syntactic approaches. Others vacillate between the inclusivity of semantics, typically concentrated in broad historical chapters or encyclopedic film lists, and the increased explanatory benefits of syntactic analysis, especially visible in long chapters devoted to one or two films deemed representative by virtue of their syntax. Implicitly, both groups of critics affirm that genre is located either in semantics or in syntax.

More satisfactory results may be derived from an alternative hypothesis: while regularly used to designate separate semantic or syntactic resemblance, the term *genre* takes on its full force only when semantic and syntactic similarities are simultaneously operative. In other words, instead of seeing these as alternative treatments, we need to see semantic and syntactic approaches as co-ordinated. It is not by chance that the film genres attracting the most popular and critical attention – the Western, the musical, the horror film – have been those that feature both a high degree of semantic recognizability and a high level of syntactic consistency. What is most fascinating about these genres is the way in which they retain a certain coherence over multiple decades in spite of constant variation in semantics and syntax alike. Only a co-ordinated semantic/syntactic analysis can facilitate understanding of this interaction. At its most forceful, then, genre is located neither in a common semantics nor in a common syntax, but in the intersection of a common semantics and a common syntax, in the combined power of a dual correspondence.

Genre as institution, institutions as genre

The history of film (and literary) genres repeatedly demonstrates the stabilizing role played by coinciding semantic and syntactic connections. When several films are united solely by their semantic elements (for example, newsroom films) or their syntax (Manichaean dual-focus confrontations), the individual films are easily wooed away from the newsroom or dual-focus corpus towards a generic identification simultaneously involving semantic and syntactic affiliation. Conversely, when a group of films shares both semantic and syntactic characteristics, it usually forms a strong and durable unit. The Western is a long-lived genre, multiple times resuscitated by its ability to conflate semantic and syntactic concerns; the *eastern, on the other hand, doesn't exist as a category, for no group of films has ever been recognized as combining East Coast locations with sufficiently consistent themes and structures.

Critics who locate genre in textual properties usually conclude that the bond of semantics and syntax is by itself capable of stabilizing generic vocabulary and attribution (thus providing strong – but circular – proof that genre is indeed located in the text). Two alternative hypotheses also deserve consideration. The first is offered by critics who insist that genres gain their power from the fact that they incarnate basic human needs and concerns. Many such critics, including Northrop Frye, invoke Jung's archetypal psychology; others, such as Torben Grodal, appeal to cognitive psychology. Both sides treat textual elements as no more than the temporal manifestations of permanent human structures. Whether in reaction to archetypes or to cognitive schemata, according to this approach genres are in an important sense transhistorical categories.

A second alternative takes an opposite tack. Textual structures, this approach asserts, are not in the text, but in a particular reading of the text. They are thus heavily dependent on the institutions that govern and support specific reading strategies. Wellek and Warren understood perfectly well that 'the literary kind is an institution' (1956, p. 226), but genre critics have not always recognized that genres can serve as institutions only because they are in turn backed up by other institutions, far more material in nature. Among these material institutions, the most active are production companies, exhibition practices, the critical establishment and government agencies.

Noël Burch's claim that 'the close-up was a self-contained genre from the very start' (1979, p. 28), for example, is primarily a statement about production packaging. It's not just that close-ups had been invented, were regularly used or attracted special attention, but that producers consistently repeated a single recognizable strategy in order to take advantage of that attention. Each new film built around a single close-up had the effect of reaffirming and thus reinforcing the apparent existence of the 'close-up' genre. A genre abandoned by producers tends to disappear from viewers' active vocabulary, while continued production serves as the most common institutional reinforcement of an existing genre. Classical genres like the dithyramb, paean, encomium, epithalamium, threnody and pastoral all made it through the Renaissance by virtue of revived production, only to fall prey in subsequent centuries to a change in production preferences. In the film domain, a similar fate awaited the scenic, the tab musical and the newsreel. It's not that today's poets produce no verses of praise, or this generation's film-makers no travel documentaries, but we no longer identify them as an *encomium* or a *scenic* because of an earlier rupture of production that virtually destroyed the genre.

Even when production institutions continue to support a genre, exhibition circumstances may destabilize generic identification. Recognizing the importance of high-profile public exhibition for the film-makers of emerging film industries, Peter Wollen postulates the existence of 'a new genre of films: the Festival Film genre' (1997, p. 10). Neither comedies nor musicals, 'festival' films are defined by their exhibition venue rather than by their textual characteristics. Indeed, a quick look at festival flyers or independent film catalogues demonstrates just how heavily exhibition circumstances weigh on genre. The typical museum- or university-sponsored festival recognizes only three entry categories: narrative, documentary and experimental (with the occasional addition of animation). This festival line-up is reinforced by independent rental and sales catalogues like that of San Francisco's Frameline Distribution, which divides titles into features, documentary, experimental and shorts. Clearly, certain films in the *narrative* and *feature* categories might be assimilated by some viewers to specific Hollywood genres, but in the context of this particular exhibition venue such an identification is not sanctioned.

Considered by itself, almost any genre breakdown will appear complete and logical. Only when compared to the exhibition system that sustains it does a particular generic configuration reveal its debt to exhibition institutions. Before 1910, the simple term *moving picture* served as a generic designator, by opposition to the other form that regularly shared the nickelodeon programme, the *illustrated song*. By 1911, however, *Moving Picture News* reflected the new tendency towards film-only programmes, and thus the need to distinguish among moving pictures, by separating films into dramatic, comedy, Western and educational types. Throughout the silent period, genre lists retained one or more terms designating short films (for example, educational, scenic and newsreel), because silent film programmes depended so heavily on shorter films. Changing exhibition practices fostered in part by Hollywood's conversion to sound eventually led to the restriction of generic vocabulary to feature-film genres. The long life of these categories sometimes blinds us to the fact that even they are tied to a specific exhibition institution.

Take the institution away and generic categories change. Because of US broadcasters' adherence to a policy of programme change on the half-hour, American television programmers (unlike many European systems) are interested first in length, and only secondarily in content. Programmes for sale to American networks are thus classified in multiples of 26 minutes (the amount of programming that will fit into a standard 30-minute block of time on US commercial TV). Meanwhile, television systems lacking predetermined programme start times pay little attention to such considerations. Bowing to the primacy of temporal considerations, Hollywood films are regularly not only re-categorized when they are shown on television, but they are even re-edited to fit television's programming needs. When recorded on videotape and rented or sold in video stores, a similar modification occurs: every possible film will be squeezed into whatever generic category happens to be fashionable.

The importance of exhibition as guarantor of generic identification usually remains entirely invisible, but it can easily be accentuated by showing a film in a venue other than the one for which it was created. Just as Duchamp's urinal took on new associations when it was transferred from men's room to exhibit, so a museum fundraising after-dinner showing of Soviet propaganda, gay pornography or a John Waters film must have a radical effect on those films' generic affiliations. When action films are listed in martial arts magazines alongside kumite documentaries, they leave the action genre in favour of the martial arts genre. When the old Blackhawk Films catalogue listed *The Lonedale Operator* and *The General* alongside railroad documentaries and train slides, Griffith and Keaton could not help but join the railroad genre. A similar exhibition strategy – scheduling Hollywood weepies alongside recent films made by women directors – helped to create the woman's film genre. Too often we have underestimated the role of exhibition institutions in anchoring generic affiliation.

The critical establishment plays an equally important role, always heavily (though usually implicitly) supported by its readers. When Nino Frank and other French post-war critics referred to certain American films as being *noir*, they were hardly making generic claims, but instead using a normal French adjective that had through the expressions *Série noire* and *roman noir* taken on the psychological connotation of *dark* rather than the original denotation of *black*. Repeated use of the term *film noir*, however, eventually had durable generic consequences – in part because, affirms Jim Naremore, 'film noir has been useful to the movie industry, providing artistic cachet and spectacular opportunities for both the "New Hollywood" auteurs of the 1970s and the sex-and-violence specialists of the 1980s' (1996, p. 24).

The individual critic may be incapable of creating or reviving a genre, but the critical community and its readers can. Consider Tom Gunning's suggestion that early films be divided into three main genres: non-continuity, continuity and discontinuity. On the one hand, this is just one man's opinion. On the other hand, the essay has repeatedly been reprinted, translated and referred to by other critics, thus lending it the suffrage of all those who have 'voted with their eyes' by choosing to read, purchase or assign this essay. When Ed Guerrero organizes much of his writing around what he calls 'Hollywood's plantation genre, spanning approximatively sixty years' (1993, p. 10), he is implicitly appealing to the critical community to rally behind his conflation of historical epics, musicals, melodramas, animation and adventure films into a new genre. Thomas Cripps is doing the same thing, but in a slightly different direction, by proposing to treat all *Black Films as Genre* (1978).

Just as a careful comparison of generic terminology to exhibition practices discloses strong connections between nomenclature and programming, so a close study of genre labels cannot help but reveal close ties between generic categories and the cultural currents with which critics are affiliated. *Blaxploitation* was identified as a cultural category during the liberal backwash of the civil rights movement. *Woman's film* as a genre term was spawned by the feminist movement. Films featuring close friends of the same sex have been produced for decades, but not until the era of gay liberation did the *buddy film* come out as a genre. Even apparently personal or idiosyncratic genre terms reflect current cultural standards. Consider the film-goer who proclaimed: 'I like Chick-Flicks, but I loathe Chick-Flick-Wanna-Be's' (Kim, 1997). Only a strong single-sex support group could authorize such a comment.

How do such terms gain currency and influence? Perhaps the most important step towards entering the genre pantheon is for a generic designator to be adopted by our generation's most important arbiters of generic taste: *TV Guide* (and similar throwaway programmes), *Leonard Maltin's Movie & Video Guide* (and other film-by-film reference books) and *Blockbuster Video* (including the anonymous writers of videocassette cover copy). For most viewers, genre is located in these classifications, along with the appendices of mass market coffee table tomes and introductory film course books. If Leonard Maltin says *Thelma and Louise* is a road movie (rather than a chick-flick or a buddy film), who are we to disagree?

Perhaps the most insidious of classificatory schemes are the film ratings established by the State, the Church, special interest groups, or even (particularly in the United States) the film industry itself. While many would reasonably claim that an 'H' or an 'X' (Great Britain), a red square in the lower righthand corner of the television screen (France) or a 'G', 'PG', 'R' or 'X' (United States) hardly constitute genre distinctions, it is important to recognize that such designations do have a genre-like effect on producers, exhibitors and audiences. In the case of producers, ratings serve to funnel production decisions into clearly separate categories, for example excluding the mixing of a plot likely to attract the 14-and-under crowd with images likely to place the film in the 'R' category. Ratings have the same kind

Susan Sarandon and Geena Davis in Ridley Scott's Thelma and Louise *(1991): is it a chick-flick, a buddy film, a road movie, or something else?*

of scheduling effect on exhibitors as other generic classifications; the Sunday midnight slot on France's Channel Five is regularly reserved for a 'red square' (i.e., soft-core pornographic) film, just as the Saturday matinee show was once reserved for 'children's' films. In response, audiences learn what to expect of a particular rating – not just in terms of violence, nudity or strong language, but also in terms of plot type, pace and sophistication of dialogue.

In countries that provide financial support for film production, a list of authorized genres often appears on official documents. Once identified with the Soviet Union and other Communist countries, this approach passed in the 70s and 80s to what we might call the Uganda-Chile-China axis, where official genres are not only specifically identified, but also carefully defined by the government. In the United States, such designations are far from absent. They exist, for example, in the funding literature distributed by local Humanities Councils funded by (and thus responsible to) the National Endowment for the Humanities. They exist in the language of National Endowment for the Arts grant announcements. They exist in the generic terminology deployed by such large privately funded organizations as the Metropolitan Museum of Art and the Getty Museum, sponsors of the 'Art on Film' project and guarantors of the genre perpetuated under the *art on film* label. All in all, though, governmental institutions have had a limited effect on American film genre terminology, partly because, unlike most other countries, the United States government has financed precious little film production, and partly because Hollywood has done a good enough job creating the impression that it successfully regulates itself for the government to leave it alone.

The British have not always been so fortunate. In the early days of the genre, horror films were (like other 'adult' films) rated 'A' by the British Board of Film Censors, meaning that those under sixteen could attend if accompanied by an adult. Introduced in 1937, the 'H' rating (for 'horrific') simultaneously reinforced the coherence of the horror genre and altogether banned those under sixteen. When in 1952 the new 'X' rating was applied to films with sexual as well as horrific content, an important support mechanism for the horror genre was cut off, resulting in the genre's dismemberment and distribution into surrounding genres (science fiction, film noir, melodrama and the like).

Then in 1984, after a two-year campaign spearheaded by *The Daily Mail*, the Video Recordings Bill sought to assure the rating of all videotapes available for purchase in Great Britain. This measure was necessary, its sponsors claimed, because of the increasing distribution of 'nasty' videos, which (following the substantification process outlined in Chapter 4) soon came to be known as 'video nasties'. Like other genrifiers, censorship proponents turned their backs on previous categorizations and medium specificity, attaching the label 'nasty' not only to feature fiction films (such as *Cannibal Holocaust, Death Trap, The Evil Dead, I Spit On Your Grave, Last House On the Left* and *SS Experiment Camp*), but also to documentaries (*Faces of Death*), and even to television programmes (*The Day After*). Because they are available on videocassette, detractors alleged, such films can have a particularly deleterious effect on younger viewers. In other words, locating the *nasties* genre in a putative effect on a specific audience, supporters saw the Video Recordings Bill as a way to concretize generic identification through official government action.

Meanwhile, in the United States, *The Day After* (1983) was presented by ABC and received by a record-breaking audience as a social problem film, investigating one of the era's most highly charged political and social questions, the threat of nuclear war. Though it might well have been positioned in relation to the melodrama, science fiction or disaster genres, or located in what Gregory Waller terms the 'genre of future war' (1987, p. 10), Nicholas Meyer's telefilm was instead pushed by the network and the press in the direction of the social problem genre. The importance of this stance comes clear only in comparison to British commentary, as analysed by Martin Barker. Identifying *The Day After* as a video nasty invites viewers (a) to restrict their attention to scenes of violence and suffering, (b) to accept the censors' evaluation of those scenes, and (c) to abandon both textual and cultural analysis as a means of establishing the film's broader meaning.

As Barker repeatedly shows in his analyses of *SS Experiment Camp* (1984, pp. 30–1), *Faces of Death* (pp. 35–6), *Cannibal Holocaust* (pp. 106–10) and *I Spit On Your Grave* (pp. 112–16), these films may not be aesthetic masterpieces, but they do use violence to make fairly clear and not uninteresting points. Of course, these points systematically critique the practices and power of patriarchal society and the Conservative government. Whereas all of these films could be seen as social problem films, the Video Recordings Bill seems designed to keep them from being considered in that context. Whereas most observers attribute the violent fascinations of British youth to unemployment and social unrest, the Tory government under Margaret Thatcher and *The Daily Mail* did everything in their power to divert attention from governmental complicity, instead blaming the availability of 'dangerous' videos.

The striking saga of the video nasties genre no doubt represents an extreme case, rare in the history of cinema. However unusual it may be, the genre's invention and its legislated institutionalization reveal a problem that has not yet surfaced in this chapter on the location of genre. As long as genre appears to be a natural outgrowth of production and exhibition practices, or an inherent quality of texts, the question of genre seems quite neutral and objective. With the extreme form of institutional support for a particular genre construction that we find in the video nasties story, however, the location and nature of genre become more than just an academic matter. Invested in genre questions, institutions actively labour to establish the truth values of their claims regarding texts and genres. As noted in the video nasties case, some kind of political positioning often underlies apparently objective claims regarding the nature, structure and effect of particular films. If each genre location turns out to be no more than the claim of a particular institution, could genres possibly be located in those institutions as well as in production, exhibition, criticism and texts themselves?

More than just a game?

Among influential genre theorists, none has expressed himself about the question of genre location more clearly than Ludwig Wittgenstein. In the quote at the beginning of this chapter, he admonishes us to '*look and see*' what games have in common if we want to understand why different activities share the same name. 'Don't think, but look!' he says, clearly locating 'gameness' not in our thought but in something that can be seen in the games themselves.

Taking Wittgenstein quite literally, I set out to 'look and see' just what *nuts* are. At my local supermarket I found a sign identifying the nut aisle. About halfway down the aisle I located the two bays apparently indicated by the sign. One was entirely filled with cans and jars, labelled 'cashews', 'peanuts', 'almonds', 'roasted sunflower seeds' or 'mixed nuts'. The other displayed dozens of hanging bags, some containing nuts in the shell and labelled 'walnuts', 'brazil nuts', 'pecans', 'peanuts', 'chestnuts' and 'hazelnuts', while others were without shells and variously identified as 'walnuts', 'pecans', 'hazelnuts' and 'trail mix'. From one extremity to the other, the side of the aisle where the nuts were located looked like this:

drink mixes
      cake mixes
            ready-made icing
                  powdered chocolate
                     chocolate morsels
                        nuts
                            cooking oils
                                low-cholesterol oils
                                      diet products

Though the aisle as a whole revealed no single organizing factor, as I stood in front of any given part of the aisle I could readily see a common factor in the products displayed before me. First came *mixes*, then *cake supplies*, then *chocolate products*, and so forth. Attending to this series of overlapping commonalities, and concentrating on nuts, I was able to reach the following conclusions:

- *nuts* are edible (like all the other items in the aisle);
- *nuts* are contained in jars, cans or bags (unlike the mixes which are in boxes);

– *nuts* are small and morsel-like (like the chocolate morsels to one side of the nuts);

– *nuts* are oily (like the items on the other side).

While waiting in line to pay, I noticed a number of other nut products: beer nuts, nut bars and doughnuts. I wasn't quite sure how to fit these nuts into my looking and seeing experiment.

Still contemplating my somewhat contradictory and inconclusive observations, I arrived home. The process of putting my groceries away only increased my frustration. After storing the cake mix in the pantry (next to the pasta), the icing in the refrigerator (next to the eggs), the bagged nuts in one cabinet (next to the spices) and the oil in another (with the other oversize bottles), I proceeded to store the canned nuts with the potato chips and the pretzels (next to the bourbon and scotch). As far as I could tell, I was not seeing at home the same things that I saw at the store. The nut aisle made me think of mixes (drink and cake) as *items in boxes*, whereas at home I immediately put them in the pantry with all the other *dry* items. At the store, the oil seemed defined by its *oiliness*, a factor shared with the neighbouring nuts, but at home its container *height* instead came into play.

Having looked twice and seen two different things, I resolved to visit the grocery store warehouse. There I found the oils stored on the ground level with other heavy non-perishables like soups and canned vegetables. Most of the nuts were in another part of the warehouse, on a second level devoted to medium-weight cans and jars. The cake mixes and bagged nuts were on the top level with lighter products like breakfast cereals.

It bothered me that nuts should be classified in so many different families, so I consulted a scientific treatise to get at the truth. Imagine my frustration when I found cashews and peanuts treated in entirely different chapters. Classified as a fruit, cashews were located with the peaches and pears, whereas the peanuts were classified as legumes and grouped with the peas and beans. I did get a measure of revenge when I turned to my trusty one-volume encyclopedia, where the peanuts were listed squarely between the peaches and the pears.

What did I learn from this attempt to look and see? First, each new location brings out a differing aspect of nuts: their size, weight, composition, growth patterns, packaging, perishability, orthography, social functions, and so forth. This is precisely what Wittgenstein predicted. Instead of finding a single common characteristic defining all nuts, we discover a large number of characteristics common to some nuts and certain other items. Instead of a scientific species, defined by unique characteristics shared only by nuts, the category of *nuts* represents the intersection of several separate lines of reasoning, each grouping nuts with items not usually considered as nuts.

Curiously, the looking process led me to note several characteristics that I cannot possibly understand as actual properties of nuts. I started out eager to look at nuts, but what I saw was shelves, containers and words. While some nut locations called attention to the characteristics of the nuts themselves, others seemed to derive from social and economic customs of a much broader nature. In short, my looking experience caused me to pay less attention to the innate properties of nuts than to the physical and social context in which nuts are used (i.e., named, sold, stored and consumed).

The more I actually *looked* at nuts (i.e., not nuts in the abstract, but nuts as they are available to me at a particular historical time and place), the more I was forced to *see* the particular purposes and practices of those who actually use them. This recognition suggests several general hypotheses:

1. 'Family resemblances' derive not only from an independent, apparently natural and seemingly objective family history; they also depend heavily on the uses to which the members of the family are put.

This is not surprising when we recall that Wittgenstein's initial query relates not to 'games', but to 'the proceedings that *we call* "games" ' (my italics). The emphasis on naming reminds us that the very notion of games is a social construction, with authors and purposes.

2. Like nuts and games, genres too are heavily dependent on the purposes of those who name, package, store, serve or consume them.

Whatever intrinsic characteristics generic material may have had prior to its recognition as a genre, it is actively modified by those who pronounce the genre's name, describe its traits, exhibit it, reproduce parts of it, or otherwise make use of its potential.

3. Just as the varying storage locations of nuts depend on the ability of nuts to be imaged in a variety of different ways (in terms of size, shape, weight, composition and use), so the constitution and continued existence of genres depend on the multifariousness of the texts associated with the genre.

Differing generic identifications correspond to different uses, placement in different series and emphasis on diverse characteristics. In order to understand generic identity and function, we must attend to the ways in which diverse genre users have placed texts in widely divergent contexts.

4. The fact that nuts (or genres) can be imaged in a variety of different ways suggests the possibility that Wittgenstein's 'look and see' begs a basic epistemological question: do we really move straight from looking to seeing to knowing?

Just as Wittgenstein assumes that the term *game* is a culturally shared term, used similarly by all speakers of the language, so he takes for granted a single, uniform process of analysis leading everyone unerringly from looking to knowing. But suppose different individuals or groups, by virtue of their differing designs on a genre, were to use it differentially. Wouldn't they *look* at different parts, *see* different aspects, and finally become convinced that they *know* different things? In short, it may be that Wittgenstein's common language approach takes too much for granted. In fact, it is precisely the notion that language is *common* (i.e., shared) that we must question.

5. The perceived nature and purpose of genres depend directly and heavily on the identity and purpose of those using and evaluating them.

In speaking of 'the proceedings that *we* call "games"' (my italics), Wittgenstein oversimplifies the situation. Who are *we* in the case of genre? The producers? The exhibitors? The viewers? The critics? It is hard to imagine how any of these genre users could possibly be excluded. Applied to a particular film genre (the Western, for example), Wittgenstein's phrase would then read as follows: 'the proceedings that we producers, exhibitors, viewers, and critics call "the Western"'. But such a formulation creates a clearly factitious togetherness, falsely assuming shared vocabulary, similar purposes and transparent communication. We know perfectly well that these groups have radically different goals, methods and philosophies.

To paraphrase Wittgenstein: 'What is common to all these genre users? Don't say: "There *must* be some thing common . . ." but *look and see* whether there is anything common to all.' In the past, it has simply been taken for granted that genres are broadly shared categories, assuring clear communication between

- administrative and production personnel ('make this as a comedy, not a melodrama');
- producers and exhibitors ('the package includes two Westerns, two musicals and two comedies');
- exhibitors and audiences ('come see the biggest adventure film of the year');
- critics and readers ('it's a gangster film like they don't make any more').

When we look more closely at generic communication, however, it is not sharing and understanding that appear, but competing meanings, engineered misunderstanding and a desire for domination rather than communication.

All genre terms are implicitly authored; that is, they are always the product of a specific user group. Yet when generic terms are used they are rarely signed by their authors. Instead, they are typically presented as universal terms, and said to be dictated by tradition or to arise spontaneously out of textual structure.

Instead of a transparent vessel of communication between sender and receiver – like the unproblematic 'message' at the centre of the Jakobsonian communication model – genres must be seen as a site of struggle among users. Our challenge is to discover the ways in which the authors and consumers of generic terminology disguise their interests and their activity. Wittgenstein's 'family resemblances' model unfortunately proves complicitous in this regard, because it systematically conceals generic agency behind an apparently natural process (the development of family resemblances through genetics). Only by adopting an overt user-oriented approach can genre studies recover the discursivity that Wittgenstein and so many other genre theorists studiously avoid.

7
How are genres used?

> Generic differences are grounded in the 'use-value' of a discourse rather than in its content, formal features, or its rules of production.
>
> Thomas O. Beebee, *The Ideology of Genre* (1974, p. 7)

The title of this chapter seems to ask a simple, straightforward question. 'How are genres used?' sounds just like 'how are hammers used?' An object exists, say a hammer. Everybody knows what it is. You can buy it in a store. I keep one in the kitchen. Ask me how I use it and I'll tell you that I mainly pound nails with it, though I have been known to use it to start a screw or two. The existence and identity of hammers is so evident that the question seems to interrogate only my use of a well-known object, not that object's nature or purpose. After all, when I use the hammer to start a screw I'm never tempted to call it a screwdriver, or even a 'screwstarter'. It forever remains a hammer, an object whose identity and purpose are clearly and continually confirmed by the culture in which we live.

We think of objects and their uses as radically separate, but since language is ultimately defined by use, every use has potential ramifications for (our understanding of) the object used. Though it seems that objects and their names precede use, all are caught up in a circular process that makes each mutually dependent on the others. When producers, marketers and consumers of an object share a single sense of the object's use value, the circular nature of the process remains quite invisible. Yet the entire system is predicated on this circularity and the attendant invisibility. Change one part of the loop and the whole system can break down.

What gives hammers a sense of hard-and-fast existence is not so much the hard material of which they are composed, but the social contract binding producers, marketers and consumers into a single interpretive community with regard to the notion of 'hammerness'. Each knows what the other expects a 'hammer' to be; each performs 'hammerness' in the same way. But this example clearly lies at one end of an extended spectrum. At this extremity, users are so firmly aligned that the identity of objects and the accuracy of language remain unquestioned. The social benefits of this alignment are manifest: when we all speak the same language to refer to the same objects, assuming that they serve the same purposes, we live in a world of assurance and understanding. Without such common ground, human society would be impossible.

But society has never been quite so simple. As useful as it may be for human beings to share terms and concepts, history reveals that an opposite tendency is also constantly at work in human communication. While some people make do with objects and language defined by previous generations, others make a name for themselves by contesting inherited notions. Inventing, renaming, redefining, recategorizing and remapping, these renegades energize an otherwise stable system. Culture itself, and the very history of language and society, depend on this continued invention of objects, concepts, names and uses. If one end of the spectrum is occupied by questions like 'how are hammers used?', implying that hammers are both permanently defined and unaffected by use, the opposite pole is inhabited by questions like 'what shall we call this?', asking for a performative response where use dictates label and definition rather than vice versa. In between stand questions that combine the attributes of both poles. On the one hand these questions recognize the relative stability of objects and words; on the other hand they acknowledge their potential mutability. Whenever a reversible, process-oriented, interactive question like 'how is language used?' is asked, the inverse question 'how does usage modify language?' is always implicitly present.

In the past, virtually all work on genre has assumed that genres enjoy the cultural determinacy of hammers; this chapter shows why a broader approach is needed. Genres are not inert categories shared by all (though at some moments they certainly seem to be), but discursive claims made by real speakers for particular purposes in specific situations. Even when the details of the discourse situation remain hidden, and thus the purpose veiled, we nevertheless do well to assume that generic references play a part in an overall discursive strategy. Note that most genre users work very hard to preclude such attention: perhaps the most important tactic in the genre world consists in naturalizing one's own discursive claims. Most typically, this is done by attributing to the text itself goals and functions proper to producer, exhibitor, spectator or critic. Each of the basic meanings of the term genre – blueprint, structure, label, contract – has its own spokesperson, save one: textual structure. Into this vacuum rapidly rush all those who speak for the other meanings, thus hiding their own purposes behind the apparently neutral text.

The history of genre theory may thus conveniently be retold as the history of user attempts to conceal their own activity and purpose. Aristotle dissimulates the distance between structure and reception by equating cathartic reception with tragic structure. Horace and the neoclassical critics attempt to assure identity of production and reception genres by legislating the duties of gentlemanly producers and receivers. Treating genres as species, Brunetière subordinates all genre users to an apparently natural, organic, pre-existing series. Frye hides the difference between two antithetical social uses of comedy by burying Aristophanes' Old Comedy in favour of Menander's New Comedy. Leo Braudy, John Cawelti and Thomas Schatz reduce genre to a magic language that the tribe uses to talk to itself, thanks to the selfless co-operation of the studios. Steve Neale destroys the independence of critical user groups in favour of slavish adherence to practices previously established by producers. In its own way, each of these positions represents genre as a single entity, unified and transparent. This chapter suggests instead that generic practice and terminology are the sites of constant struggle. Instead of conflating the work of producers, exhibitors, viewers and critics, we need to recognize their differing purposes and the resultant differences in generic categories, labels and uses.

A day at Walt Disney World
Spring vacation, 1996. Morning. Along with every other film fan on the planet (or so it seems), we're waiting in line to take the Backstage Studio Tour at Disney

World's Disney-MGM Studios. Snaking our way through endless corridors, we are surrounded by an extraordinary collection of posters for Disney films. With nothing better to do, I decide to see how Disney handles the genre question. To my amazement, I am hard put to locate even the most oblique reference to genres. After nearly an hour of poster ogling, I have had my fill of Disney characters, Disney titles, and the Disney style, but of genre, nary a trace. Perhaps this was the perfect preparation for what followed: a backstage studio tour that miraculously manages to concentrate on films from Disney, the Hollywood studio with the smallest backlot.

Afternoon. I'm excited about finally taking The Great Movie Ride. Unfortunately, about a half-million others seem to have had the idea first. So it's a relief finally to enter a big room where movie trailers help pass the time: Paramount's *Raiders of the Lost Ark*, MGM's *Singin' in the Rain*, Disney's *Fantasia*, Warners' *Footlight Parade* and *Casablanca*. Finally, it's our turn to take the ride. This time my genre desires aren't disappointed. In fact, the entire display is organized by genre: musical, gangster film, Western, sci-fi and action movie. Like the earlier trailers, featured films are borrowed from every major Hollywood studio.

Why the difference? Why should one attraction do everything possible to hide generic connections, and the next one go out of its way to highlight genre? Why is one ride configured as if Walt Disney were the only film-maker in Hollywood, while the next represents the entire Hollywood film-making enterprise? The answer, I suggest, lies in the *discursive* status of all generic claims. Pronounced *by* someone and addressed *to* someone, statements about genre are always informed by the identity of speaker and audience. Hollywood studios are not single entities, speaking a uniform discourse. On the contrary, studios speak with multiple voices. Sometimes we hear the voice of the studio-as-individual-studio (the strategy adopted by the Disney posters and the Backstage Studio Tour); at other times we listen to the studio-as-participant-in-the-Hollywood-system (as we do in The Great Movie Ride). One language is used when studio employees address each other, but we hear something quite different when the studio interpellates potential consumers. Surprisingly, critics and producers employ entirely different terms. Far from misusing generic terminology, these apparent contradictions simply reveal the discursively inflected nature of genre use.

Primarily *referential* in nature, traditional genre study has addressed questions of apparent fact: Which genres existed when? What films does each genre include? Which studios produced which genre films when? How did genres change over time? The basic questions addressed by a *discursive* approach to genre are quite different: Who speaks each generic term? To whom? For what purpose? Why is the same term handled divergently by different users? Why are the same films sometimes described generically and at other times covered by an entirely different terminology? Only by asking questions like these can we hope to discover how (and why) genres are used.

Majors and independents

A glimpse at the *Film Daily Year Book* for 1925 reveals a range of practices that come into clear focus only when we investigate their discursive status. On

WARD LASCELLE
PRODUCTIONS

Now Releasing

TWO SERIES OF SURE FIRE
OUTDOOR AND WESTERN
FEATURES

STARRING   STARRING

LESTER CUNEO   SHORTY HAMILTON

WARD LASCELLE PRODUCTIONS
BEVERLY HILLS   CALIFORNIA

In the twenties, independent producers like Ward Lascelle Productions, reduced to states rights distribution, counted on generic designation to identify their products (Film Daily Year Book, *1925, p. 302*).

one end of the spectrum we find several full-page ads placed by long-forgotten independent producers, each announcing its 1925 roster of generically identified film series. Weiss Brothers' Artclass Pictures Corporation offers 'Eight Five-Reel Rough Riding Romances' and 'Eight Five-Reel Thrillo-Action Features' (p. 297). Gerson Pictures touts 'a series of Romantic Thrill Comedy Dramas' (p. 298). Ward Lascelle Productions features 'TWO SERIES OF SURE FIRE OUTDOOR AND WESTERN FEATURES' (p. 302). Jesse J. Goldburg's Independent Pictures Corporation lists 'Eight BILL CODY Westerns', 'Eight Franklyn Farnum Westerns' and 'Eight Stunt Dramas', to go along with 'Eight Society Dramas' (p. 303). At Sierra Pictures the roster includes 'a series of six 5-reel Western Adventures', 'a series of twenty-six 2-reel Western Thrillers', and 'a series of twelve 2-reel Comedies' (p. 315). Virtually every independent producer clearly conceives, labels and advertises films in generically identified batches.

Whereas the independent ads provide an education in 20s genres, the major studios seem oblivious to generic categories. Paramount's ad, for example, highlights each film's specific selling point rather than its generic affiliation (p. 162). Sometimes a pre-sold title or a famous director is capitalized ('J. M. Barrie's PETER PAN', 'CECIL B. DeMILLE's The Golden Bed'). More often it is the star that is featured ('POLA NEGRI in East of Suez', 'BEBE DANIELS in Miss Bluebeard', 'RICHARD DIX in A Man Must Live'). First National Pictures manages to fill a thirty-two page supplement without once having recourse to generic terminology (pp. 129–60). Similarly, Warner Bros. presents its 1925 lineup without ever admitting that its films have generic connections (p. 172).

Why such a radical difference in studio publicity policy? The answer is easily found within the pages of the *Film Daily Year Book*. Whereas the major studios control their own chain of theatres, 'the first run situation in many of the larger cities is practically blocked out ... to the independent producer' (p. 289). Independent films are reduced to distribution on a 'State Rights' basis through an alternative network of independent exchanges (listed separately on pp. 321–2). Whereas the major feature film producers work hard to differentiate their products from their competitors' offerings, the independents try to fit their products into the ready-made categories applied to the only remaining exhibition slots (for short films, second features or inexpensive productions). Because the independents speak to a different audience from the majors, they use generic terminology in a radically divergent manner. When double features became commonplace in the 30s, the major studios sometimes adopted the independents' generic language when speaking of their 'B' productions, while refusing to apply generic labels to their prestige products.

The logic of generic discourse may interestingly be brought to the fore by comparing the ads of Carl Laemmle's Universal Pictures and William D. Russell's USLA Company. Eschewing generic labels for its most ambitious productions, Universal instead identifies each prestige picture as 'A Universal Jewel' (p. 194). Always near the bottom of the studio heap, however, Universal could not make ends meet on the basis of high-class offerings alone. Next to its Jewels we find a number of films designated as 'A Universal Western' and destined to fill exhibition needs not unlike those met by independent companies. But not all the films we would recognize as Westerns are so identified. Anxious to capitalize on the notoriety of actors under contract to the studio, Universal instead lists *The Hurricane Kid*, *The Saddle Hawk*, *Taming the West* and *Let 'Er Buck* as Universal Gibson Productions, after their leading man, Western favourite Hoot Gibson. Depending on the type of production (and thus implicitly on the potential market), Universal modulates its vocabulary between the fully-fledged generic labelling practised by the independents and the major studios' avoidance of generic terminology.

Just as Carl Laemmle reaches down into the independents' repertory to maintain his position, so William D. Russell takes a page out of major studio practice in order to elevate his status (p. 309). Because his USLA Company specializes in generically identified groupings ('A Series of Six High Class Dramas', 'A Series of 8 Melodramas', 'A Series of 6 High Class Society and Melodramas', 'A Series of 6 Westerns "That Are Different From the Rest"', and 'A Second Series of Westerns That Will Be in a Class By Themselves'), Russell's films were typically reviewed in the restrictive generic context reserved during the 20s for independent offerings and throughout the remainder of Hollywood's classical period for 'B' pictures. *The Valley of Hate* had been typed by *Film Daily* as 'a most excellent picture *of its kind*' (my emphasis). As a manner of lauding *The Courageous Coward*, *Billboard* could find nothing more conclusive than to rate it as 'at least fifty percent better *than the usual features of this class*' (my emphasis). In a similar manner, *Billboard* had highly recommended *His Own Law*, but only for exhibitors 'who can use a cracker-jack little Western'.

Eschewing generic designators, major studios like Paramount preferred self-publicity, including reference to studio stars, properties, and previous successes (Film Daily Year Book, *1925*, p. 162).

104

Carl Laemmle's
The White List

Smoldering Fires — Pauline Frederick, Laura LaPlante, Tully Marshall, Wanda Hawley, Malcom McGregor and Bert Roach. Story by Sada Cowan and Howard Higgin. A Clarence Brown Production. Universal Jewel.

The Hurricane Kid — Starring Hoot Gibson, with Marion Nixon, William Steele, Arthur Mackley, Harry Todd, Fred Humes and Violet LaPlante. Story by Will Lambert. Directed by Edward Sedgwick. A Universal Gibson Production.

Oh Doctor! — Starring Reginald Denny, with Mary Astor, Otis Harlan, Wm. V. Mong, Mike Donlin, Lucille Ward and Tom Ricketts. From the Saturday Evening Post story and novel by Harry Leon Wilson. A Harry Pollard Production. Universal Jewel.

Secrets of the Night — James Kirkwood and Madge Bellamy, with Zasu Pitts, Rosemary Theby, Tom Wilson and Edward Cecil. From the sensational stage success "The Night Cap" by Guy Bolton and Max Marcin. Directed by Herbert Blache. Universal Jewel.

The Mad Whirl — May McAvoy, Jack Mulhall, Barbara Bedford, Myrtle Stedman and George Fawcett. From the story "Here's How" by Richard Washburn Child. Directed by William Seiter. A Universal Jewel.

Ridin' Thunder — Starring Jack Hoxie with Katharine Grant and Francis Ford. Directed by Clifford Smith. A Universal Western.

The Price of Pleasure — Starring Virginia Valli and Norman Kerry, with Louise Fazenda, T. Roy Barnes, George Fawcett, Kate Lester and Ward Crane. Story by Marion Orth and Elizabeth Holding. Directed by Edward Sloman. Universal Jewel.

The Saddle Hawk — Starring Hoot Gibson, with Marion Nixon, G. Raymond Nye, Josie Sedgwick, Charles K. French, Frank Campeau and others. Directed by Edward Sedgwick. A Universal Gibson Production.

House Peters in Raffles The Amateur Cracksman — With Miss DuPont, Walter Long, Hedda Hopper, Winter Hall, Freeman Wood and others. From the novel by E. W. Hornung. A King Baggot Production. Universal Jewel.

The Clash — Alma Rubens and Percy Marmont, with Jean Hersholt, Cesare Gravina, Rose Rosanavo, Zasu Pitts and Ardre DeBeranger. From the story "Miracle" in the Ladies' Home Journal by Clarence Buddington Kelland. Directed by Edward Laemmle. Universal Jewel.

I'll Show You the Town — Starring Reginald Denny. From the novel by Elmer Davis. Directed by Erle Kenton. A Universal Jewel.

Fifth Avenue Models — Starring Mary Philbin and Norman Kerry, with Rosemary Theby, Joseph Swickard, Rose Dione and Jean Hersholt. Based on the novel "The Best in Life" by Muriel Hine. Directed by Svend Gade. A Universal Jewel.

The Meddler — Starring William Desmond, with Dolores Rousay, Jack Daugherty, Claire Anderson, Albert J. Smith, Kate Lester and others. Story by Miles Overholt. Directed by Arthur Rosson. A Universal Western.

Brass Buttons — Herbert Rawlinson and Madge Bellamy, with Cesare Gravina, Martha Mattox, Dorothy Brock, Jackie Morgan, Harry Mann and Nick deRuiz. From the Red Book Magazine story "The Flower of Napoli" by Gerald Beaumont. Directed by Edward Laemmle. A Universal Jewel.

Taming the West — Starring Hoot Gibson. Story by B. M. Bowers. Directed by Arthur Rosson. A Universal Gibson Production.

HOUSE PETERS in OVERBOARD! — With a brilliant supporting cast including: Patsy Ruth Miller, Arthur Hoyt, William Austin, Lydia Yeamans Titus, George Kuwa, Togo Yamamato. From the novel, "Head Winds," by A. M. Sinclair Wilt. Directed by Herbert Blache. A Universal Jewel.

Don Dare-Devil — Starring Jack Hoxie, with Cathleen Calhoun, William Steele, Cesare Gravina and Duke Lee. Story by William Gittens. Directed by Clifford Smith. A Universal Western.

Let 'er Buck — Starring Hoot Gibson, with Marion Nixon, Josie Sedgwick and G. Raymond Nye. With exclusive action scenes of the thrilling 1924 "Pendleton Round-up." Directed by Edward Sedgwick. A Universal Gibson Production.

Dangerous Innocence — Laura LaPlante and Eugene O'Brien. Based on the novel "Ann's an Idiot" by Pamela Wynne. Directed by William Seiter. Universal Jewel.

Red Clay — Starring William Desmond, with Marcelaine Day, Billy Sullivan, Lola Todd and Albert J. Smith. Story by Sarah Saddoris. Directed by Ernst Laemmle. A Universal Western.

Up the Ladder — Starring Virginia Valli, with Forrest Stanley, Holmes Herbert, Margaret Livingston, George Fawcett and Priscilla Moran. Owen Davis' Big Broadway Stage Hit. Directed by Edward Sloman. Universal Jewel.

Universal has the Pictures

Never quite a full-fledged major, but never reduced to the status of independent either, Universal split its terminology between studio-centered and generic vocabulary (Film Daily Year Book, 1925, p. 194).

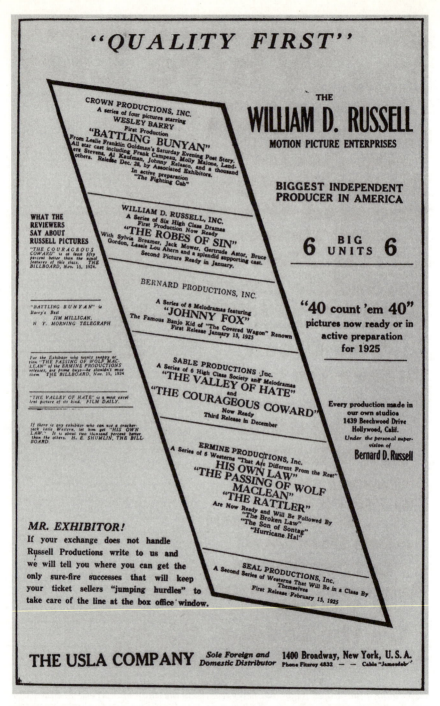

"QUALITY FIRST"

THE
WILLIAM D. RUSSELL
MOTION PICTURE ENTERPRISES

CROWN PRODUCTIONS, INC.
A series of four pictures starring
WESLEY BARRY
First Production
"BATTLING BUNYAN"
From Leslie Franklin Goldman's Saturday Evening Post Story.
All star cast including Frank Campeau, Molly Malone, Land-
ers Stevens, Al Kaufman, Johnny Relasco, and a thousand
others. Release Dec. 28, by Associated Exhibitors.
In active preparation
"The Fighting Cub"

WILLIAM D. RUSSELL, INC.
A Series of Six High Class Dramas
First Production Now Ready
"THE ROBES OF SIN"
With Sylvia Breamer, Jack Mower, Gertrude Astor, Bruce
Gordon, Lassie Lou Ahern and a splendid supporting cast.
Second Picture Ready in January.

BERNARD PRODUCTIONS, INC.
A Series of 8 Melodramas featuring
"JOHNNY FOX"
The Famous Banjo Kid of "The Covered Wagon" Renown
First Release January 15, 1925

SABLE PRODUCTIONS Inc.
A Series of 6 High Class Society and Melodramas
"THE VALLEY OF HATE"
and
"THE COURAGEOUS COWARD"
Now Ready
Third Release in December

ERMINE PRODUCTIONS, Inc.
A Series of 6 Westerns "That Are Different From the Rest"
"HIS OWN LAW"
"THE PASSING OF WOLF
MACLEAN"
"THE RATTLER"
Are Now Ready and Will Be Followed By
"The Broken Law"
"The Son of Sontag"
"Hurricane Hal"

SEAL PRODUCTIONS, Inc.
A Second Series of Westerns That Will Be in a Class By
Themselves
First Release February 15, 1925

BIGGEST INDEPENDENT
PRODUCER IN AMERICA

6 BIG 6
UNITS

"40 count 'em 40"
pictures now ready or in
active preparation
for 1925

Every production made in
our own studios
1439 Beechwood Drive
Hollywood, Calif.
Under the personal super-
vision of
Bernard D. Russell

WHAT THE
REVIEWERS
SAY ABOUT
RUSSELL PICTURES
"THE COURAGEOUS
COWARD" is at least fifty
percent better than the usual
features of this class. THE
BILLBOARD, Nov. 15, 1924.

"BATTLING BUNYAN" is
Barry's Best
JIM MILLIGAN,
N. Y. MORNING TELEGRAPH

For the Exhibitor who wants snappy action "THE PASSING OF WOLF MAC-
LEAN" of the ERMINE PRODUCTIONS
releases, are prime buys—he shouldn't miss
them. THE BILLBOARD, Nov. 15, 1924

"THE VALLEY OF HATE" is a most excellent picture of its kind. FILM DAILY.

If there is any exhibitor who can use a cracker-
jack little Western, let him get "HIS OWN
LAW." It is about two thousand percent better
than the others. H. E. SHUMLIN, THE BILL-
BOARD

MR. EXHIBITOR!
If your exchange does not handle
Russell Productions write to us and
we will tell you where you can get the
only sure-fire successes that will keep
your ticket sellers "jumping hurdles" to
take care of the line at the box office window.

THE USLA COMPANY Sole Foreign and 1400 Broadway, New York, U.S.A.
Domestic Distributor Phone Fitzroy 4832 — — Cable "Jamesdab"

*Working hard to rise above independent status, William D. Russell Motion Picture Enterprises
divided its advertising space between a genreless special production (Battling Bunyan, released
by Associated Exhibitors) and several generically identified series (Film Daily Year Book, 1925,
p. 309).*

Attempting to break out of this generic corset, Russell's headliner for 1925 is announced as

A series of four pictures starring
WESLEY BARRY
First Production
'BATTLING BUNYAN'
From Leslie Franklin Goldman's Saturday Evening Post Story
All star cast including Frank Campeau, Molly Malone ...

This time Russell uses the language of proprietary characters, contract players, pre-sold stories and recognizable personnel regularly practised by the major studios. Why should he change his language for just this small portion of his ad? And why should a handful of other independents, like Bud Barsky (p. 308), systematically advertise their actors and directors rather than the genre of their stories? Again, the answer may be found in discursive considerations. Who is it that Russell and Barsky are addressing? To be sure, they are speaking directly to their potential clients, the state rights distributors and independent exhibitors who frequent the independent exchanges.

At the same time, though, they are obliquely addressing another audience, with quite different standards and tastes. In the mid-20s, films made by the most successful independents were regularly released through major studios. While increasing sales to the independent market might appear the ultimate goal for the independent producer, in fact the true objective for ambitious independents was to free themselves from the state rights market altogether by gaining access to the theatre chain of a major studio. In 1925 alone, for example, First National Pictures released films made by Alfred E. Green Productions, Edwin Carewe Productions, Inspiration Pictures, John Francis Dillon Productions, M. C. Levee Productions, Rockett Productions, Sam E. Rork, Inc., and United Studios. Why not Bud Barsky or William D. Russell in 1926? In fact, a close look at the fine print reveals that Russell's *Battling Bunyan* was indeed distributed by Associated Exhibitors – not exactly a major studio, but nevertheless a conduit to the Pathé circuit and exchange.

Differences in exhibition circumstances lead studios to advertise in radically different ways, according to differential classification needs. Those with easy access to exhibition venues seek to individualize their products, thus distinguishing them clearly from those shown next door. But those who have no exhibition guarantees need to communicate the nature of their product as clearly as possible. In the former case, genre can actually impede success; in the latter, genre is a practical necessity. Yet, as the William D. Russell case demonstrates, the same ad may actually address multiple audiences simultaneously, through diverse terms and with disparate goals.

Hollywood and Washington

Turning to the 1943 version of the same *Film Daily Year Book*, we find that even more diverse deployment of generic terminology may sometimes serve studio interests. Reporting on its production efforts during the first year of the war, 20th

Century-Fox categorizes its films in a manner that diverges significantly from pre-war practice:

> A breakdown of the bigger pictures shows that the themes of eight were directly concerned with the glorification of the U.S. Armed Forces, seven had themes or locales of the United Nations Allies, two were set in Axis countries, three interpreted life on the home front, five were the biggest song and dance musicals ever produced by Twentieth Century-Fox in any year and six were escapist dramas of universal theme.
>
> (*Film Daily Year Book*, 1943, p. 226)

Replacing traditional genres with a generic vocabulary clearly geared to wartime conditions, the studio nevertheless manages to evoke familiar generic contexts. For example, among films classified under the rubric 'U.S. ARMED FORCES' *Ten Gentlemen from West Point* is identified as a 'dramatic story', *United We Stand* is described as a 'documentary feature', *Iceland* is a 'musical comedy', *Manila Calling* a 'melodrama', and so forth. We see here at work the genre-creation process described earlier. Films already associated with entirely different genres – and thus perceived as belonging to mutually exclusive categories – are brought together by virtue of a new identification with some common feature, in this case the presence of the US armed forces. Thus the Sonja Henie vehicle *Iceland*, for example, is torn from its obvious classification as a musical and reconfigured as a 'U.S. ARMED FORCES' film.

In dealing with this revised generic vocabulary, traditional genre study would call for careful description of the textual characteristics justifying such revisionism. Semantic/syntactic analysis might be in order, revealing the importance of semantic wartime settings and themes, along with the near total absence of syntactic consistency. Following this type of analysis, it would appear obvious why this new generic categorization failed to outlive the war: genres based on semantics alone lack the coherence necessary for longevity. Though such an analysis might be quite useful in configuring the text, it would fail to recognize the discursive dimension underlying that textual configuration. Instead of concentrating on the question 'how are texts organized?' we do well to remember that textual organization is controlled by discursive goals. In short, we need always to ask 'who speaks this generic vocabulary? to whom? and for what purpose?' This is true not only when genre terms are used in an anomalous fashion, but especially when they are used in what seems an appropriate, accurate and transparent manner.

To whom might 20th Century-Fox be speaking this revisionist typology? A first indication comes from the same studio's four-page ad (pp. 235–8), in which films are identified neither by traditional genres nor by wartime genres, but instead by author ('John Steinbeck's *THE MOON IS DOWN*'), director ('Ernst Lubitsch's *HEAVEN CAN WAIT*'), or stars ('Orson Welles [and] Joan Fontaine in *JANE EYRE*'). The audience for this ad does not appear to be the same as for the studio's yearly report. A second indication comes from the reports submitted by other studios. Warner Bros, for example, divides its films into categories almost identical to those used by 20th Century-Fox:

1. The Enemy.
2. Our Allies.

3. The Armed Forces.
4. The Production Front.
5. The Home Front.
6. The Issues.

(pp. 233–4)

Surprisingly, the exact same terms are again used by Universal, and in the same order (pp. 232–3). Even an amateur sleuth easily recognizes in such a high level of apparent coincidence the influence of an outside agency.

Once again, we need look no farther than the pages of *The Film Daily Year Book* to discover that agency: the West Coast bureau of the Office of War Information Motion Picture, established in June 1942.

> Better to serve the industry, a Hollywood office was opened under Nelson Poynter, former Scripps-Howard publisher and more recently with the Coordinator of Information. Perhaps the most important function of the Hollywood office is the furnishing of research data to producers, on request. OWI studies on such matters as manpower, salvage, taxation, transportation and various other wartime problems have proved invaluable to producers and writers on many occasions.
>
> Research furnished Hollywood by the OWI has been classified by Poynter under the following six headings. The Issues – why we fight – the peace; The Enemy – his nature; United Nations and United Peoples – our brothers-in-arms; Work and production; The Home Front – sacrifice; and The Fighting Forces – the job of the fighting man at the front.

(Older, 1943, p. 185)

One can legitimately doubt whether the OWI's office was opened 'better to serve the industry'. On the contrary, it is well known that Hollywood production was severely restricted by the OWI. In fact, Hollywood's biggest problem during the war was the difficulty of obtaining materials for and government approval of its production plans. Whether Poynter's six headings were provided 'on request' is not known, but the 1943 *Film Daily Year Book* certainly confirms the studios' slavish adherence to the new genre vocabulary provided by the OWI. As now becomes obvious, the *Film Daily Year Book* statements made by 20th Century-Fox, Warner Bros. and Universal all indirectly address the US government.

Whereas textual analysis suggests that wartime generic revisionism failed because of its lack of syntactic substance, discursive analysis of the same phenomena reveals that the new genres were from the beginning mandated by the government itself, and disappeared as soon as the government no longer had any reason to 'encourage' their use, or rather as soon as the film industry no longer feared for its life and thus necessarily made Washington an audience of choice. In fact, government-mandated wartime genres disappeared even before the end of the war, whenever the industry was addressing another interlocutor. For example, in the twenty-second annual report of the Motion Picture Producers and Distributors Association, a 1944 internal document titled the *Motion Picture Industry in Wartime America 1943–1944*, Will Hays provides an entirely different categorization of 1943 production from the *Film Daily Year Book* review aimed at the government. Here we find that the major 'types and kinds of feature-length films' are once again the familiar melodrama, Western, drama, crime, comedy, musical comedy, horror, documentary, fantasy and travelogue. The only remaining sign of government intervention lies in the enormous number of sixty-three social problem dramas for 1943, which together with eighteen social problem melodramas and five social problem crime films makes the social problem genre the most popular genre of the year (pp. 36–7). Here we have, reconfigured, films that in another document, with another audience, had previously been labelled 'The Production Front', 'The Home Front' and 'The Issues'. To simplify, we may say that new wartime genres corresponded to a new audience for studio discourse: the US government. Once Hollywood went back to its more traditional audience – distributors, exhibitors and paying spectators – genre vocabulary also returned to pre-war norms.

Genres as good *and* bad objects

Treating genres as fixed categories, traditional accounts configure genres as a shorthand assuring rapid and accurate communication between producers and

Ratings as genre

Originally created to forestall threatened government intervention into the film industry following a series of public scandals, the Production Code promulgated by the Motion Picture Producers and Distributors Association turned every Hollywood film into an implicit act of discourse obliquely addressed to the government. Until a ratings system was established in 1968 by the Motion Picture Association of America (MPAA), however, this nod towards Washington had little direct effect on generic concerns.

As practised for the past thirty years, the ratings system has affixed to every film, film trailer and film poster a letter designating the film's appropriate audience, as determined by the MPAA's Classification and Rating Administration (CARA). Like government-imposed wartime categories, this rating serves an important generic purpose. Just as the material circumstances of wartime life heighten interest in such common denominators as presence of the US armed forces, so, it is assumed, the process of parenting attracts potential viewers to such concerns as the presence (or lack) of strong language, nudity and violence.

Yet ratings categories are neither sought, displayed nor used similarly by all film-makers or at all points in history. Originally, ratings were addressed primarily to theatre owners and parents. 'G' (for 'General audiences') meant that it was all right for parents to bring their children, whereas 'PG' invited 'Parental Guidance'. A rating of 'R' 'Restricted' the film to viewers seventeen and over unless accompanied by an adult, thus calling for yet another level of parental decision-making. The dreaded 'X' rating informed theatres that children under seventeen must be eXcluded. As the system has evolved, however (with an added PG-13 category and replacement of the 'X' designation by NC-17), producers have increasingly enlisted the ratings as a weapon in their appeal to youth audiences.

For some years now, studios have gone out of their way to avoid the very technicians, studios and audiences, critics and readers. Certainly, such communication does at times exist. There is sufficient cultural agreement on the existence and nature of certain genres to subtend clear understanding – especially in the case of genres combining easily recognizable semantic features with a consistent syntax (for example, the Western and the musical). Unfortunately, genre theories have all too often been based almost exclusively on such special cases. Ironically, a more satisfactory understanding of genre may be built around generic miscommunication, for it is precisely in the apparent contradictions between differing genre practices that genre's discursive investment becomes apparent. As a demonstration of that claim, the remainder of this chapter will confront an important disparity and the widespread discursive practices that it elucidates. Chapter 8 will examine yet another contradiction.

Is genre a good object or a bad object? Read virtually any academic treatise on genre and you will come away with the conviction that, at least for producers, genres are very good things indeed. According to Richard Maltby, 'the advantages to

ratings (G, PG and PG-13) that apparently open film viewing to a wider range of spectators, because they have learnt that the most sought-after demographic group (viewers between 15 and 25) avoid films that are so rated. Recognizing the usefulness of addressing the youth audience rather than their parents, producers have routinely added to films just enough violence, nudity or strong language to ensure an R rating. (One wonders how long it will take for the US television ratings system to be similarly subverted.) Neither content nor structure alone can make sense of this case, because both depend directly on changes in the discursive situation and the identity of the audience addressed through studio manipulation of ratings.

Ratings usually constitute only a small part of overall studio discourse. The average film poster thus displays the rating in very small type in a lower corner; only X-rated films regularly diverge from this general practice. In fact, whereas major studios downplay ratings and other generic attributions, adult film producers have almost always flaunted their genre. By magnifying the rating indication (in some cases, the X is as large as the whole poster), or by multiplying it (in the familiar triple XXX designation), makers of adult films firmly identify the genre with the rating itself. They have been aided in reaching their target audience by a little known fact about MPAA ratings: though the ratings are registered with the United States Patent and Trademark Offices, and thus may not be used without CARA agreement, the X rating alone could be self-applied (while it existed). Linda Williams may be right in principle when she says that 'those in power construct the definition of pornography through their power to censor it' (1989, p. 12), yet once X-rated films became a marketable commodity, their producers discovered how easy it was to turn that very censorship into profits. Operating in a market dependent on clear generic designation, like independents during the 20s, adult film-makers thus take advantage of the most convenient available vocabulary in order to label their wares.

producers of the principle of classifying movies by type are clear. Firstly, they offer a financial guarantee: generic movies are in a sense always pre-sold to their audiences because viewers possess an image and an experience of the genre before they actually engage any particular instance of it' (1995, p. 112). Repeatedly, critics return to this concept of genre 'as a pre-sold property' (Wyatt, 1994, p. 55). As Bruce A. Austin points out, 'Research has consistently demonstrated that people cite a film's plot or story and its genre as both their most important reason for moviegoing in general and as their reason for attending a specific film' (1989, p. 74). Indeed, there exists an extensive library of literature on this topic (summarized by Austin and Gordon, 1987).

Unfortunately, studies claiming the importance of genre as a positive influence on film-goer decisions typically hide half the story. As we have seen in comparing the publicity of major studios and independents during the 20s, the importance of genre in industrial discourse depends heavily on the targeted type of exhibition. Whereas movie-goer decisions based primarily on genre are sufficient to sustain independent film-makers, generic appeal never suffices for major studio feature films. This difference is further complicated by significant changes in financing and publicity occasioned by the demise of Hollywood's vertically integrated production-distribution-exhibition arrangement.

Throughout Hollywood's golden years, films were made relatively inexpensively and returned a fairly small but dependable profit. Operating like other manufacturers, even the largest studios avoided risk, seeking instead a guaranteed, if limited, return on their investment. In that climate, where movie-going was frequent and alternative entertainment relatively rare, generic identification might indeed serve to preclude a loss on any given film. Today, the situation is markedly different. Hollywood's books are now balanced not by making a small profit on almost every film, but by making a large profit on one film out of ten. For recent films the publicity budget alone often surpasses the entire budget of a production made in the 50s. The relative importance of simple genre identification has thus diminished significantly, because genre alone can never guarantee success. In both periods, generic affiliation may help a film to achieve an average or slightly better than average income – but the median classical Hollywood film always made a small profit, while today's median film actually loses money.

In spite of substantial research apparently demonstrating the marketing usefulness of genre recognition, genre is not treated by viewers as the uniformly good object that critics tout. Part of this confusion derives from the type of questions typically asked by pollsters. From the beginning, movie-goers have consistently been asked either 'What kind of moving pictures do you like best?' (Foster, p. 27, on Portland in 1914; Short, *passim*, on Iowa City in 1916; Hepner, p. 896, on an unidentified city in 1928, quoted in Koszarski, 1990, pp. 30–1), or 'On what basis did you choose this particular film (or theatre)?' (for example, several mid-20s surveys quoted in Koszarski, 1990, pp. 28–31). Multiple-choice questions of this type cannot help but provide apparent evidence of genre's positive influence on movie-going decisions.

But suppose a survey were to be conducted in a more open-ended manner, asking such questions as 'What effect does genre have on your choice of movies?' Would such a study produce different results? To my knowledge, the only existing survey of this type was conducted by Susan Kim in Iowa City during summer 1997. One hundred movie-goers waiting in line for a film or filing out of a screening were asked to fill out a survey including open-ended questions designed to elicit responses regarding genre knowledge, genre preference and the role of genres in movie choice. While a number of respondents allowed as to how genre is 'helpful in picking out a movie that correlates with my mood', an equal number of respondents voiced negative – and even more vociferous – comments about genre. One movie-goer said that 'genre is important only when it's some sappy Hollywood "boy-meets-girl" kind of movie – then I know to avoid it like the plague'. Another respondent said that genres served her not so much to help decide what to see, but to classify 'don't sees' – which for her included horror, Second World War, sword and sorcery and romance films. It would appear that genre's capacity for positive identification is matched by a tendency to view certain genres, and thus genre production in general, as bad objects.

Given the amount of verbiage that has been dedicated to explaining the usefulness of genre terms as studio shorthand, such critical treatment of genre may seem surprising. Yet even a cursory look at any collection of studio memos must reinforce a vision of genre as bad object. When Robert Lord reported to Warners studio chief Hal Wallis in October 1939 on a proposed production, he employed straightforward generic terminology: 'in the past, the Lubitsch type of sophisticated light comedy has almost always failed to impress mass audiences' (Behlmer, 1985, p. 117). Fulfilling a similar function with regard to a property titled 'Everybody Comes to Rick's', Robert Buckner reported to Wallis his doubts about the future *Casablanca* in a generic manner. The play's big moment, he maintained, is 'sheer hokum melodrama' (*ibid.*, p. 198). Remembering that the creation of film genres has often been triggered by negative publicity (the Western as silliness appropriate only for children or foreigners, the musical as the type of film that everyone was tired of), it should hardly surprise us that studio executives too would see generic identification as a synonym of out-of-date, oversimplified and ossified production. Indeed, certain genre labels have in our society systematically become pejorative terms. In some circles, to qualify a film as 'melodramatic' is to make a deprecatory comment. Labelling a comedy 'slapstick' no longer primarily constitutes a generic designation, for all too many genres eventually lose the specificity of their reference in favour of a 'generic' negativity.

Name-brand marketing strategies

Recent marketing uses of the term 'generic' may help us to understand how genre can at one and the same time be perceived both as a good and as a bad object, and why film industries have deployed genre in such an uneven and apparently idiosyncratic manner. Look around a supermarket today and you will notice two countervailing tendencies in product packaging and labelling. On one extreme are the so-called 'name brands', the more expensive products with an enormous national media advertising budget. The names of these products are trademarked; they are presented in containers displaying distinctive printing and copyrighted designs; the small print extols the number of patents pending or held by the manufacturers.

At the opposite extreme are a group of simple plain-wrapped packages containing products termed *generic*. Contrary to the name-brand products (but like store brands and other inexpensive items), generic products are so simply labelled that there is often no design at all – just an identifying name and a list of contents. In fact, the list of contents almost always constitutes the most salient aspect of generic packaging; generic products pay little attention to colour, shape and texture, instead straightforwardly stressing the nutritional contents of each item. One other difference between name-brand and generic products stands out. Every word on a generic package is properly spelt, while name-brands consistently feature labels that are purposely misspelt.

So common is the process of deforming the English language in order to create a recognizable brand name that it would be possible to construct a veritable typology of name-brand origins. Perhaps the most common source of brand-name products and services is simple misspelling, as in Cheez Whiz, Diet Rite Cola, Heet, Kix, Kleenex, L'eggs, Oven Krisp, Pak Mail, Rice Krispies, Scotchbrite, Stanley Steemer, Trix, U-Haul and Velveeta. Indeed, certain words are invariably misspelt in brand names, including cheese (cheez), clean (kleen), guard (gard), you (u) and the trio of bright, light and right (brite, lite and rite). A second category of brand names is derived by the extension of existing descriptive terms (often accompanied by misspelling or deformation): Baggies, Donettes, Clearasil, Clorox, Grrravy, Jell-O, Müeslix, Steamatic, Tampax, Wheaties. A third group of labels derives from a process of combination (sometimes in conjunction with a misspelling): Butterball, Kit Kat, Krusteaz, Manwich, Pennzoil, Rice-a-roni, Rubbermaid, Skintastic, Sunkist. A final category results from contraction (with or without the apostrophe): Amoco, Beggin' Strips, Charmin, Cracklin' Oat Bran, Esso, Kibbles 'n Bits Bac'n Cheez, La'James, Land O Lakes, O-Cel-O.

Once the brand name has been established, it can easily be extended to dynastic proportions. At first there was only one type of Cheerios; now we have Apple Cinnamon Cheerios, Honey Nut Cheerios and Multigrain Cheerios. Once the innovative spelling 'Chex' gained recognition, it could be used for every grain available: corn, rice, wheat and even multi-bran. Fritos spawned both Doritos and Tostitos. The Fruit Newton family began with no more than a fig, but it now includes apple, cranberry, raspberry and strawberry.

A fascinating pattern arises from the aisles of the local supermarket. First of all, 'generics' share a number of characteristics:

a. generic products provide only basic nourishment or services;
b. their labels describe the contents directly and accurately;
c. the labels display what we might describe as the zero level of creativity;
d. the labels respect English grammar and orthography.

Brand-name products likewise share a number of characteristics, diametrically opposed to those of the generic products:

a. along with basic nourishment, brand-name products purport to provide an unspecified supplement of care, charm, design, quality, or other benefit;
b. while they usually reveal some information regarding the product's basic contents, labels labour to produce positive consumer attitudes towards supplementary benefits;

c. labels are virtually always sufficiently distinctive to merit trademark registration;

d. they achieve this distinctiveness either by simulating family names or through deformation of the language.

Comparing the two lists, we readily recognize the extent to which genres, in a brand-name culture, fail to offer all the desired qualities. Though generics use correct English, offer truth in advertising, meet basic human needs and guarantee consumers against starvation, brand-name products promise something more fascinating: fantasy, quality, style and individuality.

The key to brand-name success lies ironically in an ability to make fun of generic products and to take liberties with the proper English associated with generics. For in order to devise a registerable brand name, it is precisely necessary to do violence to standardized language. It is through this deformation of language and other related differences (brand-name 'stylish' design as compared to generic blandness) that brand-name products distance themselves from the generic. And indeed that is quite specifically their goal. In order to have something special to sell, something justifying a higher price, brand-name manufacturers must actively differentiate their wares. Whereas anyone can produce generic products, only brand-name owners can take advantage of the brand name and its faithful clientele. In the consumer world, nothing is less desirable than generic products. The American supermarket is clearly far removed from the Hollywood world described by critics, where genres are reputed to provide a helpful shorthand.

Brand-name movies

A careful look at studio terminology confirms that supermarket treatment of generic products much more nearly approximates Hollywood practice than the familiar critical saw about generic shorthand. Far from making and advertising genre films, major studios systematically avoid associating their films with any single genre. Like generic supermarket products, genre films can be made and distributed by any producer. When one genre film has been exploited, the producer is faced once again with the necessity to create an audience based solely on audience fidelity to a particular genre. If the exhibition situation highlights genre, then this may be an acceptable strategy, but even then the producer must compete on equal grounds with all other producers of genre films. How much more rewarding is a strategy of avoiding generic identification, instead stressing the particular plus that the studio brings to the genre.

By definition, genres can never be fully controlled by a single studio, whereas individual studios have exclusive access to contract actors, house directors, proprietary characters and patented processes. By stressing these restricted qualities in the publicity for each film, a studio automatically develops a pre-sold audience for the next film featuring the same in-house star, character or look. Instead of starting over again, publicity for the next film need only point to its continuity with the previous film in order to assure a strong audience. Following this logic, Hollywood regularly eschews genre logic for production and publicity decisions, in favour of series, cycles, remakes and sequels.

From the beginning, film-makers have understood the value of film cycles. In the early days, however, there was no question of basing studio specificity on stars or directors. Instead, the film industry tore a page out of the daily paper and adopted the method regularly used to particularize comic strips: idiosyncratic and easily identifiable characters (sometimes actually borrowed from the comic strips) were created so that each individual film could contribute to marketing the next. In the United States, the process virtually inaugurates commercial cinema. Before the turn of the century, Edison had created characters called simply 'The Tramp' and 'Jones', while American Mutoscope and Biograph had inaugurated their 'Burglar Bill' and 'Little Willie' series. In rapid succession, Edison introduced a progression of comic characters: 'Uncle Josh' (1900), 'The Old Maid' (1901) and 'Uncle Reuben' (1901). The new century was also a period of intense cinematic adoption of characters born in the newspaper, including 'Happy Hooligan' (Edison, 1900), 'Foxy Grandpa' (Biograph, 1902), 'Buster Brown' (Edison, 1903) and 'Weary Willie' (Edison, 1904). This strategy, designed both to simplify production and to enhance distribution, unfortunately had its limitations in an America unclear about the copyright status of popular entertainment. Again and again, one studio would simply steal another's character. After borrowing both 'The Tramp' and 'Happy Hooligan' from Edison, Biograph found its own 'Burglar Bill' holding forth in a Vitagraph film.

Another cycle-creation strategy involved the use of formulaic titles starting with the same word. Biograph's 'How' series began in 1898 with *How the Athletic Lover Outwitted the Old Man*, *How the Ballet Girl Was Smuggled into Camp* and *How Bridget Served the Salad Undressed*. Starting in 1900, Edison's rival 'Why' series included *Why Mrs. Jones Got a Divorce*, *Why Mr. Nation Wants a Divorce* and *Why Bridget Stopped Drinking*. From 1902 on, Biograph capitalized on two related series, promising 'Love in' a hammock, the cornfield, the dark, and the suburbs, or hijinks 'In a' manicure parlour, massage parlour, boarding school gym, German bath, or the Raines Law Hotel. Lacking legal protection, however, these cycles proved no more successful than recognizable characters at guaranteeing the benefits of proprietary creations. Almost immediately, Edison copied Biograph's 'How' titles, and since in those days turnabout was still considered fair play, Biograph simply borrowed Edison's 'Why' strategy.

As this limited example demonstrates, the value of a series-oriented production and marketing strategy depends on the legal situation. Without clear-cut copyright and trademark protection, generic labels were almost as productive as more individualized identifiers. During this early period, the same catalogue would regularly offer both a semi-proprietary series title, and an entirely sharable genre designation. A number of historical developments would rapidly change this practice, however. The creation of the star system, followed rapidly by star treatment of directors, had the effect of weakening the importance of genre for publicity purposes (and thus for production as well). With better legal protection, a mature Hollywood found it both possible and lucrative to design and protect proprietary characters. Early examples include Fox's Charlie Chan (1929), MGM's Tarzan (1932) and The Thin Man (1934) and Warners' Perry Mason (1934). In the late 30s, nearly every studio joined the band wagon. Again adopting comic strip characters, but this time also borrowing from radio and popular fiction as well, Columbia had The Lone Wolf (1935) and Blondie (1938), Warners featured Torchy Blane (1936) and the Bowery Boys/Dead End Kids (1937), MGM had Dr. Kildare (1937) and Andy Hardy (1937), Fox boasted Mr. Moto (1937) and Michael Shayne

Indiana Jones—the new hero from the creators of JAWS and STAR WARS.

Shunting generic references to shadowy adventure graphics, the text for this Raiders of the Lost Ark *(1981) poster concentrates instead on the George Lucas/Steven Spielberg collaboration.*

(1940), RKO offered The Saint (1938) and Paramount had Henry Aldrich (1939). While many of these series were eventually demoted to 'B' picture status, they all succeeded in serving the studios' major goal: to assure a continuous influx of profits without offering any assistance to competitors.

In more recent years, proprietary characters named James Bond, Rambo, Indiana Jones, Conan, Batman or Superman, along with such repeatable titles as *Godfather, Grease, Jaws, Halloween, Star Trek, Lethal Weapon, Predator, Robocop* and *Die Hard* have helped Hollywood to reap record profits, thanks to the legal protection that the system now offers. Though it has been generally assumed that Hollywood makes and publicizes genre films, careful inspection of advertising campaigns reveals that generic claims have never constituted a substantial portion of feature film publicity strategy, except when capitalizing on some other studio's success. Although even the most rudimentary posters and the shortest trailers provide *some* information about a film's generic connections, even if only through clothing and setting (Western togs and a horse versus a sword and sandals or formal attire and a dance band), poster texts and trailer voice-overs systematically stress *proprietary* characteristics (star, director and related successful films by the same studio) over *sharable* determinants like genre. *Dr. Ehrlich's Magic Bullet* was not billed by Warner Bros. as a biopic – even though by 1940 the genre was generally recognized – but as a fitting heir to previous Warners films about Pasteur and Zola. Paramount doesn't call *Raiders of the Lost Ark* an adventure film; instead it touts 'Indiana Jones – the new hero from the creators of *JAWS* and *STAR WARS*'. The function of publicity is as much to advertise a film's makers as the film itself.

Advertising campaigns for the highly successful 60s James Bond films and their imitators provide an illuminating example. United Artists' *Dr. No* is not identified by genre, but as 'THE FIRST JAMES BOND FILM'. The poster for *From Russia With Love* adds the star to the mix; on the upper right corner those who don't recognize the title of Ian Fleming's novel are told that 'JAMES BOND IS BACK', while on the lower left corner we are reminded that the film stars 'SEAN CONNERY as JAMES BOND'. Within a few months, other studios anxious to cash in on Bond's success go out of their way to characterize their films in relation to Bond. The poster for *The Ipcress File* quotes both a comparison to the Bond series ('"A THINKING MAN'S *GOLDFINGER*, FUNNIER BY FAR THAN ANY OF THE BOND FILMS AND MORE REWARDING, TOO!" – *Newsweek*') and the resultant generic designation ('"AN ADMIRABLE THRILLER IN EVERY RESPECT!" – *The New Yorker*'). As this example demonstrates, genre affiliation is not some-

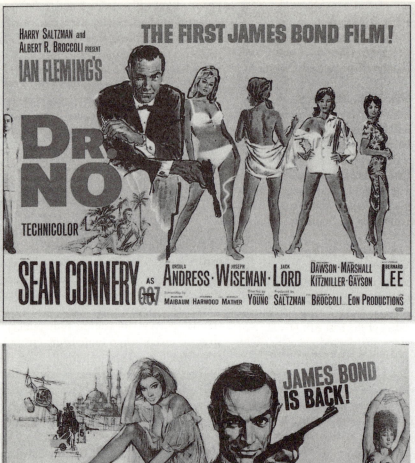

Rather than admit to any connection with an existing genre, posters for James Bond films (Dr. No, 1962; From Russia with Love, 1963) worked hard to concentrate attention instead on proprietary features, including James Bond, Ian Fleming, and Sean Connery.

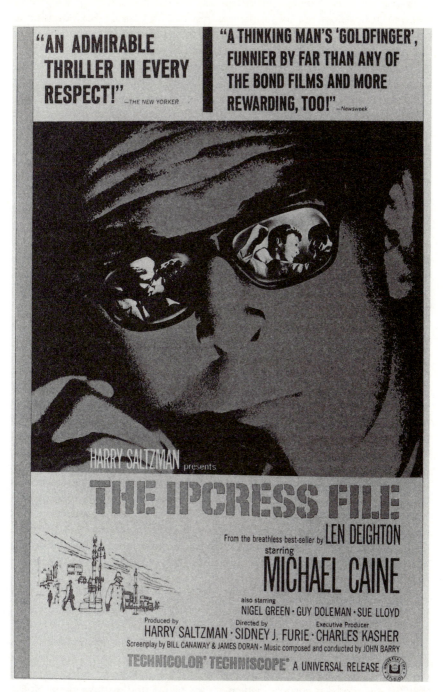

Enjoying none of the James Bond series' proprietary features, Universal's Ipcress File *(1965) had to depend on generic identification and comparison to the rival Bond films.*

thing that all films enjoy as a birthright but is a discursive strategy for gaining access to competitors' pre-sold audiences. Just as 20th Century-Fox's decision to advertise *The Story of Alexander Graham Bell* by recalling the success of Warners' *The Story of Louis Pasteur* and *The Life of Emile Zola* tended to solidify the status of the biopic, so Universal's reference to a competitor's films reinforces the identity of both studios' films as thrillers.

Examples such as these suggest that we consider genre not as a quality of texts, but as a by-product of discursive activity. Studio A produces a successful cycle of films, advertising them as a proprietary cycle based on character, plot and star; anxious to benefit from that success, studio B produces similar films and advertises them by reference to studio A's hits. The term for studio A's cycle was limited and proprietary (James Bond films, for example), so it cannot be applied to the films of studios A and B taken together. Some sort of generic term must be supplied to cover the group of films as a whole. Working retrospectively, and serving their own needs for stable, far-reaching and powerful terms, critics are quick to adopt and solidify this generic terminology, applying it indiscriminately to both studios' films. Looking back even farther, and having their own needs, film scholars have often failed to distinguish that critical use from the initial studio's scrupulous avoidance of generic terminology. It is all too easy to forget that most genre labels began life attached to a limited cycle.

Convinced that Hollywood has always produced and publicized genre films, many scholars have exhibited surprise on hearing these claims. Yet the process described here is entirely predictable, as long as one understands the logic involved. Most people image a Hollywood studio as operating like a factory: from a set of standardized molds the studio produces recognizably similar films, labels them according to their similarity and sells them under that label as long as a market subsists. Such an understanding is fundamentally misleading, for it assumes that studios create one type of product only: films. In fact, studios strive to create at least one other type of product.

Besides films as such, studios also create labels, characters, plots, theme songs, techniques, processes and devices that may in the long run have greater value than the films in which they were first deployed. The most important of these proprietary creations is undoubtedly the studio name itself. Every production thus targets two interdependent but quite separate goals: not only to make money from this particular picture, but also to guarantee a future income by identifying this film's success with a proprietary feature (title, character, star) that can be reused to pre-sell the next.

This process may be understood by reference to methods of creation and exchange of property under capitalism. The traditional understanding of Hollywood production recognizes only two sources of wealth: manufacture and sale. The studio makes the film and sells it to distributors and/or spectators. This approach treats film studios like artisans, charging only an hourly fee dependent on skill level, plus materials. Reasonably accurate for Hollywood independents in the 20s, this model is entirely inadequate for major studios throughout Hollywood's history, because capitalism involves something more (or less?) than an equal exchange of labour for money.

In order to understand the name-brand strategy of most film producers, it is necessary to recognize two additional sources of wealth: invention and theft. While inventions of many sorts bring income to Hollywood studios, by far the most important are trademarks that the studio has created *ex nihilo* and invested with its own content. While some of these proprietary labels last for decades, most last only for a short time, but during that time may have great financial value. Some – like Kodak and Esso, Mickey Mouse and the MGM logo – have stood the test of time, but Postum and Shirley Temple failed to survive the war, and the 'Die Hard' title may not continue into the next century.

Note that the value that is being referred to here is *not* the value of material products, but the value of the term itself. It is safe to guess that the trademark Jell-O would cost more to purchase than all the packages of Jell-O on super-market shelves. Similarly, it would probably cost less to buy the contract of every Dallas Cowboys player than to acquire the team name. In the late 80s, producer Joel Silver might have preferred to sell Silver Pictures rather than give up the rights to the 'Lethal Weapon' title and his contracts with actors Mel Gibson and Danny Glover – except for the fact that through the success of the *Lethal Weapon*, *Die Hard* and *Predator* films, the Silver Pictures label itself had become a surefire box-office attraction. Though they offer no material sustenance, brand names are the quintessential form of modern property. For almost a century, Hollywood studios and producers have used every primary product – every film – to create an even more lucrative secondary product: a brand-name-like feature that can be inserted into subsequent films, thus guaranteeing audience fidelity and continued income.

If Hollywood studios usually work hard to produce films with a 'signature', i.e., films that will produce not only income but also a supplementary saleable commodity which can in turn be sold, there are nevertheless times when it is more lucrative simply to steal a property already developed by another studio. This is what happens when Universal compares *The Ipcress File* to United Artists' James Bond films and reduces the entire resultant group of films to the more general category of 'thriller'. Perhaps theft is too strong a word here; perhaps the proper term is instead 'squatting'. If they are careful, squatters can make a good living in Hollywood, just as they have long done in the super-market by imitating the names, products and packaging of name brands, thus capitalizing on their success. Indeed, the term 'capitalize' says it all: whereas cycles create capital through invention, generic terminology serves to redefine proprietary characteristics in sharable terms, thus forcing the sharing of capital.

Generic discursivity

Though all too rapid, this look at genre use suggests a number of important con-clusions.

1. Genres must be understood discursively, i.e., as language that not only pur-ports to describe a particular phenomenon, but that is also addressed by one party to another, usually for a specific, identifiable purpose.
2. What we usually think of as single entities (the studio, the spectator) actually comprise multiple discursive sites.

3. Variations in generic affiliation, evaluation and terminology usually derive from differences in discursive situation.
4. Genres in general, as well as generically affiliated films, are sometimes treated as good objects, sometimes as bad objects; this difference may be attributed to differences in genre users and their goals in using genre norms or terminology.
5. The tendency of some genre users to avoid generic terminology (especially major studios speaking on their own behalf), whereas others regularly identify films by genre (studios speaking on behalf of the industry as a whole, Hollywood studios abroad, independent studios, producers of short films or critics), may be explained by the economic dimension of their discursive situation (and particularly by reference to trademark and copyright protection).
6. Genres are often created or reinforced as by-products of industrial imitation. Seeking to equate their films with the brand names they imitate, clone producers typically employ generic terms reducing both originals and clones to the same common denominator.
7. Generic terminology is often disseminated by critical acceptance of the broader, non-proprietary terms chosen by clone producers.

While they capture the question of generic use from a production-oriented point of view, these seven conclusions hardly touch the manner in which genres are used by other groups, including critics and spectators. The following two chapters will offer an opportunity to expand this limited view of genre use.

8
Why are genres sometimes mixed?

> Suppose for a moment that it were impossible not to mix genres. What if there were, } lodged within the heart of the law itself, a law of impurity or a principle of contami- } nation?
>
> Jacques Derrida, 'The Law of Genre' (1980, p. 57)

In the history of criticism, genre mixing is primarily associated with European romanticism. Conceived as a critique of neoclassical generic purity, romantic genre mixing served as the foundation of a new aesthetic inspired in part by medieval mixed genres. As a model for the study of film genre, the historical opposition of neoclassical pure genres to romantic mixed genres is not without its problems, however. Justifying an explanation of genre mixing that stresses historical contingency, the classical/romantic opposition makes it all too easy to conclude that genre mixing results from no more than the stylistic preferences of a particular period, studio or director. Thus one regularly reads that classical Hollywood was a period of distinctly generic production, while recent American cinema has either avoided genres or recombined them willy-nilly (for example, see Schiff, 1994, p. xiv, ff). Some Hollywood directors, it is said, have a predilection for pure genres (Ford, Hawks, Hitchcock, Lubitsch, Minnelli, Sirk), while others excel at mixing genres (DeMille, Renoir, Welles). While these comments are neither uninteresting nor entirely lacking in accuracy (though the former claim will be subjected to intense scrutiny and significant revision later in this chapter), they often miss the point because they start from an assumption that generic mixing is only a historical question.

Before it reaches the level of history, this chapter will reveal, genre mixing is first a discursive problem. That is, our notion that genres are more or less mixed in the films of any given period or director derives heavily from the way in which those films have been described, categorised and labelled. The descriptions, categories and labels in question of course appear in texts that have their own audience and purpose. Only by attending to this discursive orientation can we understand what is at stake in identifying films as examples either of pure genre or of genre mixing. In other words, we will do well to consider the mixing of generic terminology prior to inspection of specific genre mixing instances.

Critical investments

How do we learn about genre? How is it that we come to know a long list of genre terms, that we have a more or less clear sense of what each genre involves, and that we can easily classify many films into generic categories? Most people undoubtedly assume that what we might call 'generic competence' derives from film watching, but our experience in other domains belies such an assumption. Certainly, playing sports teaches us something about them, but the language we use to describe sport is informed by sportswriting and sportscasting. Listen to fans talk about their favourite sport and you will recognize the language of sports announcers and their journalistic colleagues. Ask people about marriage or life styles and the answers will reflect the opinions of newspaper agony aunts and daytime TV talk shows. War is experienced and explained primarily through the media that bring war into our homes, but war is not alone in being mediated: everything from politics to commercial products are increasingly described according to categories and terminology provided by the mediators who deliver them to us. Cinema is no exception. Our terms and our concepts derive not so much from cinema itself, but from those who represent cinema to us.

Just who are the people and the institutions that teach us how to talk about cinema? Primary sources would certainly include the studio-financed, studio-configured statements that no movie-goer can avoid, including newspaper ads, marquee posters and trailers for coming attractions. During Hollywood's heyday, this list would need significant expansion, for the copious pressbooks distributed by the studios offered not only posters and pictures, but also ghost-written copy for newspaper articles and radio programmes, carefully selected photos and graphics and blueprints for promotions and contests. As we have seen, however, these sources rarely offer much training in the meaning and use of genre vocabulary. Instead, they stress attributes particular to the producing studio, including previous film titles, studio stylistic traits, and the names of stars, directors and characters, set in a crown of superlatives ('first', 'best', 'most').

Our primary knowledge of genres comes instead from our culture's commitment to comment on and conserve cinema. Whereas studio discourse has only short-term memory and is always primarily forward-looking, criticism and categorization are typically turned towards the past. Studios may mention a recently successful film, but in the production world films quickly become dated; very few of yesterday's films are worth remembering until tomorrow. Critics, by contrast, often take it on themselves to locate a film in a more extended past. Genre terms concretize and concentrate this commentary. For library reference purposes, genre terms offer a useful form of categorization, permitting simpler and more efficient configuration and consultation of our long-term cinema memory. For this reason, any understanding of genre terminology must begin with the critics and compilers who constitute our major source of genre terms.

What are the requirements of critical discourse and how do they inform our understanding of genre? In his book, *Immediate Seating*, Bruce A. Austin offers an insight into the generic logic of critics. He begins the section on 'Story and Type' by pointing out that 'Research has consistently demonstrated that people cite a film's plot or story and its genre as both their most important reason for moviegoing in general and as their reason for attending a specific film' (1989, p. 74). But, as Austin proceeds to argue, people don't always define a genre in the same way, nor do they classify individual films consistently. Austin concludes that 'When attempting to measure genre preferences, it is necessary to sort the genres into meaningful, mutually exclusive, and exhaustive categories' (*ibid.*, p. 75). Although Austin approaches genre with assumptions and goals specific to social science, his desire to treat generic concerns with clarity and consistency is shared throughout the world of film criticism and categorization.

At its most extreme, the need for 'meaningful, mutually exclusive, and exhaustive' genres is clearly expressed in every film list that ever included information about genre. Many schools, libraries and archives use a computerized spreadsheet to keep track of their film and video collection. Because spreadsheets make it easy to retrieve information about the collection based on any type of data that has been entered, one of the spreadsheet's fields is typically devoted to genre. As long as a single individual makes all the genre entries, this procedure works fairly well, but as soon as multiple users start entering genre information, the system goes awry. What happens when one person labels all action/adventure films with the term *adventure*, while another employs *action* as well? What if someone restricts the *gangster* genre to the 30s, using *film noir*, *action* or *thriller* after that, while another applies the *gangster* label to films throughout the history of cinema? One person may carefully distinguish between *melodrama* and *women's film*, whereas another may never use the *women's film* designation, regularly referring instead to *weepies*. The only way out of this quandary is to establish, as Austin suggests, a standard list of genre terms. Thus the keepers of most spreadsheets ultimately decide to restrict the choice of genre field terms, forcing users to choose from a relatively short list of labels shared by all.

For example, the World Wide Web site called 'The Genres List', when maintained by Lars Joergen Aas, provided a restrictive menu of only fourteen 'main' genres, followed by a longer list of genre keywords to be used in further detailing an individual film's generic identity. Coupled with the suggestion that participants should 'try to use genres already used', rather than 'make up new genres like "Cop" when there is already a genre called "Police" ', these consensual terms were necessary for The Genres List to provide 'easier searching in the movie database' – a goal achieved only when all users employ the same labels for the same phenomena. Scholars who treat genres as transhistoric categories might well retort that a short list of genres is built into the human race, that Aas was simply providing orthographic consistency to an even more deeply ingrained homogeneity. But what of the fact that the short list of primary genre terms governing The Genres List includes neither melodrama, romance nor the gangster film? Demoted to secondary status, these familiar terms were lost in the longer listing of no less than 235 genre keywords, ranging from 'adult-humor' to 'zombie'.

Imposing a rather idiosyncratic consistency rather than deriving it from human nature, The Genres List adopts a strategy shared by many similar compilations. Repertories such as Wes Gehring's *Handbook of American Film Genres* or Daniel Lopez's *Films by Genre: 775 Categories, Styles, Trends and Movements Defined, with a Filmography for Each*, reveal a similar pair of compulsions: to use a sufficient number of categories to assure that every film will be covered, while limiting labels to the smallest number possible. For the sake of clarity and simplicity, each film is routinely classified under a single rubric. Books like these, along with the genre lists sometimes found at the end of film textbooks, typically use every possible device to justify identifying each film with a single genre (a pitfall happily avoided by the Library of Congress's *Moving Image Genre-Form Guide*, compiled by Brian Taves, Judi Hoffman and Karen Lund). Mixed genre films are usually classified according to a 'dominant' genre; films labelled differently in different periods are identified with only a single genre; films whose original genre label is no longer used are uncomplicatedly assimilated to another genre not yet invented when the film was produced. Unlike film studios, which sell films and thus stress their own individuality rather than genre affiliation, the authors of these compilations (and *a fortiori* the presses that sell them to libraries around the world) sell books and 'knowledge', products admirably served by clear generic attribution.

Most film reviews follow a similar generic labelling tradition, though perhaps for different reasons. A typical film review calls on readers' genre knowledge to position an as yet unseen film, and the films are labelled with the name of a single well-known genre, as can be seen in these examples from Richard T. Jameson's *They Went Thataway: Redefining Film Genres: A National Society of Film Critics Video Guide* (my italics):

> It's been many a moon since Hollywood has produced a *comedy* as black as *The War of the Roses*. (David Ansen, p. 102)

> In one of those odd ironies of film distribution, just as peace was breaking out across half the globe in the fall of 1989, a number of impressive *war movies* were released: Kenneth Branagh's post-Falklands reinterpretation of *Henry V*; Edward Zwick's *Glory*, an account of a black regiment's service in the Civil War; and Oliver Stone's *Born on the Fourth of July*. (Morris Dickstein, p. 272)

> *Roxanne* is one of the most beautiful, elating *romantic comedies* ever made in this country. (Peter Rainer, p. 116)

> Everything that's good and bad about *Backdraft*, the *action picture* about fire fighters, is there to see in the picture's opening sequence. (Julie Salomon, p. 216)

> There's scarcely a genre more sleazy than that of the *women's prison picture*, which today is made mainly in the Philippines and which features women degrading women in the context of sex-and-violence fantasies for the delectation of male audiences. Consequently, *Caged Heat* is especially gratifying. (Kevin Thomas, p. 283)

> This wincingly funny, pertinent, and heart-breaking *road movie* [*Thelma and Louise*] means to get under your skin, and it does. (Peter Travers, p. 297)

> Not just another Walter Hill action movie, *Trespass* is a post-Rodney King *action movie*. (Armond White, p. 221)

> *Dances with Wolves* has the same appeal as most classic *Westerns*, even the same sort of flaws. (Michael Wilmington, p. 74)

Typically, these genre attributions are located at the beginning of a review, often in the opening sentence. As such, they easily overwhelm details or demurrers provided in the rest of the review. However openly a reviewer might gesture in the direction of other genres, the initial generic attribution tends to subordinate all else to a single genre identity.

Why should commentators share the categorizing zeal of encyclopedists? Why should critics so regularly treat genres as watertight, unproblematic categories? And in particular, why should reviewers, whose most obvious task is to particularize each film, rush to identify films with stable, monolithic and non-particularizing generic categories? Though it may at first appear as nothing more than a curiosity, I believe that this 'reviewer's paradox' holds an important key to the understanding of genre. In the past, genre theorists regularly assumed that genre labelling was initially imposed by a film's producing studio. To the contrary, as we have noted, studios generally avoid identifying a film with a single unadulterated generic label. Only when a film is subjected to critical reception is its generic potential concretized and stabilized by reviewers. In short, critics and not studios lie at the origin of most generic language.

Unlike studios, critics have nothing obvious to sell. While they may provide a certain amount of information for people who have not yet seen the film, reviewers would lie low indeed on the cinema totem pole if all they had to offer were priority of viewing. In fact, the first regular film reviewers offered just that and thus found themselves at the bottom of the heap, lumped together anonymously in trade journals like *The Film Index* and *The Moving Picture World*. Not until *The Dramatic Mirror* began to publish more complex reviews would an individual reviewer gain a specific identity (as 'The Spectator') and finally a by-line (as Frank E. Woods). How did Woods emerge from anonymity, and how do today's critics achieve recognition? Woods had a product to sell beyond priority of viewing (an advantage that disappears as soon as the reader has viewed the film). On the one hand he elevated the status of his object of study by regularly linking cinema to the other arts; on the other hand he individualized his own writing by describing cinema techniques in a distinctive manner. In this way, he helped the critical profession to join directors and actors in a massive individuation movement beginning around 1910.

Today's critics follow directly in Woods' footsteps. On the one hand, they go out of their way to establish the value of their medium. On the other hand, they try to create their own 'brand-name' style. While critics have used a number of strategies to raise the status of cinema, such as the art film and auteurist approaches of the 50s and 60s, the most durable ploy has been to attach cinema to the narrative and mythical roots implied by generic identification. Generic attribution raises the stakes of reviewing, connecting cinema to well-established, deeply rooted categories. Not by chance have so many reviewers written strong general pieces designed in part to enhance the reputation of a particular genre: André Bazin on the Western, Arlene Croce on the musical, Molly Haskell on the women's film, Pauline Kael on epic films, Andrew Sarris on screwball comedy, Richard Schickel on animation, Paul Schrader on film noir, David Thomson on the gangster film, Parker Tyler on underground film, Robert Warshow on the Western and the gangster film and Robin Wood on the horror film. The critical enterprise is immeasurably boosted by strong genres and clear generic affiliation. By and large, the same critics who bring us genre are the source of our tendency to identify each film with a single dominant genre. After all, how can the critical purpose of genres be served if they cannot be directly connected to specific films?

Studio strategies

It must be remembered, however, that Hollywood studios are far from sharing the discursive position of critics. Whereas critics have a vested interest in strong genres and single genre affiliation, studios have markedly different investments. If critics are like political analysts, dependent on their ability to differentiate among candidates and their platforms, studios are like candidates for political office, above all concerned to avoid alienating any particular group of voters. Whereas political analysts are paid to call a spade a spade, candidates go out of their way to defer the naming act that might cause controversy and thus a loss of votes. This is precisely the attitude that governs studio approaches to genre. Since naming a genre is tantamount to taking a political stand, and always risks alienating potential spectators who systematically avoid that genre, Hollywood studios prefer instead to imply generic affiliation rather than actually to name any specific genre (excepting films specifically designed to take advantage of a 'hot' genre). The goal is of course to attract those who recognize and appreciate the signs of a particular genre, while avoiding repulsion of those who dislike the genre.

In Chapter 4 I explored Hollywood's classical era tendency to imply the simultaneous presence of enough different genres to assure a film's appeal to the three recognized audience sectors: male viewers, female spectators and the *tertium quid* audience with interests lying outside of traditional male and female domains. During Hollywood's golden years, studio publicity campaigns would thus implicitly choose from something like the following menu:

Male genres (choose at least one):
    Action adventure
    Gangster film
    War film
    Western
Female genres (choose at least one):
    Drama
    Musical
    Romantic comedy
    Weepie
Tertium quid (choose at least one):
    Fantasy
    Historical/costume
    Slapstick comedy
    Travel adventure

Although never to my knowledge codified by studio publicity heads, this amalgamation system operated for multiple decades, until the 60s and new methods of measuring and conceiving audience demographics. The old approach recognized only two variables, age and sex: either you were a sexually defined adult (and either male or female) or not (and thus part of the *tertium quid*, which was sometimes broken down into children and older audiences). The more recent approach recognizes far more variables (not just age and sex, but also race, ethnicity, class, education, preferred activities, geographical location and income level), and breaks those categories down into much smaller portions (for example, the old system had only three basic age groups – child, adult and older audience – but the new system recognizes as many as eight different age ranges). Though the detailed information provided by the new system makes it possible for producers to target their audiences more accurately, the splitting of the audience into multiple small sectors also induces publicity departments to imply the presence of an even broader selection of genres or sub-genres.

The desire to aim publicity at a wide range of narrowly defined audiences in turn puts pressure on producers to conceive films as a mix of as many genres as called for by targeted audiences. Though critics have consistently claimed that generic templates undergird Hollywood's profit-assuring, assembly-line production practices, careful inspection suggests that Hollywood prefers romantic genre-mixing to the classical ideal of genre purity. Deliciously captured in Robert Altman's version of Michael Tolkin's screenplay *The Player*, Hollywood's basic script development practice involves (a) attempts to combine the commercial qualities of previously successful films, and (b) the consequent practice not only of mixing genres but of thinking about films in terms of the multiplicity of genres whose dedicated audiences they can attract. The first script pitched to

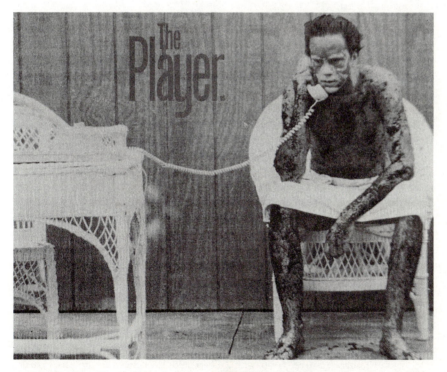

As portrayed by Tim Robbins in Robert Altman's The Player *(1992), today's producers spend all their time listening to writers trying to identify their scripts with as many genres as possible.*

producer Griffin Mill (Tim Robbins) in the opening scene of *The Player* is described as '*Out of Africa* meets *Pretty Woman*' (Tolkin, 1995, p. 16), Hollywood code for that perfect film capable of reaching every possible spectator by virtue of its ability to combine opposites: Africa and L.A., romantic drama based on a real autobiography and formulaic fantasy based on the world's oldest daydream, a seasoned actress with real talent and a newly discovered pretty face, intellectual quality and popular appeal. The next pitch takes us to new heights – or depths. 'So it's kind of a psychic political thriller comedy with a heart,' says Mill, translating

The genre-mixing game

Perhaps a simple game will explain the ease with which Hollywood mixes genres. Imagine a new parlour entertainment in which each player draws the name of a genre, then adds to a cumulative film synopsis a sentence true to the genre label drawn. Here's how such a game might develop.

Player 1 (draws historical costume drama)
   The film opens on Gilbert and Jacqueline in period dress exiting a sumptuous mansion in New Orleans' garden district.
Player 2 (draws war film)
   Dissolve to Civil War battle sequence as Gilbert explains in voice-over how he came by his fortune.
Player 3 (draws drama)
   'Now,' he says, 'my partner is out to get me; he thinks I cheated him out of half the booty.'
Player 4 (draws film noir)
   Cut to rundown part of city where detective Beaugars and his sultry secretary are solicited to find Gilbert and the hollow statue in which he hides his cash.
Player 5 (draws Western)
   Intercut chase, starting on the pier in St Louis, with Beaugars on horseback chasing the stagecoach in which Gilbert and Jacqueline are discussing their plans.
Player 6 (draws weepie)
   The dialogue reveals that Gilbert and Jacqueline are on their way to buy her illegitimate but much loved daughter Cosette out of San Francisco prostitution.
Player 7 (draws slapstick comedy)
   When the stage stops to change horses, an eastern dude (played by Leslie Nielsen) provides a comic interlude.
Player 8 (draws musical)
   Song: 'The Code of the West', sung to the dude first by the stage drivers, then by the innkeepers, and finally by Gilbert and Jacqueline, who do a trick-shot two-step in Buffalo Bill and Annie Oakley costumes.
Player 9 (draws travel adventure)
   Episodic sequence showing the stagecoach crossing the plains, the mountains, the desert and, finally, a high-angle long shot of San Francisco and the ocean beyond.
Player 10 (draws romantic comedy)
   Before Beaugars can catch up with Gilbert and Jacqueline, he protects Cosette from her abusive pimp, catches her eye, catches her in his arms, and catches her drift as she points to her hope chest; they embrace as Gilbert and Jacqueline

the screenwriter's every word into his own generic jargon. 'With a heart,' affirms the writer. 'Not unlike *Ghost* meets *The Manchurian Candidate*' (*ibid.*, p. 18). The wildly successful 'comedy-romance-thriller' *Ghost* (Wyatt, 1994, p. 106) is now to be mated to a 'tingling political paranoia thriller' (Maltin, 1997, p. 833) in order to assure yet greater returns. In spite of the film's multi-layered irony, we quickly understand this piling up of genres as the stock-in-trade of today's producer.

In this day and age it is a compliment for a film with the already composite title of *Kiss and Kill* to be called 'a film noir thriller, a love story, a psychological drama,

deposit the hollow statue in the hope chest, to a reprise of 'The Code of the West'.

As this tongue-in-cheek example suggests, genres are easily mixed because

a. popular notions of genre are heavily invested in one or two characteristic and easily identifiable elements, thus permitting genre cueing with minimal material;

b. a film needn't obey a genre's logic throughout in order to be identified with that genre;

c. because they depend on diverse elements (plot material, themes, images, style, tone, etc.), different genres may be combined with only minimal interference;

d. certain scenes or motifs (for example, the love-conquers-all final clinch), being common to multiple genres (the Western, the musical, the weepie, the romantic comedy, etc.), are capable of reinforcing audience perception of several different genres.

MGM's 1954 *western/musical/romance* Seven Brides for Seven Brothers *looks for all the world as if it were generated by Hollywood producers playing the genre-mixing game.*

a whodunit, and even a bit of a Western' – so much so that this litany of genre labels made its way into the films's newspaper ads, in spite of the pervasive publicity tendency to downplay specific generic terms in favour of provocative images or suggestive language. Whether in the 30s or the 90s, popular film producers have always understood the value of merging the qualities of multiple successful films. As Mae West would have said, in this case too much of a good thing isn't nearly enough.

What is it about genres that makes them so easy to mix? Many category types simply don't mix at all, because they are designed to be mutually exclusive in nature. Though genres are often compared to species, it is simply not possible to mate fruit flies with timber rattlesnakes as Hollywood regularly combines genres. Other category types, based like shot scales on a single spectrum of possibilities, may induce hesitation between two categories (is this a medium shot or a close-up?), but not the kind of indiscriminate category mixing practised by Hollywood. Still other category types, such as nationality, are so dependent on history that they may give rise to such anomalies as dual citizenship or statelessness, but nobody is free to mix nationalities in the way Hollywood mixes genres.

As category types go, genres lack the mutual exclusivity of genus and species, the linear configuration of shot scales, and the firmly drawn and defended borders of nations and nationalities. On the contrary, each genre was not only confected out of found materials, which may be introduced into any film at virtually any time (in conjunction with any other genre), but in the popular mind genres are so tightly identified with certain readily recognizable semantic traits that they may easily be represented by no more than a suggestive element here or there. The history of Hollywood genre evolution might easily have followed the model of neoclassical genre specificity and separation; instead, Hollywood has throughout its history developed techniques that make genre mixing not only easy, but virtually obligatory.

Hollywood cocktail

Since Hollywood began to apply the television industry's careful audience research methods to its own products, its publicity has increasingly targeted specific audience sectors. But this is a question of more than just promotional strategy. When mass advertising first appeared with mid-nineteenth-century increases in newspaper circulation, publicity simply announced the availability and described the qualities of a product designed to fulfil a particular consumer need. Current practice assigns a far more active role to publicity. Once a successful advertising angle has been discovered, that information is fed back into the system in order to increase marketability, i.e., to generate products that are more easily and successfully advertised. Once keyed to primary consumer needs, products are now designed to match purchasing habits, as discovered and defined by publicity and audience research departments. When cinema was born, products determined publicity strategy; a century later, publicity determines product design.

This is of course a well-known pattern. Less recognized is the important role played by genre in this process. One reason for our limited insight into recent

TOM CRUISE When he pours, he reigns.

Cocktail

No matter how the film was described to potential spectators, Tom Cruise proved the strongest appeal of Touchstone Pictures' Cocktail (1988).

Hollywood practices is studio secrecy regarding marketing strategies and the documents that reveal them. My ability to study these matters was facilitated by the generosity of my colleague Dell Edwards, who shared with me a series of particularly revealing audience research documents prepared by Joseph Farrell and The National Research Group for Walt Disney Productions. Analysing audience surveys, television commercials, a theatrical trailer and the general advertising strategy for the Touchstone Pictures Tom Cruise vehicle *Cocktail* (1988), these studies reveal with uncommon clarity the generic orientation of Hollywood's current approach to marketing.

Seeking to determine 'the strength of moviegoer interest in seeing *Cocktail* ... and the type of moviegoer most interested' (Farrell, 1988a, p. 1), the 'Advertising Strategy' report maps out a clear battle plan: instead of testing the film as made, the researchers reconceptualized the film, turning it into four separate but concurrent films, each featuring a distinctive plot corresponding to a recognizable genre.

> Four alternative concept descriptions were presented to moviegoers with each concept description representing a potentially different advertising strategy approach. The four alternative concept approaches referred to in this report are as follows:
>   '*Tom Cruise/Romantic Drama*'
>   '*Saturday Night Fever*'
>   '*Success Is Not Enough*'
>   '*Like Brothers*'
> In the '*Tom Cruise/Romantic Drama*' version, emphasis is placed on the romantic aspect of the story, with love lost and regained. The '*Saturday Night Fever*' concept focuses on the young man's desire to make it in the big city and how his definition of success is changed by his experiences. In the '*Success Is Not Enough*' version, the conflict between love and financial success is highlighted. The '*Like Brothers*' version focuses on the relationship between the young man and his mentor, the older bartender.
>   (Farrell, 1988a, p. 1)

The subjects of this survey never saw any portion of the film itself. While there were separate tests conducted of the film, the trailer and several TV spots, the overall advertising strategy was based instead on The National Research Group's critical analysis of the film (probably suggested by Walt Disney Productions, but available documents do not permit me to confirm this supposition).

The report's first take on the film ('Tom Cruise/Romantic Drama') specifically identifies its generic orientation. The second, invoking the then recent John Travolta success, points to the *Bildungsroman*/Horatio Alger tradition underlying

The National Research Group, Inc.
March 21, 1988
Page 13   0310R

-- Total positive interest, while similar based
   on all four concepts, is highest in response
   to the "Success Is Not Enough" concept at an
   above average level.

	Title/Stars Int. %	Norms %	"Romantic Drama" %	"Sat. Night Fever" %	"Success Is Not Enough" %	"Like Brothers" %	NRG Norms %
Definite	22	20	29	29	30	31	25
Probable	38	35	30	33	36	32	35
Total Positive	60	55	59	62	66	63	60

-- Younger females express the highest interest
   in the movie based on all four concept
   descriptions, at similar and exceptionally
   strong levels. Older males express the lowest
   interest at well below average for all four
   concepts.

-- The "Success Is Not Enough" concept generates
   strong younger female interest, who express an
   outstanding 53% "definite" interest, but below
   average "definite" interest among all other
   sex/age groups. The next most interest is
   expressed by younger males and younger females
   but mostly just "probable" interest.

-- The "Like Brothers" description generates
   strong younger female interest (49%) and the
   highest level of "definite" interest among
   younger males at an above average 34% level,
   and the interest based on this concept clearly
   skews to younger moviegoers. The "definite"
   interest is slightly below average among older
   females (22%).

-- The "Saturday Night Fever" description is
   again quite effective among younger females
   (46%) and averagely effective among older
   females. It is not effective among males.

-- The "Tom Cruise/Romantic Drama" concept is
   very effective among younger females (51%) and
   not particularly effective among the other
   sex/age groups except that younger males are
   about averagely interested.

This page from pre-release audience research for Cocktail *features the four generic concepts used to describe the film to prospective viewers.*

Saturday Night Fever's plot. The 'Success Is Not Enough' label evokes a 50s melodrama, and the description confirms that connection. The final concept ('Like Brothers') refers to one of the late 80s genres: the buddy film.

How is it possible to represent the same film as four different stories deriving from four different genres? Several different devices are used to assure the multivalency not only of *Cocktail* but of Hollywood films in general. First, the film offers *excess material*, more than is necessary to any given reading. The research report summarizes the romantic drama concept in the following manner:

134

Cocktail, starring Tom Cruise, is a new romantic drama. Cruise plays a young bartender. ... But Cruise finds the party life leaves him empty. Wintering as a bartender at a fancy Jamaican resort, he falls in love with a pretty young woman who is a struggling New York artist – not the rich woman he always thought he should marry, but this is true love. But when she sees Cruise date a rich woman, she does not know it is to win a meaningless bet with his bartender friend. Heartbroken, she flies back to New York without seeing him again. Back in the city that spring, Cruise finds her, but she turns him away, saying he loves money more than her. He persists, and follows her to her parents' house where he discovers she is from a very wealthy family. Her father offers Cruise money to leave his daughter alone. He turns it down flat, determined to prove his love is sincere. As the movie builds to its emotionally-charged climax, Cruise's life is turned upside-down before he and his true love are re-united for good.

(Farrell, 1988a, p. 9)

Were *Cocktail* restricted to this narrowly focused narrative, it might be hard to see it through more than one generic lens, but the film is more multi-layered than this.

It begins with a sequence detailing Cruise's attempts to get first a job and then an education. Off and on throughout the film, Cruise spends time with an avaricious bartender uncle in his native Queens. In Manhattan he receives high concept bartender training from a flamboyant bartender, played by Bryan Brown, a man with his own personal style, his own glossary of sayings and rules, his own romance and marriage, and his own money problems, eventually leading to an attention-grabbing suicide. In addition to his true love, Cruise dallies with several bar-goers and carries on an extended affair with an attractive businesswoman; not only is his first conquest seduced by Brown, but Brown's wife will later come on to Cruise. From the standpoint of the romantic drama concept, most of this material is excessive; as such it tends to destabilize the romantic drama reading, offering other interpretive configurations and generic associations. David Bordwell has called Hollywood cinema 'an excessively obvious cinema' (Bordwell *et al.*, 1985, p. 3); in fact, it is precisely because Hollywood cinema provides excess material that it must instead be termed *a deceptively obvious cinema.*

A second device favouring filmic multivalency is what we might call *multiple framing.* By virtue of the context in which it is presented, any given event appears to be 'framed' by more than one narrative series, as if a single object were repeatedly photographed, but always against a different background, thus calling into question the sameness of the object across multiple photographs. *Cocktail*'s early bartending sequences, for example, easily fit into all of the film's generic concepts:

– The glitz and hollowness of the bar scene offer an example of what the romantic Tom Cruise will not settle for.

– Brown's experience serves as both a model and a caution for the young and naïve Cruise, reinforcing the stereotypes of the film's '*Saturday Night Fever*' initiatory narrative.

– Contrasted to the uncle's rundown Queens bar, the yuppie Manhattan bar effectively represents the 'success' part of the 'Success Is Not Enough' concept.

– The 'Like Brothers' relationship between the two bartenders invokes the buddy film genre, including clichéd sibling rivalry over the same girl.

Not only the events, but the characters and dialogue are susceptible to the logic of multiple framing, both in terms of textual strategies and in terms of spectator processing.

One of the textual strategies facilitating multiple framing deserves to be recognized as a third device favouring filmic multivalency. We might call this tactic *fertile juxtaposition*. Traditional accounts of classical narrative (whether literary or filmic) invariably describe narrative events in terms of linear metaphors, like that of the narrative 'chain'. Often associated with structuralist narratology (Barthes, Todorov and Prince), this Aristotelian conception of narrative has long held a stranglehold on narrative theorizing. By stripping texts down to a single narrative framework, this approach treats each link in relation only to immediately preceding and following links. But suppose the text were, like *Cocktail*, full of extra material? Instead of a chain, we would have something more like a puzzle, where each piece is valorized not by a single cause and a single effect, but by several surrounding pieces. Typically treated according to a temporal (and linear) model, Hollywood narrative gains from being seen instead through the more complex and more open spatial model of juxtaposition. More akin to multiple-plot medieval Grail romances and nineteenth-century serial novels than to the linear psychological novels on which most narrative theory has been based, Hollywood films gain much of their power from a careful interlacing of multiple characters, plots and themes.

Instead of defining each event in terms of a preceding cause and a succeeding event, juxtaposition offers the permanent possibility of multiple interactions. Every screen moment is caught up in a multidimensional loom, in which several elements – foreground and background, shot scale and lighting, *mise en scène* and editing, dialogue and music – are woven together into a multidimensionally reversible fabric. With each new juxtaposition new connections are made, and concepts are reinforced or relegated to storage, potentially leading to that magic moment of conceptual reframing when the spectator-weaver presses on the pedal, raising some threads while lowering others and thus initiating a new series of juxtapositions and reframings. Only when understood as interlaced narratives characterized by multiple intersections and juxtapositions can Hollywood films fully reveal their polygeneric strategies.

A final device facilitating filmic multivalency involves *multifocalization*, or the multiplication of points of view and identification possibilities. Hollywood cinema is characterized by a fundamental alternation between shots of events or objects (including people conceived as objects) and faces, with their characteristic features of eyes and a mouth pointing to mental activity that seems in some way to surround, to capture, to engulf the object or event represented in the previous shot. Widely recognized as an important aspect of Hollywood style, this rhythm rarely concentrates on a single character; on the contrary, Hollywood films systematically feature facial close-ups of multiple characters. In literature, a clear distinction must be made between inside views of characters (providing privileged access to their thoughts or feelings) and more distant treatment limited to description of external features. In Hollywood films, however, no such distinction holds; similar images must serve both purposes. There is no automatic method of deciding – as there is in most novels – whether the face we see is simply an object of someone else's gaze, speech, or thought, or whether it is the locus of a thought process that perceives, processes and thus swallows up the other characters in the film. On the contrary, the lack of a clear difference between internal and external views means that the same footage is easily constructed in more than one way. To any given character, spectators typically apply both approaches, producing a reversible narrative (a is part of b's story, but b is also part of a's story) and thus potentially quite different stories. This means that a single event will often be turned by Hollywood into a *Rashomon* affair, implicitly experienced by several characters and thus requiring integration into each one of their stories (and thus potentially into different genres as well).

The Jamaican outdoor bar scene halfway through *Cocktail* offers a good example of this process. Anxious to realize his fantasy of opening a bar called 'Cocktails and Dreams', Tom Cruise has left New York for the Caribbean where, it is alleged, a flashy bartender can earn up to four hundred dollars a day. There he has met his true love. One day at the bar, Bryan Brown appears and crows about his own successful love match with a beautiful, rich wife. He tells Cruise that he will never know such good fortune because he is not a 'finisher'. Taking the dare, Cruise bets that he can pick up an attractive woman who just then sits down at the bar. Cruise wins the bet with style, yet turns out the ultimate loser. Cut to his girlfriend, who happens on the scene just as Cruise proves himself a true 'finisher' by escorting his new conquest off to her room. Visibly upset, Cruise's love match flies back to New York that very night.

In one sense, this can be viewed as just a single scene. Yet this solitary episode is multiplied when we consider the eyes through which it is filtered. At first, the rival bartenders engage in a cockfight; as they spar their muscles ripple, their colours are intensified, their eyes bulge – a stock scene from the buddy film tradition. We then focus on Cruise and his patter as he finally hooks up with the wealth he has coveted from the start, even if she is significantly older – thus fulfilling a familiar initiation plot expectation. Unfortunately, his girlfriend happens along at the wrong time, just long enough to display her dismay, to elicit our complicity, and to divert our reading in yet another direction. Since Shakespeare, romantic drama has depended on such misunderstandings. Just one scene – but, multiply focalized, that one scene turns into at least three, in the process providing grist for three different genre mills.

Aptly named, *Cocktail* serves its genres anything but straight. Although not a complex film as Hollywood offerings go, it nevertheless manages to provide all the materials and connections for constructing multiple genres. This polyvalency is reinforced by the studio's decision to produce multiple television commercials, whose titles ('Father/Romance', 'Buddies/Team', 'Success/Relationship', etc.) suggest a close match to the generic 'concepts' tested by The National Research Group. With another study determining which ad would be likely to have the greatest impact on each specific demographic sector, these television spots were in all probability programmed according to the known demographics of particular slots in the TV grid (though actual scheduling information is unavailable, this is standard industry practice). While such careful targeting may have the effect of skewing the reaction of any particular group towards a specific genre, on the whole it assures a multi-generic reading of the film, as does the continued practice of a single theatrical trailer, which fits all four generic concepts into a single ninety-second miniaturization of the film. Taken together,

Like Cocktail*'s television campaign, publicity stills are balanced between the film's star and the various narrative constructions built into the film, along with their implied generic affinities: (opposite top) Cruise and romantic match Elisabeth Shue, (opposite bottom) young man on the way to the top Cruise learning to bartend and (above) Cruise and bar buddy Brian Brown.*

Cocktail and its publicity material demonstrate a basic Hollywood strategy: even if the film boasts a strong proprietary draw (such as a star, a character or a plot), it never hurts to maximize opportunities for success by building an interlaced, multi-generic plot offering every possible chance for positive audience response.

Classical versus postmodern

But isn't the *Cocktail* strategy just a typical example of postmodern mixing? Aren't genres used very differently now from the way they were used in Hollywood's classical era? These are not simple questions, as they involve considerations both of kind and of degree – and the corresponding answers are quite divergent. Let's begin with questions of kind: did film producers during Hollywood's golden age mix genres in fundamentally the same way as they do today? In one sense, surprisingly, this question must be answered in the affirmative.

As outlined in Chapter 4, Hollywood producers have always had an incentive to produce film cycles clearly identified with the studio. Throughout the 30s Warner Bros produced a series of extremely popular biographical films, modelled first on international political figures, then on well-known scientific personalities. Not until other studios followed suit towards the end of the decade – first with musicians and musical producers (in imitation of MGM's 1936 Best Picture Academy Award winner, *The Great Ziegfeld*) and then with statesmen and inventors –

139

did Warners' cycle become consecrated as an industry-wide genre. In other words, until the very end of the decade, when the biopic was recognized as a separate genre, biographical films would always have been associated with a primary genre in addition to biography. They were thus always designated by at least two names, such as biographical drama, or musical biography. Recognition of the biopic category dissolved that double status, making it possible henceforth to label biographical dramas and musical biographies alike with the single term 'biopic'.

As this scenario reveals, the films we now label *biopics* (with the confidence that only hindsight can inspire) went through a period when their generic status was far less certain – precisely because it was in the process of changing. In fact, as we have seen, the creation of new genres regularly involves the attachment of some adjective (representing the new genre) to a variety of different nouns (naming the old genres), thus routinely identifying even the simplest films with multiple genres. Yet today, forgetting their formative period, these very films are regularly chosen to demonstrate the purity of classical Hollywood genres.

Consider the number of times that the genrification process has taken place over the course of the last century. Even if one accepts for this purpose the doubtful claim that genres existing in other media are simply borrowed as is by film, the number of new film genres is staggering. Listed more or less chronologically, the list would have to include at least boxing films, chase films, educational films, scenics, newsreels, college films, musicals, gangster films, newspaper films, screwball comedies, biopics, film noir, stag movies, art films, exploitation films, big caper films, blaxploitation, concert films, disaster films, political conspiracy films, road movies, buddy films, women's films and action films – and the list would quadruple if it were to include subgenres (for example, zombie films, spaghetti Westerns and campus comedies), minor genres (such as surfing films, baseball films and female prison films), or forgotten genres (like Indian films before 1910, sex dramas in the 20s, or radio star films in the 30s). With the development of each new genre, films go through a predictable pattern in which they are initially identified with two or more quite different categories before eventually stabilizing into the generic identity with which they are associated today.

This process is typically forgotten for genres created in the past, leaving us with what seems like an uncomplicated genre identified by a single name. Furthermore, this process is invisible during the creation process (and there are always many genres in this situation simultaneously, even though nobody can say for sure which ones will eventually reach generic status), making it easy to assume that the multiplicity of genre labels assigned to some recent films is a function of their complexity and genre-mixing tendencies rather than the result of an as-yet-incomplete historical development. Are the buddy film action comedies produced by Joel Silver a product of postmodern genre mixing or a new genre in the making, or both? Are the comic horror films analysed by William Paul in his book *LaughingScreaming* (1994) destined to become a new genre, thus erasing their apparent earlier genre-mixing status? Like the novel, which Bakhtin labels 'the genre of becoming' (1981, p. 8), film genres are perpetually caught up in the process of becoming. The near invisibility of the genrification process while it is underway facilitates a too easy assumption that radical differences separate classical and contemporary generic practices.

A second apparent difference in kind between golden age and recent genre practices regards the postmodern tendency towards bricolage, pastiche and intertextuality. Surely, this is the very heart of the postmodern style, not yet present a half-century ago. No doubt there is an element of truth in this statement, but only if the difference is understood as of degree rather than kind. We have already seen how Hollywood studios appealed to at least three separate audiences by publicising (and usually inserting into each film) three independent sets of genre cues. Note that this is true of canonical genre films as well as obvious composites. What Western is not at some points a melodrama? What musical can do totally without romance? The typical screwball comedy stitches together a series of episodes each of which has its own generic character. As a matter of course, Hollywood studios hired multiple screenwriters for each film, in order to combine their known talents for different genres. Just because we systematically use a single generic label to identify a particular film doesn't mean that the film has always been associated with a single genre, or lacks other generic characteristics.

In the past, genre labels have primarily served critics who preferred strong genres and clear-cut designations. Perhaps this is why so many film genre terms seem more like a communicative covenant of silence than a reasoned description. It's as if they were saying: 'If you agree, when we use the term "Western" we'll pledge blindness to the presence of action, adventure, comedy, disasters, drama, gangsterism, melodrama, music, newspapers, or anything else that might point towards another genre. Once the "Western" button is pushed, we agree to disengage all the other generic buttons.' Today, pandering to postmodern taste, some critics have discovered the delights of intertextuality and multi-genericity, but we must not allow a change in critical paradigm to stand in for textual difference. Genre mixing has long been a standard Hollywood practice.

It would be wrong, however, to conclude that fundamental similarities in classical and contemporary genre use preclude differences of degree. In fact, Hollywood's early mixing of genres for publicity purposes was rudimentary at best, typically involving a small number of genres combined in an unspectacular and fairly traditional manner. Only rarely was attention drawn to disparities among the genres thus combined. Recent films, on the contrary, often use intertextual references and conscious highlighting of genre conventions to stress genre conflict. From *Raiders of the Lost Ark* to *Naked Gun* and *Die Hard*, in the 80s studios consistently sought to mix comedy into action films, with the wise-cracking tough guy becoming the modern genre-mixing equivalent of the singing cowboy. [For almost three decades, from *Airport* (1970) to *Titanic* (1998), disaster films have transformed the personal concerns of multiple trapped characters into an excuse for piling on material borrowed from many different genres.]

Following a long tradition of comic pairings of big and small (Chaplin and Campbell, Keaton and Arbuckle, Laurel and Hardy, Abbott and Costello), singer and comedian (Crosby and Hope), straight man and comic (Martin and Lewis), the buddy film has in recent years brought together new categories (based on race, gender, class and age) and conflated new genres. *Butch Cassidy and the Sundance Kid* crossed buddies with the Western, *48Hrs.* introduced racially differentiated buddies into police drama and *Thelma and Louise* crossed the buddy film with the road movie. The use of distant or closed universes already identified with a specific genre (such as spaceships, deserted houses, submarines or frontier forts) has facilitated the combination of genres typically identified by location (science fiction, horror, the war film, the Western) with other genres usually identifiable by plot type (comedy, drama, film noir, melodrama, suspense, thriller).

Evolving technology has also contributed to generic combination and destabilisation. The increasing use of documentary footage in fiction films and of digitally generated images in documentaries and docu-dramas further muddies the waters, as does the ease of translating films from one medium to another. A melodrama on the big screen may become an educational film or even a comedy when exhibited on television or a home computer. Interspersing commercial messages or newsbreaks into a film invariably activates new generic contexts; channel surfing compounds the felony.

Mixing instructions

It will come as no surprise that the conclusions to be reached at the end of this chapter are varied. Indeed, the question of genre mixing is anything but the simple topic that it is often taken to be. Most important among possible conclusions are the following:

1. Studio proclivity towards mixed genres differs markedly from the critical tendency towards pure genres because of the difference in purpose and audience between studios and critics.
2. Ever subject to the reviewer's paradox, critics must simultaneously particularize films and establish their connection to valued, established traditions and categories; they thus gravitate towards strong genre recognition and clear generic affiliation.
3. Many aspects of film criticism and theory seem specifically designed to impede perception of genre mixing. The accepted treatment of Hollywood classical narrative as linear, temporally ordered and clearly motivated, for example, predisposes viewers to experience films as unified around the familiar structure of a single genre. The use of generic terms condensing multiple generic components into a single designator dissimulates or even represses recognition of genre mixing.
4. Traditional critical preference for genre purity notwithstanding, genre mixing constitutes a fundamental stage in the standard genrification process.
5. Hollywood's golden age was a period of intense genre mixing, primarily to increase a film's marketability.
6. At the level of production, this mixing was facilitated by the use of easily recognizable semantic genre cues, parallel or sequential deployment of cues based on differing aspects of the film, a tendency to base genre identification on a small fraction of a film, and the fact that certain types of scene fit easily into multiple different genres.
7. Textual features promoting multiple genre identification include the use of excess material, multiple framing, fertile juxtaposition and multifocalization.
8. At the level of film promotion, studios preferred to imply the presence of multiple genres, while naming none.
9. Recent stylistic developments – connected to changes in the conception and measurement of audience demographics – have led to still greater dependence on and self-consciousness about genre mixing.
10. The perception of genre mixing has also been enhanced by changes in critical practice; reviewers increasingly attribute multiple generic affiliations to a single film.

Genre mixing, it now appears, is not just a postmodern fad. Quite to the contrary, the practice of genre mixing is necessary to the very process whereby genres are created. After a century of cinema it is all too easy to forget that today's pure genres came out of the cinematic mother lode fused to other, clearly different forms. It took decades of careful assaying and refinement to produce the current canon of 24-carat genres. Though it may be hard to perceive on the human scale of three-score-and-ten years, the magma that produced that lode is still in movement. What we perceive as a mixture of pre-existing genres is often nothing less than the liquid lava of a new genre still in the creation process. What remains to be seen is just how that molten rock might possibly be of any use to generic spectators, the subject of the next chapter.

9
What roles do genres play in the viewing process?

> Genre is important because it helps me feel part of something larger than myself.
> Anonymous (Susan Kim, 'Genre Survey', 1997)

The two previous chapters have concentrated on the use value of generic vocabulary and constructs for producers, distributors, exhibitors and critics, but they have had little to say about the roles that genres play in the experience of readers and viewers. Like most genre-oriented questions, this area has been marked by a high level of agreement among theorists and critics. Most commentators on genre base their treatment of the reading process on familiar assumptions about genre circulation:

a. genre films are mass-produced according to a standard generic template;
b. producers systematically identify each film with a single genre;
c. distributors and exhibitors respect and perpetuate the producer's generic identification of a film;
d. consumers choose films based on that identification;
e. spectators follow a single set of generic cues unproblematically through each genre film;
f. critics, like other spectators, correctly recognize each film's generic identity.

Disarmingly simple, straightforward and logical, this account does not square, however, with the genre practice described in earlier chapters of this book.

While some films – principally low-budget and independent productions – are assembly-lined, most films now associated with a particular genre were produced either *prior to* the establishment of genre norms or *against* an existing generic paradigm (though often in keeping with a proprietary cycle). Far from explicitly identifying an individual film with a specific genre, studios work hard to multiply the number of genres with which a film is implicitly identified. Though distributors and exhibitors during Hollywood's golden years rarely violated the generic contexts implied by the parent studio, the exhibition practices of other periods and locations regularly recast a film generically. Whereas consumers often choose films on the basis of genre, the process is more complex than usually suggested. Far from simply replicating industry categorization, pre-viewing notions of a film's generic identity depend on multiple, often contradictory sources: studio discourse (which, because it targets multiple audiences, usually offers conflicting genre cues), claims made by critics (who do not necessarily deploy generic discourse for the same reasons or in the same manner as other sectors of the film industry), and several networks of genre viewers (with no guarantee of alignment among home, office, church and bar evaluations). Typically engineered to take advantage of multiple affiliations, most Hollywood films are sufficiently complex from a generic viewpoint to preclude simple processing.

Based all too heavily on the musical, the Western and slapstick comedy – the only genres that Hollywood ever came close to unproblematically mass-producing – most writing about film genre has been unduly reductive. The clarity of communication suggested by the above model represents an extreme case on which no general claims may appropriately be based. Indeed, this problem has haunted genre theory for centuries. Striving for certainty, commentators on genre have consistently based their conclusions on the most obvious cases, the most formulaic texts, and the most durable genres. Blinded by the very light that it seeks, most genre theory has failed to note the shadow play that gives genres their depth. In compensation, this chapter will attend to three major aspects of generic spectatorship that have been eclipsed by the more obvious cue-and-response process. For simplicity these are termed the generic crossroads, generic economy and the generic community.

The generic crossroads

To the extent that they are indebted to specific genres, Hollywood films incorporate a series of paradigmatically designed and often repeated 'crossroads'. Each one of these moments depends on a crucial opposition between two paths open to the text, each representing a different type of pleasure for the spectator. Strategically simplifying, we may say that one fork offers a culturally sanctioned activity or value, while the other path diverges from cultural norms in favour of generic pleasure. While invisible to viewers lacking in knowledge of the generic traditions invoked, crossroad events loom large in the experience of the genre fan, for they represent both a clear threat to generic pleasure and, with the spectator's complicity, a clear triumph over the cultural limits blocking generic pleasure. In other words, any given generic crossroads will be experienced as a genre versus culture opposition only by a certain percentage of viewers, those with an investment in this particular kind of generic pleasure. Though they may remain unaware of the process, those who delight in a particular genre are always affected by crossroad experiences involving that genre, simply because their continued pleasure depends on 'proper' negotiation of those crossroads.

It is important to distinguish between generic crossroads and similar structures that have characterized narrative since Chrétien de Troyes and the rise of Arthurian romance. When characters reach a fork in the road – literally (as in Grail romances and picaresque novels), morally (as in *The Princess of Cleves* or *Moll Flanders*), psychologically (as in *The Red and the Black* and *The Red Badge of Courage*), or metaphysically (as in *The Human Condition* and *Nausea*) – their own destiny is at stake, dependent on the direction they choose. This type of decision is thus central to what we might call the character's itinerary, whereas the generic crossroads is a highlight of the spectator's itinerary. The same event seen in differing ways may of course constitute an important element of both itineraries; the distinction between the two itineraries is more a question of viewpoint and definition than of actual textual difference.

For example, in Warners' *The Public Enemy* (1931) young Tom Powers repeat-

In Warners' The Public Enemy (1931) James Cagney and Edward Woods provide the illegality and violence that the gangster film audience seeks,

edly eschews the model of his upstanding brother Mike in favour of one criminal activity after another. In 1909 a childish department store binge includes the random theft of ice skates, a pipe, salt and pepper shakers and even a brassiere. Soon Tom and his friend Matt Doyle turn to more purposeful crimes, stealing watches in order to sell them to a fence. In 1915, now played by James Cagney and Edward Woods, Tom and Matt stray still further from the straight and narrow, with armed robbery eventually leading to the murder of a policeman. In one respect this is familiar *Bildungsroman* territory, each scene offering a new opportunity for the protagonist to choose between right and wrong, innocence and experience, pastoral virtues and urban vice. This character itinerary is not the only thing happening here, however. Because criminal activity is necessary to the gangster genre, Tom's and Matt's increasing hoodlumism is experienced by spectators not only as breaking the law, but also as facilitating genre pleasure. What appears as a cautionary moral tale when defined as a function of character choices looks more like a generic crossroads when considered as part of the spectator's itinerary.

For anyone who would experience *The Public Enemy* as a gangster film, illegal activities are necessary steps along the path to generic pleasure; even though we remain part of a culture that condemns crimes, we condone them in this context because they play to our generic desires. Since illegality is required for our pleasure, we actually seek it out, thereby producing the split subjectivity characteristic of genre spectatorship. One side continues to judge as the culture has taught us to judge, while the other bases its judgments on generic criteria, often diametrically opposed to cultural norms. Perhaps crime doesn't pay, as Hollywood films regularly remind us, but the crime genre certainly does. (I do not mean to suggest that genres somehow escape cultural influence, but simply that they are repeatedly presented as alternatives to cultural norms, as if their very existence were dependent on viewers' counter-cultural complicity. In the next section I will double back on this question and show how viewers' genre-based reaction against culture is eventually used to lock them ever more securely within cultural limits.)

RKO's *Top Hat* (1935) provides a particularly clear view of this conflict between cultural and generic values. Simultaneously offering dance music, images of dancing feet, and the familiar generically coded names of Fred Astaire and Ginger Rogers, the credit sequence provides an obvious cue. 'This is a musical', it states. 'Don't watch this film if you don't like musicals, but if you do your musical pleasure is henceforth guaranteed.' Now a musical, as the genre's critics regularly remind us, cannot exist without its three constitutive moments: boy meets girl, boy dances with girl, boy gets girl. But in *Top Hat*, from the very start, this process runs into trouble. When Astaire awakens Rogers with his nocturnal tap dancing, she does what any proper young lady in a posh hotel would do in the 1930s; rather than complaining directly to the offending noise-maker, she complains to the management. According to this scenario, the manager would silence Astaire, report back to Rogers, and the incident would be closed. But there would be no musical, because the boy would never meet the girl. The spectator's allegiances are already being tested. Should Rogers obey proper etiquette? Or should she shun society's notion of acceptable behaviour in favour of conduct becoming the musical? The spectator hesitates not a moment: generic pleasure is always preferable to social correctness.

Throughout *Top Hat*, this strategy is repeated. Generic pleasure becomes increasingly distant from and eventually antithetical to society's mores. When Astaire invites Rogers to dance, she believes that he is married to her best friend (though the spectator knows otherwise). Rogers at first hesitates to dance with Astaire, once again jeopardizing our generic pleasure, which depends on the boy dancing with the girl. When Rogers' best friend encourages her not only to dance with Astaire, but to dance closer, the spectator is delighted, for Rogers' sense of participating in a forbidden act only heightens viewing pleasure. So far, we spectators have been successful in keeping clear of any unauthorized desires by projecting them on to Ginger Rogers.

Shortly, Rogers will 'do the right thing' by marrying her employer in order to avoid the temptation of further flings with Astaire, thus jeopardizing our generic pleasure yet again by keeping the right boy from getting the right girl. We are thus delighted when Astaire and the now married Rogers go for a boat ride together. This time we have quite literally condoned an adulterous liaison in order to guarantee continued generic pleasure. Earlier, we did not desire the forbidden; we only desired Rogers' desiring the forbidden. Now we find ourselves openly celebrating the emotional consummation of an adulterous love affair, just so we can enjoy continued access to generic pleasures.

When we are in the world, we follow its rules. When we enter into the world of genres, we reveal tastes and make decisions of an entirely different nature, to the point where familiar norms directly conflict with another kind of satisfaction that

Ginger's not sure she should dance with the man she takes for her friend's husband, but she does anyway, to the delight of viewers who came to see Top Hat *(1935) precisely to watch Astaire and Rogers dance together.*

looks nothing short of 'dirty' when seen from a cultural viewpoint. It's not just that 'dirty dancing' is opposed to socially acceptable activities, but that *Dirty Dancing*'s (1987) proper vacation lodge society promises only vapid parlour games, whereas the dirty dancing of the lower-class and ethnically marked staff quarters is the stuff that musicals are made of (even if it happens to be delivered in the same package with an adulterous affair and an unwanted pregnancy). Though the definition of the term evolves constantly, the musical genre owes its very life to slightly 'dirty' dancing – from the waltz and the can-can to breakdancing and the lambada. Similarly, every cop show has its Dirty Harry. Westerns

Like many earlier musicals, Vestron Pictures' Dirty Dancing *(1987) divides dances into the old-fashioned kind that parents do and the 'dirty' kind that enchant youths . . . and film audiences. Here Patrick Swayze and Cynthia Rhodes teach Jennifer Grey (centre) the mambo.*

would not exist without a Dirty Billy or Dirty Dingus Magee. During peace time, it takes a Dirty Dozen to make a war film. Want some comedy thrown into an adventure film? Mate Dirty Mary with Crazy Larry.

Hollywood genre connections regularly rely on actors and actions defined by their eccentricity with respect to some cultural circle. The Western depends on outlaws, science fiction needs aliens, war films thrive on foreigners, adventure films require wild men and beasts, horror films count on mad scientists, strange beings or the uncanny. Tragedies belong to the flawed. According to their type, comedies feature characters who are either odd, queer, nutty or screwballs. Cartoon characters are daffy or goofy, their tunes are looney and their symphonies are silly. Melodrama characters are systematically either *under-* (underfed, underhanded, underpaid, underprivileged, underrated), *over-* (overbearing, overconfident, overdue, overextended, overpowering, oversensitive, oversexed, overwhelming), or just plain *un-* (unappreciated, unashamed, unbalanced, uncooperative, ungrateful, unhappy, unjust, unnatural, unrelenting, unrepentant, unruly, unspeakable).

Even Hollywood's heroes and role models buck authority (biopic, detective film, slapstick comedy), engage in idiosyncratic behaviour (screwball comedy, fantasy, melodrama), or seek out the very dangers that society exists to minimize (adventure film, war film, Western). Ironically, the 'good guys', the very characters charged with defending cultural norms (sheriffs, soldiers, policemen, secret agents), excel at activities normally limited by society – fighting, shooting, speeding, sleeping around – but that they exercise with great gusto. In a world where peace is the apparent ideal, Hollywood genres offer a full menu of accidents, ambushes, battles, catastrophes, conflagrations and wars. In spite of a peaceful ending, a film replete with bullets, guns, bombs, knives, fists and other implements of destruction offers its devoted spectators experiences of anything but peace.

Modern society may be built around an ideal of logic and progress, but comedy turns on illogic and repetition compulsion. Culture involves controlling nature through science; so-called 'male' genres instead feature nature gone wild (disaster film, wilderness adventure) and mad or fantastic science (horror, science fiction). Social standards severely limit the acceptable range of emotional interchange; so-called 'female' genres (melodrama, musical, weepie) provide an arena in which it is acceptable to substitute strong emotions for the mild sensations sanctioned by society.

An understanding of the generic crossroads mechanism may be gained from comedy's repeated miscommunication trope. A standard feature of the comedy of manners since Shakespeare and Molière, miscommunication was raised by Marivaux and Restoration comedy to a thematically rich device central to romantic or sophisticated comedy. From the Marx Brothers to Chevy Chase and from Astaire and Rogers to the recent Jane Austen revival, mistaken identity and miscommunication have been staples of film comedy and romance. Within this tradition, a clear distinction is made between characters and spectators; while the former suffer from misunderstandings, the latter are almost always privy to the truth. Scene

Genre films on television

It is extraordinarily instructive to watch genre films on commercial television, where ads, news flashes and public service messages provide a constant reminder of the cultural values that genres flout. It is as if television were designed to actualize the very counter-cultural tendencies and activities that genre films flaunt. Watch American television long enough and you are sure to experience such eerily significant juxtapositions as these:

cut from a holiday safety message to *Hallowe'en*;
from a peace conference to *Full Metal Jacket*;
from a list of automobile safety features to the gory accidents of *Speed*;
from a discussion of child care to *Home Alone*;
from the weekly news segment on local radar traps to the high-speed chases of *The French Connection*;
from a homeowner's insurance commercial to *The Hurricane*;
from a pickup truck ad to the closing sequence of *Easy Rider*;
from a happy family enjoying a new breakfast cereal to the dysfunctionality of *Giant*;
from a gun safety public service spot to *The Wild Bunch*.

The relief that we feel with every return to the film is precisely the delight experienced by some viewers at every generic crossroads. Putting culture's values behind us, we look forward to at least a few more minutes of excitement, danger and fear.

after scene offers the opportunity to do away with this imbalance by clearing up the characters' mistakes, but since the comedy arises out of the miscommunication itself, both the genre and the spectator's generic pleasure would be destroyed by revealing the truth – ostensibly society's greatest value. With each repeated incident of miscommunication not only does our enjoyment grow, but so does our disdain for the value society normally places on clear communication. Our pleasure has come into conflict with society's pleasure, and for once we apparently wield the power necessary to ensure our own choice.

Of course not everyone actualizes this generic potential; some viewers may refuse the generic path entirely, in favour of the cultural fork (perhaps by washing the dishes instead), while others simply switch to a different generic pleasure (for example by attending to other aspects of the film or by choosing another film). Contrary to appearances, generic crossroads are not simple textual structures (which by themselves would be insufficient to determine audience reaction), but a specific mode of processing textual structures. Initially free to take a genre cue or leave it, viewers progressively lose that freedom once they venture down a generic pathway. Operating in a Pavlovian manner, a film's repeated invitations to generic processing train those who accept them both to enjoy generic pleasures and to disdain the cultural positions presented as alternatives.

My purpose in this section is not to dictate how spectators must experience genre, but rather to describe the interaction between audience and text at the moment when viewers are actually experiencing a film generically. For arguments to be advanced later, it is crucial to note the role that generic pleasure plays in this process. Viewers who dislike a particular genre will have different crossroad experiences from those who gain pleasure from the genre. Those who don't care for the genre will never undergo Pavlovian conditioning, because their lack of interest in the genre is tantamount to not feeding Pavlov's dogs. Yet another genre (perhaps actualised by different crossroads within the same film) might offer just the sustenance necessary to entice them into a slightly different version of the process.

In other words, genres don't provide the energy necessary to generic experiences; that must instead come from viewers, who, being different, can be expected to invest their energy in extremely diverse modes. What genres are adept at, however, is funneling towards a homogeneous experience those viewers who invest in a similar type of generic pleasure. As we will see in the final section of this chapter, the ability to choose one's genre pleasures lies at the very heart of generic operations. This I say in clear opposition to the many genre theorists and critics who assume that genres serve to level *all* viewers, transforming the entire audience into a single homogeneous block.

The process described in this section is reminiscent of comments often made about narrative itself. Plots, it is said, require opposition or exception; they cannot be built around uniformity. It is thus hardly surprising that some classes of text should feature counter-cultural characters and activities. In one sense, this comment is not only justified but extremely insightful: most genres do indeed work narratively; their ability to involve and steer audiences derives directly from the narrative drive that they harness in a particularly effective manner. In another sense, though, an approach reducing genres to their narrative component fails to capture generic specificity.

However much they may deploy narrative strategies, films perceived as having generic affinities do so in a way that is all their own, precisely characterized by the operations that take place at the generic crossroads. Even when not read generically, texts offer many crossroads events: romance or career? advance or retreat? city or country? the lady or the tiger? The difference lies in the self-serving, circular nature of the genre experience. Most narrative crossroads lead to a new event, a new road, and a new and different fork; for genre viewers, however, every crossroads is formulaic, with one path always leading to renewed generic activity. Each crossroads thus serves both as a test of viewer allegiance and as an advertisement for the genre in question. Though self-consciousness and reflexivity are hardly the first words that come to mind when one thinks of genre, it's important to recognize just how often genres use the familiar resources of narrative to advertise their own wares.

Generic economy

As a locus of conflict between generic and cultural values, each generic crossroads is a work site, a place where cultural labour is performed. Though not all spectators can be expected to recognize or accept the invitation extended by any particular generic crossroads, those who do participate implicitly activate at each crossroads both cultural and generic standards. Within the real world, cultural values of course reign supreme. In the genre world, however, generic values systematically dominate – as long as we consider crossroads experiences individually. This section will take up the broader challenge of describing the overall system coordinating separate generic crossroads.

An incremental logic would appear to regulate the crossroads sequence in individual films. The first crossroads always takes place long before the start of the show. In a workaday world, implicitly overseen by a Weberian logic, spending time on a Hollywood film already constitutes a meaningful choice, an investment in popular entertainment with no obvious redeeming social value. As I have suggested in the final chapter of *The American Film Musical* (1987), traditional American beliefs place entertainment not only beneath but in clear opposition to culturally valued activities. The fork in the road that takes solid citizens off the main street of economic endeavour and through the lobby of moving picture leisure implicitly positions film viewing as the antithesis of productive behaviour.

From this initial opposition, the antagonism grows constantly between the culturally acceptable and the generically serviceable. As we have already witnessed in the cases of *The Public Enemy* and *Top Hat*, initial differences between the needs of culture and genre are often inconsequential. Two boys shoplift a few inexpensive items in a fancy department store; a proper young lady rejects custom and complains directly to the individual disturbing her sleep. So what? These are just peccadillos. While they may be necessary to generic pleasure, they are not sufficient to guarantee it. Requiring constant intensification, genre viewers can be satisfied only by an increasing opposition between (generic) pleasure and the (cultural) interdictions that restrict it. Thus *The Public Enemy* takes us from juvenile pranks to robbery to homicide to murder, and *Top Hat* leads us from a breach of etiquette through indiscretion to an apparent adultery.

It is instructive that the two genres most noted for their incremental logic – the horror film and the thriller – should be designated by terms describing the spectator's reaction rather than filmic content, for it is precisely on heightening viewer sensation that generic logic depends. The original *Frankenstein* (1931) begins by warning viewers about the sensations that the film may inspire.

> Van Sloan: It is one of the strangest tales ever told. It deals with the two great mysteries of creation. Life and death. I think it will thrill you. It may shock you. . . . It might even – horrify you! So then, if you feel that you do not care to subject your nerves to such a strain, now is your chance to – well – well – we've warned you.
>
> (Anobile, 1974, p. 9)

Implicitly opposing this strange and dangerous tale to more traditional and culturally acceptable fare, Van Sloan forces us from the start to make a choice in favour of horror. The film then leads us from a pair of minor offences (grave robbing and theft of a laboratory specimen) through a series of increasingly horrible events, beginning with the monster's provoked attack on the perverse servant Fritz and culminating in the unmotivated murder of a defenceless girl.

Throughout the film, a series of crucial oppositions self-consciously establishes the film's increasing counter-cultural thematic stakes. At first defined solely by his scientific pursuits, Dr Frankenstein is soon revealed to be neglecting his fiancée and the proper life she represents.

Universal's Frankenstein *(1931) consolidated the monster's twin careers: murdering his fellow cast members, thereby fascinating his audiences.*

153

BARON: Why does he go messing around in an old ruined windmill when he has a decent house, a bath, good food and drink and a darned pretty girl to come back to – huh! Will you tell me that?

ELIZABETH: Baron, you don't understand.

BARON: I understand perfectly well – huh – there is another woman, and you're afraid to tell me. Pretty sort of experiments these must be! Huh!

(Anobile, 1974, p. 97)

Dr Frankenstein's conduct is thus simultaneously counterposed to decent conduct, sanctioned sexuality and normal science. Were he faithful to these ideals, society would be satisfied, but genre viewers would be cheated of the strong emotions that many seek in films like *Frankenstein*. Not until the monster threatens his very creator will one of the film's crossroads be negotiated in a non-generic manner, resulting in the monster's death, the film's conclusion, and the end of the viewer's generic pleasure.

Under the strong influence of Alfred Hitchcock, thrillers often begin with a crime and the accusation of an innocent bystander. Were the accused to contact the authorities, no doubt the case could be promptly solved, but instead the poor bystander runs from the law thus further jeopardizing life and limb. Parallel to the comic device of miscommunication, the suspense film technique of misaccusation serves to prolong spectator pleasure within the specific bounds of the genre. Each plot twist not only increases the character's danger (and the spectator's thrill), but it also offers a way off the film's crazy ride. At every turn spectators must make an implicit choice: more thrills (in the continued company of an outlaw) or safety at last (under the societally sanctioned protection of the law and its defenders).

Why do we so consistently choose thrills over safety? Why do we seek out fear and the unlawful or inhuman when we could have security and the company of our kind and culture? This question can be answered only in the context of the overall forking pattern of generic plots. Through nine-tenths of the film each crossroads leads to the same generic path and pleasure, yet virtually every genre eventually abandons generic pleasure in favour of its cultural counterpart. In *Top Hat*, Ginger turns out not to be married to her employer, so it's all right for her to spark with Fred after all. In *The Public Enemy*, Cagney pushes his luck just a little too far, killing the film and the genre by too often endangering himself. *Frankenstein* the film burns up along with the monster. From *The Thirty-nine Steps* to *Three Days of the Condor*, suspense films abandon both thrills and suspense when the falsely accused character finally reaches safety.

Hollywood genre films are usually described as driven by a cause-and-effect chain of events. I have argued to the contrary (Altman, 1989) that Hollywood films are more indebted to popular theatre than to classical novels, and that their structure owes more to the dual-focus configuration of melodrama than to the single-focus arrangement of Aristotelian narrative. The generic crossroads case eloquently bears out this contention. Instead of specific causes leading to necessary effects, culminating in a fully logical conclusion, generic situations offer instead a process of intensification and release. Each crossroads simply replicates previous crossroads situations with added intensity, until the point where cultural standards (including appropriate textual length) dictate a reversal (precisely the opposite of an effect). Of course, genres do sometimes deploy cause-and-effect logic, but primarily to cover up their principal strategy of offering an increasingly intense counter-cultural genre pleasure experience, only eventually to reverse that pattern and revert to cultural dominance. Cause-and-effect plot construction is not a primary Hollywood process; instead it is like the secondary elaboration dissimulating the central signifying systems of the Freudian dream-work.

The overall generic crossroads system may in fact be usefully described in Freudian terms. Recognizing that it costs us psychic energy every time we bend to the requirements of culture or reality, Freud noted that pleasure results from a reduction in our expenditure of psychic energy. From these twin findings, he developed a notion of 'psychic economy' according to which the level of pleasure corresponds to the amount of psychic energy saved. In *Jokes and their Relation to the Unconscious* this notion is further developed and fruitfully applied to comic situations. Without necessarily accepting the psychoanalytic trappings with which Freud surrounds this notion, we may borrow the psychic economy framework as a useful model for what I term 'generic economy'. Whereas psychic economy governs relations between the reality principle and the pleasure principle, generic economy relates cultural criteria and generic pleasures.

As we have seen, the crossroad experiences so prevalent in film genres regularly entice viewers into choosing between social standards and generic pleasures. Each time viewers choose the generic fork over the lawful path they experience pleasure in a quantity measured by the distance separating cultural expectations and generic transgression. The pleasure we take from Ginger's breach of etiquette at the beginning of *Top Hat* is thus small indeed, since etiquette constitutes the least of society's requirements. With each generic crossroads, though, the distance increases between the intensity of social standards and the counter-cultural activities required to assure generic pleasure. From etiquette we proceed to morals and thence to adultery laws, just as in other genres we progress from verbal prattle to physical pranks, from the uncanny to the unbearably horrible, from cattle rustling to cold-blooded murder, or from the Cold War to World War III. As the stakes are raised, the pleasure of generic activity increases. No longer are we simply playing hooky; now we are choosing crime over the law, nonsense over communication, war over peace. We thus undermine the very foundations of the culture limiting our free range – and that is precisely what pleases us. It is only through this escalating denial of cultural values that we reach the highest levels of generic pleasure.

Yet genre films almost never end at their greatest distance from cultural norms, the point where generic pleasure is at its height. On the contrary, genre-based films virtually always follow a long period of intensification with a rapid and definitive restoration of cultural values. How are we to understand this reversion to the norm, in light of the previous comments on generic economy? Ironically, it is precisely the notion of generic economy that permits us to understand the typical generic ending. Since according to our definition pleasure is not absolute but differential in nature, generic reversals produce pleasure in proportion to the distance that must be traversed in order to restore order, to disculpate the accused, to clear up the lovers' quarrel, to free the hostages, or to kill the monster/villain/culprit. The greater the risk, the greater the pleasure of the return to safety. The greater the wrong, the greater the pleasure taken in righting it. The greater the chaos, the greater the pleasure of restoring order.

Generic economy thus not only operates like psychic economy, with pleasure measured by the degree of reduction in energy expenditure, but it does so twice over. For ninety minutes, Hollywood films offer generic pleasure as an alternative to cultural norms. This pleasure derives from a perception that the activities producing it are free from the control exercised by the culture and felt by the spectator in the real world. For most of the film, then, the genre spectator's pleasure grows as norms of increasing complexity and cultural importance are eluded or violated. In this respect, film genres join amusement parks, carnivals and sporting events as special venues offering authorized opportunities for counter-cultural activity, albeit within a context created by the culture itself. Film genres not only offer a chance to take counter-cultural pleasure, they actually equate the amount of pleasure with the extent to which the activities producing it may be perceived as counter-cultural.

Later in the same film, however, something quite different takes place. The long process of escalating escape from cultural norms produces sufficient tension to compromise viewers' appetite for generic pleasure, which is soon replaced by an equally strong desire for resolution. During earlier portions of the film, generic activity constituted a desirable flight from social standards; the level of pleasure was measured by the amount of cultural pressure avoided. Now, however, it is the tension produced by snowballing generic endeavours that must be avoided; reduction in energy expenditure is at this point produced by a return to cultural norms. The intensity of the pleasure to be gained is measured by the distance separating the tension produced by ninety minutes of generic intensification and the repose of a return to peace, order and community.

Careful manipulation of opportunities for generic pleasure and eventual return to cultural values is what makes film genres such devastatingly successful hegemonic devices. Who can resist all generic temptation? Few people savour all genres, but whichever genres we relish, we can be sure that our very pleasure in fleeing culture will eventually be used to seduce us into celebrating culture's very values. The built-in reversibility of generic economy also accounts for the fervour with which critics have proposed apparently contradictory theories of genre, either ritual or ideological in nature. The extent to which genres sequentially promote two different value systems, each providing pleasure by virtue of its difference from the other, explains not only why critics should see genres so differently, but also how genres can simultaneously perform two different functions.

The generic community

Thoughtful readers may well question the extreme generality of the 'cultural' and 'counter-cultural' notions employed thus far in this chapter. Is there really such a neat and unified thing as 'culture'? Hasn't postmodernism taught us that there are instead many divergent definitions of culture, with no single version ever achieving centrality? These are important concerns, which I share. They require two separate answers.

First, I would suggest that Hollywood genre logic has always been – and remains in the 90s – strongly modernist (as opposed to postmodern) in nature. That is, it thrives on the positing of a norm which it then violates or reverses. Is this in fact a cultural norm? In some cases it clearly is. For example, condemnation of unjustified violence and revulsion towards those who cause it have enjoyed virtually unbroken and universal support throughout this century. Building films around broadly shared values of this type increases the likelihood that audiences will recognize the norms against which generic activity is to be measured. Similarly, commentary about cultural norms is often imbedded within films in order to standardize the conduct recognized as normative. Still, even the apparent universality of cultural condemnation of violence is attenuated during the war years, challenged by special interest groups like boxing promoters or followers of the Marquis de Sade, and contradicted by violence-praising avant-garde movements like the Futurists.

More important still stands Hollywood's consistent use of cultural norms as narrative devices. Just as certain assumptions about films must be shared by all spectators in order for them together to share the experience we call cinema (suspension of disbelief, understanding of the process of representation, recognition both of the role played by the apparatus and the need to bracket and ignore that role), so genres require certain shared perceptions in order to be perceived as genres. Recognizing this principle, Hollywood has over the years designed techniques assuring a certain uniformity of perception, even if this involves chastizing conduct that in the real world may under certain circumstances be entirely acceptable, or recommending behaviour that is far from universally recognized as desirable.

Genres are not the real world, but a game that we play with moves and players borrowed from the real world. Hollywood's masters of genre are not claiming that 'this conduct presented as normative is in fact accepted as such throughout the culture', but instead that 'this conduct presented as a cultural norm and in fact so recognized by some will be used as a fundamental element of this particular game'. Each genre game begins by positing a cultural norm, in order to permit the construction of generic pleasure as in some way contradicting that norm. In order to avoid undermining spectator suspension of disbelief, the conduct in question must have some legitimate real world claim to normative status, though it need not be accepted by the entire society as the rule. In practice, this leads to a genre game that many viewers agree to play. Yet not all viewers of a film associated with a particular genre experience the film through that genre. Why should this be? And what difference does it make for this chapter's concern to detail the role that genres play in the viewing process?

In describing the process of viewing genre films, critics regularly use generalizing terms like 'the audience', 'one', or simply 'we'. Reflecting the fact that genre spectatorship is by definition a group affair, an expression like 'we are terrified' (Buscombe 1970, p. 20, apropos of a scene in *Psycho*) begs a fundamental question: who constitutes the 'we' thus evoked? Far from representing society at large, or American society as a whole, or even all filmgoers, this 'we' stands in for a different group in the case of each separate genre. Everyone knows that audiences for women's prison films are radically different from those for folk musicals, yet standard generalizing terminology tends to hide this difference. In order to understand the role genres play in viewer experience, it is necessary to break down the universalizing 'we' into its component parts.

To accept the premises of a genre is to agree to play within a special set of rules, and thus to participate in a community precisely *not* coterminous with society at large. Choosing to view a film of a particular genre involves more than just an agreement to purchase, consume and construe in a particular manner. Approaches that image viewers as nothing more than consumers are too narrow, unless the very process of consuming is understood as an event involving the pleasure of being the type of person who buys this particular kind of product. The generic contract involves adherence to particular codes and, through that adherence, identification with others who so adhere. As one of the interviewees in Susan Kim's 'Genre Survey' (1997) put it, 'Genre is important because it helps me feel part of something larger than myself'.

In the past, critics have often assumed that genres are both self-interpreting and universal in effect. Recognition of genres' counter-cultural appeal justifies a quite different conclusion. Because most generic spectatorship involves a break with social standards – however imaginary and temporary – it also creates an implicit tie among those who find pleasure in breaking this particular cultural norm in this particular manner. Two experiences recently recounted by genre theorists are revelatory in this regard. At the outset of her fascinating article on 'Film Bodies: Gender, Genre, and Excess', Linda Williams (1991) explains how she came to think of pornography, horror and melodrama as belonging to a single 'body genre' category. All three types of film, she says, are considered either by herself or by her seven-year-old son as 'gross'. He finds nothing 'more obscene than kissing'; films with monsters who rip apart teenage girls 'both fascinate and scare him', says Williams, who admits that she herself enjoys weepies 'in a guilty, perverse sort of way' (1995, p. 140). With regard to respectability, each one of these genres is excessive; viewers thus respond differentially, according to their willingness to participate in each particular type of excess. Thus Williams' son rejects sad movies, while his mother has built around melodramas not only part of a career but also an extended network of dedicated melodrama lovers.

Excess is one of many ways in which genres embody counter-cultural expression. Not only 'body genres' and what Bill Paul calls 'grossout films', but every genre film is in some sense 'gross'. Genre fans thus often sense the importance of hiding their predilections. 'One of the surprises of this project,' writes Carol Clover in the Introduction to *Men, Women, and Chain Saws*, 'has been the number of what I once thought of as unlikely people – middle-aged, middle-class people of both sexes – who have "come out" to me about their secret appetite for so-called exploitation horror' (1992, p. 7). Because genres engender 'secret appetites', public revelation of genre tastes always takes on the nature of a 'coming out'. Not just body genres, 'grossout' films and exploitation horror, but much less controversial genres as well participate in this phenomenon. Thanks to my own published work, I have been 'out' for years as a musical aficionado; now every few months I am subjected to the following confession: 'I don't usually tell people this, but for years I've been a closet musical fan.' As in the case of Carol Clover's informants, this is precisely not a fully public 'coming out'. On the contrary, confessions of genre proclivity (like those in Henry Jenkins' *Textual Poachers* [1992]) are

The upper right-hand corner of this 1938 poster for the first entry in Warners' Nancy Drew series offers a clear example of the behaviour expected of Nancy Drew fans.

usually made to individuals or groups known to share those same genre pleasures. In other words, the generic *coming out* process simultaneously involves *coming into contact* with a select group of genre fans.

While primarily appealing to potential audience members one at a time, Hollywood advertising campaigns commonly also imagine a fully face-to-face relationship among viewers. Predicting that Robert Z. Leonard's 1930 MGM Norma Shearer vehicle *The Divorcee* is 'Destined to be one of the most talked of pictures in years', the film's poster follows the Hollywood tradition of constructing positive reception as community interaction. Studio publicity campaigns regularly aim at actually engineering viewer contact beyond the confines of the theatre. Pressbooks distributed to exhibitors thus propose contests, meetings and clubs as a way to assemble like-minded viewers.

When Warners' popular youth detective Nancy Drew series debuted in 1938, the pressbook exhorted local theatres to form Nancy Drew clubs. The posters positioned Nancy Drew and her sleuthing as a desirable alternative both to childish female activities ('NANCY'S THROUGH PLAYING WITH DOLLS!...SHE'D

RATHER PLAY WITH DANGER!') and to traditional (male) modes of success ('She may get the wrong answers in school ... but she gets the right men in jail!' 'Her homework may not be so hot ... but her policework is 100%!'). A Nancy Drew fan is actually given a speaking role on one poster. Shown pushing out of her way a group of men identified as Sherlock Holmes, Perry Mason and Philo Vance, a stylishly dressed young lady says: 'One side, flatfeet, ... let a real sleuth show you how it's done! She may be just sixteen, but she's got something you guys never had ... feminine intuition!' Once initiated into the national Nancy Drew Club, each modern young woman would easily recognize fellow fans by their membership card, detective badge and the teen slang detailed in the pressbook.

While genre fandom sometimes involves this type of actual face-to-face contact, genre buffs more commonly imagine themselves communing with absent like-minded fans. This process often depends on styles, activities or objects that function both as a generic insignia permitting easy recognition among enthusiasts of the same genre, and as a symbolic representation of other genre fans in their absence. This is how sheet music operates, for example. At some point, musical lovers may actually get together to sing the song, but solitary playing, singing or simply possessing the song may stand in adequately for the absent fan group, thus providing the sheet music owner with an essential personal identification element. The same scenario holds for the many styles championed by diverse genres, whether of clothing (weepie, musical, Western), language (gangster film, film noir, science fiction), or conduct (Western, film noir, action film). Today, this process has been trivialized by the systematic sale of stuffed animals, action figures, soundtrack albums, music videos, novelized versions, and other tie-ins as part of the marketing strategy for every major Hollywood film. Flashing an action figure has become a surefire method of quickly discovering whether the neighbourhood sandbox is a generically friendly venue or not.

The face-to-face contact of the piano party or sandbox is not required, however, to set in motion the pleasures of participating in a genre community. Critics regularly pair genre terms with categories of viewers, inviting readers to imagine themselves as somehow connected to other members of those groups. 'Kung fu aficionados should enjoy it,' says Leonard Maltin of the 1983 *Revenge of the Ninja,* 'otherwise beware' (1997, p. 1117). If you enjoyed a given genre film, this and many other reviews imply, you are part of a larger group of similar-minded viewers. When the conservative British press endeavoured to throw together all video representations of sex and violence into a single 'video nasties' genre, the *Daily Express* provided a highly indicative definition of a 'nasty': 'video which is "grossly offensive" to all reasonable people'. By appealing to those who consider themselves part of a 'reasonable' majority, critics equate film viewing with participation in a specific and recognizable community.

The farther we range from live entertainment (that is, the more we deal with separate audiences, absent to each other, yet sharing the 'same' experience), the more powerful are appeals to an absent and yet implied genre community. Television's laugh-track provides comedy viewers sitting alone in separate family rooms a surrogate audience and thus an *in praesentia* stand-in for the *in absentia* members of each viewer's far-flung genre community. Both Hollywood genres and their musical counterparts reveal increasing attempts to compensate for the disappearance of the folk, the country and their music by offering products, images, styles and shared experiences evocative of vanishing or departed face-to-face communities.

Most of the time, flesh-and-blood genre communities remain beyond reach. Though we may have intermittent contact with others fond of the same genre, we are usually reduced to only imagining their presence and activity. While Carol Clover and I temporarily embodied the larger genre fan group for the genre enthusiasts who 'came out' to us, such direct contact is exceptional. Instead of regular participation in an actual group, genre spectatorship more often involves constructing an image of such a group out of fragments gleaned from every possible field. Not only industry discourse, but critical language, passing comments and chance encounters provide the reference points that permit genre fans to imagine – perhaps unconsciously – the absent community with which they share a particular taste. Though genre viewing in some cases leads to contact with actual community members, and though the meaning of genre viewing may be fundamentally caught up in nostalgia for a specific absent community, most genre spectators maintain only an imagined contact with the broader generic community. Isolated from each other, reduced to imaging the larger group on the basis of a few faint sightings, generic communities constitute what I call *constellated communities*, for like a group of stars their members cohere only through repeated acts of imagination.

Just what is the nature of a constellated community? I am tempted to point to the attitude of medieval Christians, all simultaneously facing east towards a symbolically synonymous altar. This example is clearly insufficient, however, because the community in question is so homogeneous and so dependent on regular *in praesentia* relationships. A panoptical view of diasporic Muslims would offer a better example, separately facing Mecca while simultaneously voicing the same prayers. But this example also suffers from the physical nature and clear identity of the participants. In the sky, constellations don't always have the same appearance; nor do they appear the same way to all viewers. One viewer's Big Dipper is another's Big Bear. Some of the stars that I think of as constituting a single constellation may be split by another star gazer into two or more separate constellations. Even though generic communities clearly enjoy a physical as well as an imagined existence, they are for the most part nowhere near as identifiable or dependable as the members of an organized church. Nor are participants limited to a single generic community. The same individual may, at different times, be part of a screwball comedy community, a musical community, an exploitation community and a gay porn community.

The more appropriate image of generic communities would thus be a selective view of telespectators, all separate, and all facing in the same figurative direction – towards the screen – but implicitly broken into separate groups according to the programme they are watching, the way in which they are watching it, and the other spectators they imagine watching the same programme in the same way at the same time. Each viewer's version of this scene would be different, with a few known fellow spectators providing each constellation's fixed points, and an imagined community filling the interstices.

When genres are understood as a primary factor in unifying a constellated community, the very process of spectatorship becomes a symbolic method of communication with the other members of that community. By taking a particular type of film-viewing pleasure I imagine myself as connected to those who take a similar type of pleasure in similar circumstances. For some members of the community thus constituted, the films in question may sustain face-to-face encounters, but for many genre fans communication with other members of the community occurs only indirectly, through a common orientation towards the genre. If direct experience of a film involves what we might call *frontal communication*, exchanges between viewers of the same film or fans of the same genre may conveniently be termed *lateral communication*.

Considered in this manner, films are not just a content and a form transmitted by producers to consumers, they are also the medium of an additional mode of communication that groups of consumers carry out with each other. Showing that *Written on the Wind* (1956) took on different generic meanings when read by diverse groups, Barbara Klinger simultaneously implies that Sirk's film serves different communicative purposes for each of those groups. Even when seen in solitary confinement, far from the companionship of similar spectators, the process of viewing a film generically serves as symbolic communication with other spectators who read the film through the same generic lens.

Genres are commonly taken to come into being when a body of texts shares a sufficient number of semantic and syntactic elements. This *production-driven definition* needs to be matched by a *reception-driven definition* recognizing that genres do not exist until they become necessary to a lateral communication process, that is until they serve a constellated community. Only when knowledge that others are viewing similar films similarly becomes a fundamental part of the film-viewing experience does lateral communication exist; only then does viewing films generically become a method of commun(icat)ing with other genre film spectators.

Once genre spectatorship is recognized as an indirect mode of communication, the inadequacy of existing genres becomes apparent. As long as generic categories are determined by production patterns and critical concepts, the average genre user is under pressure simply to enter into an extremely broad, already constituted constellated community, corresponding to the definition previously provided by studios and critics. While millions of fans have been content to disappear into such broad and borrowed identities, others have banded together to rewrite the generic map. 'Fandom generates its own genres', affirms Henry Jenkins (1992, p. 279). During Hollywood's golden years, dozens of localized genres rivalled canonical categories. While these were often jump-started by a remark in the press or the existence of a supporting institution, they clearly ran counter to established industry practices.

The popular railroad genre, for example, included films (and other media) offering exterior shots of trains. Sustained by magazines, model train clubs, narrow-gauge railways and distributors of railroad paraphernalia, the railroad genre served as an imaginary meeting place for hundreds of thousands of spectators. Anyone who has seen Blackhawk's version of Griffith's *Lonedale Operator*, with its incessant intertitles describing the engine and the railroad operations depicted in the film, will understand just how radically railroad genre fans could reformulate a film according to alternative genre expectations.

A similar process – and similar constellated communities – underlie golden-age genres built around many other categories: musical styles (jazz films, including shorts and Soundies), technological innovations or limitations (sound films until sync sound became generalized, part-sound films around 1930, 3-D films in the 50s), social conventions (stag films, union films, all-black or biracial films), or the particularities of viewer identity ('tits-and-ass' wartime soldiers' favourites and films featuring handicapped characters, as well as regional, national or occupationally defined films). Since regular genre viewers have a vested interest in influencing their chosen generic language and corpus, the process of redefining genres never ceases.

The rise of television has intensified the genrification process. In collaboration with television programming practices and the music industry, Christian groups have established a de facto Christian genre, while others have combined multiple media in a country genre. Hamid Naficy (1989) has shown how manipulation of television programme flow in the 80s favoured creation of a 'nuclear family' genre, whereas 90s TV has worked hard to establish what we might call an 'alternatives to the family' genre (stressing non-family groupings in bars, police stations, apartment houses, and the like). The same logic extends to other television attempts to mandate or at least encourage constelled genres: the scheduling of election movies on election night, baseball movies after World Series games, and football documentaries after Monday Night Football.

While mass media participation clearly assists mightily in the constitution of any community, similar results may be had from academic, underground or cyberspace networks. Using the woman's film as both a real and figurative meeting place, feminist critics continually expanded its definition to assure maximum lateral communication and a broad constelled community. Circulating films privately and reading mainstream films in terms of shared interests, the gay community created a corpus of films that eventually proved too big for the closet. Using a campus film festival in support of the thesis advanced in his dissertation, Peter Lunenfeld (1994) attempted to rally Los Angeles fans around the bloody 'film rouge' genre. Others have championed a 'midwestern' genre (Privett, 1997), a 'transnational' film genre (Naficy, 1994), and a 'world cinema' genre (Roberts, 1995). With the advent of e-mail and the World Wide Web, it will be increasingly possible for potential communities to achieve actualization.

As the Web expands exponentially, daily spawning sites with generic potential, and as the fragmentation and personal control of modern media – from fax machines and citizen's band radios to cellular phones and e-mail – reduce the number of participants needed to create and maintain a community, one of the basic principles of generic life once again asserts itself: the smaller and narrower the group sustaining a particular genre and its associated constelled community, the weaker the power of that genre to embody significant human problems and solutions. What we might call 'private genres' have always existed: the films we saw together while we were dating, films containing pictures of X, films that support the theses of my dissertation, and so forth. The more private these categories, however, the less likely they are to sustain lateral communication, subtend a durable community, and thus pass the twin tests of time and space on which generic significance depends.

Constellated communities are difficult to maintain; while face-to-face meeting may be possible in the expanded folk world of academia, and direct address is increasingly facilitated by networked cyberspace, most constellated communities must operate by means of postmodern bricolage, turning whatever the media offer to the furthering of imagined communities. Whether viewers dissolve into already constituted communities, or develop their own alternative communities, genres continue to play an important role in the self-identification and communication processes necessary to maintaining a constellated community.

In today's world film genres are of course not the only vehicles for lateral communication or constellated communities. The very language we use, the clothes we wear, the purchases we make, the way we spend our leisure time all afford opportunities to express our alignment with others who speak, dress, consume or play in a similar manner. When my father first read a draft of this chapter, he protested that his film viewing was an entirely individual affair, and not the expression of some hidden community participation. Indeed, he may be right that film genres are not the vehicle of his particular mode of lateral communication. Yet the pleasure he takes in using language carefully and creatively clearly aligns him with an absent community of writers and speakers who still (his word) respect the English language. His spontaneous gift to me of David Crystal's *Cambridge Encyclopedia of the English Language* was a way of saying: 'See, this community does exist; there are people out there who still respect the language.' My father achieves self-expression through choice of a particular language genre, anchored in an absent community. My mother attains a similar goal through the type of purchases she makes. My nephew connects with an absent community through the choice of music that he listens to and plays on his drum set. The lateral communication system established by Hollywood cinema has now become a basic part of our culture.

Modern marketing methods work very hard indeed to establish the broad desirability of this or that soft drink or sports shoe. Ads pay less and less attention to the qualities of the product and more to the quality of its consumers, thus constituting an instant absent community for each potential purchaser. Richard Dyer (1981) has suggested that musicals give viewers a sense of what utopia might be like. With their emphasis on a community of contented consumers, today's advertisements offer viewers a particular sense of utopia, by giving them an instant sense of what belonging might be like. In fact, the ad implies, that sense of belonging can be replicated at any time for the price of the advertised product. People used to be concerned to keep up with the Joneses, who lived down the street; now they aspire to take part in a 'community' known only through the media. Madison Avenue's ability to imply the existence of an absent constellated community further reinforces the importance of lateral communication as a quintessential modern mode, even though the communication and the community alike may be more implied than real.

How spectators use genres

The two preceding chapters outlined ways in which producers, exhibitors and critics use generic texts, generic terminology and the very notion of genre to serve their (shifting) purposes. This chapter has analysed instead the varied ways in which spectators use genres and genre films to satisfy their own needs. Of course, the notion of a clear separation between user groups and generic functions can never be anything more than a fiction, since producers systematically pander to viewer needs and spectators find ways to serve their own purposes even with texts designed to serve other groups' goals.

Several general conclusions may be drawn from the analyses presented in this chapter:

1. Even though genre films commonly conclude by a return to cultural norms, genre spectators typically seek (and find) in genre films some sort of counter-cultural pleasure.
2. Genre films are structured as a series of 'generic crossroads', each proposing an alternative between continued generic pleasure (based on counter-cultural character activity) and cessation of generic pleasure (due to cessation of counter-cultural activity).
3. According to the principle of 'generic economy', genre spectator pleasure is increased by the escalating distance between cultural and counter-cultural alternatives.
4. Returning to a culturally sanctioned position, the *in extremis* reversal characteristic of genre films produces further spectator pleasure while folding spectators back into cultural norms.
5. The counter-cultural commitments involved in generic spectatorship create an invisible bond among fans of the same genre.
6. Membership in the resultant 'constellated community' surrounding each genre constitutes an important source of spectator pleasure.
7. Genres thus serve indirectly as a form of 'lateral communication' among constellated community members.

This view of genre varies so enormously from received notions that it is doubtful whether current communication models can adequately support it. The next chapter considers whether an alternative model might be necessary.

10
What communication model is appropriate for genres?

> Lasswell . . . argues that to understand the processes of mass communication we need to study each of the stages in his model:
> *Who*
> Says *what*
> In *which channel*
> To *whom*
> With *what effect?*
> This . . . model . . . sees communication as the transmission of messages. . . . Most mass-communication research has implicitly followed this model.
>
> John Fiske, *Introduction to Communication Studies* (1990, pp. 30–1)

In the previous chapters I have painted a picture of genre(s) that varies signifi-cantly from traditional notions. Claiming that genres actively signify, function and reinforce solidarity for diverse constituencies, I have stressed the transactional process whereby conflict and negotiation among user groups constantly trans-form generic designations. On the production side, we have discovered that genres are not produced in the straightforward manner of texts; instead, their very exist-ence depends on a complex conflation of studio cycle creation, exhibitor multi-generic advertising appeals and critics' reductive labelling practices. On the reception side, we have noted that generic spectatorship is always implicitly a group affair, even when – perhaps especially when – group members are separated or unknown to each other.

One unfortunate result of these conclusions is that genres can no longer be considered according to the romantic model that has dominated literary study for the last two centuries. In a world where poems and novels were both written and read by solitary individuals, it perhaps made sense to consider literature as a per-sonal affair, but collaborative confection and consumption of genres clearly precludes such an understanding. To our frustration, we lack an appropriate model for thinking about generic reception. It will be the task of this chapter to construct such a model.

The four-hoot call of the barred owl
The final section of Chapter 9 detailed the importance of generic communities to the process of genre reception. In order to build a model around the interpersonal implications of this process, however, we need to know considerably more about its mechanisms. In order to tease out important aspects of the generic reading process, I will begin with an example apparently distant from the realm of film genre. I beg the reader's indulgence for this allegorical strategy.

When students write dissertations, they often seek out quiet and isolation. One of my advisees might very well have written me a letter like this one from his hideaway in the north woods.

Dear Rick,
This place is truly gorgeous. In fact, I've become quite a bird watcher. At first I thought it would be interesting to walk around the woods and look at all the trees, but I couldn't tell one from the other. Then I found an old bird book in my cabin. That really started me going. Now I sort of specialize in owls. Did you know that all owls are divided into two families? In one family there are the barn owls, with heart-shaped faces, while all other owls fall into a second family. Say, I'll bet you didn't know that the barred owl has a four-hoot call.

Since I started I've seen at least three of the famous spotted owls. But my high point as a bird watcher came one day when I was testing out the new binoculars that I ordered from a special bird-watcher catalogue. On one owl I was able to read the numbers on a metal leg band – 147622. I asked around a little bit and finally discovered somebody who's a member of the Audubon Society. She called in and found that the bird I saw was a three-year-old snowy owl that had been banded in Alaska last year sometime, and seen since in Washington and Idaho.

When I first started, I couldn't tell the difference between a male screech owl and a female great horned owl. Now I go down to Great Falls every now and then to meet with a bird watchers group. In fact, the high point of my month is when my bird-watching magazine arrives. I sure have learned a lot about birds. Believe it or not, Sharon and I have even taken to telling each other bird stories over supper!

I don't want you to think I'm not working on my thesis. I'm sure that by the end of *this* summer I'll have a draft of the whole thing ready.

Jim

In spite of the natural beauty of the trees around him, Jim ended up paying far more attention to the birds nesting in them. Whereas the trees remained undifferentiated, little by little the birds took on identities that made them seem more worthy of consideration. What once had been just plain 'birds' became identifiably different species of owls. Concurrently, Jim's interest in owls began to overflow the woods where he actually observed owls, invading other portions of his life. Several expenses were occasioned by his new passion. Jim happily spent time learning about bird species and telling supper-time stories; he spent money on dedicated equipment and specialized magazines; he spent energy contacting other birdwatchers.

Since two players clearly dominate this model – Jim as subject and the owl as object – it apparently makes sense to represent, remember and configure this case as the simple story of Jim's increasing interest in owls. A closer look reveals more than two players, however. In addition to Jim and his owls, the story also mentions or implies the following components:

- the old bird book found by Jim in his cabin (along with those responsible for the book's classifications);
- the catalogue from which Jim bought his binoculars (along with those who wrote and supplied it);
- the environmentalists who made spotted owls famous;
- leg band no. 147622 (and the person who attached it);
- the people who saw the same snowy owl in Washington and Idaho and reported it to the Audubon Society;

- the member of the Audubon Society whom Jim met;
- the Audubon members who keep bird-banding records;
- the Great Falls bird watchers with whom Jim meets;
- the bird-watching magazine subscribed to by Jim;
- Jim's supper-mate Sharon and their bird stories.

As this list makes clear, Jim is hardly alone with the owls. On the contrary, if he showed interest in birds at all, it is because he was by chance exposed to descriptive, evaluative and classificatory statements that made him distinguish between trees and birds. Though beautiful and majestic, trees offered Jim so little intellectual satisfaction and so few opportunities to meet others that he eventually found them uninteresting. At first blush, birds would seem to offer even less incentive. Whereas trees can be counted on to stay put, birds are notoriously elusive and difficult to observe. But Jim found in birds two intriguing characteristics that he had by chance not discovered in trees: not only are they categorizable, but behind those dry categories lies an extensive human community. Instead of configuring this story around two fundamental players, Jim and the owls, we must make room for a third instance, those who lift birds out of the forest's anonymity, thus becoming part of the community that sustains Jim's bird-watching.

The presence of this third group of players changes Jim's experience in an important way. When Jim looked at trees, he never saw anything but trees. When Jim looks at birds, however, he also implicitly sees the activity of an absent bird-watching community. This symbolic presence does not require the material reminder of a bird band, for it is imbedded in Jim's very viewing activity. As Jim assesses the shape of an owl's face, looking for the familiar heart shape of barn owls, he carries with him the baggage of his bird book, and thus a whole community of bird-watchers, illustrators and categorizers. Even the simple process of naming birds rehearses an earlier naming and illustrating process, thus symbolically bringing Jim into the presence of bird-loving naturalists all the way back to Audubon.

Concretized by the Great Falls bird-watchers, his Audubon Society contact, and his supper partner Sharon, Jim's bird-watching community may depend to a certain extent on face-to-face contact, but it certainly doesn't disappear just because the members of that community are physically absent. On the contrary, Jim's bird-watching community is crystallized and deposited on the surface of every bird-watching experience. Through bird-watching lore (terminology, stories, illustrations, paraphernalia), and through Jim's repetition of activities previously engaged in by others, Jim's bird-watching colleagues remain symbolically present to him in the form of a remembered, imagined, constellated community. If Jim finds birds interesting, it is precisely because they have become more than just birds; they are now the conduit through which Jim maintains regular contact with an absent community. The birds have become signs of the constellated community.

Genres operate in a similar manner. Until viewers gain some knowledge of genres, films are like trees: wonderful and interesting, but differentiated only by personal observation. The very process of learning about a genre necessarily changes that configuration twice over. Not only does genre knowledge modify our perception of individual films, but it also creates a more or less powerful bond with a part-real, part-imagined group of genre viewers. While genre experience must necessarily pass through the phenomenological process of actually perceiving individual films, film viewing is not the ultimate measure of genre power. A genre's strength depends far more heavily on the vigour of the generic community, which in turn depends on the way in which a genre is represented and reinforced in the society at large (or in a specific subset of that society). The intensity of Jim's bird-watching activity derives both from the possibility of face-to-face contacts reinforcing his birding interests, and from a complex support system recalling or simply suggesting the existence of real community members even when they are absent.

Genre-viewing pleasure grows out of quite similar processes. Established genres suggest the existence of a generic community through decades of critical texts, graphic representations and residual products (Western styles, sheet music and records, gangster accents, and the like). Traditional genres are so good at this process that little face-to-face interaction is needed to coat genre viewing with a heavy imagined-community layer (as demonstrated by foreign emulation of the styles and language popularized by American genres). Stabilization of most new genres, on the contrary, requires regular face-to-face or indirect (for example, Internet) reinforcement, as does the reconfiguration of established genres according to the interests of a current real-world community (women's film, gay cinema, many experimental film genres). Whether established and content to project a broad but largely imagined community, or new and dependent on nearby evidence that others share a similar generic viewpoint, genres always subtend some form of community.

Before leaving Jim and the north woods, we need to recognize a further similarity between bird-watching and film-viewing. In both cases, there is a strong tendency to confuse the absent authors responsible for establishing bird categories and film genres with the present community members who rehearse them. Just as the continuity between John James Audubon and current Audubon Society members hardly justifies their equation, so the radical power difference between film critics and genre fans should preclude slippage between the two categories. Yet the process of genre community constitution is so carefully hidden behind the commercial practices of journalistic critics, clothing designers, toy manufacturers, radio and television broadcasters and the publishers of everything from books and music to comics and video games, that genre viewers understandably fail to see how these commercial interests inform the face-to-face community buttressing generic reading practices. In this sense, the term 'community' is most certainly misleading, for it implies both an equality and a non-commercial nature belied by actual practice. Indeed, it is precisely the community-like nature of face-to-face genre contact that makes genres appear so benign, thus making it possible for commercial and ideological intent to pass unnoticed.

Modelling generic communication

For centuries, with very few exceptions, a single model has dominated our understanding of the communication process. Though major differences separate

Aristotle, Roman Jakobson and Stuart Hall, by and large they share a two-party model clearly indebted to face-to-face communication situations. According to this model, a single sender communicates directly with a single receiver, as represented in Figure 10.1.

Figure 10.1

This frontal configuration has so dominated serious study of the communication process that non-face-to-face communication situations have simply been grafted on to the face-to-face model.

In spite of the fact that it is in certain ways diametrically opposed to face-to-face communication, mediated communication is commonly figured as a simple variation on the face-to-face model. As represented in Figure 10.2, the disseminating medium is typically located like some vast distorting lens between the sender and the receiver.

Figure 10.2

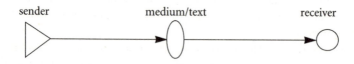

Of course, most users of this model recognize that it is only a convenient reduction of a more comprehensive broadcasting model, according to which a sender may simultaneously address multiple receivers. The broadcasting model is schematically represented in Figure 10.3.

Figure 10.3

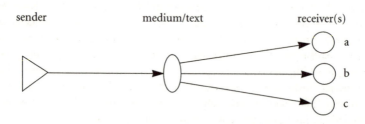

This more complete version reveals the previous models' limitations. When communication is assumed to take place one receiver at a time, in the form of separate *frontal* communications, it is difficult to account for relationships between receivers sharing the same text. This is especially important for the process of genre viewing, which depends so heavily on *lateral* communication among members of the reception community.

Figure 10.4

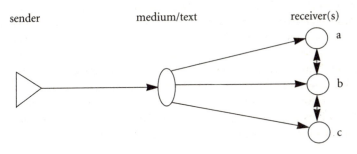

sender   medium/text   receiver(s)

Our model needs to include not only a multiplicity of receivers, but also the many interactions among them, as represented in Figure 10.4.

Substituting a T-shaped configuration for the familiar straight-line approach, and a triadic arrangement (sender–receiver–fellow receiver) for the traditional dyad (sender–receiver), this model captures direct relationships among receivers, but it fails to recognize either the role of imagined connections to other members of the generic community, or the role of genre viewing in prompting that imagination. Somehow, our model needs to take into account the fact that genres depend at least as heavily on constellated communities as they do on face-to-face contact.

Do birds or films announce 'I am a spotted owl'? or 'I am a musical'? On the contrary, birds and films simply provide opportunities for viewers to reactivate the discourse of the absent speakers who first defined the characteristics of spotted owls and musicals, as well as those whose continued viewing implicitly reinforces that definition. That is, frontal sources like owls and films offer a medium through which we can be addressed (or imagine we are being addressed) by lateral speakers. When we use the term 'discourse' in connection with films, we are usually referring to the frontal relationship that films entertain with their spectators, but the concept of lateral communication requires recognition of a second type of discursivity. We may conveniently label traditional discursivity 'primary', while the type of discursivity associated with lateral communication may be termed 'secondary'. *Primary discursivity* describes the spectator's relationship to the film; *secondary discursivity* addresses the spectator's relationship to other spectators.

As we saw in Chapter 9, Hollywood is particularly adept at using secondary discursive appeals to attract viewers, especially in connection with generic logic and audiences. Treating constellated communities as sources of comfort for individual viewers, the film industry has long done everything possible to imply that a given film will maximize isolated viewers' symbolic integration into a larger and much-valued audience. Sometimes, Hollywood's use of secondary discursivity even takes on the nature of a conscious campaign. For example, Jay Beck has shown that Paramount built its massive 1937 *Life* magazine ad campaign entirely around secondary discursive appeals. Yet in *Variety* Paramount continued to emphasize the more traditional primary discursivity, clearly assuming that distributors and exhibitors are less concerned with questions of community than are 'individual' spectators.

Secondary discursivity is important to genre because it anchors the dispersed communities characteristic of generic viewing. Indeed, the continued existence of constellated communities directly depends on secondary discursivity, that is on the ability of generic texts to imply or reflect the existence of absent community members and thus serve as a symbolic community meeting place. Somehow we need to take account of the fact that for some spectators genre films become signs of other spectators, even when (especially when?) the two groups never meet. Figure 10.5 offers a graphic representation of the reflection process that makes it possible for viewers to communicate with each other indirectly.

Figure 10.5

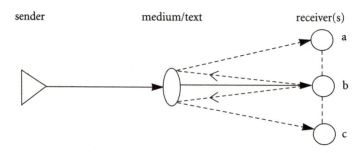

As Figure 10.5 suggests, the complexity of the situation derives from the medium's ability simultaneously to refract and reflect, to express the concerns not only of the original author but also of the constellated community that repurposes and redefines the genre.

Doubly authored, genres depend both on the encoding practices of an obvious sender and on the decoding recipes of a dispersed reception community. 'To count as communication,' affirms Eric Rothenbuhler, 'something must be read as if it were written' (1995, p. 9). To count as generic communication, however, something must be read as if it were *twice written*, first by the original authors and then again by the constellated community that 'rewrites' the genre. In this final model there are actually two superimposed communication processes, frontal and lateral. The genre text offers a double site of communication: (a) between the original producer and the film's spectators and (b) among members of the constellated community understood both as authors of the film's ability to signify the existence of other community members, and as readers of the signs thus constituted.

No wonder genre theorists have long debated whether genres are ideological constructs delivered from above or ritual experiences confected by audiences. Though an individual film may have a single (albeit usually collaborative) author, genres always depend on decoding practices shared by a broad if dispersed community. This double authorship prompts genres to lay claim simultaneously to both positions, both ideological and ritual. Only through conversion from a frontal, dyadic, straight-line communication model to a lateral, triadic, T-shaped model can these aspects of generic operation be brought to the surface.

Saussure revisited

The communication model sketched out in the previous section radically uncouples generic understanding from studio intentions. While the film industry may take its own advantage of generic formations, it never fully controls them because it always shares genre authorship with a disparate, shifting and elusive array of viewing communities. Earlier sections of this book have shown not only that genres are permanently in process and that multiple contradictory generic configurations regularly coexist, but also that generic evolution directly depends on those coexistent contradictions.

Why are individual films so regularly labelled differently, especially during periods of genre unrest and redefinition? Why is it that genres are so often defined diversely by disparate users? How is it even possible, theoretically speaking, that the same texts should give rise to radically diverse generic categories? In one sense, this question embodies the basic postmodern challenge to traditional semiotics. On one side the beleaguered semioticians have simply reinforced their trenches, claiming that cinema or literature or daily life constitutes a coherent system with rules that can be analysed and understood. They have been increasingly attacked by a generation of critics armed with evidence of diverse reception and out to prove that no such overriding system exists. A single coherent system would not produce fundamentally different constructions, the postmodern logic reasons; *ergo*, no single coherent system exists.

What is at stake here is nothing less than the very notion of system. Based in Saussurean linguistics, the notion of system has been treated by many current thinkers as both utterly necessary and absolutely compromised – necessary because reasoned communication seems to require the sharability and consistency characteristic of systems; compromised because every attempt to describe such a system ironically generates evidence of inconsistency, miscommunication and thus a distinct lack of sharability. While this problem is far too large to address here in all its complexity, genres may have something useful to contribute. A rapid look at this question will also provide an opportunity to expand the communication model presented in the previous section.

Distinguishing between *langue* or language system, and *parole* or individual utterance, Saussure built his linguistics on the assumption that any given speech act is simply a specific application of the overall language system. The adjective 'overall' is key here. According to Saussure's notion of system, language is larger than any given individual; nobody can possibly know the language completely, yet what we apply when we speak is an overall language system. Language operates differentially, Saussure affirms; that is, any specific utterance can make meaning only by comparison to the other utterances permitted by the system in that particular context. This Olympian view makes sense for linguists, who happily take on the responsibility of transcending their own individuality in favour of a broader description. Yet it is precisely attention to individual viewpoints that might have preserved Saussurean linguistics from dwelling exclusively on systems so large that they remain fundamentally irrelevant for most textual applications.

For a moment, let us dwell not on Saussure's theories of language as a whole, but instead on his descriptions of the way understanding takes place (and by extension, the way systems are built). Simplifying somewhat, we may say that the entire Saussurean system rests on two distinctions: the opposition of syntagma to paradigm, and the difference between language levels (labelled phonemic and morphemic by Martinet and others working in the Saussurean tradition). While these oppositions remain quite static in nature, a dynamic impulse is provided by the notion of commutation, which involves a constant shifting between levels, all the while assessing the differences made at one level by changes in another. Individuals learn what counts as a syntagmatic unit, what is contained within a paradigm, and what sounds have what meaning by virtue of the ability to go back and forth from the level of sounds to the level of meaning, each time implicitly assessing the context in which particular combinations of sound are used and the effects of changing sounds, phonemes or morphemes.

Suppose we were to substitute for Saussure's emphasis on *langue* – the overall language system – a notion of language based instead on *parole* and the commutation process through which individual speech acts are assessed by real language users. Whereas a *langue*-based linguistics assumes a single stable system, a *parole*-based understanding of language would at first concentrate instead on an ongoing system-learning process, since each new utterance potentially opens the way, through commutation, to new conclusions about the way the language is constructed. If we were to take the time to compare the learning achieved by several different language users, we would soon note that, contrary to expectation, they are not reaching the same conclusions about the language.

Instead of finding that language users take different paths to learning the same system, we would find that the difference in paths actually leads individuals to practise differing systems, all nevertheless designated by the same language name. Instead of *learning* a single pre-existing system, we must conclude, these language users are *building* multiple different systems. Rejecting Saussure's totalizing notion of system, but adopting his commutative, layered model of system construction, we would be equipped to understand language conceived as a large number of competing systems-in-process. Saussure makes everyone a teacher with constant access to a complete textbook. I suggest that we instead imagine a classroom full of students, each one learning something slightly different.

If *langue* is a fiction, unknowable and unknown, and if everyone's understanding of the language is dependent instead on a different selection of *paroles*, then we must all speak slightly different languages, since the speech acts on which different people's knowledge depends cannot possibly be the same. While we may share many perceptions about the language – and to that extent the language appears to operate like a fully Saussurean language system – other perceptions vary according to language users' experience with the language. Since everyone's analysis is based on different examples, and thus on different partial knowledge, every word must vary slightly when spoken or understood by different users. What we call communication, then, is actually in part miscommunication. Instead of a single language system, there are always a very large number of slightly different overlapping language-systems-in-the-making.

Conceived as what Jurij Lotman calls 'secondary modeling systems', literary or cinematic texts forged out of verbal or graphic languages have repeatedly been treated as using those primary languages to build a textual system in much the same way that language systems are built out of sounds or other primary materials. Based on a totalizing language system model, however, attempts to apply Saussurean logic to literature and film never fulfilled their promise and have largely been abandoned by post-structuralist, post-semiotic and post-modernist theoreticians. If we were to abandon overall systems in favour of continued system-building, however, the Saussurean model would not only become more viable, it would offer answers to several troublesome questions.

Having learnt meanings of a word like 'chair' by commuting the givens of daily life and language, viewers approach genre concepts similarly. But they don't necessarily all reach the same conclusion. Whereas one group of viewers may have learnt about Westerns by viewing singing cowboy films and reading the popular press of the 30s, another group may accomplish the same task while reading recent film theory and viewing *The Searchers, The Wild Bunch, The Shootist, Once Upon a Time in the West* and *Unforgiven*. While these two groups may well share terminology, they will not actually be using the same words to designate the same phenomena. In fact, because there is little to anchor generic commutation other than critical statements that rarely reach any more than a small percentage of the genre public, genre definitions remain inconsistent even among fans. While scholars and encyclopedists strive to eradicate contradictions, such differences necessarily constitute a basic component of genre reception.

How it works in practice

Imagine a rectangular space made up of millions of dots, equidistant but with slight differences in size and shape. Experience has taught us that this dot matrix may hold meaning, but how do we establish meaning? It would be nice to be able to fully analyse this array as traditional Saussurean semiotics recommends, but none of us has the time, the memory or the analytical capacity to take into account all possible commutations. At first most of us would probably attend to pretty much the same concerns, commonly practised in our culture: similarity of dot shape and size, horizontal or vertical continuity, and other familiar configurations. Subsequently, however, our understanding of this rectangular array of dots might well be inflected by the shapes and objects we see juxtaposed to it – triangles and diagonals, letters and numbers, patterns based on the spaces rather than the dots – along with the incentives we might have to process the dots in a particular manner (perhaps because we are being paid or indirectly compensated for constructing a particular type of meaning). However we connect the dots this time, we will surely roll that experience into our next dot-reading exercise.

Now imagine that the dots are the grain that makes up a film image, or the pixels that constitute a television picture. While the complexity of these rectangular

The dynamic dimension of genre grows precisely out of these differences. While some viewers may be convinced of the need to define a given genre in one way, others will have come in contact with quite dissimilar 'generic speech acts' and thus will see both texts and genre in a different manner entirely. Only through inconsistencies of this type can a genre be redefined through one of its subsets, thus giving rise to a new genre. It is precisely because there are no master systems but only diverse system-building paths that new generic categories remain constantly possible.

Even within an overall atmosphere of imprecision, difference and contradiction, however, varying levels of agreement among viewers are possible. Just as the

arrays may seem overwhelming, we still make sense of them by the methods described above; meaning still depends on several broadly shared or personal reading patterns and the need for incentives to energize the interpretation process. Of particular interest here is a modest but challenging question: how can the same array support multiple different readings by diverse groups or at differing points in time?

The biopic provides a simple but elegant example. Whatever broadly shared interpretive processes *Disraeli* may have engaged in 1929, subsequent films starring George Arliss offered alternative models for reading the Warner Bros blockbuster: through juxtaposition, *The Green Goddess* made it a British colonial film; *Old English* made it a period pecuniary drama; *The Millionaire* made it a madcap financial comedy. In each case, the new Arliss film provided the material necessary for a quite predictable Saussurean commutation process. Setting film B (or C, or D) next to film A can have the effect of guiding the commutable material to which real spectators with limited analytical capacity will actually attend. *Old English* implicitly says 'Test *Disraeli* to discover whether financial manipulation is meaningful'. Quietly we imagine *Disraeli* with and without financial shenanigans (in an informal but effective version of the commutation test), and conclude that they are important at a higher level of analysis, that is, that they are essential to the overall meaning of the film. Roughly speaking, this is how contemporary viewers were at one point convinced to interpret *Disraeli* as a financial drama.

Though Warners' Disraeli (1929) may now appear to us as a biopic, it took a protracted historical process to bring that category to the surface.

But what about *Alexander Hamilton*, *Voltaire* and films without Arliss, such as Warners' own *Pasteur* and *Zola*? Implicitly,

176

Audubon Society offers a support network guaranteeing shared terminology and attitudes among bird-watchers, so studio and critical discourse, along with face-to-face contact among viewers, stabilizes generic assessment and assures a certain similarity of terminology and corpus building among genre fans. In fact, the very process of recognizing and naming genres is an important method of stabilizing generic 'languages'. As we saw earlier, viewers cannot consume films generically without activating and thus reinforcing terms and concepts borrowed from other genre viewers. It is precisely for this reason that genre viewing infallibly invokes an absent like-minded audience. This constellated community thus specifically reflects both the viewer's alienation from anything that might claim to be an over-

every film – as well as every critical term – considered along with *Disraeli* may initiate a new commutation process, but only when the conclusions about that process are generally shared and consecrated by formulaic production and critical vocabulary will a new genre emerge. It took millions of commutation operations concentrating on the biography of eccentric but successful public figures to replace perceptions of *Disraeli* as financial drama, dizzy comedy or diplomatic romance with a clear and durable image of *Disraeli* as biopic.

It is tempting to end the story here: a shared commutation process has established the repeated importance of certain textual characteristics and patterns, thus constituting a genre. In one sense such a hiatus is entirely justifiable, since once a genre is formed and supported both by repeated production and critical vocabulary, the commutation process becomes automatized. Instead of effecting the cluster of commutations associated with the biopic genre only after many years and on a trial-and-error basis, most viewers begin to accept the biopic pattern as a shared schema called for by certain arrays of dots.

While this automatization could theoretically last forever, many influences militate against permanence. Consider the importance of television commercials, news and safety messages for anchoring our perception of genre films' counter-cultural investment (see Chapter 9). While this institution currently supports the genres that we know, as do many other texts regularly juxtaposed to the films we see (toys, games, clothing styles and other elements of fashion, but also sports, news and even politics), there is every reason to believe that changes in these supporting institutions can eventually transform genres massively or even wipe them out entirely.

In order to understand how genres develop as they do, why some take longer to reach fruition than others, and why different spectator groups emphasize diverse genres, we must analyse the texts and terms successively brought into contact with those genres and those spectators, thereby assessing the types and range of material commuted by particular spectators with regard to specific films and sets of films. In this way we can make simultaneous sense of a situation that at one point looks like a fully shared system and yet at other times seems to depend entirely on individual perception. This versatility can be assured only by a *parole*-based semiotics.

arching master system, and the limited relief derived from localized and partial agreement on the meaning of individual 'genre utterances'. In short, lack of absolute assurance or accuracy both in defining genres and in expressing their meaning simultaneously establishes the need for generic constellated communities and the context within which those communities can be established.

A new communication model

Although this chapter is insufficient to fully justify and construct an entirely new model of the communication process, it has suggested a number of directions that must be considered by anyone who would build a discursive communication model consistent with the approach to genre developed here.

1. Because they are doubly authored, once by the original producer and then again by a genrifying instance, genre texts require a model recognizing both primary and secondary discursivity.
2. A complete communication model must adequately represent the superimposition of two signifying systems, frontal and lateral.
3. While one of these signifying systems may be said to operate according to familiar linear principles, the process whereby spectators turn texts into signs of absent imagined spectators requires separate recognition, lest communication among constellated community members be excluded from the model.
4. The multi-level configuration of Saussurean semiotics, along with the notion of commutation, may conveniently be pressed into service as a model to describe spectator processing of textual material.
5. In order to respect individual and historical variation, however, the emphasis on an overarching language system (*langue*) must be abandoned in favour of the *parole*-oriented aspects of Saussure's model.
6. Differential commutation, whether based on individual, group, or historical differences, may be invoked to explain both generic durability and generic fluctuation.
7. Recognition of the role played by criticism and other cultural institutions in stabilizing and destabilizing generic and other forms of communication is a necessary aspect of an adequate communication model.

Rather than conclusions, these seven statements should be considered as principles, as food for the thought of anyone who would share my temerity in revisiting such basic and important questions. In a sense, they constitute one logical conclusion of a book-length reflection, but I prefer to see these hypotheses as the beginning of what I hope will be an even longer reflection by other theorists concerned about these very general problems.

11
Have genres and genre functions changed over time?

> If all philosophy is a footnote to Plato, then all genre theory is little more than a footnote to Aristotle. The current tendency to figure genres transhistorically simply extends Aristotle's intention to note the *essential* quality of each poetic kind. It is precisely the notion that genres have essential qualities that makes it possible to align them with archetypes and myths and to treat them as expressive of broad and perdurable human concerns.
>
> Rick Altman, *Film/Genre* (1999, p. 20)

One of the most attractive aspects of genre as a critical category is its broad applicability. Not only have genre terms withstood a multi-millennial test of time, but the same generic labels are regularly deployed across multiple media. Over the course of centuries, genres have taken on such a passkey role that cultural critics who wouldn't think of applying Gay Nineties terminology to a Roaring Twenties phenomenon readily evoke Aristotle or neoclassical genre usage in support of Hollywood film study. Of all the critical concepts applied to cinema, genre is perhaps the only one that regularly escapes history. Individual genre studies may not always be oblivious to historical concerns (though many are), but while detailing a genre's internal development genre histories typically fail to ask a broader but no less important series of questions. Does the word 'genre' itself mean the same thing when used by Aristotle and Zanuck, by Boileau and Linda Williams? Do film genres function like literary genres? Do twentieth-century genres have the same purpose as earlier genres? Unaskable from within the analysis of a particular film genre, these questions can only be asked by a broad study, such as this book, devoted to the problem of film genre in general.

In this chapter I will forward the unexpected claim that generic functions have indeed changed over time. Taken as a whole, consumer genres do not operate quite like classical genres. The (neo)classical genres of choice were epic, tragedy and comedy, while melodrama, adventure and romance are the film genres of choice. Why does the range of prevalent genres change with the rise of the mass media? What function does this generic drift play in the overall generic economy? Genres are deployed differently by diverse user groups; producers, exhibitors, critics and spectators all have their own purposes for using generic constructs and terminology. If genre were an unchanging, transhistorical category, then we might expect consistency among genre users; instead we find that film genres are deployed differently from their predecessors. How do these changes impact the very meaning of the term genre in the modern world? Has the development of mechanical reproduction had the same effect on genre that it has had on other aspects of representation?

The neoclassical nature of standard genre theory

Over the last century, most treatises on genre have based their claims on what we might loosely label neoclassical genre practice. As we saw in Chapter 1, neoclassicism considered literary composition to be circumscribed by Aristotelian and Horatian critical norms. Production thus proceeded by imitation of recognized generic models. Labelling their products generically, neoclassical authors successfully communicated with an audience trained by public institutions in the interpretation of genre terminology. Within this system, genres were considered as transhistorical categories defined by dead critics. Authors don't create genres, according to this viewpoint, they only deploy already existing genres as a model for composition and as a method of instructing audiences. Audiences don't create genres either, but they do have to learn about them in order to understand what they are being told by authors.

It is precisely this critic-to-author-to-audience model of generic functionality that has been adopted by canonical genre theory. Treated as fixed signifiers, genres are primarily seen in terms of their dual production purposes: to provide a blueprint for the creation of art works and a language to explain them to audiences. Since the critics of the past have already accomplished the task of defining genres, today's critics are restricted to the role of secondary commentator or educator, either refining our notion of what Aristotle, Horace and their successors really said, or training each new generation to understand genre terminology properly. Imaging genre as flowing directly from critic to author to audience, this neoclassically inspired model stresses what I have called primary discursivity.

If neoclassical literary practice were our only example of generic usage, then this straight-line, production-oriented, primary discursive model might seem justified. However, three separate factors combine to argue both for a broader understanding of genre in general and for recognition that generic functions have changed significantly with the break-up of the social, economic and political structures subtending the neoclassical system:

- a theoretical critique of the neoclassical model's straight-line nature;
- historical changes in the nature of audience identity and the importance accorded by society to audiences in general;
- the long-term effect of important modifications in distribution modes.

Together, these elements suggest not only an expanded and more versatile notion of generic operation, but also a significant shift in the overall function of genres since neoclassical times.

The neoclassical view of history was always foreclosed on both ends; as such it actually negated the very possibility of history. Aristotle and Horace were not seen as thinking men reacting to situations that preceded them; instead, they were treated as the origin of thoughts that lacked a real history. Similarly, a world that simply perpetuated configurations defined by the ancients could have no true history. This pattern served the neoclassical system well, not just generically but politically and economically too, by assuring continued reproduction of the conditions necessary for successful power management. In this pre-revolutionary era, women were not created equal, but valued differentially. Like the King's word, the decision of the ancients was taken as final and omnipotent. Like the serfs, the generic public was restricted to thoughts authorized by their superiors and their education.

At the height of the system, late in the French seventeenth century, an initial critique of the neoclassical model gave rise to a public debate labelled the 'Quarrel of the Ancients and the Moderns'. While such conservatives as Boileau declared the wisdom of the ancients sufficient for modern needs, free spirits like Charles Perrault sought to empower his contemporaries by asserting that a new era needs new thoughts. For Perrault's modern camp, the claims of the much-revered ancients were necessarily marked by their bygone time and deserved to be evaluated according to modern needs. Though generic concerns were hardly touched by this famous quarrel, the modern position has important ramifications for genre questions.

Conservative thinkers saw a fundamental difference between Aristotle and contemporary audiences, the ancient Greek being styled as a speaker while Frenchmen were reduced to listening. Instead of splitting humanity into speakers and listeners, lords and serfs, the modern camp recognized a fundamental commonality among all people. Providing the basic theory that would lead to the Revolution a century later, the moderns refused to accept the notion that free speech had been once and for all curtailed by the authority of the ancients. Whereas the conservatives saw contemporary spectators as listening only, the moderns sought to endow all people with the right of speech, thereby implicitly equating the least modern spectator with the mighty Aristotle.

The theoretical importance of this position – and its continued modernity – become apparent when translated into the encoding/decoding terminology of Stuart Hall (1980). Hall categorizes the various types of decoding strategies that readers perform in reaction to the encoding of literary texts. Dividing the world into two mutually exclusive groups, Hall unconsciously replicates the neoclassical system whereby the ancients encode and all others are reduced to decoding. The moderns recognized that all encoding results from decoding (Aristotle is of necessity reacting to the specificity of his times, which were different from ours), and that decoders may themselves become encoders simply by speaking and enacting their own times. Splitting the world into fixed classes of encoders and decoders implicitly perpetuates the neoclassical neglect of history and with it the neoclassical power structure, in spite of Hall's apparent emphasis on resistant decoding strategies. By contrast, recognition of the universal right both to listen and to speak undermines neoclassical inequalities and restores a true sense of history, where every generation defines the world anew rather than permanently replicating a predefined pattern.

Though I have approached this problem historically, it clearly involves a clash between two fundamental theoretical models, whose differences may be perceived most clearly through graphic representation. The straight-line neoclassical system works as follows:

Figure 11.1

| ancient critics | - - - - - - - -> | producers | - - - - - - - -> | modern spectators |
| (encoders, speakers) | | (conforming to the ancients' rules) | | (decoders, listeners) |

Repeated over and over again, this pattern lends nobility and power to the genres prescribed by the ancients, but predefines spectator reaction to the point of disenfranchisement. Leaving out producers temporarily for the sake of clarity, the model implicitly adopted by the moderns looks quite different:

Figure 11.2

```
------> ancient
        decoders ------> ancient
                encoders ------> modern
                        decoders ------> modern
                                encoders ------>
```

With the continuous process implied by this model, the very terms 'ancient' and 'modern' no longer seem appropriate. As Stendhal's romantic rallying cry would eventually put it, all classical authors were romantics in their time. All 'ancients' were just the moderns of an earlier day. All encoders were once decoders; all decoders are potential encoders.

Just as this new model destabilizes previous notions regarding the separateness of speaking and listening classes, so it radically complicates the function of production within the system. Neoclassical producers were considered as craftsmen who learnt the rules and then produced careful imitations of the ancients. From a generic point of view, they could be counted on to respect existing principles and canons. The modern approach makes producers – like everyone else – into a complex combination of listener and speaker, imitator and creator, decoder and encoder.

Audience or 'audience'?

Not until the age of revolutions and the rise of romanticism did the principles debated in the Quarrel of the Ancients and the Moderns begin to affect genre directly. New production practices led the way, not only as an extension of the celebrated romantic love for mixed genres, but also through the development of such new genres as melodrama, the fairy tale, the folk song, the gothic novel, the short story and the prose poem. Anxious to liberate literary production, the romantics proclaimed artists' freedom to follow their inspiration wherever it might lead. But even the romantics never went so far as to consider the role that readers and spectators might play in the development of new genres.

The nineteenth century, however, was characterized by a series of technological and social developments that would eventually enfranchise audiences and give them a powerful voice in the constitution and maintenance of new genres. Massive changes in printing technology and practice made it increasingly possible for small groups to express their opinions publicly; not only were unit costs significantly reduced, but revolutionary ideals led to relaxed censorship in many

182

countries. By mid-century, the success of mass-produced and widely distributed newspapers had produced a degree of specialization conducive to the self-expression of smaller and smaller groups. At first the penny press simply provided the masses with a new source of information and entertainment, but eventually the evolution of printing and related marketing and postal developments would make it possible for every club, political group and trade union to have its own publication.

Like pronouncements about genre, all communication once emanated from an established centre of power, eventually rippling out to all corners of the state. With the development of the telegraph and the telephone, however, a true republic of letters finally came into being, a *res publica* or 'public thing' based on a two-way communication between citizens rather than the one-way state pronouncements that had characterized the monarchy. Organizations with shared interests had always existed within the centralized state, but these were usually geographically localized small groups. The new communication technology enhanced the ability of separated individuals to remain part of a coherent group, thus reinforcing group unity and lending new importance both to remote relations and to lateral communication. Long before the recent attention to demographics, the national audience was being carved into a series of overlapping populations, defined not by their 'primary' identity as citizens, but by temporary and partial shared interests or characteristics.

The development of recording and broadcasting radically intensified this effect, while shifting its overall impact. By and large, the lateral communication of nineteenth-century disseminated groups grew directly out of shared experiences. Based heavily on conventions, rallies, revivals, camp meetings, Chautauquas and other instances of physical co-presence, American political, religious and social life before broadcasting featured face-to-face contact and real-life common interests. When disseminated, coherent groups could span the gaps separating them, at least temporarily, by using the mail, the telegraph or the telephone. Recording and broadcasting complicated this situation. Instead of real memories of group consumption, of remembered elbow-to-elbow experiences with other listeners, phonograph records fostered a new kind of audience, or rather 'audience', because those who listened to the same record did not enjoy the simultaneity and face-to-face relationships previously implied by the very definition of the term. Radio and television generalized this situation to the point where the term *audience* eventually abandoned any implication of physical co-presence.

With the early twentieth-century rise of the mass media came new respect for disseminated 'audiences'. Whereas the previous century had lionized authors, this century began very early to concentrate on consumers. Record sales and record audiences were regularly analysed and soon divided into increasingly detailed categories. Nickelodeon audiences were ceaselessly described and evaluated. Radio and television audiences were first measured only in terms of brute numbers, but soon were broken down into smaller and smaller listener and viewer categories. With Hollywood's rise to international domination came an increased commitment to assess the reaction first of the general audience and eventually of recognizably separate audience sectors.

This intense scrutiny of enormous 'audiences' whose only consciousness of each other was provided by the media itself actually served to foster a new kind of audience identification. Identified by the media as part of the 'Steel Belt' audience, a Western Pennsylvania farmer found himself lumped in a category with thousands of others whom he had never seen and with whom he had little in common. Finding that the recorded versions of his favourite folk music were identified as 'Country and Western', he entered into yet another identity-stretching virtual category. Abandoning the general store, he bought his provisions in increasingly specialized shops, department stores or from the pages of a Sears Roebuck catalogue carefully divided and organized by category. In fact, during his lifetime, the very language he spoke evolved significantly, with the creation of thousands of words designed to identify and advertise general classes of products to consumers. The rise of advertising undergirded this new concern both to describe audiences and to categorize products so that products and audiences could be more lucratively matched.

Abandoning the neoclassical model of the audience as unified and automatically processing texts in a predictable manner, the capitalist logic of this consumer century immediately required taking the audience seriously. While audience freedom was hardly the goal – in fact audience manipulation was the name of the game – constant attention to consumer preferences, accompanied by the development of a sophisticated vocabulary to designate types of consumers and consumer articles, concentrated unaccustomed attention on audiences. Ironically, the audiences of this century have been unified not by face-to-face contact, but by the need of commodity producers to treat specific groups of disparate individuals, unknown to each other, as a unified market.

Genre in the age of remote consumption

Walter Benjamin's formative analysis of 'The Work of Art in the Age of Mechanical Reproduction' (1974) is based primarily on the difference between painting and photography, and thus on the gap between the unique work of art and the mechanically reproduced artifact. It has not generally been recognized that Benjamin's choice of example limits his argument and channels his reasoning in a particular direction. Because he concentrates on uniqueness and its disappearance, Benjamin concludes that the primary effect of mechanical reproduction lies in an art work's loss of aura. What if he had instead stressed some other aspect of the modern technological revolution, such as the gap between live performance and remote consumption of recorded or broadcast performances – how would such a shift have modified his argument?

Though Benjamin makes a great deal of the difference between painting and photography, the two are in one sense quite similar. When we look at a painting or a photograph, the author is usually absent and the mode of contemplation is typically personal and individual. With the transition from live performance to recorded or broadcast representation, however, a radically new set of characteristics is deployed. Face-to-face relationships (between the performer and the audience and among audience members sharing exhibition space) disappear, while gaps of time and space are more easily bridged. If moving from painting to photography causes a loss of 'aura', we might say that the change from live performance to recording or broadcasting engenders a loss of 'presence'. Most commentators on this characteristic modern loss have stressed the distance that records, radio and television interject between performer and spectator. For an understanding of twentieth-century generic drift, however, the modification in intra-audience relations looms much more important.

From the start of commercial radio, commentators recognized that something had been lost in the constitution of a disseminated audience. As early as 1927, in the prestigious *American Journal of Sociology*, Marshall Beuick insisted that radio cannot possibly compete with theatre, concerts, cinema or church services, since it doesn't involve assembling people in the flesh. Within a matter of months, broadcasters would apply to the first soap operas the 'virtual intimacy' technique so essential for giving listeners the sense of being present in someone else's house. As long as we can overhear the intimate conversations of the Goldbergs wrestling with family problems in the privacy of their own home, who needs face-to-face assemblies? As long as we can share FDR's fireside, why should we worry that we can't rub elbows with others doing likewise? By its ability to provide presence, coherence and a clear sense of other 'audience' members, radio quickly proved its capacity to replace the lost face-to-face audience.

In fact, the prevalence with which the modern media all introduce narratives of community suggests the extent to which they take seriously the actual demise of elbow-to-elbow viewing and the togetherness for which it serves as an apt figure. Radio compensates for the loss of liveness and presence by assuring continued lateral communication through virtual intimacy, pseudo-live programming, town meeting formats, and programmes with a pre-constituted following and daily newspaper follow-up (such as sports, news and celebrated trials). Whereas Hollywood cinema almost never permits a direct gaze into the camera, the rhetoric of American television depends on friendly faces looking directly at me (and at several million other 'audience' members). Announcers, advertisers, newscasters and talk show hosts thus recreate a sense of commonality and community. Where the prevalence of Hollywood representational codes makes eye contact with the 'audience' impossible, television's virtual intimacy offers an appropriate substitute, whether in the home (*The Goldbergs, Life with Father, All in the Family, The Waltons*) or, starting with *The Mary Tyler Moore Show*, in a family-substitute location (*WKRP in Cincinatti, Cheers, L.A. Law, thirtysomething, NYPD Blue, Night Court, Ellen*).

The case of cinema is more complicated. As Tom Gunning has demonstrated (1998), the Lumière brothers conceived their cinematograph for an amateur market, as a proto-camcorder destined to take pictures of 'baby' and 'a game of cards with the neighbours' or 'the train you arrived on last summer' and 'our friends at the factory'. In other words, one version of cinema began as an extension of face-to-face folk activity, just as radio began as a walkie-talkie-like point-to-point medium, carrying personal messages from ship to shore, between individuals known to each other. Before they became a mass entertainment medium, moving pictures thus constituted an illustrated extension of the letter and a storable version of face-to-face contact. Initially conceived as memories of real experiences, films were designed to be shown only to friends of the figures on the screen.

This spectre of what cinema could have been – had cinema followed the Kodak model and aimed at individual consumers and amateur practitioners – offers an interesting way to understand the early history of American cinema. Fundamentally Benjaminian, in that it begins with a loss associated with the rise of mechanical reproduction, this approach abandons Benjamin at two crucial points. First, it is built around the loss of presence rather than the loss of aura. Second, it stresses the deployment and application of new technologies – including exhibition, programming and other socially imbedded uses – rather than purely ontological or technical considerations.

As a recording technology, cinema might have been used to record, remember and relish the movements of loved ones. That is, it might have provided a direct reflection of its viewers' own lives, thus bridging the loss of presence implicit in all mechanical reproduction. In fact, for a decade or so, it did just that. In spite of the Lumières' decision to forsake amateurs in favour of a commercial market, thus transforming the cinematograph from a tool into a service, cinema's early years still regularly reflected the importance of face-to-face events, particularly in the production of actualities and in itinerant exhibitors' use of locally shot footage. The definitive departure from an aesthetic of home movies (and the direct recording of vaudeville, boxing or Passion Play scenes) did not come until around 1905, with the development of the chase film and other narrative genres. A decade later, this movement would be consecrated in what we now call the classical Hollywood style.

Condemned by its mechanical nature to substitute spatial and temporal absence for an originary presence, cinema began with the implicit charge to restore presence. Through the choice of familiar topics and projection to familiar audiences, early cinema met this obligation well. Yet within a few short years, the problem of lost presence apparently disappeared into narrative films organized into neat generic categories. In fact, the problem of lost presence did not disappear at all, but is simply caught up in questions of narrative and generic organization.

The increasing narrativization of American cinema goes hand in hand with the development of editing techniques defined precisely to restore the sensation of presence. When a turn-of-the-century merchant from eastern Pennsylvania attended one of Lyman Howe's famous travelling shows in the local Lyceum, he could count on seeing his friends both in person and on the screen. Sometimes he might literally see a picture of himself and his friends, taken a week earlier by Howe's advance man; at other times he would see his world represented in an offset manner – either through objects, people and landscapes related to him spatially, or through representations of scenes which he might himself have witnessed in another time frame.

A decade later, the same merchant would most likely attend a nickelodeon with continuous shows rather than a Lyceum with only one or two shows at each twice-yearly visit. No longer could our merchant count on encountering his friends, his own picture, or even representations of his life. In fact, if he looked around, he would find the store-front theatre filled with unfamiliar faces, so much so that no single image could possibly satisfy everyone's desire for films apparently chosen specially for them. Yet at the same time the film would have provided a new satisfaction. In the earliest films, the camera saw and recorded what it saw. By the time

186

of the first purpose-built cinemas, however, the camera would increasingly be located in such a way as to stand in for a character, and through that character, for the spectator. Through an increasingly complex and standardized pattern of shot/reverse shots and point-of-view shots, narrative films succeeded in providing a specific place for the viewer, albeit not specific to any particular viewer. Eventually codified and consecrated in the Hollywood classical narrative technique of suture, this process simplified the producer's task (it's easier to edit an anonymous viewer into the fabric of every film than to shoot footage of each town on your exhibition route), while directly addressing spectator regret at the loss of presence.

Concurrently, genres began to perform an extremely similar function for producers and consumers alike. Exploited with increasing frequency, narrative genres offered producers the dual benefit of reduced production costs (through standardization and reuse of concepts, costumes, props, sets and scripts) and stabilization of audience response (a significant problem for producers anxious to wrest control of textual meaning from exhibitors accustomed to complete control). Though the immediate effect of early twentieth-century enhancement of copyright protection was to encourage proprietary cycles rather than shared genres, as suggested in Chapter 7 increased legal protection of intellectual property eventually lent support to genres as well. For spectators, the rise of film cycles, stars and genres offered a new and innovative approach to the loss of presence implicit in cinema's new narrative look.

When our merchant attended Lyman Howe's show, he saw the familiar faces of his neighbours. A decade later he would instead see characters who had little by little become the regular companions of his visits to the cinema. Soon he would be calling actors and actresses by name and recognizing them more easily than his business acquaintances. Increasingly, he would be comforted by an atmosphere that he found familiar. Instead of puzzling out ever novel situations, he would know from the opening scenes what to expect. The remainder of each genre film – whether comedy, melodrama or Western – would thus remind him not of home but of his new affective 'home' located in previous film-viewing experiences.

Not only did genres prove particularly adept at replacing the experience of presence, but the knowledge that others found pleasure in the same genre even made it possible for genres to stand in for an absent community. With the growth of cinema culture, favoured not only by commercial interests but also by the need to constitute constelled communities in response to a loss of presence, genres concretized cinema's promise of community. Journalistic critics offered imaginary discussion partners; fan magazines established an instant peer group; film-related paraphernalia offered an interpenetration between the film world and the daily world that would eventually lead to a virtual disappearance of any barrier between the two.

Our merchant would already have experienced something like this phenomenon with novels, theatre or comic strips – all of which boast repeated settings, plots, characters and fans – but only the movies combined contact with a real audience and imaginary contact with an absent constelled community. Well before the First World War, film genres were on their way to becoming the site of a new mode of life, an imagined existence capable of supplanting the one we used to call real.

Pseudo-memorials

In the past, it was commonly asserted that genres arose from specific ritual practices. Both comedy and tragedy, it was said, had their origin in the Attic religious festivals held in honour of Dionysus. Largely abandoned by scholars (though see Fowler, 1982, p. 149ff), such claims stressed an aspect of genre overlooked by most recent genre theorists. Whether they originally derive from specific religious rituals or not, genres do serve what we might call a *memorial* purpose; that is, they recall a society's collective experience, by rehearsing the stories, characters and topics that the culture deems important.

For example, take the genre of chancel drama, developed in western Europe around the turn of the millennium. Intercalated into the Mass, the first versions simply acted out the familiar story of the three Maries arriving at the tomb to find the stone rolled away:

Quem quaeritis?	Whom do you seek?
Jesum Christum crucifixum.	Jesus Christ who was crucified.
Non est hic. Resurrexit.	He is not here. He is resurrected.

Bearing witness to the physical existence of the absent Christ and other Christian faithful, chancel dramas rehearse a collective past while evoking the larger body of worshippers who share in that collectivity. Of course, the spectators to this brief drama know the story perfectly well, but by reliving the experience of the three Maries they are invited to recall the knowledge and the awe of Christianity's central mystery.

One aspect of this process deserves particular attention. Like many other genres, chancel drama draws power from its close connection to other aspects of spectator life. It represents not only a well-known story, but an annually repeated aspect of Christian life as well. To a non-Christian audience, chancel drama might make linguistic sense, but it would fail to make generic sense, since generic meaning depends on correct alignment of text and audience. If the text fails to serve as a memorial both to a collective past and to a current collectivity, then it is not fulfilling a generic role.

Have genres changed in a consumer-oriented mass-mediated world? Three closely related shifts revealed by film genre texts and their uses suggest that a major transformation in the very nature of genres takes place during the twentieth century.

First, earlier attention to the presence of sameness has been replaced by an absence of difference. For centuries, generic texts were generated and maintained by the homogeneity of their authors and audiences. In order to provide the mutual reinforcement on which genres depend, social and generic structures were carefully aligned. Arising out of relatively unified cultural contexts (Attic religion, medieval courts, Paris theatre, the British bourgeoisie), genres like tragedy, lyric poetry, tragicomedy and the novel served as a coded yet nevertheless clear expression of that unity. Along with several other turn-of-the-century transformations, the rise of the nickelodeon theatres radically unsettled that situation. Perhaps for the first time ever, a permanent cultural institution offered continuously available entertainment to all sectors of the society. Carnivals facilitating the promiscuous mixing of diverse populations had existed for centuries, but as their special place in the Christian calendar implies, carnivals are short-lived and temporary, like the fairs, festivals and expositions that have increasingly taken their place in the secular world. Cinemas, however, offered a permanently carnivalized venue. Not only did they attract all classes, but they also opened the way to a radically diverse combination of live and recorded entertainment.

Starting with the nickelodeon era and increasing throughout the century, American film genres have with few exceptions abandoned the traditional generic strategy of reflecting audience unity. Instead of seeking topics and strategies that would exploit whatever similarities existed among movie patrons, producers very early discovered that larger audiences could be built by offering topics that simply avoided obvious disparities among filmgoers. While a small percentage of film production continued to depend on projected audience coherence (such as the substantial African-American and Yiddish silent film industries), an increasing proportion of films (especially after the coming of sound destroyed regional and independent production) eschewed actual points of similarity among audience members, preferring instead simply to avoid anything that would underscore difference among separate audience sectors. Concerned to maximize audience size, producers were responding to an economic mandate associated with the capital investment required by all mechanical reproduction systems. Thus were born the 'sharable unspecifics' for which Hollywood genre production is so justly (in)famous.

Second, though they were once configured as collective memorials, genres now increasingly offer only pseudo-memorials. Genres have always been marked by conflict between two opposed tendencies. Genres succeed and endure because they are properly aligned with real world institutions. Whether or not genres derive from specific cultural rituals, they clearly serve a memorial function, commemorating key aspects of collective history. Romantic comedy evokes the courtship process central to democratic standards of kinship and reproduction. Recalling no specific couple, romantic comedy nevertheless implicitly harks back to actual courtships experienced or imagined by spectators (their own, those of their parents and forebears) and to the wedding ceremonies in which those courtships culminated. Matched up with the social, legal and religious traditions of the societies in which it has flourished, romantic comedy serves as a reminder of and a monument to those traditions. In this sense, all genres share the epic function of recalling the origins and justifying the existence of current practices.

Opposed to this referential dimension is an intertextual framework without which genres cannot exist. However much genre texts may recollect events, locations or relationships, they must also recall previous texts or they will fail to assure the genre's continued existence. In order to play the role of genre spectator properly (i.e., in such a way as to engage individual texts as part of a genre), each spectator must have a double experience: experience of the culture and its assumptions, rules and myths, as well as experience of other genre texts. These two necessities and the two resultant genre construction tendencies may of course be combined in differing proportions.

I suggest that the rise of consumerism and the mass media, along with the extraordinary proliferation of narrative entertainment that they have brought, have tilted the typical generic mix of life experience/textual experience radically towards the experience of previous texts. This situation results in part from a familiar pattern whereby enduring genres offer a greater choice of possible intertexts and thus stress generic intertexts over social rituals and experiences. Showing *The Searchers* or *The Shootist* to an audience unfamiliar with the classical Western rapidly reveals the extent to which those films depend on a knowledge of the Western tradition. The ability to recognize quotations and understand transformations is necessary in order to activate the generic potential of Westerns that quote and transform earlier Westerns. But the same is true of any long-lived genre: neoclassical tragedy as opposed to classical tragedy, Miltonian or Joycean epic versus Virgil or Homer, the novels of Flaubert and Proust as compared to those of Austen and Balzac.

More is at stake here than a simple question of 'maturity'. Producers' interest in enlarging audiences drives them to offer sharable unspecifics as an acceptable meeting point for larger and larger groups of viewers. When trying to bring together spectators who actually share less and less, what better meeting place than the common past provided by the genre itself? The science fiction film glutted the 50s with stories of human fear in the face of monsters generated by nuclear weapons and other military experiments, actual or imagined. Instead of direct identification with the embattled citizens of our world, clearly seen against recognizable American landscapes and sharing American experiences and fears, films in the 90s offer us computer graphic images of imaginary worlds inhabited by beings who are costumed and genetically engineered to resemble spectators as little as possible. Today our students have little notion either of the nuclear dysphoria or the moon-walking euphoria once evoked by science fiction films, but they do have

The passed-along song

It is worth considering the history of the musical's most characteristic throwback device, the passed-along song. Borrowing the opening that he had originally worked out for the stage version of *Porgy* (1927), and that he would use again later for *Porgy and Bess* (1935), Rouben Mamoulian begins *Love Me Tonight* (Paramount, 1932) with an orchestrated city-symphony-like number in which the daily sounds of awakening Paris are magically combined into a single musical composition. As we move from one contented citizen to another we recognize the extent to which their common interests have synchronized their every movement. Anyone who has ever fought Paris traffic knows that Mamoulian's version decidedly paints *la vie en rose*, but the mythic purity of that version nevertheless offers an apt representation of a world with only one show in town at a time.

During the 40s this vision of societal coherence was regularly figured by the characteristic folk musical technique of passing a song from one character to another. *Meet Me in St. Louis* uses the title tune to introduce us to the Smith family, as one after the other takes up the song where the previous singer had left off. This is a world, the device implies, of shared songs and synchronized hearts all singing in the same key, united by sheet music, pianos and the families who gather around them. In subsequent years, the same technique would carry the a crystal-clear sense of the connection between today's version of outer space and the fanciful spaceships, computer-generated images and imaginary sounds of *Star Wars, Star Trek* and their imitators. Forty years ago, it was possible to meet in a backyard bomb shelter to discuss science (that didn't seem totally) fiction. Today's students meet on the holodeck of Starship Enterprise, via the World Wide Web, thus giving the genre an entirely new spin.

Whereas genres once served as a monument to real world configurations and concerns, today's genres have increasingly taken on what we might call a pseudo-memorial function. That is, they count on spectator memory to work their magic, but like the 'Organization' in an increasing number of futuristic and spy films, they themselves implant in spectators the necessary memories, in the form of other genre films. Their minds filled with prepackaged memories provided by generic memory-masters, genre film spectators have become the true twentieth-century cyborgs.

Third, whereas genres previously depended on constituted communities, they now anchor constellated communities. How are communities constituted? As a rule, they are created by a combination of direct interaction and shared interests. What would happen if interaction were eliminated? Would the inability to learn about others' interests impede community formation? On the contrary, communities would continue to be formed, but their nature would change. Today, traditional communities based on face-to-face communication and shared interests are complemented by far larger communities based on similarity of taste but not buttressed by direct interaction. Wearing Nike sports shoes guarantees initiation into a fraternity far exceeding the number of Nike wearers in an individual's immediate entourage. The definition and stability of the Nike community

same message in *State Fair, Centennial Summer, Summer Holiday* and many lesser films.

Updating the technique, the opening of *American Hot Wax* (Floyd Mutrux, 1978) differs markedly from the classical passed-along song. On the soundtrack we hear Little Richard singing 'Tutti Frutti', while the images show a series of radio listeners: a teenage white girl, black youths in an apartment, a bourgeois white family in a suburban house, the son cooped up in his own room. Like other films of the 70s and 80s, including *American Graffiti, FM* and *Do the Right Thing, American Hot Wax* ironically uses synchronized simultaneous radio listening as a device to strip listeners of any possible common interest or personal contact, save their devotion to Alan Freed and the music he chooses. Whereas the characters in *Love Me Tonight* and *Meet Me in St. Louis* all succeed in making music together because of their commonality, the characters of *American Hot Wax* are brought together only by simultaneous listening and radio station choice. One situation depends on an already constituted community, while the other is itself constitutive of a constellated community of people who may never enjoy face-to-face contact. In fact, the careful choice of characters implies, they probably wouldn't recognize each other and certainly wouldn't enjoy each other's company if they should ever chance to meet.

derive not from direct contact with other Nike buyers, but from a shared vision of Michael Jordan going airborne in his own signature Nikes. This new brand of community depends less on shared interests and direct contact than on similarity of consumption habits.

When the mass media reserved the microphone for the chosen few, spectators were reduced to the type of expression that comes from commodity choice alone. Where communication once was a two-way affair, the media have reduced receivers to a single sort of self-expression: programme selection. Self-definition once depended on our choice of face-to-face experiences and the common goals and beliefs that led to them. Today, self-definition is increasingly a matter of twisting the dial or manipulating the remote control. Personal satisfaction and a supportive community must be conjured up through film preference, channel surfing and video rental choice. While our every decision still aligns us with a specific community, we no longer expect actually to meet the other members of that group face-to-face.

In a mass-mediated commercial world where presence has gone the way of aura, and where economic success depends on audience size, genres serve as a stand-in for *in praesentia* community and as a vehicle of lateral communication. Though they maintain familiar generic forms, modern genres nevertheless operate in a markedly different manner, supplementing radio announcers and talk-show hosts as a method of 'bringing together' the members of a far-flung 'audience'. Operating throughout the entertainment industry, this method of assuring the coherence and survival of constellated 'communities' is employed not only by cinema, but by radio, TV and recorded music as well. There have always been differences in musical styles, for example, but only since the rise of recording have musical styles become genres correlated with specific constellated communities (and boosted by competing labels, magazines, clubs, products and cable channels). Indeed, this configuration actually extends into domains not normally thought of as subject to generic analysis, including virtually everything that is sold and consumed in the modern world.

Sports, stars and advertising

By virtue of their narrative complexity, multimedia nature and close connection to diverse commodity forms, film genres are especially important for constituting alternative public spheres in response to the rise of recording and broadcasting. They are certainly not alone, however. A similar function is fulfilled by sports, stardom and advertising. The popularity of participatory sports skyrocketed around the turn of the century. Participation in many sports, however, was a single-class affair, as were many sports audiences. Only with the rise of spectator sports, the generalization of sports reporting and the development of sports statistics as a predictable and easily produced form of journalism did sports become a mixed-class event. But this mixing of classes is based in large part on imaginary contact. As with film genre, we are dealing here with constellated communities, existing without physical interaction among fans of the same sport or team. It is hardly surprising to discover that the rise of spectator sports takes place virtually simultaneously with the development of film genres.

The same claim may be made regarding the development of the cinema star system – and for that matter the modern notion of celebrity in general. Though the last century had its public appearance stars, celebrity increased markedly in breadth, power and functionality with the advent of recording and broadcasting, and their ability to reach a far larger 'audience'. The growth of film's star system during the teens and 20s had a particularly strong effect, for it was ably supported by references throughout the other media to the personal lives of the stars. As with spectator sports, cinema celebrity crosses class lines and substitutes virtual contact for actual presence. Thus generations of American young women have responded to the secondary discursivity of Hollywood star texts by adopting a particular hairstyle certain to identify them (not to just anybody but especially to those who understand the code) as devotees of that particular star. To attend that star's films, to read about that star, to participate in that star's favourite activities is implicitly to communicate with the like-minded members of the star-worshipping community. Even without the physical evidence of fan magazines, fan mail and fan clubs, individual fans take their place within the star's constellation.

Consumers within a capitalist society do not just accept what is offered. Their choice of products is a source of pleasure, pride and even identity. This is why genres, sports and stars loom so large in the twentieth-century firmament. Whatever power they have comes from their users, who need the identity – albeit imagined – provided by these phenomena. A similar role is played by advertising. Normally seen in terms of its primary discursive role of pitching products to potential purchasers, advertising also fills an increasingly important secondary discursive role. Earlier advertising simply identified products and the locations where they were available (still advertising's major role in many countries), but when capital mated advertising with the mass media a radically different situation was created. Every ad became not just a plea to buy a particular type of merchandise but also an appeal to identify with a specific consuming group. As consumers we constantly evaluate products according to the type of people who own them. The question used to be only: 'Do I need one of those?' With the new century the question changed significantly: 'What community do I become a part of by buying one of those?' Thorsten Veblen was right about the Leisure Class. What he could not foresee is the extent to which we would strive to join a class whose other members are only imagined.

Genre in the new millennium

Built on a fundamental paradox, genre subsists because it seems to provide firm anchorage in a transnational, transhistorical substratum oblivious to the vagaries of time and place. Yet those who actually pronounce generic terms and invoke generic categories do so in such a fundamentally contradictory way as to preclude associating permanence or universality with the notion of genre. This chapter has raised a question that transhistorical generic tendencies have virtually precluded in the past: is it possible that not only specific genres but even the very notion and function of genre have changed over the course of centuries? This is of course an enormous question, impossible to cover fully in the space of a few pages, especially given the paucity of assistance provided by previous genre theorists.

Where does this chapter's rapid overview put us? It would be presumptuous to claim that such an abbreviated discussion has led to anything that might appropriately be called conclusions. Still, it may be useful to summarize the points made during the course of this penultimate chapter.

1. Though genre theorists have long assumed that both genre theory in general and specific genres are transhistorical, the past century has seen major changes in the definition and deployment of genres.
2. Genre theory, with support from a commodified culture, is currently in the process of effecting a major move from neoclassical to postmodern presuppositions, and in particular towards increased sensitivity to audience needs and influence.
3. Neoclassical inclination towards epic, tragic and comic genres has given way to cinema's predilection for melodrama, adventure and romance.
4. This transition corresponds to a more general shift from textual structures assuming audience coherence to preference for topics and treatments offering audiences new causes for coherence.
5. Once identified by their ability to provide collective memorials, genres now fulfill instead a pseudo-memorial function, based on a substantial increase of generic intertextuality.
6. Generic intertextuality has increased in importance so that the media can offer viewers a new 'home' located in previous media-viewing experiences and the comfort of recognizing generic references.
7. In this century, with the rise of recording and broadcasting, coherent face-to-face genre audiences have increasingly been replaced by disseminated 'audiences'.
8. As a result, texts and genres have laboured to provide substitutes for lost 'presence', primarily by making genres and genre texts essential to communication among members of constellated communities.
9. Increased copyright protection in this century has significantly altered the importance accorded to proprietary cycles, thus establishing a new dialectic between brand-name and generic interests.
10. Many of the functions increasingly fulfilled by genre in this century are also satisfied by sports, stars and advertising.

All these changes point to a significant transformation in the roles that genres play for their diverse users.

What will these changes mean for genre in the new millennium? It hardly surprises me to note the rapid rise of generic thinking over the past decade or so. The technological and representational explosion of recent years only reinforces earlier patterns of alienation and lost presence. In this atmosphere, genre can easily appear to represent a safe harbour in which to ride out the storm. While genres are certainly not as simple as most people think they are, many a placebo has provided a successful cure. Because people see safety in the apparent stability of genre, they find genre films useful as signs of successful constellated community communication. Though no one can possibly imagine what the generic landscape will look like in another century, it seems clear to me that generic logic will continue to prove useful for a broad spectrum of user groups.

12
What can genres teach us about nations?

My first memory of 'The Star-Spangled Banner' embellished, and thereby diminished, is Jimi Hendrix's famous riff at Woodstock. Did anyone at the time see his performance as anything but protest? True, it was both effective and timely, but protest nonetheless – the musical equivalent of flag-on-the-butt jeans. Since then, however, we've heard all manner of 'variations on a theme' passed off as national tribute. I haven't heard a baroque or rap version yet, but this year's winter sports season has hardly begun.

John Barylick, 'Oh, Say, Can You Sing?' (1996, p. 16)

Taking generic categories themselves for granted, traditional genre criticism concentrates on the manner in which separate genres are embodied in specific films, stressing historical changes, directorial tendencies and textual idiosyncracies. Genres are typically seen as unproblematically regimenting both the process of production and that of reception. This book has sought to destabilize the apparently clear and fixed relationship between genres and their practitioners. While in some periods genres play a predictable formative role, at other points they are mashed, twisted and reshaped into unrecognizably new forms. Investigation into the origins of this process has led to a heuristically powerful but virtually unprovable hypothesis: that genres increasingly make their meaning through secondary discursivity and lateral communication, thus providing a common focus for constellated communities. This chapter will broaden still further the speculation that led to those conclusions.

The preceding chapters in this book have described genres not as formal patterns or as textual canons, but as system and process. Every generic system is made up of an interconnected network of user groups and their supporting institutions, each using the genre to satisfy its own needs and desires. While at any given point a generic system may appear perfectly balanced and thus at rest, the look of stability is actually produced only by a momentary equilibrium of countervening concerns. Because a genre is not one thing serving one purpose, but multiple things serving multiple purposes for multiple groups, it remains a permanently contested site. In fact, it is precisely the continued contestation among producers, exhibitors, viewers, critics, politicians, moralists, and their diverse interests, that keeps genres ever in process, constantly subject to reconfiguration, recombination and reformulation.

This chapter is based on an outrageous but logical extrapolation from the previous chapters' treatment of genre as system and process. Genres are not only formal arrangements of textual characteristics; they are also social devices that use semantics and syntax to assure simultaneous satisfaction on the part of multiple users with apparently contradictory purposes. That is, genres are regulatory schemes facilitating the integration of diverse factions into a single unified social fabric. As such, genres operate like nations and other complex communities. Perhaps genres can even teach us about nations.

Hegel's newspaper

In recent years two powerful models have dominated discussion of the ways in which private citizens come together to constitute a national public. Jürgen Habermas' description of a bourgeois 'public sphere' and Benedict Anderson's notion of 'imagined communities' will serve here as background for an inquiry into the relationship between genres and nations. Habermas and Anderson agree that a new order, whether nation or public sphere, cannot arise until certain ancient habits are put away. Sacred languages must be discarded and replaced by the language of reason. The concentric organization characteristic of monarchies must be abandoned in favour of a secular society counterposed to the state. Finally, in place of a consistent pattern of communication between centre and periphery (state and subject) there must arise a new mode of regular interaction among those who inhabit what was once considered the periphery.

However, Habermas and Anderson concentrate on radically different types of interactions among private individuals. Whereas Habermas stresses the face-to-face interaction of French salons and British coffee houses, Anderson emphasizes the shared but separate experiences that permit individuals to imagine the other members of a broader community. The difference between these two scholars' approaches to newspapers is of particular interest. For Habermas, newspapers are simply an extension of coffee-house dialogue. Full of letters to the editor, such publications as the *Tatler*, the *Spectator* and the *Guardian* simply extend direct interchange to a wider public. Seen as primarily epistolary in nature – as little more than private letters made public – newspapers concretize the notion of 'society' by assuring regular contact among private citizens. To this discursive model Habermas assimilates not only the so-called 'moral weeklies', but the essay and all public sphere literary production as well (1991, p. 42ff).

Whereas Habermas bases his treatment of newspapers on face-to-face models, Anderson treats the press as a particular type of commodity. Unlike sugar, he points out, newspapers are subject to a mode of simultaneous, scheduled consumption that unites otherwise diverse populations. 'Hegel observed,' he notes, 'that newspapers serve modern man as a substitute for morning prayers.' The process of reading takes place silently and individually, yet 'each communicant is well aware that the ceremony he performs is being replicated simultaneously by thousands (or millions) of others of whose existence he is confident, yet of whose identity he has not the slightest notion' (1991, p. 35). Where newspaper content is of the essence for Habermas, since the debate over issues bearing on state authority is key to his notion of the public sphere, Anderson's newspaper might as well be entirely lacking in content. As long as simultaneous consumption ties readers together, it matters little what they read. The power of this vision of simultaneous activity is such that Anderson adopts it as a symbol for his entire analytical enterprise, asking 'What more vivid figure for the secular, historically clocked, imagined community can be envisioned?' (*ibid.*).

However vivid Anderson's figure of simultaneous newspaper reading, the reference to Hegel highlights its historical limitations. Hegel died in 1831, only a few years prior to radical changes in printing technology and the subsequent transformation of newspaper layout, financing and distribution. Perhaps, as Anderson implies, Berlin in the 1820s offered only a single newspaper of limited proportions and undifferentiated pages. The high-speed printing press revolution changed that situation forever. During the 1830s, Paris newspapers began to offer serial novels in a space previously reserved for political or cultural analysis. Coupled with a speculative reduction in newspaper pricing and an increase in advertising space, the success of this arrangement led to a radical expansion of the newspaper audience and a rapid multiplication of newspaper titles and formats. During the 1840s, London publishers followed suit. By mid-century, the modern mass media made their debut. Not only did individual newspapers begin to take on a recognizable character through graphic conventions, content specialization or political affiliation, but they systematically abandoned their unitary structure in favour of increasingly diverse rubrics.

Whereas, according to Anderson, Hegel and his contemporaries all read the same paper from cover to cover, thus participating in a single cult, subsequent readers had to imagine their communities through a series of choices. The first was selection of a newspaper from the many available. While initially confusing, this choice was soon facilitated by standard product differentiation devices (characteristic mastheads, recognizable layouts, distinctive graphics). Growing in size with audiences and increasing economies of scale, newspapers also began to offer readers an expanding range of rubric choices. Early nineteenth-century newspapers were monopolized by political, cultural and business news understood as important to every *honnête homme*. Before the century was over, newspaper readership had expanded beyond the affluent few; with this expansion came topics that no longer targeted the entire reading public: fashion, sports, comic strips, fiction of various types and advertisements of increasing diversity. Soon each newspaper section would be larger than any whole newspaper published in Berlin before 1831. Most readers would henceforth scan certain parts of the paper and skip others entirely, while reading word-for-word only their rubrics of choice. One wonders what Hegel would say about the Sunday New York *Times*.

By stressing the newspaper characteristics that contribute most notably to the constitution of, respectively, public spheres and nations, Habermas and Anderson unintentionally reveal a fascinating pattern reminiscent of genre history. Before the elaboration of a bourgeois public sphere, the people who came together already knew each other by virtue of family or class ties (virtually the same thing in a world dominated by birth). Their interchanges simply replicated, symbolically, the ruler's one-way communiqués to his court. A bourgeois public sphere could not appear until people from different classes (but sharing an ability to reason) began to assemble to discuss their common interest in issues of state authority. This assembly of thinking people who had been on the periphery of the previous system gave rise to newspapers conceived as a method of extending the dialogue to absent members and slack times.

Comes the revolution – whether economic or political – and these previously marginalized private interlocutors take over the centre and produce the prose shared by Hegel and his fellow newspaper readers. What once was an intense, reasoned discourse aimed at specific, known individuals would eventually be hollowed out and turned into an excuse for a 'secular, historically clocked, imagined community'. Like the flag that symbolically unifies the imagined communities that we call nations, the shared newspaper binds citizens invisibly, thus paradoxically restoring the concentricity initially undermined by the public sphere's reasoners. In other words, Hegel's newspaper – the kind once shared by an entire population – paradoxically undoes the individualization produced by the public sphere's enlightenment, thus restoring many of the features of the preceding regime.

But as we have seen, neither Hegel's newspaper nor his society remained stable. Differentiated and fragmented, the press eventually gave expression to a new kind of 'public' sphere. This time, however, the singular would no longer really be appropriate, and the topic of disseminated discussion would no longer be state authority. Scores of separate topics, separate rubrics, separate styles and separate genres would spring up as vehicles for the lateral communication of individual constellated communities. Once again, the centre would be challenged by those at the margins. And once again, through the Hollywoodization of America and the McDonaldization of the world, the newly resurgent margins would take over the centre.

Genres play two different roles in this scenario. In one sense, genres are simply the heirs apparent of the public sphere and imagined national communities, the next in a logical series. While Addison and Steele employed and extended the face-to-face lateral communication methods of the coffee house, however, genres must operate through the secondary discursivity and disseminated lateral communication characteristic of constellated communities. Historically, the breakdown of newspaper unity, the expansion of readership, and the introduction of serial fiction all contribute to the development of the new genres that would eventually nourish cinema, radio and television.

Just as the public sphere responds from the margins to the unreasoned exercise of centralized authority, so genrification responds from the margins to the morning prayers constitituted by unitary newspapers and the nationalistic religions that they serve. The mass media genre explosion simply extends a process that began with coffee houses and salons. The Starbucks revolution serves many of the same purposes, albeit on behalf of different values and a narrower 'public', just as the letters to 'Dear Abby' duplicate, *mutatis mutandis*, the lateral communication purposes of those addressed to the *Spectator*.

In another sense, genres provide a model for processes common to the public sphere, imagined community and constellated communities alike. Habermas devotes most of his attention to Enlightenment changes common to several established western European nations, while Anderson is more concerned with new nations born during the succeeding age of revolutions. This book has concentrated on changes associated with the still later development of the mass media. Given the differences among these objects of study, why should all three projects attend so closely to the same factors? The answer, I would suggest, lies in the fact that each of these projects, while overtly emphasizing a specific type of social organization as product, also implicitly accentuates a process common to all three. Anderson concentrates on the moment when a nation was formed and stops there, failing to acknowledge the ongoing nature of the process he has described. The nation-state environment has lasted long enough to convince us that the processes that once contributed to the constitution of existing nations are now extinct.

E pur si muove. And yet this apparently stable world continues to move; its tectonic plates continue to slide over one another, thus creating ever new volcanoes, ever new earthquakes, ever new (yet constantly recognizable) situations. The hardest thing to see is the dynamic nature of one's own era. An understanding of genres and the process of regenrification may help us to see just how subject to reformulation are the apparently stable relationships that define our lives.

Strikingly, the model developed in this book apropos of film genres might help us to understand the ways of nations. From 'public sphere' to 'imagined community' to 'constellated communities', similar processes continue to function (with variations caused by several factors, including increases in scale, economic changes and the introduction of new media). Instead of treating genres as stable or fixed, I have endeavoured to show just how volatile they can be under certain conditions, just how subject they are to redefinition and redeployment. In stressing the process of regenrification, I have described a mode of regeneration used by genres and nations alike.

All genre formation, I have suggested, begins with a process of cycle-making creolization, combining gypsy adjectives with established, land-owning generic substantives. Only when those previously marginalized adjectives plant their flag in the centre of the world are they transmuted into substantival genres, thus putting them on the map, as it were, while simultaneously opening them up to new adjectival settlements and an eventual squatter takeover. Alone, no single point on the periphery can possibly stand up to the powerful centre, but through lateral communication the margins can eventually muster the strength necessary for a takeover, only eventually to be displaced by a new set of laterally connected margins.

Regenrifying the national anthem

Anderson's book offers many figures for imagined communities. One of the most telling – and most useful for distinguishing between 'imagined' and 'constellated' communities – is the experience of unison singing.

> Take national anthems, for example, sung on national holidays. No matter how banal the words and mediocre the tunes, there is in this singing an experience of simultaneity. At precisely such moments, people wholly unknown to each other utter the same verses to the same melody. The image: unisonance. Singing the Marseillaise, Waltzing Matilda, and Indonesia Raya provide occasions for unisonality, for the echoed physical realization of the imagined community.
>
> (1991, p. 145)

When I first read this passage, I was filled with the exultation of the 'Marseillaise' as sung in *La Grand illusion* and *Casablanca*. Watching these classic films I do indeed imagine myself part of a broader community. Then I remembered the controversy in France over the inaugural 'Marseillaise' of the 1992 Winter Olympics in Albertville. Staged to emphasize Olympic harmony, the French national anthem was sung by an eleven-year-old girl after releasing a white dove into the air. The contrast with the song's vengeful, militant, blood-drenched lyrics was too much even for the French. For weeks, Parisian personalities (including first-lady

Danielle Mitterrand, homeless defender L'Abbé Pierre, and even retired general Charles Ferauge) filled the press with calls for more peaceful lyrics or even a new anthem, which only elicited a volley of variously motivated retorts. Once the symbol of French togetherness in the face of foreign threats, the 'Marseillaise' had ironically turned into the battleground itself.

The French quarrel in turn reminded me of the perpetual bickering over the American national anthem. Set to the tune of a British drinking song, the 'Star-Spangled Banner' is regularly called uninteresting, unsingable and even un-American, especially by proponents of popular alternatives such as 'America the Beautiful'. Once anchored in Fourth of July festivities, the US national anthem has now become more identified with sporting events – two generations of TV viewers remain convinced that 'Play ball!' are its final words. Unison singing has disappeared along with the link between the national anthem, the national holiday and national unity. In its place we have a 'Star-Spangled Banner' soloist taking advantage of a temporarily open microphone, implicitly equating the once hallowed moment of saluting the flag and singing the national anthem with a karaoke bar. In *La Grand illusion* and *Casablanca* the unison crowd drew all the attention; now it is a local personality, a starlet, or even a well-known recording star who grabs the spotlight. Every year, we are subjected to skirmishing over who should sing the national anthem at major sporting events like the Super Bowl.

In fact, ever since Jimi Hendrix played the 'Star-Spangled Banner' at Woodstock, the national anthem has become the target of individuals and groups anxious to give the event their particular slant. In July 1990, comedienne Roseanne Barr caused outrage by grabbing her crotch and spitting on the ground as a final touch to her performance before a San Diego Padres baseball game. Not to be outdone, and seeing that the national anthem can be reconfigured for virtually any purpose, pop singer Whitney Houston turned her 1991 Tampa Super Bowl performance into an ode to the popular recording industry. Furious to discover that Houston had pre-recorded her teary-eyed rendition (while on camera the recording star was simply lip-syncing to a record), a public debate was launched over national anthem versions that has still not abated. The tendency towards stylistically identifiable national anthem performances – from folk, gospel and country to grand opera and Native American – makes one wonder whether the term *national* anthem is still appropriate.

A national anthem's rather special ability to control the circumstances of its performance and reception has clouded Anderson's vision regarding *actual* national anthem experiences. The militant wartime meaning of the 'Marseillaise' consecrated by *La Grand illusion* and *Casablanca* will simply no longer serve as the basic model for all national anthem, since decades of mass-mediated versions of the 'Star-Spangled Banner' have shown that even the national anthem is subject to the fragmenting power of the regenrification process. Once, no doubt, the 'Star-Spangled Banner' was capable of playing the role assigned to it by Anderson. In those days, renditions of the national anthem had no style; that is, they were restricted to a standard sanctioned arrangement kept alive by military bands. The 'Star-Spangled Banner' played the role of 'grand old flag' rallying all Americans in opposition to the British and other enemies. Now, however, every high visibility sporting event is an occasion to ally the national anthem with a particular style

Whereas Uncle Sam's grand old flag outfit in Yankee Doodle Dandy *(see page 87) embodied shared belief in American causes and coherence, Peter Fonda's star-studded helmet in* Easy Rider *(1969) clearly carries an entirely different meaning, as confirmed by one of the film's final shots, parodying the common Vietnam-era image of a flag-shrouded coffin.*

and thus with a specific (sub-national) community and the rituals that support it. From time to time the marching hymn of a great nation at war, the 'Star-Spangled Banner' is now most often served with chips and salsa.

In fact, like the national anthem, even the flag itself is subject to regenrification. The repurposing of the flag may have begun during the Vietnam flag-burning era as a clear gesture of protest, but today it has turned into a battle of styles and genres. From flag-on-the-butt jeans to high fashion, from redneck patriotism to high concept oblivion, the flag has become a method of affirming anything but national cohesion. Ironically, those who display the flag on national holidays are now typically understood to be making a political statement rather than expressing national unity. Instead of recalling national glory, they are commonly assimilated to a particular politically defined group like the American Legion. When patriotism is reduced to the identifiable style of a specific constellated community, then the stage of unisonality has clearly been superceded.

The name of the father

Consider the fascinating case of Cristóbal Colón, the man sent by Queen Isabella of Spain to explore the western seas. Largely ignored in a world turned more towards the future than the past, Colón was not clearly credited with the discovery of the New World until the era of American independence, when he was rebaptized 'Christopher Columbus' and literally identified with the new nation now nicknamed 'Columbia'. On the occasion of the tercentenary of his maiden voyage, the name of Columbus served as holy water in the patriotic baptism of colleges, cities, ships, rivers, and even the nation's capital (Sale, 1990, pp. 339–40).

But wait, was Columbus really a Spaniard? In 1792 the new nation itself was the order of the day, but by the 1892 quatercentennial a century of immigration had changed the country significantly, and the question of national heritage took on a new importance. Sensing an opportunity to steal a march on their Irish, Scandinavian and German neighbours, the Italian community in America made a discovery and a claim of its own: Cristóbal Colón was really none other than the Italian-born Cristoforo Colombo. Rallying around their new hero, Italian-Americans established the Knights of Columbus, erected an Italian-designed monument in New York's newly named Columbus Circle, and launched a successful movement to make Columbus Day a national holiday. The heretofore national namesake had now become instead a symbol of sub-national pride.

Another century, yet another reuse of the same material. Insisting that his landmark voyages be labelled 'encounters' rather than by the unacceptably Eurocentric term 'discovery', quincentennial critics once again forced a revised identity on the embattled explorer. As the despoiler of pristine pre-Columbian America, Columbus served as an apt target for the everpresent PC lobby. Once the father of America, then the ancestor of all Italian-Americans, he has now

Hyphenating the margins

Nations, like genres, are born through a process that does not disappear with that birth. The imagining of community, like the genrification process, always operates dialectically, through the transformation of an already existing community/genre. Written during the War of 1812, fought like the Revolution itself against the British, the 'Star-Spangled Banner' took a century to be officially accepted as the national anthem (first by Woodrow Wilson's 1916 executive order and finally by a 1931 act of Congress). Once primarily associated with national holidays, the national anthem has in recent decades been shifted to sporting events where it is subjected to stylization and regenrification. At first impression, this process appears to remove the song from the centre, from nationally sanctioned holy days like the Fourth of July. Yet Habermas and Anderson have taught us the meaning of just such a hollowing out of hallowed ground: it is precisely the abandonment of the sacred language associated with Independence Day that makes a new order possible. That new order involves the folding of the margins (a coalition of sports fans and popular music fans) into a new centre, where the Super Bowl serves as

Christopher Columbus (Gérard Depardieu) sets foot on the New World in Ridley Scott's epic 1492: Conquest of Paradise, *one of many films that commemorated – and effectively undermined – the Columbus Quincentennial.*

been recast as the originator of all that is politically incorrect in America today. In the past, the sacrosanctity of (his) national origin would have protected him from attack, but today identity is conceived very differently indeed. A new sacredness and a new religion have once again been folded from the margins towards the centre.

national holiday of a new America. Not just national anthems and flags, but even national holidays are subject to the process of regenrification.

With national concerns as with genres, hyphenation is the vehicle of change. By 1910, a series of proto-generic hyphenated experiments – Western-epic, Western-drama, Western-melodrama – had precipitated the Western. By 1930, a pattern of generic miscegenation – musical-drama, musical-comedy, musical-melodrama – had produced an offspring regarded, surprisingly, as pure. During the same period, melting-pot America was born out of a population of Italian-Americans, Irish-Americans and Chinese-Americans, who (after many tribulations) eventually came to be known simply as Americans. Today the situation apparently repeats itself, this time with Latin Americans, African Americans and Asian Americans, but this time the hyphen has been removed by populations anxious to have their origins respected and their contributions to American life recognized rather than simply buried beneath a hyphen.

A colleague recently assured me that creolization is the answer to America's current racial, ethnic and national-origin problems. His Irish parents were prejudiced against their Italian neighbours in the next ghetto, he said, but eventually they discovered their common poverty, their common ethnic interests and their common Catholicism, so the differences were in the long run downplayed. The same thing, he contended, will happen today as Asian Americans, Latin Americans and African Americans intermarry until there is no difference remaining.

Unsatisfied with his single-problem, single-product approach, I offered a process-oriented response. Consider France, for example, I protested. France is so dependent on centuries of immigration and the absorption of Breton, Alsatian, Savoyard, Basque and other minorities, that if you read the names of players on the national soccer team you can't even tell that it's the French team. However dependent France has been on immigration and inclusion, however, the far-right politician Jean-Marie Le Pen has succeeded in persuading the French descendants of Italians, Brits, Swiss, Germans and Spaniards that North Africans, Portuguese and sub-Saharan Africans are dangerously Other.

Another otherness is always available, Le Pen reminds us. The very process of discovering similarities among rival populations, apparently a gesture of conciliation and unity, all too easily leads to overemphasis on those shared qualities, thus redefining those who don't share them as unacceptably other. In the Catholic religion that brought them together, Irish-Americans and Italian-Americans also found justification for the bloody anti-abortion battles that have increasingly divided the United States. Even such groups as feminists, who successfully moved from marginal protests to institutional recognition by playing up common concerns of an apparently sex-linked nature, have now in many universities been contested and even supplanted by new alliances among lesbian, gay and bisexual groups. For every feminist protest against established practices, there is always a lesbigay protest in the wings, waiting for feminist practices to become sufficiently established to make them a worthwhile target.

Because genre critics, like nations, have a vested interest in stability, they depend heavily on myths of distant origin, continued coherence and permanent inviolability. Satisfied with the current situation, users of generic and national terminology alike have a desire to slow the process of regenrification, while margin dwellers have every reason to speed it up. Those at the centre thus regularly exaggerate the age, rootedness and importance of current practice, openly resisting otherness, hyphenation and creolization, while those on the margins must use resistant reading practices, secondary discursivity and lateral communication to reinforce always frail constelled communities. Anderson offers Swiss nationalism as an example of this process, showing how the multilingual nation invented a six-hundred-year history in order to dissimulate its recent origins and shore up its fragile unity (1991, p. 135ff). Earlier in this book, we saw how the same logic operates with the musical, the Western and the biopic.

Genre critics have learnt that to keep generic borders closed they must concentrate on a genre's classical period, extrapolate it in both directions, and fight poachers at all costs. I admit to having regularly succumbed to these strategies myself. When nations adopt the same tactics, the results are worrisome. The US, Britain and France could not have been constituted without continued immigration, yet all have recently proposed to close their borders, as if to say: 'We wanted to make a country, now it's made, no further applications taken'. Yet the imagining of community, and of genres, cannot be stopped by mandate. A fine line separates immigration seen as nourishment for a hungry nation and immigration seen as a form of squatting – not to say poaching. Too many politicians have been comfortable preserving a mythically pure notion of nation by following the genre critics' formula: concentrate on the nation's classical period, extrapolate it in both directions, and fight poachers at all costs. Surely, there are lessons to be learnt from this unexpected concordance.

Increasingly, our identity is invented, dispersed, disseminated, as the communities that we inhabit become more imagined, constelled, ethereal. Bodies moving in time used to figure our common bodily and social coherence (reading simultaneously, singing in unison, dancing to the beat, pointing the gun the same way). Now all we have left is bodies facing in the same direction, towards the screen. Yet they continue to be brought together by a continuing chain of genres offering a type of communication particularly well suited to the perpetually reimagined communities in which we live.

Genre/nation

Tentative and suggestive rather than confident and definitive, this chapter must end with hypotheses rather than conclusions. If I had my way, these suggestions would lead to a general reconceptualization of genre problems in the widest possible context, in recognition of the continuity linking generic logic with other important forms of cultural reasoning.

1. Neither genre nor nation is a single coherent concept referring to a single coherent referent. The very notions of genre and nation depend on constant conflict among multiple competing but related notions, based on diverse user needs and varied parameters.
2. Genres are regulatory schemes facilitating the integration of diverse factions into a single unified social fabric. As such, genres share many functions with nations and other complex communities.
3. Genre formation begins with cycle-making creolization, combining gypsy

205

adjectives with established, land-owning generic substantives. Genrification and substantification take place when marginals plant their flag in the centre of the world, thus subjecting them to new adjectival settlements and permitting an eventual squatter takeover.

4. Nations, like genres, are born through a process that does not disappear with that birth. The imagining of community, like the genrification process, always operates dialectically, through the transformation of an already existing community/genre.

5. The processes and social situations designated by Habermas as the 'public sphere' and by Anderson as 'imagined communities' find both a parallel and a direct heir in film (and other media) genres and their 'constellated communities'.

6. The recurrent process of folding the margins into the centre, by which genres and nations alike are established and modified, has the power to regenrify everything from national anthems and national holidays to flags and other national emblems.

7. Satisfied with the current situation, having a vested interest in slowing the process of regenrification, entrenched users of generic and national terminology alike stress myths of distant origin, continued coherence and permanent inviolability in order to maintain stability. This denial of continued regenrification deprives the margins of the very rights and opportunities that once promoted the mobility of those now championing stability.

Genres and nations, these hypotheses suggest, are tied together in such a special way that, against all likelihood, genre theory might actually be a useful tool for analysing relationships between populations and the texts they use, for whatever purpose they might use them. Against all expectation, genre theory might actually help us think about nations.

Conclusion:
A semantic/syntactic/pragmatic approach to genre

> Far from postulating a uniquely internal, formal progression, I would propose that the relationship between the semantic and the syntactic constitutes the very site of nego-tiation between Hollywood and its audience, and thus between ritual and ideological uses of genre.... most genres go through a period of accommodation during which the public's desires are fitted to Hollywood's priorities (and vice-versa)....
>
> Whenever a lasting fit is obtained ... it is because a common ground has been found, a region where the audience's ritual values coincide with Hollywood's ideological ones. ... The successful genre owes its success ... to its ability to carry out both functions sim-ultaneously. It is this sleight of hand, this strategic overdetermination, that most clearly characterizes American film production during the studio years.
>
> Rick Altman, 'A Semantic/Syntactic Approach to Film Genre' (1984, pp. 13–15)

Some years ago I published an article proposing 'A Semantic/Syntactic Approach to Film Genre'. Reproduced as an appendix to this book, that article has enjoyed a certain success. As often happens with attempts to reduce complex phenomena to a simple formula, however, I remained haunted by certain aspects of my neat and manageable semantic/syntactic approach. 'Just where, for example, do we locate the exact border between the semantic and the syntactic?' (1984, p. 15), I asked towards the end of the article. I might also have given voice to some more obvi-ous and even more difficult questions: Of all the possible semantic and syntactic elements in a given film, how do we know to which ones we should attend? Don't different spectators notice different elements? Doesn't that change anything? I would have undoubtedly had ready answers at the time, but I now recognize that many of those answers would have been fundamentally circular in nature. The genre tells us what to notice, I would have said, and some spectators know the genre better than others.

Thus defended, the semantic/syntactic approach may serve analytical purposes admirably, offering a satisfying descriptive vocabulary useful for interpreting indi-vidual texts and relating them to existing generic groupings. When it comes to a broader theoretical and historical understanding, however, such a defence defi-nitely falls short. Even though the article made a valiant and perhaps at times successful effort to account for genre history, it ignored the threat that divergent perceptions represent not only for the overall semantic/syntactic theory, but even for its descriptive adequacy. Assuming stable recognition of semantic and syntac-tic factors across an unstable population, I underemphasized the fact that genres look different to different audiences, and that disparate viewers may perceive quite disparate semantic and syntactic elements in the same film. This blindness in turn kept me from fully investigating the possibility that genres might serve diverse groups diversely.

Because I was seeking a clear, supple, relevant terminology that could be shared by all spectators, my perspective was ironically limited *by the very nature of my project*. In search of the transparent and the objective, I couldn't possibly see that every terminology is to some extent tied to a particular use. Just as Todorov's project is compromised by his willingness to base a theory on someone else's definition and delimitation of swans, and Wittgenstein's entire enterprise is undermined by a decision to predicate his theory on the unexamined category of games, so I found my work compromised by the unspoken assumption that terminology can be neutral. So pleased was I to have figured out why the same texts are regularly treated by ritual and ideological critics in radically opposed ways that I failed to recognize in this opposition the key to the whole problem. While the article acknowledged a genre's ability simultaneously to satisfy differing needs, which I attributed to two collective singulars (the 'audience' and 'Hollywood'), I never awakened to the fact that genres may have multiple conflicting audiences, that Hollywood itself harbours many divergent interests, and that these multiple genre practitioners use genres and generic terminology in differing and potentially contradictory ways.

I continue to believe that genres embody precisely those moments/situations/structures that are capable of simultaneously benefiting multiple users. But this ability to satisfy several groups at the same time complicates the issue significantly. When we look at established genres all we can see is the coincidence, alignment and reinforcement so characteristic of successful genres. This is why it has been important in this book to look at patterns of generic change – genre origins, genre redefinition and genre repurposing – along with the more traditional topics of generic stability and structure.

My attempt to forge an objective terminology suffered from a failure to recognize the discursive nature of genres. I take some solace in reporting that I had good company in this particular doghouse. From Aristotle to Wittgenstein and from Frye to Fowler (but with the notable exception of recent forays by Rosmarin and Beebee), most genre theories have been less than fully sensitive to generic discursivity. As I have suggested in the present book, genres now appear to me not just discursive but, because they are mechanisms for co-ordinating diverse users, multi-discursive. Instead of utilizing a single master language, as most previous genre theoreticians would have it, a genre may appropriately be considered multi-coded. Each genre is simultaneously defined by multiple codes, corresponding to the multiple groups who, by helping to define the genre, may be said to 'speak' the genre. When the diverse groups using the genre are considered together, genres appear as regulatory schemes facilitating the integration of diverse factions into a single social fabric.

A semantic/syntactic/pragmatic approach

Though semantic/syntactic terminology may be useful in describing the effects of generic discursivity, it is not by itself sufficient to expose or explain them. That is why I have found it necessary to build the semantic/syntactic/pragmatic approach presented in this book. At this point, a few words about the notion of pragmatics are in order. A simple linguistic analogy will help explain this concept. Human sound-producing capacity is theoretically infinite in nature, yet individual languages recognize as meaningful only a small percentage of the sound variations actually produced by speakers. Linguists and other language users distinguish between meaningful and meaningless sound variation by way of a simple procedure called the commutation test. This test involves hypothetically substituting one sound for another and noting whether the change of sounds makes a difference in meaning; if the meaning changes, then the difference between the two sounds is recognized as significant and meaningful. As outlined more fully in Chapter 10, this process depends on the assumption that language is split into separate levels: only by interrogating the level of meaning can we identify significance at the level of sound variation.

Following Jurij Lotman (1977), I have suggested that this pattern can be extended beyond language to an understanding of texts (1981). Beyond the levels of phonemes and morphemes, one can discern further levels dependent on the use to which language is put in a particular text or group of texts. Applying the commutation test to a poem or a film, we can discover which linguistic units take on meaning at a textual level. In one sense, this logic is flawless; the same structures that make it possible for language to communicate meaning are redeployed to create meaning at a higher level. Just as the level of meaningful words is necessary to ground the commutation that identifies which sounds are significant, so a textual level is necessary to ground linguistic meaning. To put it more simply, you can't decide which sounds are significant without knowing which of all possible sound combinations have meaning as words; similarly, you can't know which sound groupings have meaning as words without knowing how those sound clusters are used in practice. Use grounds linguistic meaning just as linguistic meaning grounds sound significance. Attention to that use is what linguists call *pragmatic* analysis.

The logic and the simplicity of this claim, along with the apparent fixity of language, kept me from recognizing one fundamental fact about this process, however. Far from being permanently grounded at a high level by some universally accepted practice, this system involves an infinite regression where each level, instead of being permanently guaranteed by the next, is only temporarily buttressed by a level that is itself only temporarily grounded by a level that is itself . . . and so on. Rather than breeding stability and security, this system thrives on borrowed time and deferral. The long history and social usefulness of individual languages may give them a high degree of apparent stability, yet even they are never as stable and secure as our dictionaries imply. The farther we go from phonemes and morphemes towards textual uses and generic uses, the more problematic and unstable the system.

Though I may have paid too little attention to the exponentially increasing 'use indeterminacy' factor as we move from left to right along the noise/phoneme/morpheme/text/genre chain, I still maintain that textual and generic signification are created in a manner similar to linguistic meaning, by use of the same principles at a higher level. We know which sounds have phonemic value by testing (through commutation) their use in specific words or expressions; we know in turn which phoneme clusters count as meaningful words by testing through commutation their use in specific texts. We know which specific textual patterns count as meaningful only by virtue of their deployment in broader cultural institutions like genres. The meaning of each level is assured only through its use at a higher level.

It is precisely this 'use factor' that pragmatics addresses. Whether we are discussing literature or cinema (or any other meaning-making system), the base language(s) surpass their own structure and meaning as they are integrated into textual uses. This is the level that semantic/syntactic terminology serves so well. In order to understand which semantic and syntactic factors actually make meaning, however, it is necessary to subject them to a further analysis based on the uses to which they are put. Though the process appears entirely linear, with each level determined and defined by the next, that linearity is actually no more than a convenient fiction, for even the simplest language or text may have multiple users and branching uses.

If the whole story were told, at every level of analysis we would have to recognize that the next level up is not limited to a single use pattern against which the lower level can be commuted. Unsure which use pattern to take seriously, we would have to commute every potentially significant unit multiple times, in relation to each of the different higher-level uses with which it is associated. Leading to massive undecidability, this situation would destroy our ability to separate meaningful sounds from noise, words from jabberwocky, and textual structures from random patterns. Linguistic clarity would be sacrificed, along with shared cultural expectations. So undesirable is this situation that virtually all cultures have devised ways to reduce linguistic usage dispersion (and thus the effects of use indeterminacy) in order to guarantee continued clear communication. If every meaning depends on an indeterminate number of conflicting users, then no stable communication can take place; so society artificially restricts the range of acceptable uses, thus controlling the potential dispersion and infinite regression of the meaning-making series. If every meaning had to be deferred, then communication would literally be impossible; society far prefers to restrict communication (which is thus always slight miscommunication) rather than risk full freedom, which might destroy communication altogether.

Linguistic variation is relatively easy to restrain. At the level of texts and institutions, however, usage dispersion is virtually impossible to contain. This is why an understanding of broad-based representational practices like literature and cinema requires a separate pragmatics. Because semantic and syntactic elements are used in so many different ways, pragmatic analysis of genres cannot depend solely on commutation as its major analytical technique. Instead of looking primarily down the chain of meaning towards texts, morphemes and phonemes, pragmatic analysis must constantly attend to the competition among multiple users that characterizes genres. As such, pragmatic analysis necessarily abandons the linearity of the linguistic model on which it was originally based. Always assuming multiple users of various sorts – not only various spectator groups, but producers, distributors, exhibitors, cultural agencies, and many others as well – pragmatics recognizes that some familiar patterns, such as genres, owe their very existence to that multiplicity.

Reception, opposition, poaching

The relationship between pragmatics and reception study deserves special attention. For a long time, traditional approaches to genre study assumed that genres (a) pre-exist spectators and (b) guide audience reception. Reception study denies the latter claim but accepts the former. Because the semantic/syntactic/prag- matic approach instead treats genres as a site of struggle and co-operation among multiple users, it must deny both claims. Whereas reception study limits its attention to various individuals' or groups' processing of a text or genre, pragmatic analysis treats reading as a more complex process involving not only hegemonic complicity across user groups but also a feedback system connecting user groups. Instead of a one-way text-to-reader configuration, pragmatics thus assumes a constant (if sometimes extremely slow) cross-fertilization process whereby the interests of one group may appear in the actions of another. Thus film production and genre formation cannot be systematically and simple-mindedly located upstream from film viewing, as most reception studies would have it. Instead of raising reception to an all-powerful final position in the production/distribution/exhibition/consumption/interpretation process (as several recent theorists have done), pragmatics recognizes reception study as an appropriate way to acknowledge the activities of specific user groups, but only in order subsequently to embed reception in a broader process-oriented and interactive analysis of competing user groups.

Like reception study, a semantic/syntactic/pragmatic approach refuses determinacy to textual structures taken alone, but in addition it acknowledges the difficulty of extracting those textual structures from the institutions and social habits that frame them and lend them the appearance of making meaning on their own. While pragmatic analysis sometimes destabilizes meaning by showing just how dependent it is on particular uses of a text or genre, at other times it succeeds in revealing the meaning-grounding institutions that make meaning seem to arise directly out of semantics and syntax. Just as it is no longer acceptable to base all genre theory on the special cases of the musical and the Western, it is unacceptable to base our understanding of textual determinacy on the case of marginal reception. Yet, as I have argued, marginal reception does have a special position in the theory of genres, like that of nations, because new structures regularly grow out of spectator positions once characterized as downright eccentric.

Just as it is essential to understand the breadth of a semantic/syntactic/pragmatic approach as compared to reception study, it is important to distinguish between the systemic approach of pragmatics and the more limited (though helpful) notions offered by Stuart Hall and Michel de Certeau. Because Hall and de Certeau have concentrated heavily – especially in their most influential work – on the act of reading itself, they have often failed to address the broader problems covered by pragmatic analysis. In his article 'Encoding/Decoding' (1980), Hall has described readers as either accepting, negotiating or opposing an intended reading. For de Certeau, 'readers are travellers; they move across lands belonging to someone else, like nomads poaching their way across fields they did not write, despoiling the wealth of Egypt to enjoy it themselves' (1984, p. 174). The 'poaching nomad' metaphor proves strikingly revelatory of Hall's and de Certeau's fundamental conservatism. According to de Certeau's account, there once was a great nation named Egypt, now despoiled by a tribe of nomads. Nothing before, nothing after. But how did Egypt get to be a great nation and what happened to the nomads? De Certeau's 'snapshot' historiography occludes discussion of these questions.

Instead of describing the overall process of reading and its relationship to institutions, both Hall and de Certeau are content to enlarge a single moment of that process. How did intended readings become identifiable as such? How did some people achieve the right to encode meanings, while others are reduced to decoding? As Hall and his followers model the situation, even the most oppositional reading is still just an act of decoding, ultimately dependent on a prior act of encoding. While the connections between encoding and decoding are carefully traced, no clear path leads from decoding to subsequent encodings, from opposing to intending, from the margins of a current society to the centre of a reconfigured society. Similarly, de Certeau assumes that the map has already been drawn by others, and that no nomadic activity can ever alter it. Not even squatters, who might claim their rights and thus settle the land, readers are treated as poachers on land owned by someone else, who established claim to the land in some mythic past. But just what did happen to Joseph, Moses and their tribe of nomads?

Over the past two decades, reception study has become a growth industry. Surprisingly, however, reception-oriented theorists have failed to draw the radical conclusions of their insights. Stressing localized reception (in time as well as space) of texts produced by someone outside the reception sphere, critics have never taken seriously the ability of audiences to generate their own texts and thus to become intenders, mappers and owners in their own right. Only when we voluntarily restrict our vision to a narrow slice of history do the players appear to be Egypt and the nomads. When we take a wider view, we easily recognize that civilizations have a more complex relation to poachers and nomads. In fact, every civilization was, in an important sense, produced by the settling of nomads. But once they have settled and drawn a new map, every former band of nomads is nothing more than another Egypt now subject to the poaching of a new band of nomads. With each cycle, the nomadic poachers become property owners, and thus authors, map-makers and intenders, thereby establishing the capital that attracts still others' poaching activity.

Tales of marauding tribes on the southern reaches of the Nile may seem entirely unrelated to film genre, yet the systems operate similarly. In order to create new film cycles, producers must attach new adjectives to existing substantival genres. In so doing, producers are precisely 'poaching' on established genre territory. Yet this unauthorized, product-differentiating activity often settles into a new genre immediately subject to further nomadic raiding. Cycles and genres, nomads and civilizations, raids and institutions, poachers and owners – all are part of the ongoing remapping process that alternately energizes and fixes human perception. When cycles settle into genres, their fixity makes them perfect targets for raids by new cycles. When their wandering in the wilderness is done, nomads spawn civilizations only to be robbed and plundered by yet other wandering tribes. After their raid on existing film vocabulary, feminist film critics formed a series of successful institutions that for now protect their acquisitions but must eventually succumb to yet other raiders. Successful poachers eventually retire with their spoils to a New World where they are in turn despoiled by a new generation of poachers. Those who poached on *drama* by adding to it a nomadic *melo-* need not be surprised when a new group of nomads kidnaps the resultant *melodrama* and mates it with a wandering *family*.

Writing at a point in history when it was essential to free critics from the tyranny of textual analysis, Hall and de Certeau rightly accord to readers a degree of freedom and activity previously unavailable. To the extent that they restrict their analysis to a single category of users (readers), however, they are unable to capture the pragmatic complexity of literary and filmic systems. In their work, and that of many other critics and theoreticians writing over the last two decades, one senses a residue of the preceding text-based era. Today we have good cause to understand texts as one part of a far broader cultural enterprise. Only by shifting attention from reception practices alone to the broader – and conflicting – usage patterns of all users can we escape the residual tyranny of the text-king.

Planning and using cities and texts

When production and reception are thought of as primarily mental activities, they are not always easy to imagine. Material examples offer a more satisfying way of figuring the challenge and the promise of a semantic/syntactic/pragmatic approach. City planning offers particularly clear benefits in this regard. Take the example of Brasilia, recently recounted to me by Brazilian film scholar Ismail Xavier. As designed in the 50s by city-planner Lúcio Costa and architect Oscar Niemeyer, Brazil's new inland capital was to consist of multi-class units each with all necessary services. It soon became clear, however, that this utopian vision would not succeed, since government functionaries seeking lodging close to their centrally located offices quickly drove lower-class residents out of convenient locations. That is, the carefully developed Costa/Niemeyer plan, with a clearly identified syntactic arrangement of semantic elements, was opposed by a group of poachers. Thus far, the circumstances bear out Hall's and de Certeau's approaches.

Where the pragmatic side of semantic/syntactic/pragmatic analysis shows its mettle, however, is in its geographical and chronological expansion of use analysis. It is not enough to concentrate on the functionaries' reading of this city plan. What benefits accrued to other groups through this process? Why did the lower classes move? Did they find benefits in their new location (such as reduced cost, increased space, or intensified communication within their own group)? What interest beyond easy access to the workplace did the new inhabitants have (for example, the prestige of centrality in a city lacking more traditional markers of success, such as differentiated buildings)? The original plan clearly served the well-known leftist utopian notions of the planners; what social, economic and government purposes are served by the functionaries' poaching? The original plan represented an ideal, indeed a *genre*, of city planning characteristic of many projects around the world, before and since. The subsequent re-ghettoization just as clearly introduced a revised set of relationships among the city's users, corresponding to a different genre built on partial satisfaction of the needs of multiple user groups.

213

The above 'geographical' expansion of pragmatic analysis to other contemporary user groups must be complemented by a 'chronological' expansion to past and future city-planning projects. Costa and Niemeyer were clearly designing not just as individuals with an imagination, but also in response to the experience of previous populations in previous spaces. That is, they themselves are the site not of a single user priority but of several contradictory priorities representing practitioners of previous city plans. Their own plan is thus 'their own plan' only to the extent that such an expression can imply co-ordination of several use desires evinced by others. Moving down the flow of time, how did Costa and Niemeyer use the experience of Brasilia in their subsequent planning? How did this experiment affect others' plans? While each architect's attempt to resolve the problems addressed by Costa and Niemeyer might be thought of as a particular individual's design, it must be recognized that subsequent planners are simply the interpreters of user desires made evident by Brasilia and other related designs. To the extent that an individual planner balances those needs in a way already made familiar by other planners, a particular genre is reinforced and renewed. As opposed to the analysis of individual texts and their reception, understanding of genres requires this geographical and chronological expansion.

Just as city planners once thought that people would automatically inhabit their city as designed, so genre theorists once believed that readers and viewers would automatically follow the lead of textual producers. In fact, there was once a time when both expectations were to a great extent correct – not because use-as-planned is built into cities or texts, but because the economic and social support structures surrounding cities and texts silently and effectively exhorted populations and audiences to play their expected role. As long as audiences and critics alike regularly took the practice of use-as-directed to imply use-as-planned, we needed to be reminded of the difference between the two. Fifteen years ago, it was important to have Roger Odin, in his initial foray into the realm of semio-pragmatics, point out that 'images never tell us how to read them' (1983, p. 68).

In 1999, however, we no longer need to be reminded that different audiences can make different meanings out of the same text. Instead, what we need is an approach that

- addresses the fact that every text has multiple users;
- considers why different users develop different readings;
- theorizes the relationship among those users; and
- actively considers the effect of multiple conflicting uses on the production, labelling, and display of films and genres alike.

In constructing a semantic/syntactic/pragmatic approach to genre, I have attempted to address these very goals. This has led me to propose that what we call *genre* is in fact something quite different from what has always been supposed.

Instead of a word or a category capable of clear and stable definition (the goal of previous genre theorists), genre has here been presented as a multivalent term multiply and variously valorized by diverse user groups. Successful genres of course carry with them an air of user agreement about the nature both of genres in general and of this genre in particular, thus implying that genres are the unproblematic product of user sharing. In fact, the moments of clear and stable sharing typically adduced as generic models represent special cases within a broader general situation of user competition. While genres may make meaning by regulating and co-ordinating disparate users, they always do so in an arena where users with divergent interests compete to carry out their own programmes.

As a final point, which has ramifications far too broad to have entered fully into the argument of this book, I would simply point out that what I have just claimed about genre is true of every communicative structure in every language ever devised. Though the social utility of language has forced cultures to downplay this point, every word, every meaningful gesture, every film image makes meaning only through a process of multiple commutation engendered by the multiple usefulness of the sign in question. In spite of Saussure's claim to be presenting a *Course in GENERAL Linguistics*, our theories of language have always been theories of the exception, of the socially stabilized special case. A truly general theory would have to pass – as I have here – through analysis of contradictory usage, constant repurposing and systematic miscommunication, thus surpassing the specially determinate situation we call language.

The positions presented and defended in this book offer an avenue to a renewed general theory of meaning, one that fully recognizes the importance of competition and miscomprehension to any theory of communication and comprehension. Presented here solely with relation to film genre, semantic/syntactic/pragmatic analysis may be applied to any set of texts, because it is truly based on a general theory of meaning.

Appendix *

A semantic/syntactic approach to film genre

What is a genre? Which films are genre films? How do we know to which genre they belong? As fundamental as these questions may seem, they are almost never asked – let alone answered – in the field of cinema studies. Most comfortable in the seemingly uncomplicated world of Hollywood classics, genre critics have felt little need to reflect openly on the assumptions underlying their work. Everything seems so clear. Why bother to theorize, American pragmatism asks, when there are no problems to solve? We all know a genre when we see one. Scratch only where it itches. According to this view, genre theory would be called for only in the unlikely event that knowledgeable genre critics disagree on basic issues. The task of the theorist is then to adjudicate among conflicting approaches, not so much by dismissing unsatisfactory positions but by constructing a model that reveals the relationship between differing critical claims and their function within a broader cultural context. Whereas the French clearly view theory as a first principle, Americans tend to see it as a last resort, something to turn to when all else fails.

Even in this limited, pragmatic view, whereby theory is to be avoided at all costs, the time for theory is nevertheless upon us. The clock has struck thirteen; we had best call in the theoreticians. The more genre criticism I read, the more uncertainty I note in the choice or extent of essential critical terms. Often what appears as hesitation in the terminology of a single critic will turn into a clear contradiction when studies by two or more critics are compared. Now, it would be one thing if these contradictions were simply a matter of fact. On the contrary, however, I suggest that these are not temporary problems, bound to disappear as soon as we have more information or better analysts. Instead, these uncertainties reflect constitutive weaknesses of current notions of genre. Three contradictions in particular seem worthy of a good scratch.

When we establish the corpus of a genre we generally tend to do two things at once, and thus establish two alternative groups of texts, each corresponding to a different notion of corpus. On the one hand, we have an unwieldy list of texts corresponding to a simple, tautological definition of the genre (e.g., Western = film that takes place in the American West, or musical = film with diegetic music). This *inclusive* list is the kind that gets consecrated by generic encyclopaedias or checklists. On the other hand, we find critics, theoreticians, and other arbiters of taste sticking to a familiar canon that has little to do with the broad, tautological

---

* This text was first published in *Cinema Journal* 23, no. 3 (Spring 1984), pp. 6–18. It has since been reprinted, with slight modifications, in *Film Genre Reader*, ed. Barry Grant (Austin: University of Texas Press, 1986), pp. 26–40; in *Film Genre Reader II*, ed. Barry Grant (Austin: University of Texas Press, 1995), pp. 26–40; and in *Film Theory and Criticism: Introductory Readings*, eds. Leo Braudy and Marshall Cohen (New York: Oxford University Press, 1998; fifth edition), pp. 630–641.

definition. Here the same films are mentioned again and again, not only because they are well known or particularly well made, but because they somehow seem to represent the genre more fully and faithfully than other apparently more tangential films. This *exclusive* list of films generally occurs not in a dictionary context, but instead in connection with attempts to arrive at the overall meaning or structure of a genre. The relative status of these alternate approaches to the constitution of a generic corpus may easily be sensed from the following typical conservation:

'I mean, what do you do with Elvis Presley films? You can hardly call them musicals.'

'Why not? They're loaded with songs and they've got a narrative that ties the numbers together, don't they?'

'Yeah, I suppose. I guess you'd have to call *Fun in Acapulco* a musical, but it's sure no *Singin' in the Rain*. Now there's a real musical.'

When is a musical not a musical? When it has Elvis Presley in it. What may at first have seemed no more than an uncertainty on the part of the critical community now clearly appears as a contradiction. Because there are two competing notions of generic corpus on our critical scene, it is perfectly possible for a film to be simultaneously included in a particular generic corpus and excluded from that same corpus.

A second uncertainty is associated with the relative status of theory and history in genre studies. Before semiotics came along, generic titles and definitions were largely borrowed from the industry itself; what little generic theory there was tended therefore to be confused with historical analysis. With the heavy influence of semiotics on generic theory over the last two decades, self-conscious *critical* vocabulary came to be systematically preferred to the now-suspect *user* vocabulary. The contributions of Propp, Lévi-Strauss, Frye and Todorov to genre studies have not been uniformly productive, however, because of the special place reserved for genre study within the semiotic project. If structuralist critics systematically chose as the object of their analysis large groups of popular texts, it was in order to cover a basic flaw in the semiotic understanding of textual analysis. Now, one of the most striking aspects of Saussure's theory of language is his emphasis on the inability of any single individual to effect change within that landscape.[1] The fixity of the linguistic community thus serves as justification for Saussure's fundamentally synchronic approach to language. When literary semioticians applied this linguistic model to problems of textual analysis, they never fully addressed the notion of interpretive community implied by Saussure's linguistic community. Preferring narrative to narration, system to process, and *histoire* to *discours*, the first semiotics ran headlong into a set of restrictions and contradictions that eventually spawned the more process-oriented second semiotics. It is in this context that we must see the resolutely synchronic attempts of Propp, Lévis-Strauss, Todorov, and many another influential genre analyst.[2] Unwilling to compromise their systems by the historical notion of linguistic community, these theoreticians instead substituted the generic context for the linguistic community, as if the weight of numerous 'similar' texts were sufficient to locate the meaning of a text independently of a specific audience. Far from being sensitive to concerns of history, semiotic genre analysis was by definition and from the start devoted to bypassing history. Treating genres as neutral constructs, semioticians of the 60s and early 70s blinded us to the discursive power of generic formations. Because they treated genres as the interpretive community, they were unable to perceive the important role of genres in exercising influence on the interpretive community. Instead of reflecting openly on the way in which Hollywood uses its genres to short-circuit the normal interpretive process, structuralist critics plunged headlong into the trap, taking Hollywood's ideological effect for a natural ahistorical cause.

Genres were always – and continue to be – treated as if they spring full-blown from the head of Zeus. It is thus not surprising to find that even the most advanced of current genre theories, those that see generic texts as negotiating a relationship between a specific production system and a given audience, still hold to a notion of genre that is fundamentally ahistorical in nature.[3] More and more, however, as scholars come to know the full range of individual Hollywood genres, we are finding that genres are far from exhibiting the homogeneity that this synchronic approach posits. Whereas one Hollywood genre may be borrowed with little change from another medium, a second genre may develop slowly, change constantly, and surge recognizably before settling into a familiar pattern, while a third may go through an extended series of paradigms, one of which may be claimed as dominant. As long as Hollywood genres are conceived as Platonic categories, existing outside the flow of time, it will be impossible to reconcile *genre theory*, which has always accepted as given the timelessness of a characteristic structure, and *genre history*, which has concentrated on chronicling the development, deployment and disappearance of this same structure.

A third contradiction looms larger still, for it involves the two general directions taken by genre criticism as a whole over the last decade or two. Following Lévi-Strauss, a growing number of critics throughout the 70s dwelled on the mythical qualities of Hollywood genres and thus on the audience's ritual relationship to genre film. The film industry's desire to please and its need to attract consumers were viewed as the mechanism whereby spectators were actually able to designate the kind of films they wanted to see. By choosing the films it would patronize, the audience revealed its preferences and its beliefs, thus inducing Hollywood studios to produce films reflecting its desires. Participation in the genre film experience thus reinforces spectator expectations and desires. Far from being limited to mere entertainment, filmgoing offers a satisfaction more akin to that associated with established religion. Most openly championed by John Cawelti, this ritual approach appears as well in books by Leo Brandy, Frank McConnell, Michael Wood, Will Wright and Tom Schatz.[4] It has the merit not only of accounting for the intensity of identification typical of American genre film audiences, but it also encourages the placing of genre film narratives into an appropriately wider context of narrative analysis.

Curiously, however, while the ritual approach was attributing ultimate authorship to the audience, with the studios simply serving, for a price, the national will, a parallel ideological approach was demonstrating how audiences are manipulated by the business and political interest of Hollywood. Starting with *Cahiers du cinéma* and moving rapidly to *Screen, Jump Cut* and a growing number of journals, this view has recently joined hands with a more general critique of the mass media offered by the Frankfurt school.[5] Looked at in this way, genres are simply the generalized, identifiable structures through which Hollywood's rhetoric flows. Far more attentive to discursive concerns than the ritual approach, which remains faithful to Lévi-Strauss in emphasizing narrative systems, the ideological approach stresses questions of representation and identification previously left aside. Simplifying a bit, we might say that it characterizes each individual genre as a specific type of lie, an untruth whose most characteristic feature is its ability to masquerade as truth. Whereas the ritual approach sees Hollywood as responding to societal pressure and thus expressing audience desires, the ideological approach claims that Hollywood takes advantage of spectator energy and psychic invest-ment in order to lure the audience into Hollywood's own positions. The two are irreducibly opposed, yet these irreconcilable arguments continue to represent the most interesting and well defended of recent approaches to Hollywood genre film.

Here we have three problems that I take to be not limited to a single school of criticism or a single genre but implicit in every major field of current genre analy-sis. In nearly every argument about the limits of a generic corpus, the opposition of an inclusive list to an exclusive canon surfaces. Wherever genres are discussed, the divergent concerns of theorists and historians are increasingly obvious. And even when the topic is limited to genre theory alone, no agreement can be found between those who propose a ritual function for film genres and those who cham-pion an ideological purpose. We find ourselves desperately in need of a theory which, without dismissing any of these widely held positions, would explain the circumstances underlying their existence, thus paving the way for a critical methodology that encompasses and indeed thrives on their inherent contradic-tions. If we have learnt anything from poststructuralist criticism, we have learnt not to fear logical contradictions but instead to respect the extraordinary energy generated by the play of contradictory forces within a field. What we need now is a new critical strategy enabling us simultaneously to understand and to capitalize on the tensions existing in current generic criticism.

In assessing theories of genre, critics have often labelled them according to a par-ticular theory's most salient features or the type of activity to which it devotes its most concentrated attention. Paul Hernadi, for example, recognizes four general classes of genre theory: expressive, pragmatic, structural and mimetic.[6] In his extremely influ-ential introduction to *The Fantastic,* Tzvetan Todorov opposes historical to theoretical genres, as well as elementary genres to their complex counterparts.[7] Others, like Frederick Jameson, have followed Todorov and other French semioti-cians in distinguishing between semantic and syntactic approaches to genre.[8] While there is anything but general agreement on the exact frontier separating semantic from syntactic views, we can as a whole distinguish between generic definitions that depend on a list of common traits, attitudes, characters, shots, locations, set, and the like – thus stressing the semantic elements that make up the genre – and definitions that play up instead certain constitutive relationships between undesignated and variable place-holders – relationships that might be called the genre's fundamental syntax. The semantic approach thus stresses the genre's building blocks, while the syntactic view privileges the structures into which they are arranged.

The difference between semantic and syntactic definitions is perhaps most apparent in familiar approaches to the Western. Jean Mitry provides us with a clear example of the most common definition. The Western, Mitry proposes, is a 'film whose action, situated in the American West, is consistent with the atmosphere, the values, and the conditions of existence in the Far West between 1840 and 1900'.[9] Based on the presence or absence of easily identifiable elements, Mitry's nearly tautological definition implies a broad, undifferentiated generic corpus. Marc Vernet's more detailed list is more sensitive to cinematic concerns, yet overall it follows the same semantic model. Vernet outlines general atmosphere ('emphasis on basic elements, such as earth, dust, water, and leather'), stock characters ('the tough/soft cowboy, the lonely sheriff, the faithful or treacherous Indian, and the strong but tender woman'), as well as technical elements ('use of fast tracking and crane shots').[10] An entirely different solution is suggested by Jim Kitses, who emphasizes not the vocabulary of the Western but the relationships linking lexical elements. For Kitses the Western grows out of a dialectic between the West as garden and as desert (between culture and nature, community and individual, future and past).[11] The Western's vocabulary is thus generated by this syntactic relationship, and not vice versa. John Cawelti attempts to systematize the Western in a similar fashion: the Western is always set on or near a frontier, where man encounters his uncivilized double. The Western thus takes place on the border between two lands, between two eras, and with a hero who remains divided between two value systems (for he combines the town's morals with the outlaw's skills).[12]

In passing we might well note the divergent qualities associated with these two approaches. While the semantic approach has little explanatory power, it is applicable to a larger number of films. Conversely, the syntactic approach surrenders broad applicability in return for the ability to isolate a genre's specific meaning-bearing structures. This alternative seemingly leaves the genre analyst in a quandary: choose the semantic view and you give up *explanatory power*; choose the syntactic approach and you do without *broad applicability*. In terms of the Western, the problem of the so-called 'Pennsylvania Western' is instructive here. To most observers it seems quite clear that films like *High, Wide and Handsome* (Rouben Mamoulian, 1937), *Drums Along the Mohawk* (John Ford, 1939) and *Unconquered* (Cecil B. DeMille, 1947) have definite affinities with the Western. Employing familiar characters set in relationships similar to their counterparts west of the Mississippi, these films construct plots and develop a frontier structure clearly derived from decades of Western novels and films. But they do it in Pennsylvania, and in the wrong century. Are these films Westerns because they share the syntax of hundreds of films we call Westerns? Or are they not Westerns, because they don't fit Mitry's definition?

In fact, the 'Pennsylvania Western' (like the urban, spaghetti and sci-fi varieties) represents a quandary only because critics have insisted on dismissing one type of definition and approach in favour of another. As a rule, the semantic and syntactic approaches to genre have been proposed, analysed, evaluated and disseminated separately, in spite of the complementarity implied by their names. Indeed, many arguments centering on generic problems have arisen only when semantic and syntactic theoreticians have simply talked past each other, each unaware of the other's divergent orientation. I maintain that these two categories of generic analysis are complementary, that they can be combined, and in fact that some of the most important questions of genre study can be asked only when they *are* combined. In short, I propose a semantic/syntactic approach to genre study.

In order to discover whether the proposed semantic/syntactic approach provides any new understanding, let us return to the three contradictions delineated earlier. First, there is the split corpus that characterizes current genre study – on the one side an inclusive list, on the other an exclusive pantheon. It should now be quite clear that each corpus corresponds to a different approach to generic analysis and definition. Tautological semantic definitions, with their goal of broad applicability, outline a large genre of semantically similar texts, while syntactic definitions, intent as they are on explaining the genre, stress a narrow range of texts that privilege specific syntactic relationships. To insist on one of these approaches to the exclusion of the other is to turn a blind eye on the necessarily dual nature of any generic corpus. For every film that participates actively in the elaboration of a genre's syntax there are numerous others content to deploy in no particular relationship the elements traditionally associated with the genre. We need to recognize that not all genre films relate to their genre in the same way or to the same extent. By simultaneously accepting semantic and syntactic notions of genre we avail ourselves of a possible way to deal critically with differing levels of 'genericity'. In addition, a dual approach permits a far more accurate description of the numerous intergeneric connections typically suppressed by single-minded approaches. It is simply not possible to describe Hollywood cinema accurately without the ability to account for the numerous films that innovate by combining the syntax of one genre with the semantics of another. In fact, it is only when we begin to take up problems of genre history that the full value of the semantic/syntactic approach becomes obvious.

As I pointed out earlier, most genre theoreticians have followed the semiotic model and steered clear of historical considerations. Even in the relatively few cases where problems of generic history have been addressed, as in the attempts of Metz and Wright to periodize the Western, history has been conceptualized as nothing more than a discontinuous succession of discrete moments, each characterized by a different basic version of the genre – that is, by a different syntactic pattern that the genre adopts.[13] In short, genre theory has up to now aimed almost exclusively at the elaboration of a synchronic model approximating the syntactic operation of a specific genre. Now, quite obviously, no major genre remains unchanged over the many decades of its existence. In order to mask the scandal of applying synchronic analysis to an evolving form, critics have been extremely clever in their creation of categories designed to negate the notion of change and to imply the perpetual self-identify of each genre. Westerns and horror films are often referred to as 'classic', the musical is defined in terms of the so-called 'Platonic ideal' of integration, the critical corpus of the melodrama has largely been restricted to the post-war efforts of Sirk and Minnelli, and so on. Lacking a workable hypothesis regarding the historical dimension of generic syntax, we have insulated that syntax, along with the genre theory that studies it, from the flow of time.

As a working hypothesis, I suggest that genres arise in one of two fundamental ways: either a relatively stable set of semantic givens is developed through syntactic experimentation into a coherent and durable syntax, or an already existing syntax adopts a new set of semantic elements. In the first case, the genre's characteristic semantic configuration is identifiable long before a syntactic pattern has become stabilized, thus justifying the previously mentioned duality of the generic corpus. In cases of this first type, description of the way in which a set of semantic givens develops into a henceforth relatively stable syntax constitutes the history of the genre while at the same time identifying the structures on which genre theory depends. In dealing with the early development of the musical, for example, we might well follow the attempts during the 1927–1930 period to build a backstage or night-club semantics into a melodramatic syntax, with music regularly reflecting the sorrow of death or parting. After the slack years of 1931–1932, however, the musical began to grow in a new direction; while maintaining substantially the same semantic materials, the genre increasingly related the energy of music-making to the joy of coupling, the strength of the community and the pleasures of entertainment. Far from being exiled from history, the musical's characteristic syntax can be shown by the generic historian to grow out of the linking of specific semantic elements at identifiable points. A measure of continuity is thus developed between the task of the historian and that of the theoretician, for the task of both are now redefined as the study of the interrelationships between semantic elements and syntactic bonds.

This continuity between history and theory is operative as well in the second type of generic development posited earlier. When we analyse the large variety of wartime films that portray the Japanese or Germans as villains, we tend to have recourse to extra-filmic events in order to explain particular characterizations. We thus miss the extent to which films like *All Through the Night* (Vincent Sherman, 1942), *Sherlock Holmes and the Voice of Terror* (John Rawlins, 1942), or the serial *Don Winslow of the Navy* (1943) simply transfer to a new set of semantic elements the righteous cops-punish-criminals syntax that the gangster genre of the early 30s had turned to starting with *G-Men* (William Keighley, 1935). Again, it is the interplay of syntax and semantics that provides grist for both the historical and the theoretical mill. Or take the development of the science fiction film. At first defined only by a relatively stable science fiction semantics, the genre first began borrowing the syntactic relationships previously established by the horror film, only to move in recent years increasingly towards the syntax of the Western. By maintaining simultaneous descriptions according to both parameters, we are not likely to fall into the trap of equating *Star Wars* (George Lucas, 1977) with the Western (as numerous recent critics have done), even though it shares certain syntactic patterns with that genre. In short, by taking seriously the multiple connections between semantics and syntax, we establish a new continuity, relating film analysis, genre theory and genre history.

But what is it that energizes the transformation of a borrowed semantics into a uniquely Hollywood syntax? Or what is it that justifies the intrusion of a new semantics into a well-defined syntactic situation? Far from postulating a uniquely internal, formal progression, I would propose that the relationship between the semantic and the syntactic constitutes the very site of negotiation between Hollywood and its audience, and thus between ritual and ideological uses of genre. Often, when critics of opposing persuasions disagree over a major issue, it is because they have established within the same general corpus two separate and opposed canons, each supporting one point of view. Thus, when Catholics and Protestants or liberals and conservatives quote the Bible, they are rarely quoting the same passages. The striking fact about ritual and ideological genre theoreticians, however, is that they regularly stress the same canon, that small group of texts most clearly reflecting a genre's stable syntax. The films of John Ford, for example, have played a major role in the development of ritual and ideological approaches alike. From Sarris and Bogdanovich to Schatz and Wright, champions of Ford's understanding and transparent expression of American values have stressed the communitarian side of his films, while others, starting with the influential *Cahiers du cinéma* study of *Young Mr. Lincoln* (1939), have shown how a call to community can be used to lure spectators into a carefully chosen, ideologically determined subject position. A similar situation obtains in the musical, where a growing body of ritual analyses of the Astaire–Rogers and post-war MGM Freed unit films is matched by an increasing number of studies demonstrating the ideological investment of those very same films.[14] The corpus of nearly every major genre has developed in the same way, with critics of both camps gravitating toward and eventually basing their arguments on the same narrow range of films. Just as Minnelli and Sirk dominate the criticism of melodrama, Hitchcock has become synonymous with the thriller. Of all major genres, only film noir has failed to attract critics of both sides to a shared corpus of major texts – no doubt because of the general inability of ritual critics to accommodate the genre's anti-communitarian stance.

This general agreement on a canon stems, I would claim, from the fundamentally bivalent nature of any relatively stable generic syntax. If it takes a long time to establish a generic syntax and if many seemingly promising formulas or successful films never spawn a genre, it is because only certain types of structure, within a particular semantic environment, are suited to the special bilingualism required of a durable genre. The structures of Hollywood cinema, like those of American popular mythology as a whole, serve to mask the very distinction between ritual and ideological functions. Hollywood does not simply lend its voice to the public's desires, nor does it simply manipulate the audience. On the contrary, most genres go through a period of accommodation during which the public's desires are fitted to Hollywood's priorities (and vice versa). Because the public doesn't want to know that it is being manipulated, the successful ritual/ideological 'fit' is almost always one that disguises Hollywood's potential for manipulation while playing up its capacity for entertainment.

Whenever a lasting fit is obtained – which it is whenever a semantic genre becomes a syntactic one – it is because a common ground has been found, a region where the audience's ritual values coincide with Hollywood's ideological ones. The development of a specific syntax within a given semantic context thus serves a double function: it binds element to element in a logical order, at the same time accommodating audience desires to studio concerns. The successful genre owes its success not alone to its reflection of an audience ideal, nor solely to its status as apology for the Hollywood enterprise, but to its ability to carry out both functions simultaneously. It is this sleight of hand, this strategic overdetermination, that most clearly characterizes American film production during the studio years.

The approach to genre sketched out here of course raises some questions of its own. Just where, for example, do we locate the exact border between the semantic and the syntactic? And how are these two categories related? Each of these questions constitutes an essential area of inquiry, one that is far too complex to permit full treatment here. Nevertheless, a few remarks may be in order. A reasonable observer might well ask why my approach attributes such importance to the seemingly banal distinction between a text's materials and the structures into which they are arranged. Why this distinction rather than, for example, the more cinematic division between diegetic elements and the technical means deployed in representing them? The answer to these questions lies in a general theory of textual signification that I have expounded elsewhere.[15] Briefly, that theory distinguishes between the primary, linguistic meaning of a text's component parts and the secondary or textual meaning that those parts acquire through a structuring process internal to the text or to the genre. Within a single text, therefore, the same phenomenon may have more than one meaning depending on whether we consider it at the linguistic or textual level. In the Western, for example, the horse is an animal that serves as a method of locomotion. This primary level of meaning, corresponding to the normal extent of the concept 'horse' within the language, is matched by a series of other meanings derived from the structures into which the Western sets the horse. Opposition of the horse to the automobile or locomotive ('iron horse') reinforces the organic, non-mechanical sense of the term 'horse' already implicit in the language, thus transferring that concept from the paradigm 'method of locomotion' to the paradigm 'soon-to-be-outmoded pre-industrial carry-over'.

In the same way, horror films borrow from a nineteenth-century literary tradition their dependence on the presence of a monster. In doing so, they clearly perpetuate the linguistic meaning of the monster as 'threatening inhuman beings', but at the same time, by developing new syntactic ties, they generate an important new set of textual meanings. For the nineteenth century, the appearance of the monster is invariably tied to a romantic overreaching, the attempt of some human scientist to tamper with the divine order. In such texts as Mary Shelley's *Franken-stein*, Balzac's *La Recherche de l'absolu*, or Stevenson's *Dr. Jekyll and Mr. Hyde*, a studied syntax equates man and monster, attributing to both the monstrosity of being outside nature as defined by established religion and science. With the horror film, a different syntax rapidly equates monstrosity not with the overactive nineteenth-century mind, but with an equally overactive twentieth-century body. Again and again, the monster is identified with his human counterpart's unsatisfied sexual appetite, thus establishing with the same primary 'linguistic' materials (the monster, fear, the chase, death) entirely new textual meanings, phallic rather than scientific in nature.

The distinction between the semantic and the syntactic, in the way I have defined it here, thus corresponds to a distinction between the primary, linguistic elements of which all texts are made and the secondary textual meanings that are sometimes constructed by virtue of the syntactic bonds established between primary elements. This distinction is stressed in the approach to genre presented here not because it is convenient nor because it corresponds to a modish theory of the relation between language and narrative, but because the semantic/syntactic distinction is fundamental to a theory of how meaning of one kind contributes to and eventually establishes meaning of another. Just as individual texts establish new meanings for familiar terms only by subjecting well-known semantic units to a syntactic redetermination, so generic meaning comes into being only through the repeated deployment of substantially the same syntactic strategies. It is in this way, for example, that making music – at the linguistic level primarily a way of making a living – becomes in the musical a figure for making love – a textual meaning essential to the constitution of that syntactic genre.

We must of course remember that, while each individual text clearly has a syntax of its own, the syntax implied here is that of the genre, which does not appear as *generic* syntax unless it is reinforced numerous times by the syntactic patterns of individual texts. The Hollywood genres that have proved the most durable are precisely those that have established the most coherent syntax (the Western, the musical); those that disappear the quickest depend entirely on recurring semantic elements, never developing a stable syntax (reporter, catastrophe, and big-caper films, to name but a few). If I locate the border between the semantic and the syntactic at the dividing line between the linguistic and the textual, it is thus in response not just to the theoretical but also to the historical dimension of generic functioning.

In proposing such a model, however, I may leave too much room for one particular type of misunderstanding. It has been a cliché of the last two decades to insist that structure carries meaning, while the choice of structured elements is largely negligible in the process of signification. This position, most openly championed by Lévi-Strauss in his cross-cultural methodology for studying myth, may seem to be implied by my model, but is in fact not borne out by my research.[16] Spectator response, I believe, is heavily conditioned by the choice of semantic elements and atmosphere, because a given semantics used in a specific cultural situation will recall to an actual interpretive community the particular syntax with which that semantics has traditionally been associated in other texts. This *syntactic expectation*, set up by a *semantic signal*, is matched by a parallel tendency to expect specific syntactic signals to lead to predetermined semantic fields (for example, in Western texts, regular alternation between male and female characters creates expectation of the semantic elements implied by romance, while alternation between two males throughout a text has implied – at least until recently – confrontation and the semantics of the duel). This interpretation of the semantic and the syntactic through the agency of the spectator clearly deserves further study. Suffice it to say for the present that linguistic meanings (and thus the import of semantic elements) are in large part derived from the textual meanings of previous texts. There is thus a constant circulation in both directions between the semantic and the syntactic, between the linguistic and the textual.

Still other questions, such as the general problem of the 'evolution' of genres through semantic or syntactic shifts, deserve far more attention than I have given them here. In time, I believe, this new model for the understanding of genre will provide answers for many of the questions traditional to genre study. Perhaps more important still, the semantic/syntactic approach to genre raises numerous questions for which other theories have created no space.

Notes

1. Ferdinand de Saussure, *Course in General Linguistics*, edited by Charles Bally and Albert Sechehaye, trans. Wade Baskin (New York: McGraw-Hill, 1959), pp. 14–17.
2. Especially in Vladimir Propp, *Morphology of the Folktale* (Bloomington: Indiana Research Center in Anthropology, 1958); Claude Lévi-Strauss, 'The Structural Study of Myths', in *Structural Anthropology*, trans. Claire Jacobson and Brooke Grundfest Schoepf (New York: Basic Books, 1963), pp. 206–231; Tzvetan Todorov, *Grammaire du Décaméron* (The Hague: Mouton, 1969); and Tzvetan Todorov, *The Fantastic*, trans. Richard Howard (Ithaca: Cornell University Press, 1975).
3. Even Stephen Neale's discursively oriented study falls prey to this problem. See *Genre* (London: British Film Institute, 1980).
4. John Cawelti, *The Six-Gun Mystique* (Bowling Green: Bowling Green University Popular Press, 1970), and John Cawelti, *Adventure, Mystery and Romance* (Chicago: University of Chicago Press, 1976); Leo Brandy, *The World in a Frame: What We See in Films* (Garden City: Anchor Books, 1977); Frank McConnell, *The Spoken Seen: Films and the Romantic Imagination* (Baltimore: Johns Hopkins University Press, 1975); Michael Wood, *America in the Movies, or Santa Maria, It Had Slipped My Mind* (New York: Delta, 1975); Will Wright, *Sixguns and Society: A Structural Study of the Western* (Berkeley: University of California Press, 1975); Thomas Schatz, *Hollywood Genres: Formulas, Filmmaking and the Studio System* (New York: Random House, 1981).
5. See especially the collective text '*Young Mr. Lincoln de John Ford*,' *Cahiers du cinéma*, no. 223 (August 1970): 29–47, translated in *Screen* 14, no. 3 (Autumn 1973): 29–43; and Jean-Louis Comolli's six-part article 'Technique et ideologie', *Cahiers du cinéma*, nos. 229–241 (1971–1972). The entire *Screen* project has been usefully summarized, with extensive bibliographical notes, by Philip Rosen, '*Screen* and the Marxist Project in Film Criticism', *Quarterly Review of Film Studies* 2, no. 3 (August 1977): 273–287; on *Screen*'s approach to ideology, see also Stephen Heath, 'On Screen, in Frame: Film and Ideology', *Quarterly Review of Film Studies* 1, no. 3 (August 1976): 251–265. The most important influence on all these positions is Louis Althusser, 'Ideology and Ideological State Apparatuses', in *Lenin and Philosophy and Other Essays*, trans. Ben Brewster (New York: Monthly Review Press, 1971), pp. 127–186.
6. Paul Hernadi, *Beyond Genre: New Directions in Literary Classification* (Ithaca: Cornell University Press, 1972).
7. Todorov, *The Fantastic*.
8. Frederic Jameson, 'Magical Narratives: Romance as Genre', *New Literary History* 7 (1975): 135–163. It should be noted that my use of the term 'semantic' differs from Jameson's. Whereas he stresses the overall semantic input of a text, I am dealing with the individual semantic units of the text. His term thus approximates the sense of 'global meaning', while mine is closer to 'lexical choices'.
9. Jean Mitry, *Dictionnaire du cinéma* (Paris: Larousse, 1963), p. 276.
10. Marc Vernet, *Lectures du film* (Paris: Albatros, 1976), pp. 111–112.
11. Jim Kitses, *Horizons West* (Bloomington: Indiana University Press, 1969), pp. 10–14.
12. Cawelti, *The Six-Gun Mystique*.
13. See, for example, Christian Metz, *Language and Cinema* (The Hague: Mouton, 1974), pp. 148–161; and Wright, *Sixguns and Society, passim*.
14. This relationship is especially interesting in the work of Richard Dyer and Jane Feuer, both of whom attempt to confront the interdependence of ritual and ideological components. See in particular Richard Dyer, 'Entertainment and Utopia', in *Genre: The Musical*, edited by Rick Altman (London and Boston: Routledge and Kegan Paul, 1981), pp. 175–189; and Jane Feuer, *The Hollywood Musical* (Bloomington: Indiana University Press, 1982).
15. Charles F. Altman, 'Intratextual Rewriting: Textuality as Language Formation', in *The Sign in Music and Literature*, edited by Wendy Steiner (Austin: University of Texas Press, 1981), pp. 39–51.
16. The most straightforward statement of Lévi-Strauss' position is in 'The Structural Study of Myths'. For a useful elucidation of that position, see Edmund Leach, *Claude Lévi-Strauss* (New York: Viking Press, 1970).

Bibliography

Aas, Lars Joergen, 'Genres List'. 1995 World Wide Web page, www.msstate.edu/Movies/con-tributions_genres.html. Currently www.imdb.com or uiarchive.cso.uiuc.edu (genres.list.gz) with a new webmaster.

Alicoate, Jack (ed.), *The 1943 Film Daily Year Book of Motion Pictures*, (New York: Film Daily, 1943).

Althusser, Louis, 'Ideology and Ideological State Apparatuses', in *Lenin and Philosophy and Other Essays* (New York: Monthly Review Press, 1971), pp. 127–186.

Altman, Rick, *Genre: The Musical* (London: Routledge & Kegan Paul, 1981a).

—— 'Intratextual Rewriting: Textuality as Language Formation', in Wendy Steiner (ed.) *The Sign in Music and Literature* (Austin: University of Texas Press, 1981b).

—— 'A Semantic/Syntactic Approach to Film Genre', *Cinema Journal*, vol. 23 no. 3, pp. 6–18, 1984.

—— Expanded version of 'A Semantic/Syntactic Approach to Film Genre', (1986) in Barry Keith Grant (ed.), *Film Genre Reader*, (2nd edition, Austin: University of Texas Press, 1995), pp. 26–40.

—— *The American Film Musical* (Bloomington: Indiana University Press, 1987).

—— 'Dickens, Griffith, and Film Theory Today', *South Atlantic Quarterly*, vol. 88 no. 2, 1989, pp. 321–59; reprinted in Jane Gaines (ed.), *Classical Narrative Revisited* (Durham: Duke University Press, 1992), pp. 9–47.

—— 'Genre', in Geoffrey Nowell-Smith (ed.), *The Oxford History of World Cinema*, (Oxford: Oxford University Press, 1996) pp. 276–285.

—— 'The Musical', in Geoffrey Nowell-Smith (ed.), *The Oxford History of World Cinema* (Oxford: Oxford University Press, 1996), pp. 294–303.

—— (ed.) *Sound Theory/Sound Practice* (New York: Routledge, 1992).

Anderson, Benedict, *Imagined Communities: Reflections on the Origins and Spread of Nationalism* (London: Verso, 1983; revised version, 1991).

Andrew, Dudley, *Concepts in Film Theory* (New York: Oxford, 1984).

Anobile, Richard J. (ed.), *Frankenstein* (New York: Avon, 1974).

Aristotle, *Aristotle's Theory of Poetry and Fine Art, with a Critical Text and Translation of The Poetics*, ed. S.H. Butcher (New York: Dover, 1951).

Aumont, Jacques, and Bergala, Alain, Marie, Michel, and Vernet, Marc, *Aesthetics of Film*, trans. Richard Neupert (Austin: University of Texas Press, 1992).

Austin, Bruce A., *Immediate Seating: A Look at Movie Audiences* (Belmont, CA: Wadsworth, 1989).

Austin, Bruce A. and Gordon, F. Thomas, 'Movie Genres: Toward a Conceptualized Model and Standardized Definitions', in Bruce A. Austin (ed.), *Current Research in Film: Audiences, Economics, and Law* 3 (Norwood, NJ: Ablex, 1987), pp. 12–33.

Babington, Bruce and Evans, Peter William, *Biblical Epics: Sacred Narrative in the Hollywood Cinema* (Manchester: Manchester University Press, 1993).

Bakhtin, Mikhail, *The Dialogic Imagination*, trans. Caryl Emerson and Michael Holquist (Austin: University of Texas Press, 1981).

Barker, Martin (ed.), *The Video Nasties: Freedom and Censorship in the Media* (London: Pluto Press, 1984).

Barrios, Richard. *A Song in the Dark: The Birth of the Musical Film* (New York: Oxford University Press, 1995).

Barthes, Roland, 'Introduction to the Structural Analysis of Narrative', *Communications* 8 (1966). English translation by Stephen Heath in *Image-Music-Text* (New York: Hill and Wang, 1977), pp. 79–124.

Barylick, John, 'Oh, Say, Can You Sing?', *Newsweek*, 25 November 1996, p. 16.

Basinger, Jeannine, *The World War II Combat Film: Anatomy of a Genre* (New York: Columbia University Press, 1986).

Bauman, Richard, 'Genre', in Richard Bauman (ed.), *Folklore, Cultural Performances, and Popular Entertainments: A Communications-Centered Handbook* (Oxford: Oxford University Press, 1992).

Bazin, André, 'The Evolution of the Western', in *What Is Cinema?* II, trans. Hugh Gray (Berkeley: University of California Press, 1971) pp. 149–157.

—— 'The Western: or the American Film Par Excellence', in *What Is Cinema?* II, trans. Hugh Gray (Berkeley: University of California Press, 1971), pp. 140–148.

Beaumarchais, Pierre Caron de, *Essai sur le genre dramatique sérieux* (1767).

Beck, Jay, 'Film Advertising in 1937: Paramount Ads in *Life* and *Variety* Magazines'. Unpublished paper.

Beebee, Thomas O., *The Ideology of Genre: A Comparative Study of Generic Instability* (University Park: Penn State University Press, 1994).

Behlmer, Rudy, *Inside Warner Bros. (1935–1951)* (New York: Simon & Schuster, 1985).

Benjamin, Walter, 'The Work of Art in the Age of Mechanical Reproduction', in Gerald Mast and Marshall Cohen (eds), *Film Theory and Criticism: Introductory Readings* (New York: Oxford University Press, 1974), pp. 612–634.

Bennett, Tony, 'Texts, Readers, Reading Formations', *Bulletin of the Midwest MLA*, vol. 18 no. 1, 1983, pp. 3–17.

—— 'Texts in History: The Determinations of Readings and Their Texts', *Bulletin of the Midwest MLA*, vol. 18 no. 1, 1985, pp. 1–16.

—— *Outside Literature* (London and New York: Routledge, 1990).

Beuick, Marshall D., 'The Limited Social Effect of Radio Broadcasting', *American Journal of Sociology* 32 (January 1927), pp. 615–622.

Boileau-Despréaux, Nicolas, *Art poétique* (1674).

Borde, Raymond and Chaumeton, Eugène, *Panorama du film noir américain* (Paris: Editions de Minuit, 1955).

Bordwell, David, Staiger, Janet and Thompson, Kristin, *The Classical Hollywood Cinema: Film Style and Mode of Production to 1960* (New York: Columbia University Press, 1985).

Branigan, Edward, *Narrative Comprehension and Film* (London and New York: Routledge, 1992).

Bratton, Jacky, Cook, Jim and Gledhill, Christine (eds), *Melodrama: Stage, Picture, Screen* (London: British Film Institute, 1994).

Braudy, Leo, *The World in a Frame: What We See in Films* (New York: Anchor, 1977).

Brooke-Rose, Christine, 'Historical Genres/Theoretical Genres: A Discussion of Todorov on the Fantastic', *New Literary History*, vol. 8 no. 1, 1976, pp. 145–58.

Brooks, Peter, *The Melodramatic Imagination: Balzac, Henry James, Melodrama, and the Mode of Excess* (New Haven: Yale University Press, 1976).

Browne, Nick (ed.), *Refiguring American Film Genres* (Berkeley: University of California Press, 1997).

Brunetière, Ferdinand, *L'Evolution des genres dans l'histoire de la littérature* (1890–1894).

Burch, Noël (director), *Correction Please, or How We Got Into Pictures*, New York: Museum of Modern Art, 1979.

Buscombe, Edward, 'The Idea of Genre in the American Cinema', *Screen*, vol. 11 no. 2, 1970, pp. 33–45. Reprinted in Barry Keith Grant (ed.), *Film Genre Reader* (2nd edition, Austin: University of Texas Press, 1995), pp. 11–25.

—— (ed.) *The BFI Companion to the Western* (New York: Atheneum, 1990).

—— *Stagecoach* (London: British Film Institute, 1992).

Calhoun, Craig (ed.), *Habermas and the Public Sphere* (Cambridge: MIT Press, 1992).

Carroll, Noël, *The Power of Horror or Paradoxes of the Heart* (New York: Routledge, 1990).

Castelvetro, Lodovico, *Poetica D'Aristotele Vulgarizzata et Sposta* (1570).

Cavell, Stanley, *Pursuits of Happiness: The Hollywood Comedy of Remarriage* (Cambridge: Harvard University Press, 1981).

Cawelti, John G., *The Six-Gun Mystique* (Bowling Green: Bowling Green University Popular Press, 1975).

—— *Adventure, Mystery and Romance* (Chicago: University of Chicago Press, 1976).

—— 'Chinatown and Generic Transformation in Recent American Films', in Barry Keith Grant (ed.), *Film Genre Reader* (Austin: University of Texas Press, 1986), pp. 183–201.

Chartier, Pierre, 'Les Américains aussi font des films "noirs"', *Revue du cinéma*, vol. 1 no. 2 (November 1946), pp. 67–70.

Clarens, Carlos, *An Illustrated History of the Horror Film* (New York: Capricorn, 1967).

—— *Crime Movies: An Illustrated History* (New York: Norton, 1979).

Clover, Carol J., *Men, Women, and Chain Saws: Gender in the Modern Horror Film* (Princeton: Princeton University Press, 1992).

Cohan, Steven and Hark, Ina Rae (eds), *The Road Movie Book* (London and New York: Routledge, 1997).

Cohen, Ralph, 'Do Postmodern Genres Exist?', in Marjorie Perloff (ed.), *Postmodern Genres*, special issue of *Genre*, vol. 20 nos. 3–4 (Fall–Winter, 1987), pp. 241–258.

—— (ed.) *The Future of Literary Theory* (New York: Routledge, 1989).

Colie, Rosalie, *The Resources of Kind: Genre-Theory in the Renaissance* (Berkeley: University of California Press, 1973).

Collins, Jim, *Uncommon Cultures* (New York: Routledge, 1989).

Comolli, Jean-Louis, 'Technique et Idéologie', *Cahiers du cinéma*, nos 229–41 (1971–72).

Cook, David, *A History of Narrative Film* (2nd edition, New York: Norton, 1990).

Cook, Pam, 'Melodrama and the Women's Picture', in Sue Aspinall and Sue Harper (eds), *Gainsborough Melodrama* (London: British Film Institute, Dossier 18, 1983).

Corneille, Pierre, *Discourses* (1660).

Cripps, Thomas, *Black Films as Genre* (Bloomington: Indiana University Press, 1978).

Croce, Arlene, *The Fred Astaire and Ginger Rogers Book* (New York: Galahad Books, 1972).

Croce, Benedetto, *Aesthetic as Science of Expression and General Linguistic*, trans. Douglas Ainslie (London: Peter Owen, 1909 [Italian original, 1902]).

Culler, Jonathan, *Structuralist Poetics: Structuralism, Linguistics and the Study of Literature* (Ithaca: Cornell University Press, 1975).

Custen, George F., *Bio/Pics: How Hollywood Constructed Public History* (New Brunswick: Rutgers University Press, 1992).

Dannenberg, Joseph (ed.), *Film Daily Year Book 1925* (New York: Film Daily, 1925).

Darwin, Charles, *Origin of Species* (1859).

De Certeau, Michel, *The Practice of Everyday Life* (Berkeley: University of California Press, 1984).

Delamater, Jerome, 'Performing Arts: The Musical', in Stuart Kaminsky, *American Film Genres* (Dayton; Pflaum, 1974).

Derrida, Jacques, 'La Loi du genre/The Law of Genre', *Glyph* 7, 1980, pp. 176–232.

Dick, Bernard F., *Anatomy of Film* (2nd edition, New York: St. Martin's, 1990).

Diderot, Denis, *Entretiens sur le Fils naturel* (1757).

Doane, Mary Ann, 'The Woman's Film: Possession and Address', in Mary Ann Doane, Patricia Mellencamp, Linda Williams (eds) *Re-Vision: Essays in Feminist Film Criticism* (Frederick, MD: American Film Institute/University Publications of America, 1984), pp. 67–82.

—— *The Desire to Desire: The Woman's Film of the 1940s* (Bloomington: Indiana University Press, 1987).

Dryden, John, *Essay of Dramatic Poesy* (1668).

Dyer, Richard, 'Entertainment and Utopia', in Rick Altman (ed.), *Genre: The Musical* (London and Boston: Routledge, 1981).

Ehrmann, Jacques (ed.), 'Structuralism', *Yale French Studies* 36–37 (1966).

Elsaesser, Thomas, 'Tales of Sound and Fury: Observations on the Family Melodrama', *Monogram* 4, 1973, pp. 2–15. Reprinted in Barry Keith Grant (ed.), *Film Genre Reader* (2nd edition. Austin: University of Texas Press, 1995), pp. 350–380.

—— 'Film History as Social History: The Dieterle/Warner Brothers Bio-pic'. *Wide Angle*, vol. 8 no. 2, 1984, pp. 15–31.

Epstein, Rob and Friedman, Jeffrey, (producer and director), *The Celluloid Closet*, Columbia TriStar Home Video, 1996.

Farrell, Joseph, '*Cocktail*: Advertising Strategy' (Los Angeles: National Research Group, Inc., 1988a).

—— '*Cocktail*: Recruited Audience Surveys in Granada Hills on 6/30/88', (Los Angeles: National Research Group, Inc., 1988b).

—— *Cocktail*: Trailer Test' (Los Angeles: National Research Group, Inc., 1988c).

—— *Cocktail*: TV Commercial Test' (Los Angeles: National Research Group, Inc., 1988d).

Fenin, George and Everson, William K., *The Western: From Silents to Cinerama* (New York: Bonanza Books, 1962).

Feuer, Jane, *The Hollywood Musical* (Bloomington: Indiana University Press, 1982).

—— 'Melodrama, Serial Form and Television Today', *Screen*, vol. 25 no. 1, 1984. pp. 4–16.

—— 'Genre Study and Television', in Robert C. Allen (ed.) *Channels of Discourse: Television and Contemporary Criticism* (Chapel Hill: University of North Carolina Press, 1987).

—— *The Hollywood Musical* (2nd edition, Bloomington: Indiana University Press, 1993).

Fischer, Lucy, *Shot/Countershot: Film Tradition and Women's Cinema* (Princeton: Princeton University Press, 1989).

Fishelov, David, *Metaphors of Genre: The Role of Analogy in Genre Theory* (University Park: Penn State University Press, 1993).

Fiske, John, *Understanding Popular Culture* (Boston: Unwin Hyman, 1989).

—— *Introduction to Communication Studies* (2nd edition, London & New York: Routledge, 1990).

Flinn, Caryl, *Strains of Utopia: Gender, Nostalgia, and Hollywood Film Music* (Princeton: Princeton University Press, 1992).

Foster, William Trufaut, *Vaudeville and Motion Picture Shows. A Study of Theaters in Portland, Oregon* (Portland: Reed College, 1914).

Fowler, Alastair, *Kinds of Literature: An Introduction to the Theory of Genres and Modes* (Cambridge: Harvard University Press, 1982).

Frank, Nino, 'Un nouveau genre "policier": l'aventure criminelle', *L'Ecran français*, 61 (August 1946), pp. 8–9, 14.

Freadman, Anne, 'Untitled: (on genre)', *Cultural Studies*, vol. 2 no. 1, 1988, pp. 67–99.

Freud, Sigmund, *Jokes and their Relation to the Unconscious*, trans. James Strachey (New York: Norton, 1960 [German original, 1905]).

Frow, John, 'Michel de Certeau and the Practice of Representation', *Cultural Studies*, vol. 5 no. 1, 1991, pp. 52–60.

—— *Cultural Studies and Cultural Value* (Oxford: Clarendon Press, 1995).

Frye, Northrop, 'The Argument of Comedy', in *English Institute Essays* (New York: Columbia University Press, 1949).

—— *Anatomy of Criticism* (Princeton: Princeton University Press, 1957).

Gaines, Jane, 'Costume and Narrative: How Dress Tells the Woman's Story', in Jane Gaines and Charlotte Herzog (eds), *Fabrications: Costume and the Female Body* (New York: Routledge, 1990), pp. 180–211.

Gallagher, Tag, 'Shoot-Out at the Genre Corral: Problems in the "Evolution" of the Western', in Barry Keith Grant (ed.), *Film Genre Reader* (2nd edition, Austin: University of Texas Press, 1995), pp. 246–260.

Gehring, Wes D., *Handbook of American Film Genres* (Westport, CT: Greenwood, 1988).

Giannetti, Louis, *Understanding Movies* (6th edition, Englewood Cliffs: Prentice Hall, 1993).

Gifford, Dennis, *A Pictorial History of Horror Movies* (London: Hamlyn, 1973).

Gitlin, Todd, *Inside Prime Time* (New York: Pantheon, 1983).

Gledhill, Christine, 'The Melodramatic Field: An Investigation', in Christine Gledhill (ed.), *Home Is Where the Heart Is* (London: British Film Institute, 1987).

Goldmann, Lucien, *Le Dieu caché: Etude sur la vision tragique dans les Pensées de Pascal et dans le théâtre de Racine* (Paris: Gallimard, 1959).

Grant, Barry Keith (ed.), *Film Genre Reader* (2nd edition, Austin: University of Texas Press 1995).

—— *The Dread of Difference: Gender and the Horror Film* (Austin: University of Texas Press, 1997).

Grodal, Torben Kragh, *Cognition, Emotion, and Visual Fiction: Theory and Typology of Affective Patterns and Genres in Film and Television* (Copenhagen: Department of Film and Media Studies, 1994 [revised version, Oxford: Oxford University Press, 1997]).

Guerrero, Ed., *Framing Blackness: The African American Image in Film* (Philadelphia: Temple University Press, 1993).

Gunning, Tom, 'Non-Continuity, Continuity, Discontinuity: A Theory of Genres in Early Films', *IRIS*, vol. 2 no. 1, 1984, pp. 101–112. Reprinted in Thomas Elsaesser (ed.) with Adam Barker, *Early Cinema: Space, Frame, Narrative* (London: British Film Institute, 1990), pp. 86–94.

—— 'Primitive Cinema, a Frame-Up? or the Trick's on Us', *Cinema Journal* 28, 1989, pp. 3–12. Reprinted in Thomas Elsaesser (ed.) with Adam Barker, *Early Cinema: Space, Frame, Narrative* (London: British Film Institute, 1990), pp. 95–103.

—— 'Crazy Machines in the Garden of Forking Paths: Mischief Gags and the Origins of American Film Comedy', in Kristine B. Karnick and Henry Jenkins (eds), *Classical Hollywood Comedy* (New York: Routledge, 1984, pp. 87–105.

—— "Those Drawn with a Very Fine Camel's Hair Brush": The Origins of Film Genres', *Iris*, 20, 1995, pp. 49–61.

—— 'New Thresholds of Vision: Instantaneous Photography, and the Early Cinema of Lumière', in Terry Smith (ed.), *Impossible Presence: The Image Encounter* (Power Institute Series 2), 1998.

Habermas, Jürgen, *The Structural Transformation of the Public Sphere: An Inquiry into a Category of Bourgeois Society*, trans. Thomas Burger with Frederick Lawrence (Cambridge: MIT Press, 1991 [orig. 1962]).

Hall, Stuart, 'Encoding, Decoding', in Stuart Hall, Dorothy Hobson, Andrew Lowe, Paul Willis (eds), *Culture, Media, Language* (London: Hutchinson, 1980).

Hanks, William, 'Discourse Genres in a Theory of Practice', *American Ethnologist* 14 (November 1987), pp. 668–692.

Hansen, Miriam, *Babel and Babylon: Spectatorship in American Silent Film* (Cambridge: Harvard University Press, 1991).

Hartman, Geoffrey, 'Structuralism: The Anglo-American Adventure', *Yale French Studies* 36–37 (1966), pp. 148–168.

Haskell, Molly, *From Reverence to Rape: The Treatment of Women in the Movies* (New York: Penguin, 1974).

Hays, Will H., *Motion Picture Industry in Wartime America 1943–1944*, Twenty-second Annual Report, 27 March 1944.

Heath, Stephen, 'On Screen, in Frame: Film and Ideology', *Quarterly Review of Film Studies*, vol. 1 no. 3 (August 1976), pp. 251–265.

Hepner, H.W., 'Public Likes and Dislikes', *Film Daily Yearbook* 1929, p. 896.

Hernadi, Paul, *Beyond Genre: New Directions in Literary Classification* (Ithaca: Cornell University Press, 1972).

—— 'Entertaining Commitments: A Reception Theory of Literary Genres', *Poetics* 10, 1981, pp. 195–211.

Hirsch, E.D., Jr., *Validity in Interpretation* (New Haven: Yale University Press, 1967).

Horace (Quintus Horatius Flaccus), *Ars Poetica* (also known as *Epistle to the Pisones*), in *Criticism: The Major Statements*, ed. Charles Kaplan (New York: St. Martin's Press, 1975), pp. 94–107.

Hugo, Victor, Preface to *Cromwell* (1827).

Jacobs, Lea, 'The Woman's Picture and the Poetics of Melodrama', *Camera Obscura* 31 (1993), pp. 120–147.

Jameson, Fredric, 'Magical Narratives: Romance as Genre', *New Literary History* 7, 1975, pp. 135–163.

Jameson, Richard T. (ed.) *They Went Thataway: Redefining Film Genres: A National Society of Film Critics Guide* (San Francisco: Mercury House, 1994).

Jauss, Hans Robert, *Towards an Aesthetic of Reception*, trans. Timothy Bahti (Minneapolis: University of Minnesota Press, 1982).

Jenkins, Henry, *Textual Poachers: Television Fans and Participatory Culture* (New York: Routledge, 1992).

Johnston, Claire, 'Women's Cinema as Counter-Cinema', in *Notes on Women's Cinema* (London: Society for Education in Film and Television, 1973), pp. 24–31.

Jost, François (ed.), *Le Genre télévisuel. Réseaux: Communication, Technologie, Société* 81 (January–February 1997).

Kael, Pauline, 'Epics: *The Bible, Hawaii, Dr. Zhivago*', in *Kiss Kiss Bang Bang* (Boston: Little, Brown and Company), pp. 131–137.

Kaminsky, Stuart M., *American Film Genres: Approaches to a Critical Theory of Popular Film* (Dayton: Pflaum, 1974; revised edition 1984).

Kaminsky, Stuart M. and Mahan, J.H. *American Televisual Genres* (Chicago: Nelson-Hall, 1986).

Kaplan, E. Ann, *Women and Film: Both Sides of the Camera* (New York: Methuen, 1983).

Karney, Robyn (ed.), *Chronicle of the Cinema* (New York: Dorling Kindersley, 1995).

Karnick, Kristine Brunovska and Jenkins, Henry (eds), *Classical Hollywood Comedy* (New York: Routledge, 1994).

Kim, Susan, 'Genre Survey' (Iowa City: manuscript, 1997).

Kiss or Kill (advertisement), *New York Times*, 21 November 1997, B29.

Kitses, Jim, *Horizons West: Anthony Mann, Budd Boetticher, Sam Peckinpah: Studies of Authorship within the Western* (Bloomington: Indiana University Press, 1969).

Klinger, Barbara, *Melodrama and Meaning: History, Culture, and the Films of Douglas Sirk* (Bloomington: Indiana University Press, 1994).

—— ' "Local" Genres: The Hollywood Adult Film in the 1950s', in Bratton, Cook and Gledhill (eds), *Melodrama: Stage, Picture, Screen* (London: British Film Institute, 1994), pp. 134–146.

Koszarski, Richard, *An Evening's Entertainment: The Age of the Silent Feature Picture, 1915–1928* (New York: Scribner's, 1990).

Kracauer, Siegfried, *From Caligari to Hitler: A Psychological History of the German Film* (Princeton: Princeton University Press, 1947).

Kreuger, Miles, *The Movie Musical from Vitaphone to 42nd Street as Reported in a Great Fan Magazine* (New York: Dover, 1975).

Krutnik, Frank, 'A Spanner in the Works? Genre, Narrative and the Hollywood Comedian', in Karnick and Jenkins (eds), *Classical Hollywood Comedy* (New York: Routledge, 1994), pp. 17–38.

Kuhn, Annette, *Women's Pictures: Feminism and Cinema* (London: Routledge & Kegan Paul, 1982).

Kuhn, Thomas, *The Structure of Scientific Revolutions* (Chicago: University of Chicago Press, 1962).

Landy, Marcia, *British Genres: Cinema and Society, 1930–1960* (Princeton: Princeton University Press, 1991).

Lang, Robert, *American Film Melodrama: Griffith, Vidor, Minnelli* (Princeton: Princeton University Press, 1989).

Leach, Edmund, *Claude Lévi-Strauss* (New York: Viking Press, 1970).

Leutrat, Jean-Louis, and Liandrat-Guigues, S., *Les Cartes de l'Ouest. Un genre cinématographique: le western* (Paris: Armand Colin, 1990).

Lévi-Strauss, Claude, 'The Structural Study of Myths', in *Structural Anthropology* (New York: Basic Books, 1963).

Lopez, Daniel, *Films by Genre: 775 Categories, Styles, Trends and Movements Defined, with a Filmography for Each* (Jefferson, NC: McFarland, 1993).

Lotman, Jurij, *Semiotics of Cinema*, trans. Mark E. Suino (Ann Arbor: Michigan Slavic Contributions, 1976).

—— *The Structure of the Artistic Text*, trans. Ronald Vroon (Ann Arbor: Michigan Slavic Materials, 1977).

Lunenfeld, Peter, *Film Rouge: Genre, Postmodern Theory, and the American Cinema of the 1980s*, UCLA dissertation, 1994.

MacGowan, Kenneth, *Behind the Screen* (New York: Delacorte, 1965).

Maltby, Richard, *Passing Parade: A History of Popular Culture in the Twentieth Century* (Oxford: Oxford University Press, 1989).

—— *Hollywood Cinema: An Introduction* (Oxford and Cambridge, MA: Blackwell, 1995).

Maltin, Leonard (ed.), *Leonard Maltin's Movie and Video Guide: 1998 Edition* (New York: Signet, 1997).

Martinet, André, *Elements of General Linguistics*, trans. Elisabeth Palmer (Chicago: University of Chicago Press, 1966).

Mast, Gerald, *The Comic Mind: Comedy and the Movies* (Indianapolis: Bobbs-Merrill, 1973).

Mayne, Judith, 'The Woman at the Keyhole: Women's Cinema and Feminist Criticism', in Mary Ann Doane, Patricia Mellencamp, Linda Williams (eds), *Re-Vision: Essays in Feminist Film Criticism* (Frederick, MD: American Film Institute/University Publications of America, 1984), pp. 49–66.

McConnell, Frank D., *The Spoken Seen: Film and the Romantic Imagination* (Baltimore: Johns Hopkins University Press, 1975).

Mercier, Louis-Sébastien, *Du théâtre, ou nouvel essai sur l'art dramatique* (1773).

Merritt, Russell, 'Melodrama: Post-Mortem for a Phantom Genre', *Wide Angle*, vol. 5 no. 3, 1983, pp. 24–31.

Metz, Christian, *Language and Cinema* (Mouton: The Hague, 1974).

Minturno, Antonio, *De Poeta Libri Sex* (1559).

Mitry, Jean, *Dictionnaire du cinéma* (Paris: Larousse, 1963).

Modleski, Tania, *Loving with a Vengeance: Mass-Produced Fantasies for Women* (Hamden, CT: Archon Books, 1982).

—— 'Time and Desire in the Woman's Film', *Cinema Journal*, vol. 23 no. 3, 1984, pp. 19–30.

Muller, Eddie and Faris, Daniel, *Grindhouse: The Forbidden World of 'Adults Only' Cinema* (New York: St. Martin's Griffin, 1996).

Mulvey, Laura, 'Notes on Sirk and Melodrama', *Movie* 25, 1977, pp. 53–56. Reprinted in Christine Gledhill (ed.), *Home Is Where the Heart Is* (London: British Film Institute, 1987).

—— 'Melodrama In and Out of the Home', in Colin MacCabe (ed.), *High Theory/Low Culture: Analyzing Popular Television and Film* (Manchester: Manchester University Press, 1986).

Musser, Charles, 'The Travel Genre in 1903–1904: Moving Towards Fictional Narrative', originally published in *Iris* 2, 1984. Reprinted in Thomas Elsaesser (ed.) with Adam Barker, *Early Cinema: Space, Frame, Narrative* (London: British Film Institute, 1990), pp. 123–132.

—— *The Emergence of Cinema: The American Screen to 1907* (New York: Scribner's, 1990).

Naficy, Hamid, 'Television Intertextuality and the Discourse of the Nuclear Family', *Journal of Film and Video*, vol. 41 no. 4, 1989, pp. 42–59.

—— 'Phobic Spaces and Liminal Panics: Independent Transnational Film Genre', *East-West Film Journal*, vol. 8 no. 2, 1994, pp. 1–30.

Naremore, James, 'American Film Noir: The History of an Idea', *Film Quarterly*, vol. 49 no. 2, 1996, pp. 12–28.

—— *More Than Night: Film Noir in its Contexts* (Berkeley: University of California Press, 1988).

Neale, Stephen, *Genre* (London: British Film Institute, 1980).

—— 'Melodrama and Tears,' *Screen*, vol. 27 no. 6, 1986, pp. 6–23.

—— 'Questions of Genre', *Screen*, vol. 31 no. 1, 1990, pp. 45–66. Reprinted in Barry Keith Grant (ed.), *Film Genre Reader* (2nd edition, Austin: University of Texas Press, 1995), pp. 159–183.

—— 'Melo Talk: On the Meaning and Use of the Term "Melodrama" in the American Trade Press', *Velvet Light Trap* 32, (1993), pp. 66–89.

Nowell-Smith, Geoffrey, 'Minnelli and Melodrama', *Screen*, vol. 18 no. 2 (Summer 1977), pp. 113–118.

O'Brien, Charles, 'Film Noir in France: Before the Liberation', *Iris*, 21 (Spring 1996), pp. 7–20.

Odin, Roger, 'Pour une sémio-pragmatique du cinéma', *Iris*, vol. 1 no. 1, 1983, pp. 67–82.

Older, Andrew H., 'The OWI Motion Picture Bureau', in Jack Alicoate (ed.), *The 1943 Film Daily Year Book of Motion Pictures* (New York: Film Daily, 1943), pp. 185, 187.

Paul, William, *LaughingScreaming: Modern Hollywood Horror and Comedy* (New York: Columbia University Press, 1994).

Perloff, Marjorie, 'Introduction', in Marjorie Perloff (ed.), *Postmodern Genres*. Special issue of *Genre*, vol. 20 nos. 3–4 (Fall–Winter 1987), pp. 233–240.

Pope, Alexander, *Essay on Criticism* (1711).

Privett, Ray, 'Midwest and Midwestern: Geography and Genre in *Troublesome Creek* and *Fargo*. Unpublished manuscript, 1997.

Propp, Vladimir, *Morphology of the Folktale* (Bloomington: Indiana Research Center in Anthropology, 1958).

Radway, Janice, *Reading the Romance: Women, Patriarchy and Popular Literature* (Chapel Hill: University of North Carolina Press, 1984).

Richardson, John H. (with Kim Masters), 'The Selznick of Schlock', *Premiere*, December 1990, pp. 114–123, 152.

—— 'Silver Lining', *Premiere*, December 1991, pp. 107–116.

Roberts, Martin, 'Transnational Geographic: Perspectives on *Baraka*'. Unpublished manuscript, 1995.

Roddick, Nick, *A New Deal in Entertainment: Warner Brothers in the 1930s* (London: British Film Institute, 1983).

Rosen, Philip, '*Screen* and the Marxist Project in Film Criticism', *Quarterly Review of Film Studies*, vol. 2 no. 3 (August 1977), pp. 273–287.

Rosmarin, Adena, *The Power of Genre* (Minneapolis: University of Minnesota Press, 1985).

Rotha, Paul, *Documentary Film* (New York: Hastings House, 1952).

Rothenbuhler, Eric, 'What Makes Us Think Looking at a Television Set is Communication?' Unpublished manuscript, 1995.

Rousseau, Jean-Jacques, *Discourse on the Origins of Equality* (1755).

Ryall, Tom, 'The Notion of Genre', *Screen*, vol. 11 no. 2 (March–April 1970), pp. 22–32.

Ryan, Marie-Laure, 'Towards a Competence Theory of Genre', *Poetics* 8, 1979, pp. 307–337.

Sacks, Sheldon, 'The Psychological Implications of Generic Distinctions', *Genre*, vol. 1 no. 2 (April 1968), pp. 106–115, 120–123.

Sale, Kirkpatrick, *The Conquest of Paradise: Christopher Columbus and the Columbian Legacy* (New York: Plume, 1990).

Sarris, Andrew, 'The Sex Comedy Without Sex', *American Film*, vol. 3 no. 5 (March 1978), pp. 8–15.

Saussure, Ferdinand de, *Course in General Linguistics*, trans. Wade Baskin (New York: McGraw-Hill, 1959).

Scaliger, Julius Caesar, *Poetics (Poetices Libri Septem)* (1561).

Schaeffer, Jean-Marie, *Qu'est-ce qu'un genre littéraire?* (Paris: Seuil, 1989).

—— 'Literary Genres and Textual Genericity', in Ralph Cohen (ed.), *The Future of Literary Theory* (New York: Routledge, 1989), pp. 167–187.

Schatz, Thomas, *Hollywood Genre: Formulas, Filmmaking, and the Studio System* (New York: Random House, 1981).

Schickel, Richard, *The Disney Version: The Life, Times, Art, and Commerce of Walt Disney* (New York: Avon Books, 1968).

Schiff, Stephen, 'Introduction: The Repeatable Experience', in Richard T. Jameson (ed.), *They Went Thataway: Redefining Film Genres* (San Francisco: Mercury House, 1994), pp. xiii–xx.

Schlegel, Friedrich, *Dialogue on Poetry* (1800).

Schrader, Paul, 'Notes on *Film noir*,' *Film Comment* 8 (Spring 1972), 9–13.

Sennett, Ted, *Warner Brothers Presents* (New York: Castle Books, 1971).

Short, Ray LeRoy, *A Social Study of the Motion Picture*, University of Iowa Masters thesis, 1916.

Singer, Ben, 'Female Power in the Serial-Queen Melodrama: The Etiology of an Anomaly', *Camera Obscura* 22 (January 1990), pp. 90–129.

Sklar, Robert, *Film: An International History of the Medium* (New York: Prentice Hall and Harry N. Abrams: 1993).

Smith, Henry Nash, *Virgin Land: The American West as Symbol and Myth* (Cambridge: Harvard University Press, 1950).

Sobchack, Vivian, *Screening Space: The American Science Fiction Film* (2nd edition, New York: Ungar, 1991).

Staiger, Emil, *Grundbegriffe der Poetik* (Zurich: Atlantis Verlag, 1946).

Staiger, Janet, *Interpreting Films: Studies in the Historical Reception of American Cinema* (Princeton: Princeton University Press, 1992).

Stendhal (Henri Beyle), *Racine et Shakespeare* (1823, 1825).

Strelka, Joseph P. (ed.), *Theories of Literary Genre* (University Park: Penn State University Press, 1978).

Sweeney, Russell, *Coming Next Week: A Pictorial History of Film Advertising* (New York: Castle Books, 1973).

Tasso, Torquato, *Discorsi* (1594).

Taves, Brian, *The Romance of Adventure: The Genre of Historical Adventure Movies* (Jackson: University Press of Mississippi, 1993).

Taves, Brian, Hoffman, Judi and Lund, Karen, *The Moving Image Genre-Form Guide* (Washington, DC: Library of Congress, 1997).

Thomson, David, *America in the Dark: Hollywood and the Gift of Unreality* (New York: William Morrow and Company, 1977).

Todorov, Tzvetan, *Grammaire du Décaméron* (Mouton: The Hague, 1969).

—— *The Fantastic*, trans. Richard Howard (Ithaca: Cornell University Press, 1975 [French original, 1970]).

—— 'The Origin of Genres', *New Literary History* 8, 1976, pp. 159–170.

Tolkin, Michael, *The Player, The Rapture, The New Age: Three Screenplays* (New York: Grove Press, 1995).

Triplett, Mike, '*Die Hard* in a Newspaper', *The Daily Iowan*, 5 March 1998, 5c.

Turim, Maureen, *Flashbacks in Film: Memory and History* (New York: Routledge, 1989).

Tyler, Parker, *Underground Film: A Critical History* (New York: Grove Press, 1969).

Valenti, Jack, 'The Movie Rating System', Motion Picture Association of America, n.d.

Veblen, Thorsten, *The Theory of the Leisure Class: An Economic Study of Institutions* (New York: Dover, 1994 [original, 1899]).

Vernet, Marc, *Lectures du film* (Paris: Albatros, 1976).

Vida, Marco Girolamo, *De Arte Poetica* (1527).

Vuillermoz, E, '*La Bête humaine, Hôtel du Nord*', *Le Temps*, 14 January 1939.

Waller, Gregory A., 'Re-placing *The Day After*', *Cinema Journal*, vol. 26 no. 3 (Spring 1987), pp. 3–20.

Warshow, Robert, *The Immediate Experience* (New York: Atheneum, 1974). 'The Gangster as Tragic Hero', pp. 127–134; 'Movie Chronicle: The Westerner', pp. 135–154.

Weber, Max, *The Protestant Ethic and the Spirit of Capitalism* (New York: Scribner, 1958 [original, 1920]).

Wellek, René, 'The Concept of Evolution in Literary History', in *Concepts of Criticism* (New Haven: Yale University Press, 1963).

Wellek, René and Austin Warren, *Theory of Literature* (3rd edition, New York: Harcourt, Brace & World, 1956 [original, 1949]).

Wild West, The, by the Editors of Time-Life Books (New York: Warner Books, 1993).

'Wild West Pictures', *The Moving Picture News*, vol. 4 no. 46 (18 November 1911), p. 6.

Williams, Alan, 'Is a Radical Genre Criticism Possible?', *Quarterly Review of Film Studies*, vol. 9 no. 2 (Spring 1984), pp. 121–125.

Williams, Linda, ' "Something Else Besides a Mother": *Stella Dallas* and the Maternal Melodrama', *Cinema Journal*, vol. 24 no. 1, 1984, pp. 2–27.

—— *Hard Core: Power, Pleasure, and the 'Frenzy of the Visible'* (Berkeley: University of California Press, 1989).

—— 'Film Bodies: Gender, Genre, and Excess', *Film Quarterly*, vol. 44 no. 4, 1991, pp. 2–13. Reprinted in Barry Keith Grant (ed.), *Film Genre Reader* (2nd edition, Austin: University of Texas Press, 1995), pp. 140–158.

—— 'Melodrama Revisited', in Nick Browne (ed.), *Refiguring American Film Genres* (Berkeley: University of California Press, 1989), pp. 42–88.

Wittgenstein, Ludwig, *Philosophical Investigations*, trans. G.E.M. Anscombe (London: Oxford University Press, 1953).

Wollen, Peter, 'An Alphabet of Cinema: 26 Responses to a Self-Interview', *Point of Contact*, vol. 5 no. 1, 1997, pp. 5–17.

Wood, Michael, *America in the Movies, or 'Santa Maria, It Had Slipped My Mind'* (New York: Delta, 1975).

Wood, Robin, 'An Introduction to the American Horror Film', in Bill Nichols (ed.), *Movies and Methods II: An Anthology* (Berkeley: University of California Press, 1985), pp. 195–220.

—— *Hollywood from Vietnam to Reagan* (New York: Columbia University Press, 1986).

Wright, Will, *Sixguns and Society: A Structural Study of the Western* (Berkeley: University of California Press, 1975).

Wyatt, Justin, *High Concept: Movies and Marketing in Hollywood* (Austin: University of Texas Press, 1994).

'*Young Mr. Lincoln* de John Ford', collective text by the editors of *Cahiers du cinéma* 223 (August 1970), pp. 29–47. English translation in *Screen* (Autumn 1972), pp. 5–44.

Index

This book is indexed in three ways: by **Subject** (pp.237–8), by **Genre** (pp.238–9), and by **Name/Title** (pp.239–246).

Subject Index

advertisements, **see** publicity

approaches to genre, **see** classical, evolutionary, ideological, neoclassical, ritual, romantic, scientific, semantic/syntactic, semantic/syntactic/pragmatic, zoological

archetype, **see** myth

audiences, **see** spectatorship

'B' films 62, 104, 117

brand names 62, 113ff, 120–1, 122

classical approaches to genre 1ff, 7, 15, 49, 129, 181

comic strips 116

constellated community 161, 164, 165, 168, 171–72, 177, 178, 187, 191, 192, 194, 198, 199, 202, 205

copyright 62, 116, 122, 187, 194

corpus, generic 22ff, 38, 82, 84, 89, 216–17, 219, 221, 223

critics 3–4, 8, 9, 11, 12, 19, 21, 24, 28, 30, 38, 40, 42–3, 47, 48, 61, 71, 73, 74, 77, 82, 84, 85, 89, 99, 111, 112, 124, 127, 128, 142, 144, 166, 169, 187, 204, 216, 217

cycles, **see** film cycles

discourse, **see** genre as discursive activity

evolutionary approaches to genre 6, 21, 49, 70

film cycles 42, 59–61, 64ff, 70 71, 77, 82, 115ff, 139–40, 144, 166, 187, 199, 205, 212

film industry (major studios), **see also** independent filmmakers 15ff, 28, 30, 38, 44ff, 54, 72, 73, 102, 105, 109, 112, 115ff, 126, 128, 133, 142, 144, 173, 207, 208

flag 86–7, 195, 199, 201, 204

generic communication 169ff

generic community 156ff, 168ff

generic crossroads 145ff, 154, 155, 165

generic economy 152ff, 165

generic functions 14–15, 26, 180, 208

generic pleasure 145ff, 155, 156, 165, 169, 193

genre and culture 146ff, 154, 155, 157, 165

genre and nation 19, 69, 86, 87, 132, 195ff, 211–12

genre as discursive activity 107, 109, 121, 171, 193, 208

genre mixing, **see** mixed genres

government role in genre 28, 94ff, 107ff, 213

ideological approaches to genre 26ff, 207, 219, 222ff

independent filmmakers 102ff, 120, 122

industry, **see** film industry

institutions 8, 12, 16, 90ff, 124, 195

lateral communication 162, 164, 165, 171–72, 178, 185, 192, 195, 198, 199, 205

mixed genres, genre mixing 4–5, 7, 12, 16, 17, 18, 43, 123ff, 129

myth, archetype 8, 19–20, 26, 34, 49–50, 90, 179, 189

nation, **see** genre and nation

national anthem 195, 199ff

neoclassical approaches to genre 4ff, 101, 123, 179ff, 194

newspapers 124, 182, 195ff

novel 1, 6, 82, 83, 136, 140, 145, 182, 188, 197

poetry 1–2, 50, 82, 188

posters, **see** publicity

producers 12, 38ff, 44ff, 74, 77, 82, 99, 103, 111, 122, 144, 172, 187

publicity, advertisements, posters 30, 39, 42, 52, 54ff, 63, 65, 78–9, 84, 102ff, 115, 117ff, 124, 128ff, 132ff, 136, 137, 141, 150, 159, 164, 166, 177, 192, 193, 194

quarrel of the Ancients and Moderns 181ff

radio 33, 78, 82, 116, 124, 140, 169, 182, 185, 191, 192, 194, 198

ratings 93ff, 110–11

readers, **see** spectatorship

reception study 212

recorded music 159, 169, 182, 184, 185, 192, 194, 200

ritual approaches to genre 2, 20, 21, 26ff, 49, 188ff, 207, 218–19, 222ff
romantic approaches to genre 5ff, 7, 15, 49, 123, 129

scientific approaches to genre 6, 8, 12, 15, 28
secondary discursivity 171–72, 178, 193, 195, 198, 205
semantic/syntactic approach to genre 24, 87ff, 108, 162, 195, 207, 210, 216ff
semantic/syntactic/pragmatic approach to genre 207ff
sheet music 159, 169
spectatorship, audiences, readers, users 10, 11, 12, 14, 16, 18, 27, 40, 44, 48, 74, 75–6, 85, 91, 97ff, 100ff, 110ff, 124, 126ff, 141, 142, 144, 145ff, 153, 154, 157, 158, 159, 160, 162, 164–65, 166, 169ff, 177, 178, 180–3, 185–7, 188ff, 194, 195, 207, 210, 211, 214, 222, 225
stars 25, 30, 34–5, 39ff, 103–4, 115, 116–7, 120, 124, 187, 192–3, 194
studios, see film industry

television 77, 82, 150, 161, 169, 175, 177, 182, 185, 192, 194, 198
theatre 39, 40, 188
trademarks, see brand names

users of genre, see spectatorship

zoological approaches to genre 16, 62ff, 70, 101, 132

Genre Index

action 46, 92, 102, 103, 125, 126, 128, 140, 141, 160
adult humor 125
adventure 16, 17–8, 19, 21, 25, 52, 57, 72, 81, 93, 99, 117, 125, 128, 130, 141, 149, 179
animation 33, 91, 93, 127
art, see avant-garde
avant-garde/experimental/art/underground 86, 91, 127, 140, 169

baseball 140, 163
big caper 19, 140, 225
biopic 16, 19, 20, 30, 33, 38ff, 46, 47, 48, 51, 57ff, 62, 71, 81, 117, 120, 139–40, 149, 176–7, 205
blaxploitation 86, 93, 140
boxing 140
buddy 46, 47, 93, 94, 134ff, 140, 141
burlesque, see comedy, burlesque
cartoon, see animation
chase 52, 140, 186
chick flick 93, 94
college comedy, see comedy, college

comedy 1, 5, 8, 11, 13, 19, 24, 32, 36, 49, 51, 52, 53, 56, 57, 61, 62, 66, 67, 69, 70, 71, 78, 81, 92, 99, 101, 103, 109, 113, 126, 131, 141, 142, 149, 150, 176, 179, 187, 204
  burlesque 51, 69
  college 32, 33, 140
  romantic 17, 18, 32, 69, 126, 128, 130, 131, 189
  screwball 20, 51, 73, 127, 140, 141, 149, 161
  slapstick 51, 69, 81, 128, 130, 145, 149
concert 140
cop, see drama, police
costume drama, see drama, costume
crime/gangster 13, 23, 24, 25, 34, 37, 44, 46, 47, 99, 102, 109, 110, 125, 127, 128, 140, 141, 145–6, 160

detective 149
disaster 19, 95, 140, 141, 150, 225
docudrama 51, 62
documentary 18, 33, 50, 91, 92, 108, 110, 142, 163
drama 11, 32, 33, 51, 52, 57, 66, 67, 69–70, 73, 92, 103, 108, 109, 128, 130, 131, 141, 142, 176, 204, 213
  costume 128, 130
  police 141, 148
  romantic 133ff
  sex 140

educational 92, 140
election 163
epic 1, 6, 11, 18, 36, 49, 50–1, 52, 68, 69, 70, 84–5, 93, 127, 179, 190, 204
experimental, see avant-garde
exploitation 140

fantastic 9–10, 15, 85
fantasy 18, 110, 128, 149
festival 91
film noir 18, 27, 51, 53, 61–2, 73, 74, 75, 92, 125, 127, 130, 131, 140, 142, 160, 223
foreign 85
gangster, see crime
gay 161, 169
grossout 158

headline 44
horror 13, 24, 58, 71, 72, 73, 74, 78, 86, 90, 94, 109, 113, 127, 140, 142, 149, 150, 153ff, 158, 221, 222, 224

Indian 36, 140

lyric 11, 50, 69, 70, 85, 188

martial arts 92, 160
melodrama 5, 17, 18, 19, 20, 21, 23, 24, 32,

33, 36, 37, 51, 52, 53, 61–2, 70, 71, 73, 74, 76, 78, 80, 93, 95, 99, 104, 108, 109, 110, 113, 125, 234, 141, 142, 149, 150, 158, 179, 187, 204, 213, 221, 222, 223
'family' 17, 24, 76, 77, 80,. 82, 213
maternal 75, 76
midwestern 163
musical 13, 16, 17, 18, 19, 20, 21, 22, 23, 24, 25, 26, 30, 31ff, 36, 40, 44, 45, 46, 47, 48, 50, 51, 53, 54, 56, 57, 61, 62, 63ff, 67, 68, 69, 71, 73, 78, 80, 90, 91, 93, 99, 102, 108, 109, 111, 113, 127, 128, 130, 131, 140, 141, 145, 147, 150, 157, 160, 161, 164, 190, 204, 205, 211, 216, 221, 223, 225

newspaper 90, 140, 141, 225
newsreel 33, 91, 92, 140
noir, see film noir

plantation 93
police, see drama, police
political 140
pornography, see also gay pornography 94, 111, 158

radio star 140
railroad 35, 92, 162
road 19, 25, 93, 94, 126, 140, 141
romance 8, 11, 32, 33, 36, 42, 45, 52, 56, 57, 61, 66, 67, 68, 103, 113, 125, 131, 145, 150, 179
romantic comedy, see comedy, romantic
romantic drama, see drama, romantic
rouge 163

scenic 51, 52, 91, 92, 140
science fiction 13, 18, 20, 33, 62, 78–80, 95, 102, 142, 149, 150, 160, 190, 222
screwball comedy, see comedy, screwball
sex, see drama, sex
slapstick comedy, see comedy, slapstick
social problem 47, 95, 110
spy 18
stag 140
surfing 140
suspense 24, 142, 154
sword and sorcery 113

thriller 62, 72, 103, 117, 119, 120, 121, 131, 142, 153, 223
tragedy 1, 5, 8, 11, 49, 51, 62, 69, 71, 149, 179, 188, 190
tragicomedy 4–5, 11, 62, 69, 199
travel 33, 34, 35, 37, 57, 110, 128, 130

underground, see avant-garde

video nasties 95, 160

war 13, 16, 18, 24, 25, 72, 95, 113, 126, 128, 130, 142, 149
weepie, see women's film
Western 3, 16, 17, 19, 20, 21, 23, 24, 25, 26, 30, 33, 34ff, 48, 50, 51, 52, 53, 54, 62, 68, 70, 71, 73, 78, 86, 89, 90 92, 99, 102, 103, 104, 109, 111, 113, 117, 126, 127, 128, 130, 131, 132, 141, 142, 145, 148–9, 160, 175, 187, 190, 204, 205, 211, 216, 219ff, 222, 224, 225
  Pennsylvania 220
  singing cowboy 141, 175
  spaghetti 140, 220
wilderness 150
women's film 69, 72ff, 78, 82, 86, 93, 125, 127, 128, 130, 131, 140, 150, 160, 169
women's prison 126, 140, 157
world cinema 163

zombie 125, 140

Name/Title Index

Aas, Lars Joergen, 125
Abbott, Bud and Costello, Lou, 141
Academy Awards, 40, 139
Addison, Joseph, 198
Adolfi, John, 40, 41
Adorno, Theodor, 27
Adventures of Robin Hood, The (Curtiz, 1938), 18
Aeschylus, 5
Affairs of Cellini, The (LaCava, 1934), 43
Air Force One (1997), 47
Airport (Seaton, 1970), 141
Alexander Hamilton (Adolfi, 1931), 40–42, 176
All in the Family, 185
All Through the Night (Sherman, 1942), 222
Althusser, Louis, 26–7
Altman, Rick, 13, 19, 27, 28, 89, 154, 179, 207
Altman, Robert, 129
'America the Beautiful,' 200
American Graffiti (Lucas, 1973), 191
American Hot Wax (Mutrux, 1978), 191
Anderson, Benedict, 196–8, 199, 203, 205
Andrew, Dudley, 13, 14, 44
Andy Hardy series (MGM), 117
Annales School, 27
Anobile, Richard, 153, 154
Ansen, David, 126
Arbuckle, Charles 'Fatty,' 141
Aristophanes, 78, 101
Aristotle, 1*f*, 10, 101, 170, 179, 180, 181, 208
Arliss, George, 39*f*, 59, 176
Arnold, Matthew, 19
Aronson, 'Broncho Billy,' 34, 36
Arthur, Jean, 57
Associated Exhibitors, 107

Astaire, Fred and Rogers, Ginger, 24, 57, 147–8, 150, 223
Aumont, Jacques, 85
Austen, Jane, 190
Austin, Bruce and Gordon, Thomas, 112, 124, 125

Babington, Bruce and Evans, Peter William, 84
Baby Face (Green, 1933), 45
Back Street (Stahl, 1932), 75
Backdraft (Howard, 1991), 126
Bakhtin, Mikhail, 140
Balzac, Honoré de, 190, 224
Barker, Martin, 95
Barr, Roseanne, 200
Barrios, Richard, 54
Barry, Wesley, 107
Barrymore, John, 40, 41
Barsky, Bud, 107
Barthes, Roland, 13, 27, 136
Barylick, John, 195
Basinger, Jeannine, 16
Batman (Burton, 1989), 117
Battling Bunyan (1925), 106–7
Baudry, Jean-Louis, 27
Bazin, André, 19, 127
Beaumarchais, Pierre-Augustin Caron de, 5
Beauty and the Beast (television series), 54
Beck, Jay, 171
Beebee, Thomas O., 100, 208
Behind the Make-Up (1929), 66
Behlmer, Rudy, 25, 45, 113
Belasco, David, 78
Benjamin, Walter, 184, 186
Bennett, Tony, 15
Bête humaine, La (Renoir, 1938), 61
Beuick, Marshall, 185
Big Pond, The (Henley, 1930), 32
Big Sleep, The (Hawks, 1946), 25
Biograph, 35, 116
Blackhawk Films, 92, 162
Blanke, Henry, 44, 48
Blondie series (Columbia), 116
Bogdanovich, Peter, 223
Boileau, Nicolas, 4, 49, 179, 181
The Bold Bank Robbery (Lubin), 34
Boles, John, 33
Bonnie and Clyde (Penn, 1967), 25
Borde, Raymond and Chaumeton, Eugene, 61
Bordwell, David, 135
Born on the Fourth of July (Stone, 1989), 126
Bowery Boys series (Warner Bros.), 116
Branagh, Kenneth, 126
Braudy, Leo, 13, 16, 27, 101, 218
Brewster's Millions (Hill, 1985), 46
'*Broadway*' films, 31
Broadway Hoofer, 32, 66

Broadway Melody, The (Beaumont, 1929), 30, 32, 48, 54
Brooks, Peter, 20
Brown, Bryan, 133, 137, 139
Brunetière, Ferdinand, 6, 7, 8, 49
Buckner, Robert, 113
Burch, Noël, 91
'Burglar Bill' series (American Mutoscope & Biograph), 116
Burned at the Stake (Paley and Steiner), 34
Buscombe, Ed, 13, 34, 36, 54, 157
'Buster Brown' series (Edison), 116
Butch Cassidy and the Sundance Kid (Hill, 1969), 141

Cabin in the Cotton (Curtiz, 1932), 44
Caged Heat (Demme, 1974), 126
Cagney, James, 25, 146, 154
Campbell, Eric, 141
Candy, John, 46
Cannibal Holocaust, 95
Captain Blood (Curtiz, 1935), 25
Capture of the Yegg Bank Burglars (Porter), 34
Cardinal Richelieu (Lee, 1935), 40, 43
Casablanca (Curtiz, 1942), 102, 113, 199, 200
Castelvetro, Lodovico, 4
Cavell, Stanley, 17, 20
Cawelti, John, 13, 16, 19, 20, 21, 27, 34, 49, 101, 218, 220
Centennial Summer (Preminger, 1946), 191
Cervantes, Miguel de, 6
Chaplin, Charlie, 141
Charlie Chan series (Fox), 116
Chase, Chevy, 150
Chatterton, Ruth, 45
Cheers, 185
Children of Dreams, 32
Chong, Rae Dawn, 46
Classification and Rating Administration (CARA), 110, 111
Clive of India (Boleslawski, 1935), 43
Close Harmony (1929), 66
Clover, Carol, 158, 161
Clyde, June, 75
Cocktail (Donaldson, 1988), 133*f*
Coleman, Ronald, 43
Colie, Rosalie, 84
College Love, 32
Columbia Pictures, 55, 116
Columbus, Christopher, 202–3
Commando (Lester, 1986), 46
Comolli, Jean-Louis, 27
Conan the Barbarian (Milius, 1982), 46, 117
Connery, Sean, 117–8
Cook, David A., 34, 74
Cook, Pam, 69, 74
Courageous Coward, The, 104
Corneille, Pierre, 4, 8
Costa, Lucio, 213, 214

240

Creature from the Black Lagoon, The (Arnold, 1954), 78, 79*f*
Cripple-Creek Bar-room, 34
Cripps, Thomas, 93
Croce, Arlene, 127
Croce, Benedetto, 7
'*Crocodile' Dundee* (Faiman, 1986), 46
Crosby, Bing, and Hope, Bob, 141
Cruise, Tom, 133, 135, 137, 139
Crystal, David, 164
Culler, Jonathan, 85
Cummings, Jack, 80
Custen, George F., 16, 19, 40, 43

Damsel in Distress, A (Stevens, 1937), 57
Dances With Wolves (Costner, 1990), 126
Daniels, Bebe, 103
Dante, Allighieri, 6
Darwin, Charles, 6, 8
Davis, Bette, 45
Davis, Geena, 94
Day After, The (Meyer, 1983), 95
De Certeau, Michel, 211, 214
Delamater, Jerome, 20, 71, 78
Death Trap (Lumet, 1982), 95
DeMille, Cecil B., 57, 103, 123, 220
Depardieu, Gérard, 203
Dernier tournant, Le, 61
Derrida, Jacques, 123
Devil May Care, 32
Diderot, Denis, 5
Dickstein, Morris, 126
Die Hard (McTiernan, 1988), 46–7, 117, 121, 141
Die Hard with a Vengeance (McTiernan, 1995), 47
Dieterle, William, 42, 48, 71
Dirty Dancing (Ardolino, 1987), 148
Dirty Dingus Magee (Kennedy, 1970), 149
Dirty Dozen, The (Aldrich, 1967), 149
Dirty Harry (Siegel, 1972), 148–9
Dirty Little Billy (Dragoti, 1972), 149
Dirty Mary Crazy Larry (Hough, 1974), 149
Disney, Walt, 102
Disraeli (Green, 1929), 20, 39–43, 48, 58, 59, 81, 176, 177
Divine Lady (1929), 25, 41
Divorcee, The (Leonard, 1930), 159
Dix, Richard, 103
Do the Right Thing (Lee, 1989), 191
Doane, Mary Ann, 13, 73*f*
Don Winslow of the Navy, 212
Donner, Richard, 46
Doorway to Hell (Mayo, 1930), 44, 47
Double Indemnity (Wilder, 1944), 61–2
Dr. Ehrlich's Magic Bullet (Dieterle, 1940), 57, 58, 59, 117, 120
Dr Jekyll and Mr. Hyde (Fleming, 1941), 78
Dr. Kildare series (MGM), 116–7

Dr. No (Young, 1962), 117–8, 120
Dracula (Melford, 1931), 78
Dragonwyck (Mankiewicz, 1946), 75
Drums Along the Mohawk (Ford, 1939), 220
Dryden, John, 4,13
Dubarry, Woman of Passion (1930), 41
Duchamp, Marcel, 92
Dunne, Irene, 75
Dyer, Richard, 164

Easy Rider (Hopper, 1969), 150, 201
Edison, Thomas A., 35, 116
Edwards, Dell, 133
Edwin Carew Productions, 107
Eliot, T. S., 19
Ellen, 185
Elsaesser, Thomas, 13, 24, 71, 76, 81, 82
Essanay, 36
Evil Dead, The (Raimi, 1982), 95
Ex-Lady (Florey, 1933), 45

FM (Alonzo, 1978), 191
Faces of Death, 95
Fantasia (Sharpsteen, 1940), 102
Farnum, Franklyn, 103
Farrell, Joseph, 131, 135
Fenin, George and Everson, William K., 34
Feuer, Jane, 16, 17, 21, 22, 71, 77
First Blood (Kotcheff, 1982), 46
First National Pictures, 103, 107
Fiske, John, 166
Five Star Final (LeRoy, 1931), 44
Flaubert, Gustave, 190
Fleming, Ian, 118
Flirtation Walk (Borzage, 1934), 63
Flynn, Errol, 25
Focillon, Henri, 21
Fontaine, Joan, 108
Follow the Leader, 32
Fonda, Peter, 201
Footlight Parade (Bacon, 1933), 102
Ford, Harrison, 23
Ford, John, 24, 27, 71, 123, 220, 223
48Hrs. (Hill, 1982), 46, 141
42nd Street (Bacon, 1933), 33, 45
Foster, William Trufaut, 112
1492: Conquest of Paradise (Scott, 1992), 203
Fowler, Alistair, 11, 51, 188, 208
'Foxy Grandpa' series (Biograph), 116
Frameline Distribution, 91
Frank, Nino and Chartier, Jean-Pierre, 61
Frankenstein (Whale, 1931), 78, 153, 154
Frankfurt school, 219
Freed, Alan, 191
Freed, Arthur, 24, 71, 78, 80, 223
French Connection, The (Friedkin, 1971), 150
Freud, Sigmund, 26, 155
Frisco Jenny (Wellman, 1933), 45
From Russia With Love (Young, 1963), 117

Frye, Northrop, 1, 8*f*, 13, 15, 19, 24, 49, 78, 81, 90, 208, 217
Full Metal Jacket (Kubrick, 1987), 150
Fun in Acapulco (Thorpe, 1963), 217

G-Men (Keighley, 1935), 222
Gallagher, Tag, 71
Gallimard Press, 61
Gable, Clark, 57
Gaudio, Tony, 48
Gehring, Wes, 125
General, The (Keaton, 1927), 92
'Genres List, The,' 125
Getty Museum, 94
Ghost (Zucker, 1990), 131
Giant (Stevens, 1956), 150
Gibson, Hoot, 104
Gibson, Mel, 46, 121
Gitlin, Todd, 43
Glory (Zwick, 1989), 126
Glorifying the American Girl (1929), 66
Glorious Betsy (1928), 41
Glover, Danny, 46, 121
Godfather, The (Coppola, 1972), 117
Goldbergs, The, 185
Golden Bed, The (DeMille, 1925), 103
Goldfinger (Hamilton, 1964), 117
Goldman, Lucien, 71
Golem, The, 78
Grand Illusion (Renoir, 1937), 199, 200
Grand Slam (Dieterle, 1933), 44
Grant, Cary, 57
Grease (Kleiser, 1978), 117
Great Movie Ride, The, 102
Great Train Robbery, The (Porter, 1903), 30, 34*f*, 48, 61
Great Ziegfeld, The (Leonard, 1936), 139
Green, Alfred E., 40, 107
Green Goddess, The (Green, 1930), 40, 41, 176
Grey, Jennifer, 149
Griffith, D. W., 17, 78, 92, 162
Grodal, Torben, 90
Guerrero, Ed, 93
Gunning, Tom, 93, 185
Guns of Navarone, The (Thompson, 1961), 17–8

Habermas, Jürgen, 196–8, 203
Hale, George C., 35
Hale's Tours, 35
Half Shot at Sunrise (Sloane, 1930), 32
Hall, Stuart, 170, 181, 211
Halloween (Carpenter, 1978), 117, 150
Hamlet (Shakespeare), 83, 84
'Happy Hooligan' series (Edison), 116
Harlow, Jean, 57
Hartman, Geoffrey, 8
Haskell, Molly, 72, 74, 77, 127
Hawks, Howard, 123

Hawn, Goldie, 25
Hays, Will, 109
Hearts in Dixie, 32
Heaven Can Wait (Lubitsch, 1943), 108
Hegel, F. W., 196*f*
Hendrix, Jimi, 195, 200
Henie, Sonja, 108
Henry V (Branagh, 1989), 126
Henry Aldrich series (Paramont), 117
Hernadi, Paul, 84, 219
High, Wide and Handsome (Mamoulian, 1937), 220
Hill, Walter, 46, 126
Hirsch, E.D., 10–11
His Own Law, 104
Hitchcock, Alfred, 24, 27, 113, 154
Hoffman, Judi, 125
Hold-up of the Rocky Mountain Express, 35
Home Alone (Columbus, 1990), 150
Homer, 6, 50, 190
Horace, 1, 3*f*, 49, 101, 180
Hôtel du Nord (Carne, 1938), 61
Houston, Whitney, 200
Howard, Joe, 43
House of Rothschild (Werker, 1934), 40, 43
'How' series (Biograph), 116
Howe, Lyman, 186, 187
Hudson, Rock, 81
Hugo, Victor, 5, 8
Huizinga, Arnold, 26
Human Condition, The, 145
Hunchback of Notre Dame (Dieterle, 1939), 78
Hurricane, The, 150
Hurricane Kid, The, 104

I am a Fugitive from a Chain Gang (LeRoy, 1932), 44
I Spit on Your Grave, 95
Inspiration Pictures, 107
Interior N. Y. Subway (Biograph), 35
Invisible Man, The (Whale, 1933), 78
Ipcress File, The (Furie, 1965), 117, 119, 121
Isaiah, 5
It's a Great Life (1930), 66

Jakobson, Roman, 170
James, Henry, 83
James Bond series, 18, 117*f*
Jameson, Fredric, 219
Jameson, Richard T., 13, 126
Jane Eyre (Stevenson, 1944), 108
Jaws (Spielberg, 1975), 117
Jazz Singer, The (Crosland, 1927), 31
Jenkins, Henry, 54, 158, 162
Jessel, George, 43
Jesse J. Goldburg's Independent Pictures Corporation, 103
John Francis Dillon Productions, 107

Johnson, Samuel, 13
Johnston, Claire, 74
'Jones' series (Edison), 116
Jour se lève, Le (Carne, 1939), 61
Jumpin' Jack Flash (Marshall, 1986), 46
Jung, Carl, 8

Kael, Pauline, 127
Kalem, 36, 52
Kaminsky, Stuart, 13, 19
Kaplan, E. Ann, 77
Karloff, Boris, 25
Keaton, Buster, 92, 141
Keighley, Willaim, 222
Kelly, Gene, 25
Kim, Susan, 93, 113, 144, 158
Kit Carson, 34
Kitses, Jim, 15, 89, 220
Klinger, Barbara, 162
Koszarski, Richard, 72, 112
Kracauer, Siegfried, 15
Kreuger, Miles, 33
Kuhn, Annette, 74, 77

L.A. Law, 185
Laemmle, Carl, 78, 104
Landy, Marcia, 16
Lang, Robert, 17, 20, 74, 76
Larger, Ernst and Cassirer, Carl, 26
Last Gentleman, The (Adolfi, 1934), 41
Last House on the Left (Craven,1972), 95
Laurel, Stan and Hardy, Oliver, 141
Le Pen, Jean-Marie, 204
Leonard, Robert Z., 159
Let 'Er Buck, 104
Let's Go Native, 32
Lethal Weapon (Donner, 1987), 46, 117, 121
Leutrat, Jean-Louis and Liandrat-Guigues, S., 50
Lévi-Strauss, Claude, 26–7, 217, 218, 219, 225
Library of Congress, 125
Life Begins (Flood, 1932), 44
Life of a Cowboy (Porter, 1906), 32
Life of Emile Zola, The (Dieterle, 1937), 42, 120, 176
Life with Father, 185
Linnaeus, Carolus, 6, 16, 64
Little Caesar (LeRoy, 1930), 25, 44, 47
'Little Willie' series (Biograph), 116
Lone Wolf series (Columbia), 116
Lonedale Operator (Griffith), 92, 162
Lonesome Dove (McMurtry), 51
Lord, Robert, 113
Lost Mine, The (1907), 52
Lotman, Jurij, 175, 209
Love Me Tonight (Mamoulian, 1932), 190, 191
Love Parade, The (Lubitsch, 1929), 32
Lubin, Arthur, 34

Lubitsch, Ernst 108, 113, 123
Lucas, George, 117, 222
Lumière, Auguste and Louis, 185, 186, 187
Lund, Karen, 125
Lunenfeld, Peter, 163

M.C. Levee Productions, 107
MGM Studios, 24, 31–2, 43, 71, 78, 78, 102, 116, 121, 139, 159, 223
MacDonald, Jeannette, 25
MacGowan, Kenneth, 34
Mad Genius, The (Curtiz, 1931), 41
Madame Pompadour (1927), 41
Mairet, Jean, 4
Malinowski, Bronislaus, 26
Malone, Dorothy, 81
Maltby, Richard, 111
Maltin, Leonard, 93, 131, 160
Mamoulian, Rouben, 190, 220
Man From Blankley's, The, 40
Man Who Played God, The (Adolfi, 1932), 41
Man Who Shot Liberty Valance, The (Ford, 1962), 26
Manchurian Candidate, The (Frankenheimer, 1962), 131
Manila Calling (Leeds, 1942), 108
Marivaux, 150
'Marseillaise, La,' 199, 200
Martinet, André, 174
Marx Brothers, 150
Mary Tyler Moore Show, The, 185
Mast, Gerald, 20, 71
Match King, The (Bretherton, 1932), 44
Mayne, Judith, 74
McConnell, Frank, 13, 27, 218
McTiernan, John, 46
Meet Me in St. Louis (Minnelli, 1944), 190, 191
Menander, 78, 101
Mercier, Louis-Sébastien, 5
Merritt, Russell, 71, 72
Metropolitan Museum of Art, 94
Metz, Christian, 21, 221
Michael Shane series (Fox), 117
Michelangelo, 83
Mighty Barnum, The (Lang, 1934), 43
Millionaire, The (Adolfi, 1931), 40–2, 176
Milton, John, 50
Minnelli, Vincente, 17, 27, 123, 221, 223
Minturno, Ugento Antonio, 4
Mitry, Jean, 219, 220
Modleski, Tania, 74, 76, 77
Molière, Jean-Baptiste, 81, 150
Moll Flanders (Defoe), 145
Moon is Down, The (Pichel, 1943), 108
Motion Picture Association of America (MPAA), 110
Motion Pictures Producers and Distributors Association, 109, 110

Mr. Moto series (Fox), 117
Mulvey, Laura, 76
Mummy, The (Freund, 1932), 78
Muni, Paul, 25, 42, 57–8
Murder, My Sweet (Dmytryk, 1944), 62
Murphy, Eddie, 46
Musser, Charles, 34
My Darling Clementine (Ford, 1946), 26
My Man, 32

NYPD Blue, 185
Naficy, Hamid, 163
Naked Gun, The (Zucker, 1988), 141
Nancy Drew series (Warner Bros.), 159–60
Naremore, Jim, 61, 62, 92
National Endowment for the Humanities, 94
National Research Group, 133, 137
Nausea (Sartre), 145
Neale, Stephen, 13, 14, 16, 18, 19, 28, 30, 34,
    44, 72, 76, 82, 85, 101
Negri, Pola, 103
Niemeyer, Oscar, 213, 214
Night Court, 185
Nolte, Nick, 46
Northwest Mounted Police (DeMille, 1940), 57
Nowell-Smith, Geoffrey, 76

O'Brien, Charles, 61
Odin, Roger, 214
Office of War Information, 109
Oklahoma! (Zinnemann, 1955), 26
Old English (Galsworthy), 40, 41, 176
'Old Maid' series (Edison), 116
Once Upon a Time in the West (Leone, 1968),
    175
Only Angels Have Wings (Hawks, 1939), 54–5
Out of Africa (Pollack, 1985), 130

Palmy Days (Sutherland, 1931), 33
Paramount Studios, 41, 78, 102, 103, 117,
    171–2
Passenger 57 (Hooks, 1992), 47
Pasternak, Joe, 80
Pathé Studios, 107
Paul, William, 140, 158
Perrault, Charles, 181
Perry Mason series (Warner Bros.), 116
Phantom of the Opera, 78
Pixérécourt, Guilbert de, 78
Plato, 20, 179
Plautus, 4
Player, The (Altman, 1992), 129–30
Poynter, Nelson, 109
Poker at Dawson City, 34
Pope, Alexander, 4
Popper, Karl, 6
Porgy and Bess (Mamoulian, 1935), 190
Porter, Edwin S., 33*f*
Portrait of a Lady, The (James), 83

Predator (McTiernan, 1987), 46, 117, 121
Presley, Elvis, 217
Pretty Woman (Marshall, 1990), 130
Princess of Cleves (Lafayette), *The*, 115
Privett, Ray, 163
Propp, Vladimir, 13, 26, 217
Proust, Marcel, 190
Pryor, Richard, 46
Psycho (Hitchcock, 1960), 157
Public Enemy, The (Wellman, 1931), 25, 44,
    47, 145–6, 152, 154
Pygmalion (Rousseau), 70

Quai des brumes (Carne, 1937), 61
Quo Vadis, 17–8

RKO Studios, 43, 117, 147
Rabelais, 5
Raiders of the Lost Ark (Spielberg, 1981),
    17–8, 102, 117, 141
Rainer, Peter, 126
Rambo: First Blood Part II (Cosmatos, 1985),
    46
Rashomon (Kurosawa, 1950), 137
Rawlins, John, 222
Rebecca (Hitchcock, 1940), 81
Red and the Black, The (Stendhal), 145
Renoir, Jean, 61, 123
Rhodes, Cynthia, 149
Richardson, John H., 47
Rio Rita, 32
Ritz Brothers, 57
Roadhouse Nights, 32
Robbins, Tim, 129–30
Roberts, Martin, 163
Robinson, Edward G., 25, 42
Roddick, Nick, 40
Rockett Productions, 107
Rogue's Song, The, 32
Romance of the Rail (Porter, 1903), 30
Rosmarin, Adena, 85, 208
Rothenbuhler, Eric, 172
Rousseau, Jean-Jacques, 70
Roxanne (Schepisi, 1987), 126
Russell, William D., 104, 105, 106–7
Ryall, Tom, 14

SS Experiment Camp, 95
Sachs, Sheldon, 49
Sade, D.A.F., 157
Saddle Hawk, The, 104
Saint, The series (Fox), 117
Saint Paul, 6
Sally, 32
Salomon, Julie, 126
Sam E. Rork, Inc., 107
Sarandon, Susan, 94
Saratoga (Conway, 1937), 57
Sarris, Andrew, 127, 223

Saturday Night Fever (Badham, 1977), 133, 134, 135
Saussure, Ferdinand de, 173, 174, 215, 217
Scaliger, Julius Caesar, 4
Scarface (Hawks, 1932), 25
Schatz, Thomas, 13, 14, 16, 17, 20, 21, 27, 34, 62, 71, 82, 101, 218, 223
Schickel, Richard, 127
Schiff, Steven, 123
Schlegel, Friedrich, 5
Schrader, Paul, 127
Schwarzenegger, Arnold, 25, 46
Scott, Ridley, 94, 203
Sea Hawk, The (Curtiz, 1940), 25
Searchers, The (Ford, 1956), 175, 190
Selig, 35, 36
Selznick, David O., 46
Sennett, Ted, 40
Seven Brides for Seven Brothers (Donen, 1954), 131
Shakespeare, William, 5, 150
Shearer, Norma, 159
Shelley, Mary, 224
Sherlock Holmes and the Voice of Terror (Rawling, 1942), 222
Sherman, Vincent, 222
Shipmates Forever (Borzage, 1935), 63
Shootist, The (Siegel, 1976), 175, 190
Short, Ray LeRoy, 38
Shue, Elizabeth, 139
Sierra Pictures, 103
Silver, Joel, 46*f*, 121, 140
Silver Dollar, 45
Singer, Ben, 71, 72
Singin' in the Rain (Donen and Kelly, 1952), 102, 217
Singing Fool, The (Bacon, 1928), 61
Singing Marine, The (1937), 57, 63
Sirk, Douglas, 24, 27, 71, 81, 123, 162, 221, 223
Smart Money (Green, 1931), 47
Smith, Henry Nash, 34
Song of Roland, The, 51
Sons O' Guns (Bacon, 1936), 63, 64
Souza, Steve de, 46, 47
Speed (DeBont, 1994), 47, 150
Spielberg, Steven, 117
Spencer, Herbert, 6
Stack, Robert, 81
Stagecoach (Ford, 1939), 54
Stallone, Sylvester, 25
Stanwyck, Barbara, 45
'Star-Spangled Banner, The,' 195, 200, 202, 203
Star Trek, 117, 190
Star Wars (Lucas, 1977), 17, 18, 23–4, 117, 190, 222
State Fair (Lang, 1945), 191
Steele, Richard, 198

Steinbeck, John, 108
Stella Dallas (Vidor, 1937), 81
Stendhal (Henri Beyle), 5, 182
Stevens, George, 43
Stevenson, R.L., 224
Stone, Oliver, 126
Story of Alexander Graham Bell, The (Cummings, 1939), 59, 120
Story of Louis Pasteur, The (Dieterle, 1936), 42, 57, 81, 120, 176
Street Girl, 32
Successful Calamity, A (Adolfi, 1932), 41, 42
Sudden Death (Hyams, 1995), 47
Summer Holiday (Mamoulian, 1948), 191
Sunny, 32
Superman (Donner, 1978), 117
Svengali (Mayo, 1931), 41
Swayze, Patrick, 149
Sweet Kitty Bellairs (Green, 1930), 40

THX sound, 22
Tacitus, 6
Taming the West, 104
Tarnished Angels (Sirk, 1957), 81
Tarzan series (MGM), 116
Tasso, Torquato, 4
Taves, Brian, 16, 17–8, 19, 21, 125
Ten Gentlemen from West Point (Hathaway, 1942), 108
Tenderfoot, The (1907), 52
Terminator, The (Cameron, 1984), 46
Thatcher, Margaret, 95
Thelma and Louise (Scott, 1991), 25, 93–4, 126, 141
Thin Man, The series (MGM), 116
39 Steps, The (Hitchcock, 1935), 154
thirtysomething, 185
Thomas, Kevin, 126
Thomson, David, 127
Three Days of the Condor (Pollack, 1975), 154
Three Musketeers, The (Dwan, 1939), 54, 57
Time, the Place and the Girl, The, 32
Titanic (Cameron, 1998), 141
To Each His Own (Leisen, 1946), 75
Todorov, Tzvetan, 1,6, 8*f*, 13, 15, 85, 136, 208, 217, 219
Tolkin, Michael, 129–30
Top Hat (Sandrich, 1935), 147–8, 152, 154, 155
Top Speed, 32
Torchy Blane series (Warner Bros.), 116
Touchstone Pictures, 133
'Tramp' series (Edison), 116
Travers, Peter, 126
Travolta, John, 133
Trespass (Hill, 1992), 126
Triplett, Mike, 47
Trip Through the Black Hills, 35
Troyes, Chretien de, 145

20th Century-Fox, 43, 45, 56, 59, 107–8, 116, 117, 120
20th Century Pictures, 40, 41, 43, 47
20,000 Years in Sing Sing (Curtiz, 1933), 45
Tyler, Parker, 127

'Uncle Josh' series (Edison), 116
'Uncle Reuben' series (Biograph), 116
Unconquered (DeMille, 1947), 220
Undercurrent (Minnelli, 1946), 75
Under Siege (Davis, 1992), 47
Unforgiven (Eastwood, 1992), 175
United Artists, 41, 117, 121
United States Patent and Trademark Offices, 111
United We Stand, 108
Universal Studios, 71, 104, 105, 109, 119, 121, 153
Universal Gibson Productions, 104

Vagabond Lover, The (Neilan, 1929), 32
Valley of Hate, The, 104
Veblen, Thorsten, 193
Vernet, Marc, 220
Vestron Pictures, 148
Vida, Marco Girolamo, 4
Video Recordings Bill, 95
Vidor, King, 17
Virgil, 6, 50, 190
Vitagraph, 116
Vitaphone, 33, 39
Voltaire (Adolfi, 1933), 40, 42, 176
Vuillermoz, Ernest, 61

WKRP in Cincinnati, 185
Waller, Gregory, 95
Wallis, Hal, 44, 113
Walt Disney Productions, 133
Walt Disney World, 101
Waltons, The, 185
War and Peace (Tolstoy), 51
War of the Roses, The (DeVito, 1989), 126
War of the Worlds, The (Haskin, 1953), 78

Ward Lascelle Productions, 103
Warner Brothers Studios, 32, 33, 39*f*, 44, 45, 47, 57, 58, 59, 63, 64, 71, 81, 102, 103, 108, 113, 116, 117, 120, 139, 140, 145, 146, 159
Warshow, Robert, 21, 127
Waters, John, 92
Wayne, John, 25
Weary River, 32
Weathers, Carl, 46
Weiss Brothers' Artclass Pictures Corporation, 103
Wellek, Rene and Warren, Austin, 1, 7 13, 91
Welles, Orson, 108, 123
West, Mae, 132
What Happened in the Tunnel (1903), 35
White, Armond, 126
Whoopee! (Freeland, 1930), 32
'Why' series (Edison), 116
Wild Bunch, The (Peckinpah, 1969), 150, 175
Williams, Alan, 13, 30
Williams, Linda, 74, 111, 158, 179
Wilmington, Michael, 126
Wilson, Woodrow, 203
Winchester '73 (Mann, 1950), 26
Wittgenstein, Ludwig, 83, 96*f*, 208
Wolf Man, The (Waggner, 1941), 78
Wollen, Peter, 91
Woman in the Window, The (Lang, 1944), 62
Wood, Michael, 218
Wood, Robin, 27, 127
Woods, Edward, 146
Woods, Frank E. ('The Spectator'), 127
Working Man, The (Adolfi, 1933), 41, 42
Wright, Will, 13, 17, 20, 27, 218, 221, 223
Written on the Wind (Sirk, 1956), 162
Wyatt, Justin, 112, 131

Xavier, Ismail, 213
Yankee Doodle Dandy (Curtiz, 1942), 86, 201
Young Mr. Lincoln (Ford, 1939), 222
Zanuck, Darryl F., 43*f*, 179
Zwick, Edward, 126